THE THAMES

An Artist's Journey from Source to Sea

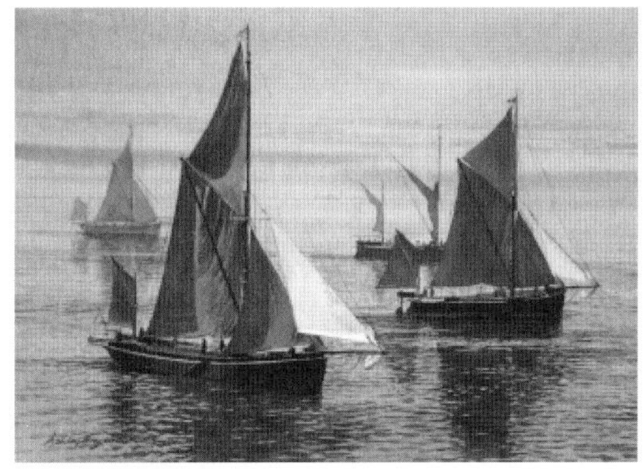

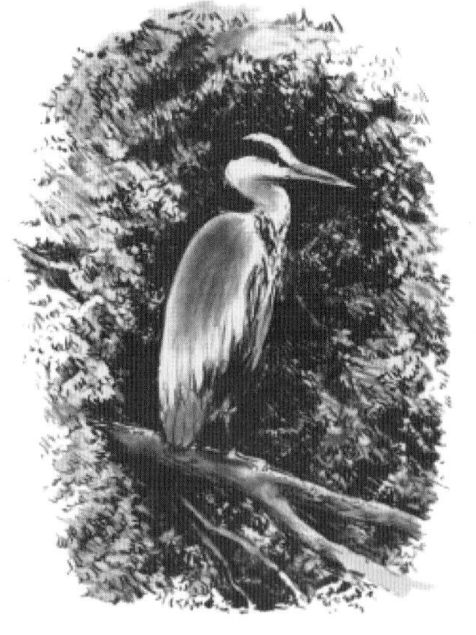

THE THAMES

An Artist's Journey from Source to Sea

Ashley Bryant

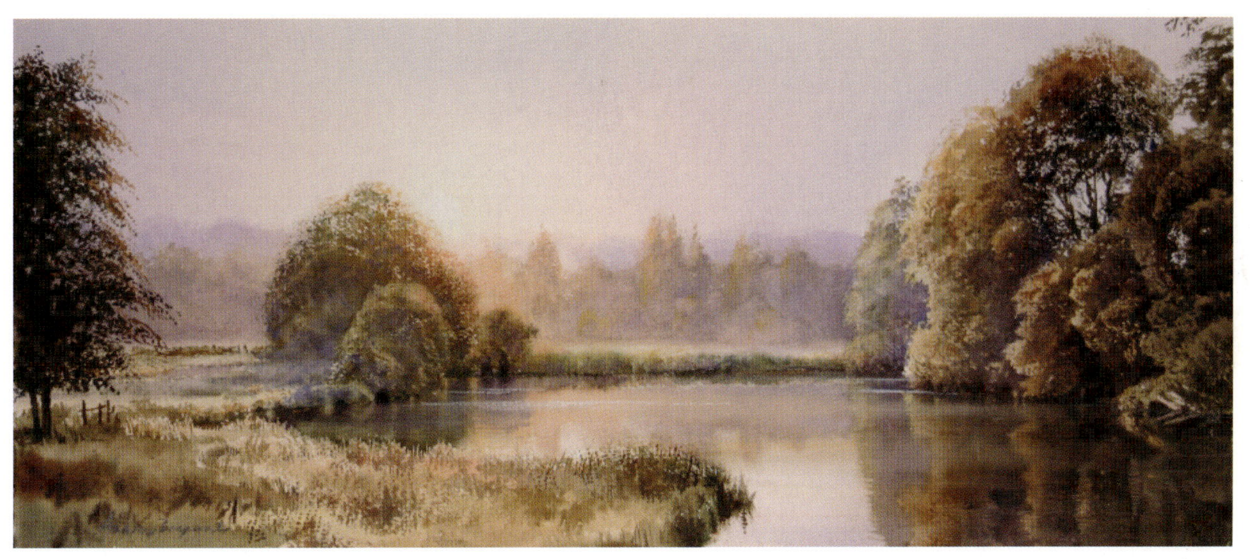

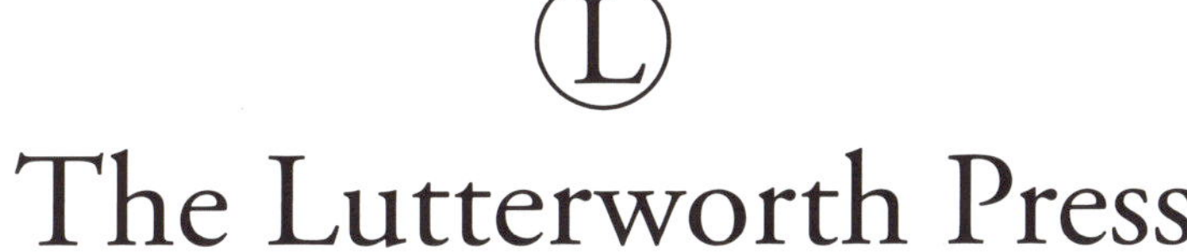

The Lutterworth Press

The Lutterworth Press
P.O. Box 60
Cambridge
CB1 2NT

www.lutterworth.com
publishing@lutterworth.com

First Published in 2006

ISBN (13): 978 0 7188 3062 5

British Library Cataloguing in Publication Data
A catalogue record is available from the British Library

Printed in the United Kingdom by
The Bath Press

CONTENTS

1. The Source to Reading

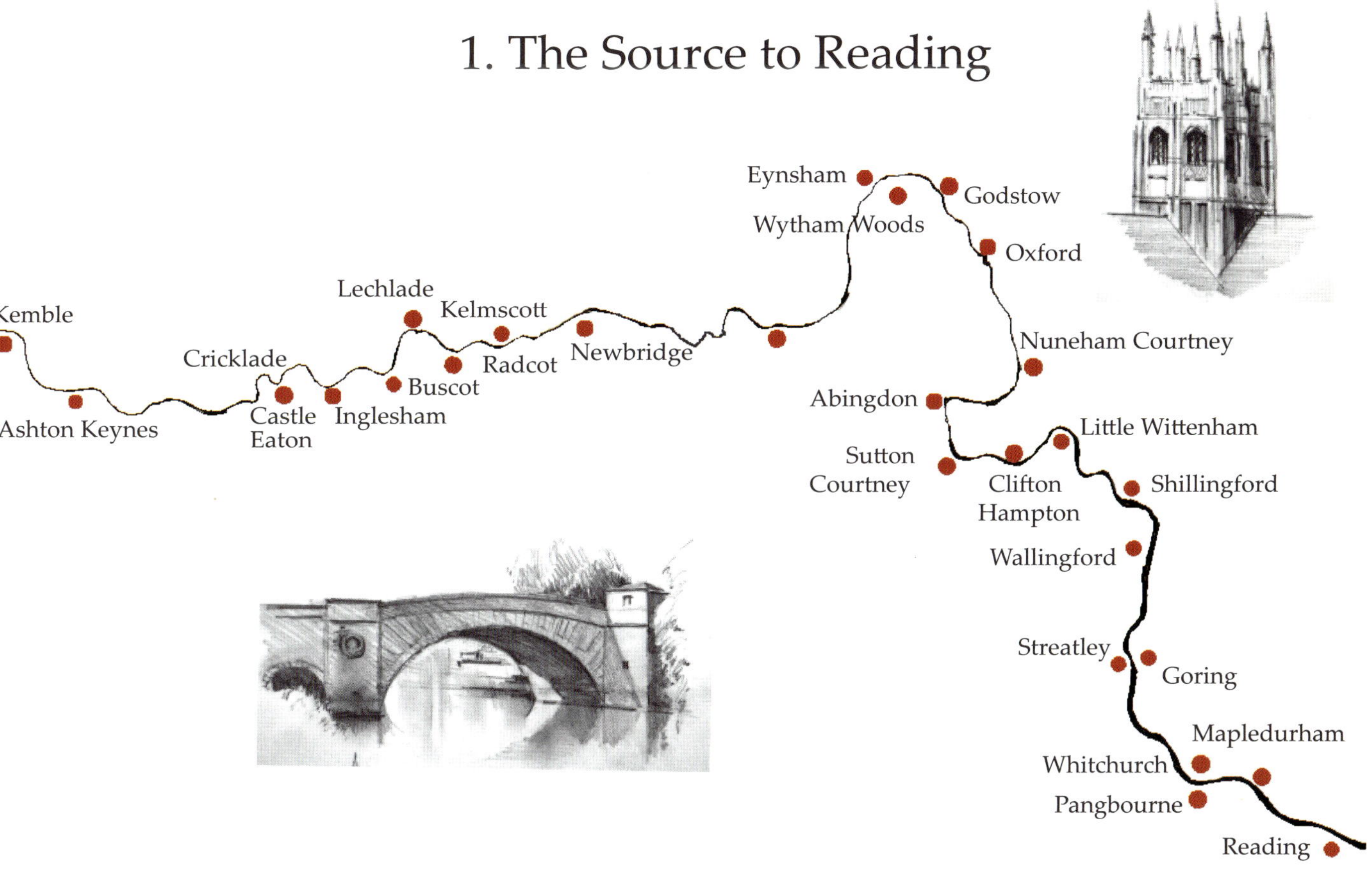

2. Reading to Central London

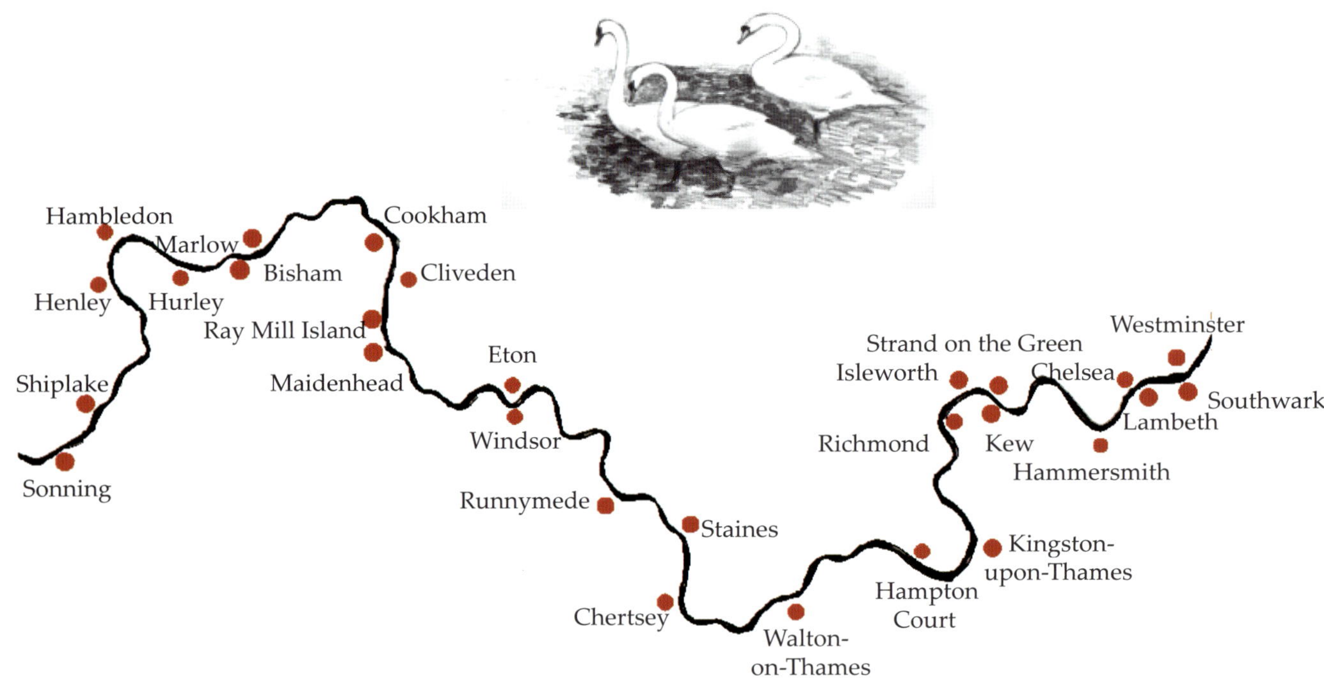

READING TO HAMPTON COURT

HAMPTON COURT TO CENTRAL LONDON

3. Central London to the Sea

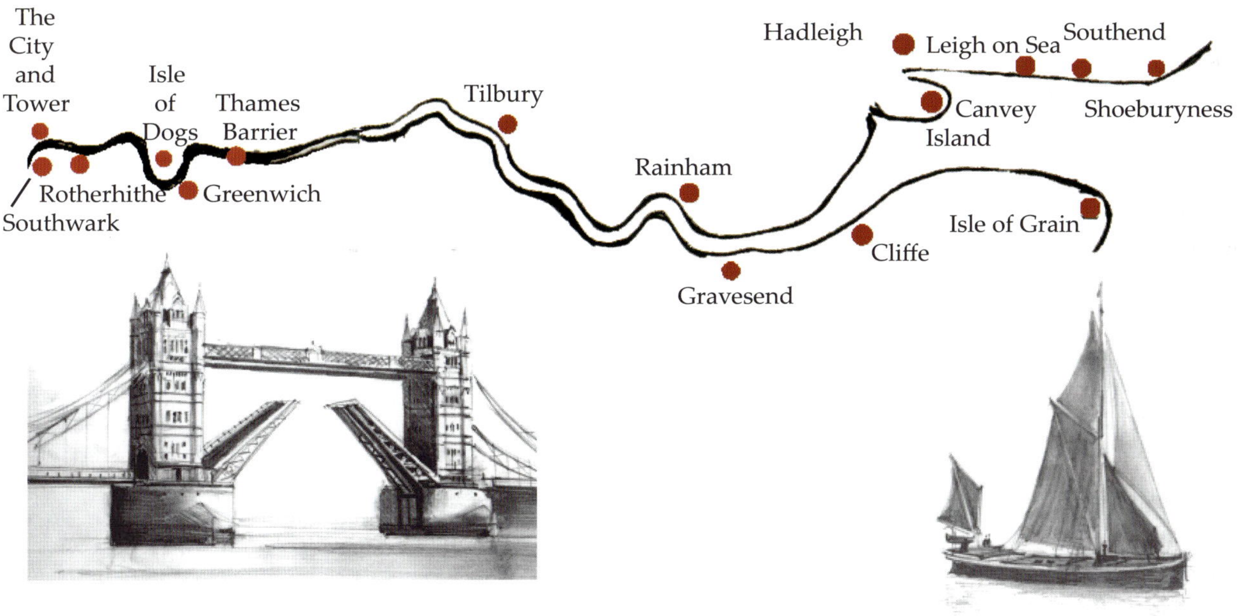

CENTRAL LONDON TO THE SEA

INTRODUCTION

For many people their first view of the Thames is a milestone in life, never to be forgotten. Whether we lean over the Embankment wall in London or sit on its grassy banks in its higher reaches, the river holds our attention with its magical and timeless qualities. Here is the great river we all heard about during our school days, the river often seen as a background in films and television programmes and the central ribbon of sporting events such as the London Marathon. It is a favourite backdrop to news reports and regularly makes the news itself with everything from dramatic riverside buildings to stranded whales.

The term 'liquid history' is often applied to the Thames. Its great highway has prompted the building of fortresses, palaces, religious institutions, places of government and commercial enterprises, and crossing points have sown the seeds of town development. The Thames has formed a boundary between kingdoms, as well as providing protection for communities and a livlihood for many thousands. From records we know about the high notes of English history, such as the lives of kings and the battles that were fought along the banks of the Thames, but much of the River's past is shrouded in mystery. It is impossible to walk along the river without feeling a sense of history; locks, warehouses and docks are features of the recent past whilst remains of abbeys and castles give a glimpse of life in earlier times.

Sporting events are held on the river, providing colourful spectacles. Henley heads the list of regattas, whilst barge races are held in the estuary from Southend Pier. One of the sporting highlights is the annual boat race between Oxford and Cambridge Universities. There are interesting customs, some with an historic foundation, such as Swan Upping, and others that are quite bizarre, like the football match played on the muddy foreshore at Leigh-on-Sea. The Thames is a superb leisure facility enjoyed by a growing number of people with a variety of interests: boating, pleasure cruising, yachting, fishing, walking along the Thames path or simply sitting and enjoying the view.

The Thames, a nature reserve in its own right, provides a rich corridor along which wildlife can flourish. This wildlife has become accustomed to people, making it easier to get close – a great benefit for photographers and artists. Thanks to tighter legislation and the work of environmental agencies, the Thames is now the cleanest major river in Europe with clear benefits to wildlife and mankind.

From an artistic point of view it is not the river itself that provides a satisfying composition but its associated landscape, buildings, bridges, boats and sky. The river is the factor which unites these elements, reflecting their features and forging a composition of line, balance and harmony. The Thames provides a huge range of artistic opportunities as it grows in stature from source to sea. Its origin could not be more modest – it rises from a tiny spring in the middle of a Gloucestershire meadow a few miles from Cirencester. Where it meets the North Sea, almost 220 miles later, the river is five miles wide.

For most of its length the Thames path clings to the riverside, providing an excellent opportunity to explore the river. This well-marked route of 184 miles starts at the source and continues to the Thames Barrier, splitting into separate routes on both banks of the river in west London. Occasionally the path takes an inevitable but frustrating diversion from the river around residential and commercial properties and private estates. An alternative way to explore the Thames, allowing the river to be seen from a variety of different views, is to take a boat. There are many opportunities to either hire your own or to take a trip on a passenger service.

London owes its status as one of the world's greatest cities and its pre-eminence as the English capital to one key factor – the river. The Thames waterfront in London, home to some of the best known buildings and bridges in the world, is a great showpiece. The section from Westminster to Tower Bridge is the greatest prime site in Britain and any new building proposed for this waterfront carries a great responsibility and is seen in an international spotlight. New schemes are on the drawing board and the future skyline looks exciting. London's riverside is constantly evolving, particularly with new residential developments to the east and west of central London. River commuter buses and water taxis provide services for these growing communities and this boat traffic is a revival of one of the old ways of travelling around London.

Over the centuries the Thames has been a magnet for some of the greatest landscape painters. As a Londoner, Turner was a prolific painter of the Thames. Constable was drawn from his beloved East Anglia to paint the river. Even the French impressionists left their mark, including Monet, whose views of the House of Parliament are amongst the most stunning examples of his work. Their paintings are seemingly beyond the abilities of mere mortals, but they are an inspiration to other artists. The work of earlier painters can provide fascinating historical information about the Thames before the age of photography.

My own association with the river started with school trips to London, when I became familiar with sections of it. Whilst working in London my interest in the river grew, and later as an artist, I had the opportunity to produce this book. My objective was to put together a collection of paintings from source to sea which illustrated the broad spectrum of the river; its beautiful scenery, the neighbouring towns, its wildlife and the customs and sporting events that take place along its course, accompanied by references to its absorbing history and dynamic present. The paintings were completed over a period of six years, from 2000-2006. Inevitably, the choice of subjects and viewpoints was a personal one and every artist would have made a different selection. I have tried to keep the text fairly brief – it is impossible to compete with so many well-researched books on the river, so I have restricted the text to subjects that have interested me, and will, I hope, also capture the imagination of the reader.

This book, though an epic task, has given me great pleasure to produce – to walk the banks with friends, to enjoy the peaceful and timeless qualities of the river, learn some of its secrets and meet many interesting people. Each painting is part of a special memory.

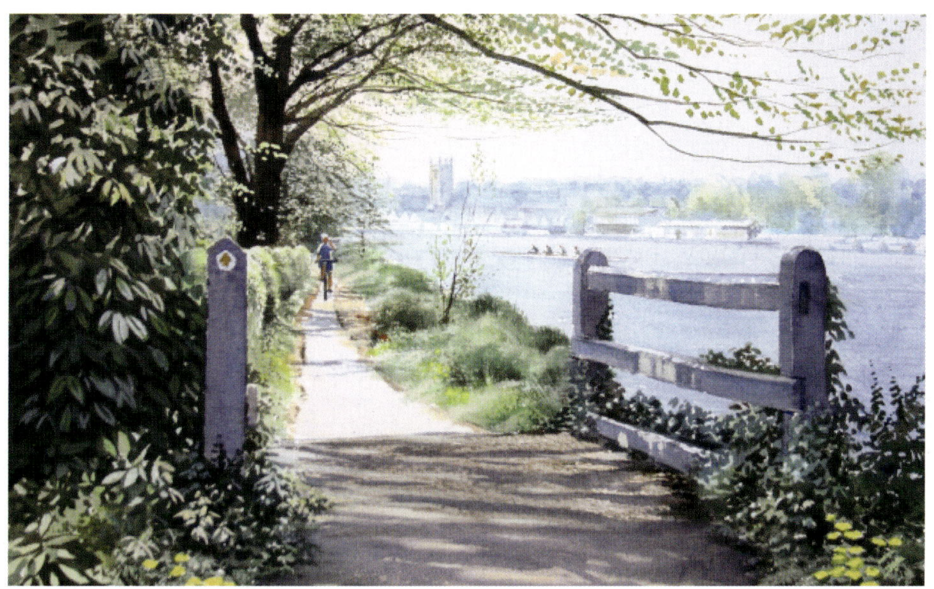

THE SOURCE

In the corner of a Gloucestershire field, known as Trewsbury Mead, near the village of Kemble, and three miles from Cirencester, stands a venerable ash tree. The boughs of the tree stretch across a depression in the ground. This hollow remains dry for most of the year, but in the winter it fills with water to create a tiny pond which provides the rather insignificant source of the great River Thames. A few scattered stones mark the spot and a nearby granite slab, erected by the Thames Conservators in 1874, confirms that this is the hallowed birthplace.

However, the infant Thames refuses to be tied down by officialdom. In a newspaper article, under the heading "Old Father Thames Keeps On Growing" (April 2001), it was reported that after a period of very wet weather another spring a mile upstream had started flowing to stake its own claim as the beginning of the river. The official source at Trewsbury Mead is regularly contested (by one rival claim in particular, as we shall see in a later chapter), and with the effects of global warming and increased winter rainfall, the debate looks set to continue.

The geology of the surrounding area comprises chalk, limestone and sandstone through which rainfall seeps and accumulates in underground reserves, thanks to an underlying and impermeable clay bed. After heavy rains the water table increases and springs start actively contributing to the river's early stages.

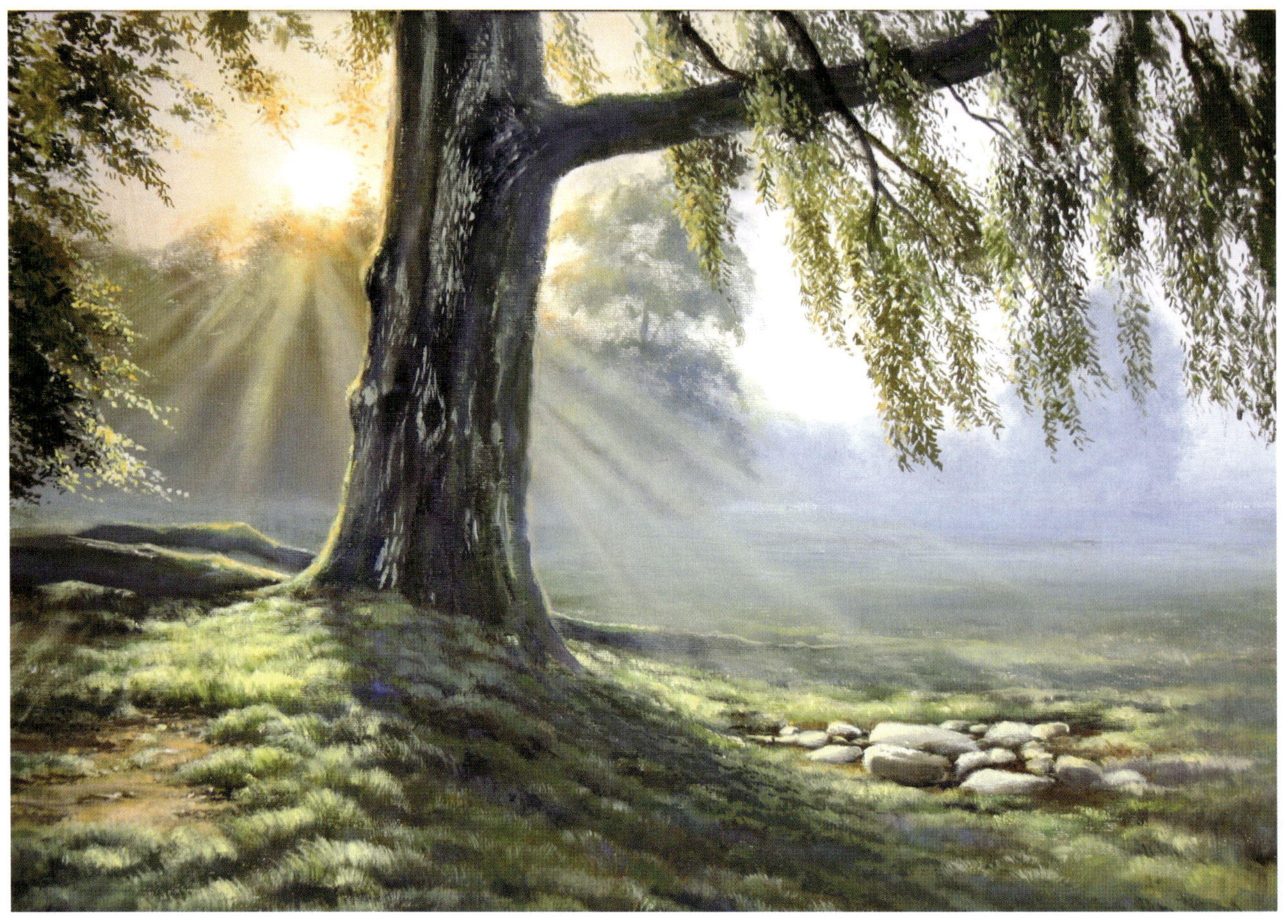

The meadow surrounding the river's source seems flat, but as we walk "downstream", it soon develops into a shallow valley interrupted at right-angles by the Fosse Way, where a larger pool forms in winter. At least on the other side of this ancient road a definite water course can be seen, but once again it is nearly always dry. Stepping across this small ditch it is amazing to think the Thames will be five miles wide at the estuary between the Essex and Kent shorelines. Before continuing our Thames journey take a look at the last few pages in this book to see the final transformation of the river.

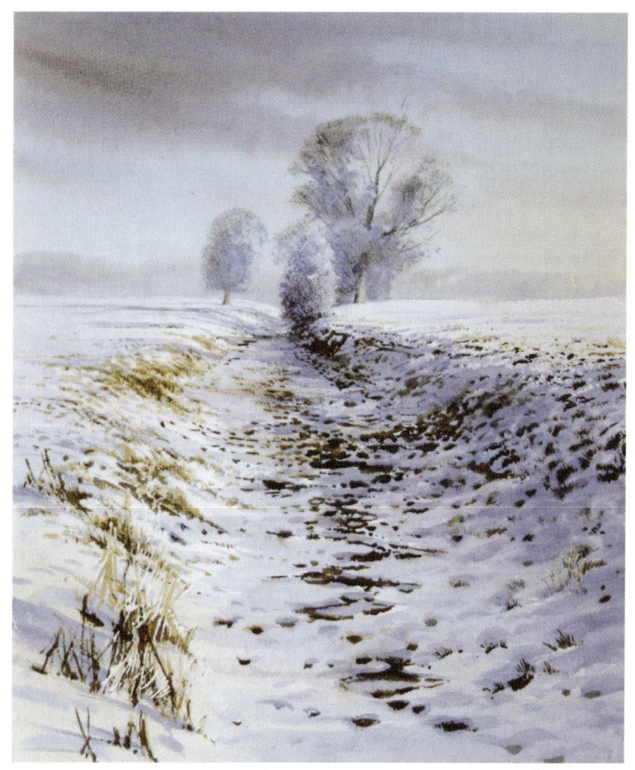

A mile further downstream, and one and a half miles from the source, the river approaches the A428 road bridge, by which time it is twenty feet wide thanks to the contribution of other springs along the way. This grassy river bed is grazed by cattle in a quiet pastoral scene, but after sustained rains, especially in the winter, it explodes into life and the young river becomes a menacing spectacle.

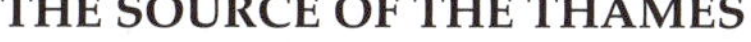

THE SOURCE OF THE THAMES
(Opposite Page)
Early morning lighting was needed to give this composition a lift. I was on the spot from 7a.m. one September morning to catch the sunlight as it broke through the trees onto the misty meadow and picked out the stones placed around the river's source.

EARLY BEGINNINGS UNDER SNOW
(Above Right)
Even after an early snowfall at the beginning of winter the course of the river is comparatively dry as it approaches the A428 road bridge.

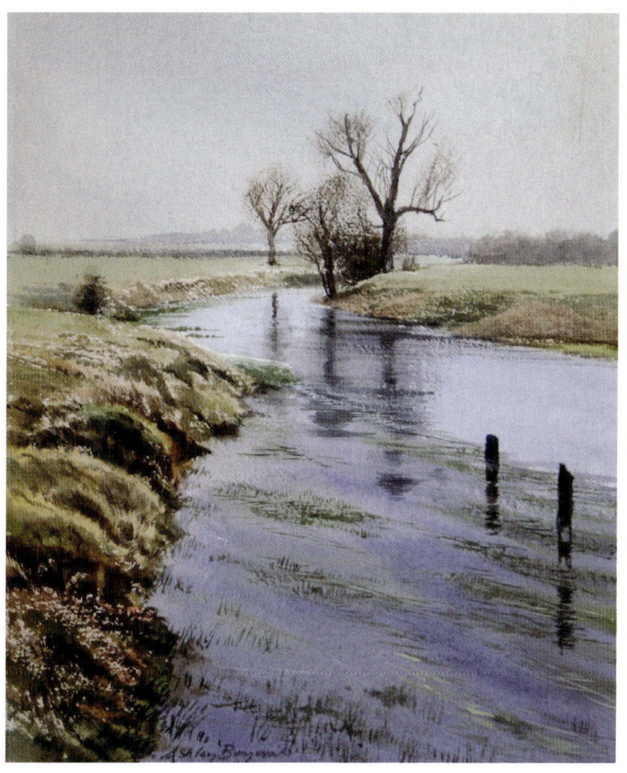

EARLY BEGINNINGS IN JANUARY
(Right)
The view from a similar location to the painting above, but after a month of rain the river is in spate with crystal-clear spring water together with surface water from the surrounding fields.

KEMBLE

THE THAMES AT KEMBLE
(Below)
This watercolour shows a view of the river just downstream from the A428 bridge. I have tried to capture the essence of a dank, misty January day, when the temperature was just above freezing and the moss-covered branches dripped with moisture.

THE HARE
(Right)
This is one of many examples of wildlife along the route. Fortunately this hare stayed still long enough for me to approach and take a photograph from which this watercolour was produced.

DOWNSTREAM FROM KEMBLE
(Opposite page)
A typical winters view of the river, looking downstream towards Ewen.

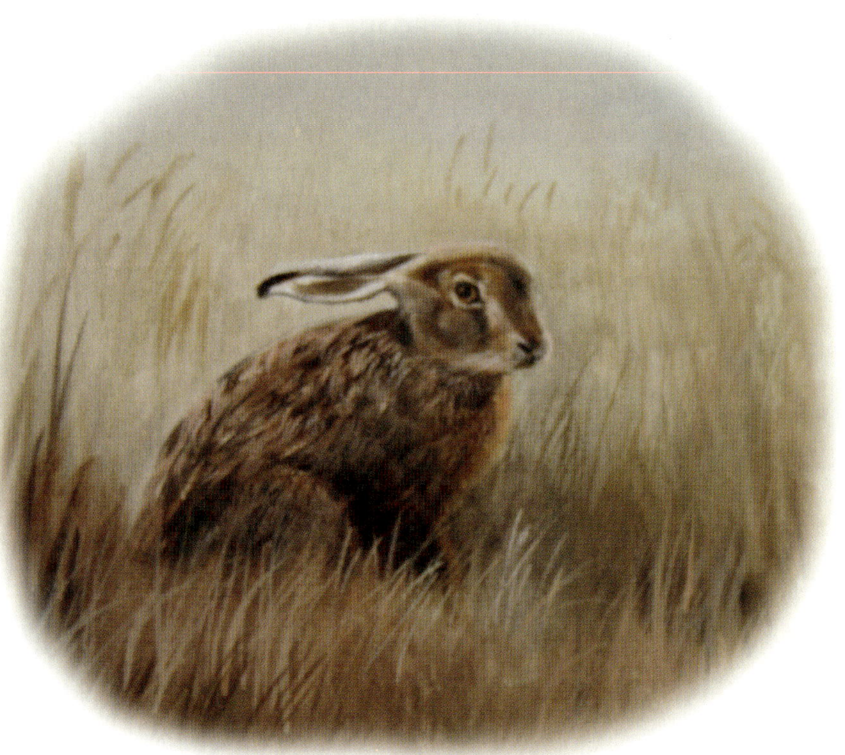

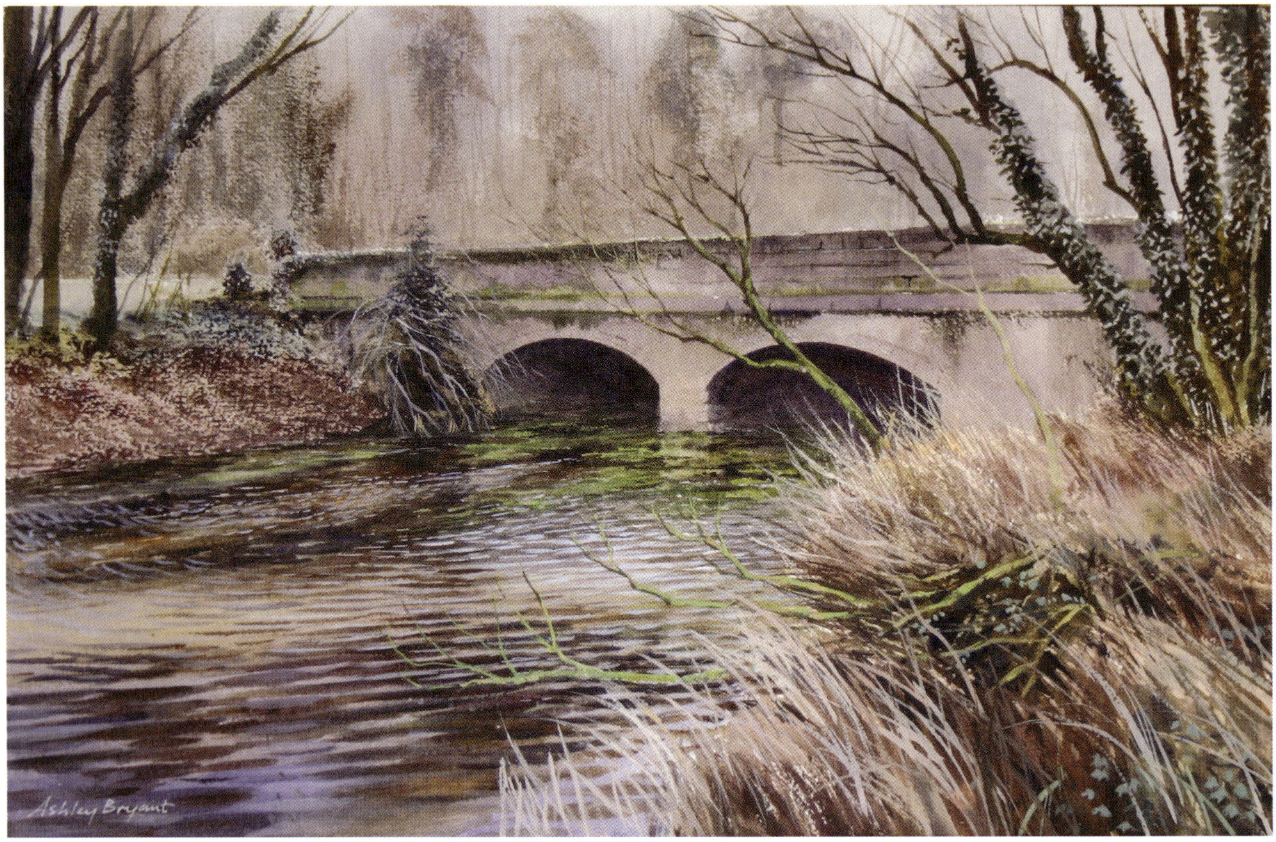

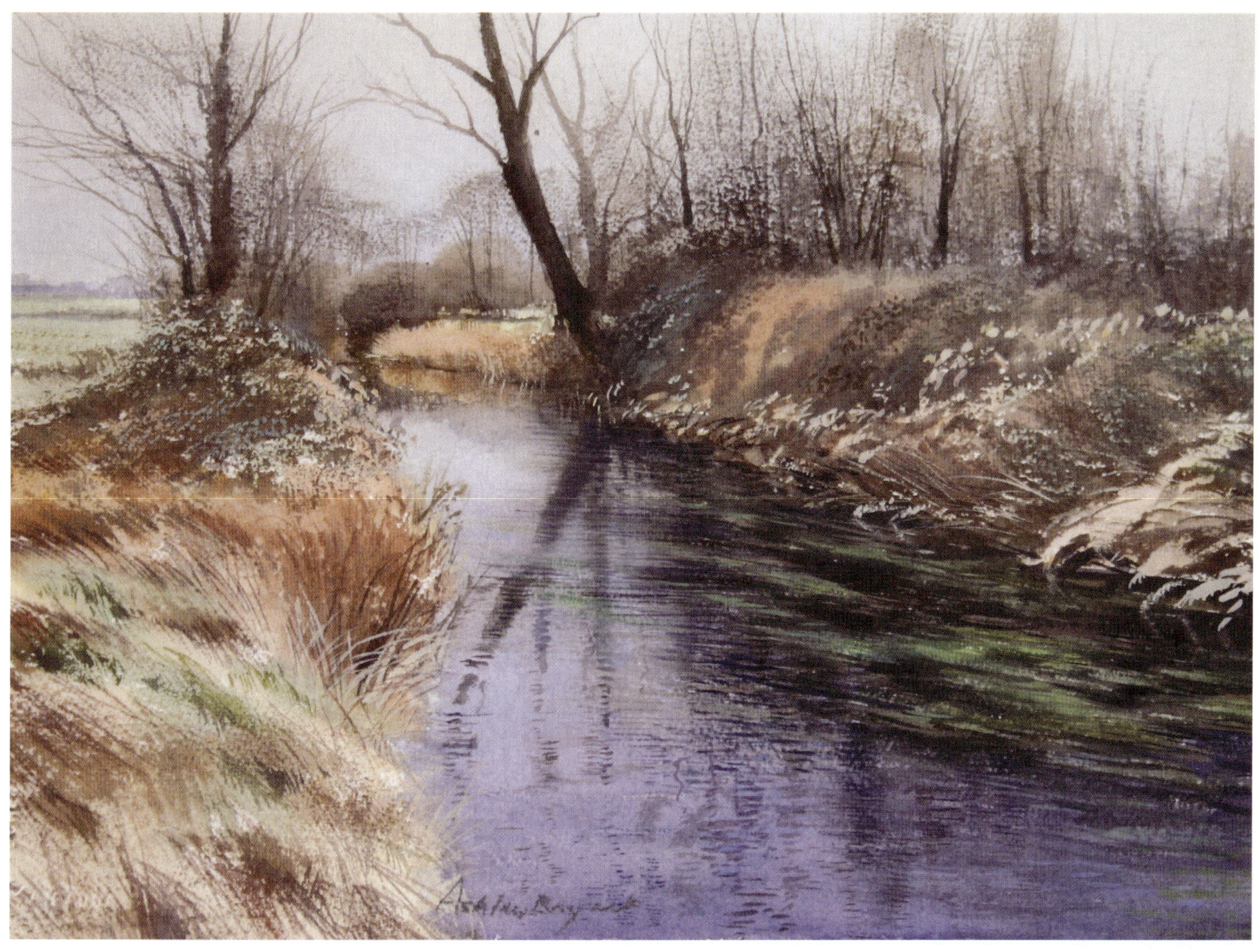

As the seasons pass, the appearance of the infant river undergoes a variety of changes. In summer the riverbed is invariably dry in these uppermost regions. The springs responsible for generating a supply of water remain dormant and a heavy shower of rain makes little difference. The banks are clothed with a wide variety of sedges, rushes and flowering plants together with a complement of trees and shrubs making the river a verdant corridor, rich in wildlife.

A visit in January provides a very different picture. Crystal-clear water surges over beds of bleached sedges, sweeping them into sinuous waves and excavating hollows of sand and gravel in its haste. The river has the appearance of a chalk stream with its gin-clear pools and swirling waters – more like the higher reaches of the Hampshire Avon or the Dorset Stour.

A winter's walk along the Thames Path is always a great pleasure. Statuesque teasels and a varied assortment of riverside plants provide food for flocks of goldfinches. Over-wintering birds such as fieldfares and redwings find berries on elder and hawthorn, and long-tailed tits explore the overhanging trees for dormant insects. Sometimes a heron is seen standing, grey and forlorn, by the waterside, an unlikely outpost for a fish supper, but there may be eels and crayfish, together with voles and mice displaced from their nests by rising waters.

ASHTON KEYNES

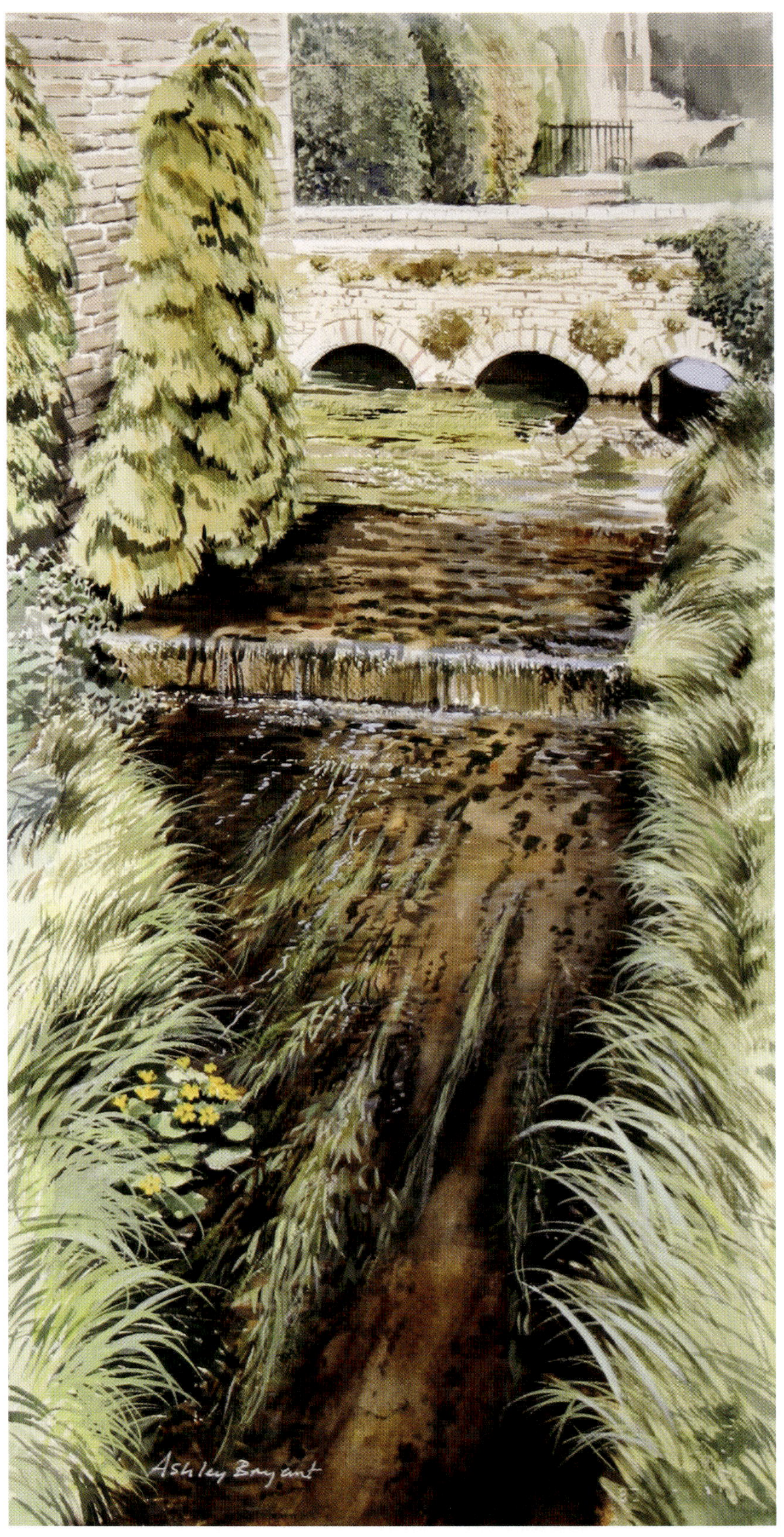

BY THE MAIN STREET
(Right)
Each house to the west of the main street requires its own bridge over this branch of the river – a delightful setting.

THE THAMES AT ASHTON KEYNES
(Opposite Page Above)
The channel of the river between the churchyard and the main street of the village is captured in this watercolour. It was painted at the end of a dry summer and the well-tended verges are brown and dry, but even so the water here flows permanently. The boys on the bridge are looking at a small shoal of fish – probably tiny roach.

OLD PREACHING CROSS
(Opposite Page Below)
This cross, one of several in the area, is located near the bridge in the painting opposite. Such crosses were erected in medieval times and used by itinerant friars as a focal point for worship and teaching.

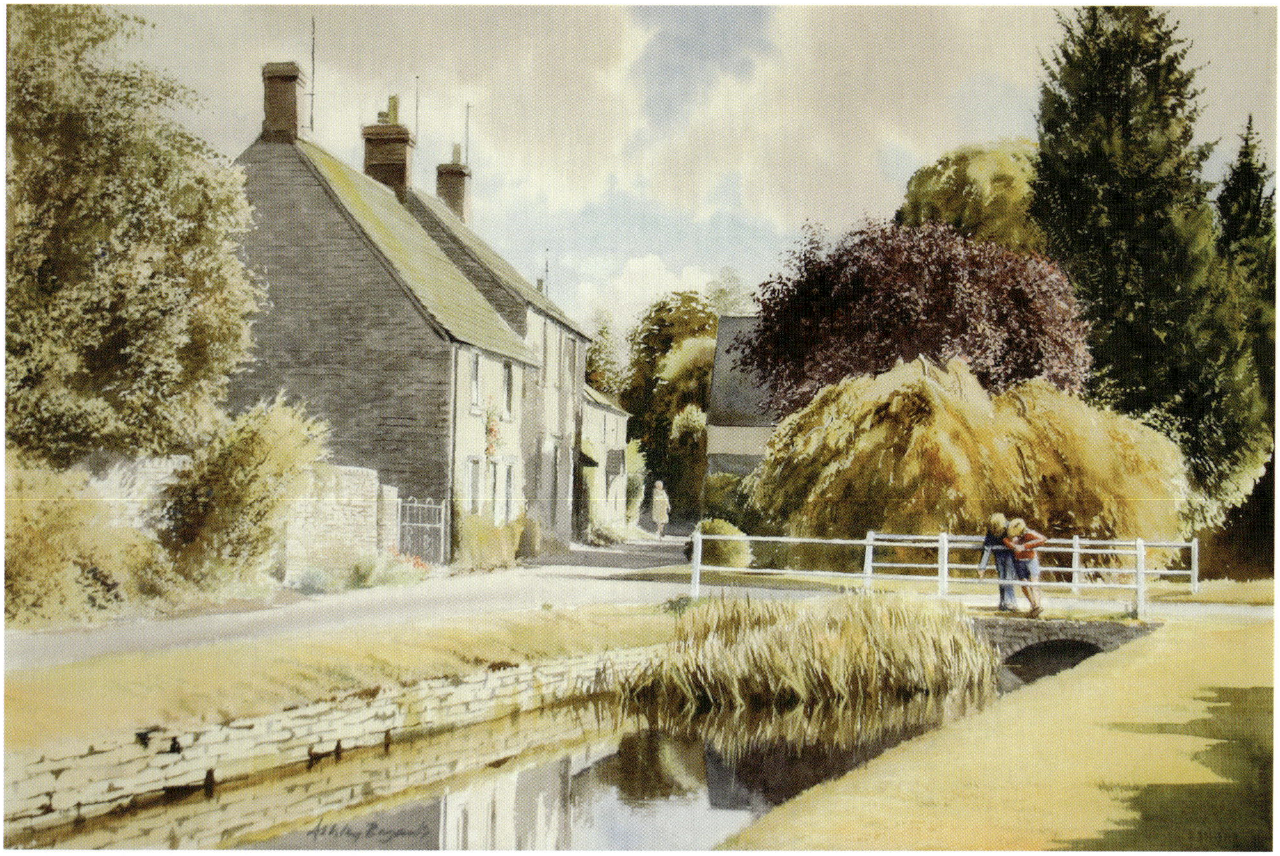

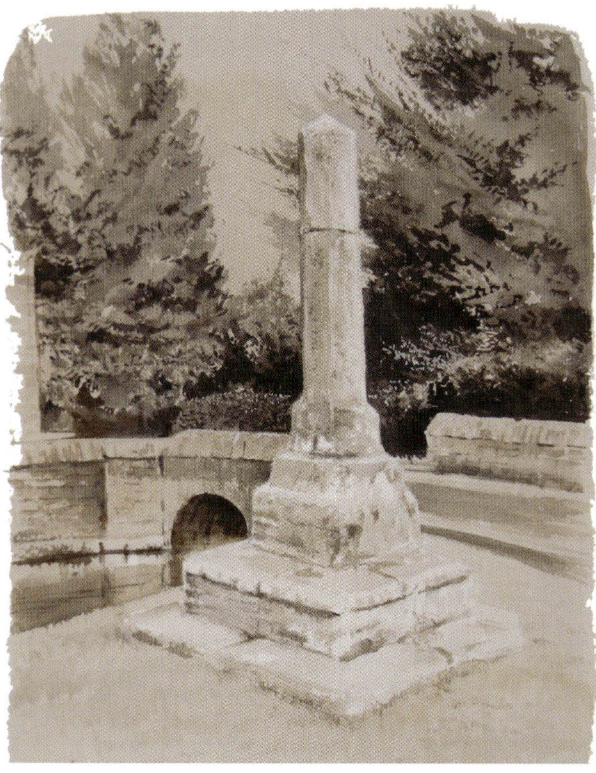

The river has already skirted around several villages and now flows directly through Ashton Keynes, a village which is largely surrounded by vast expanses of water, the result of gravel extraction in the upper Thames valley. The Thames threads its way along narrow strips of land between these flooded workings which provide extensive leisure facilities as well as havens for wildlife.

The Thames divides into separate channels as it passes through the village – man-made adaptations of the natural divisions in the river's course. The channels may have helped to disperse flood water although the village has never been a stranger to flooding. To quote the village website: "years ago, people talked of keeping their back door and front door open so the water flowed straight through, and of a foot of water standing indoors for weeks".

CRICKLADE

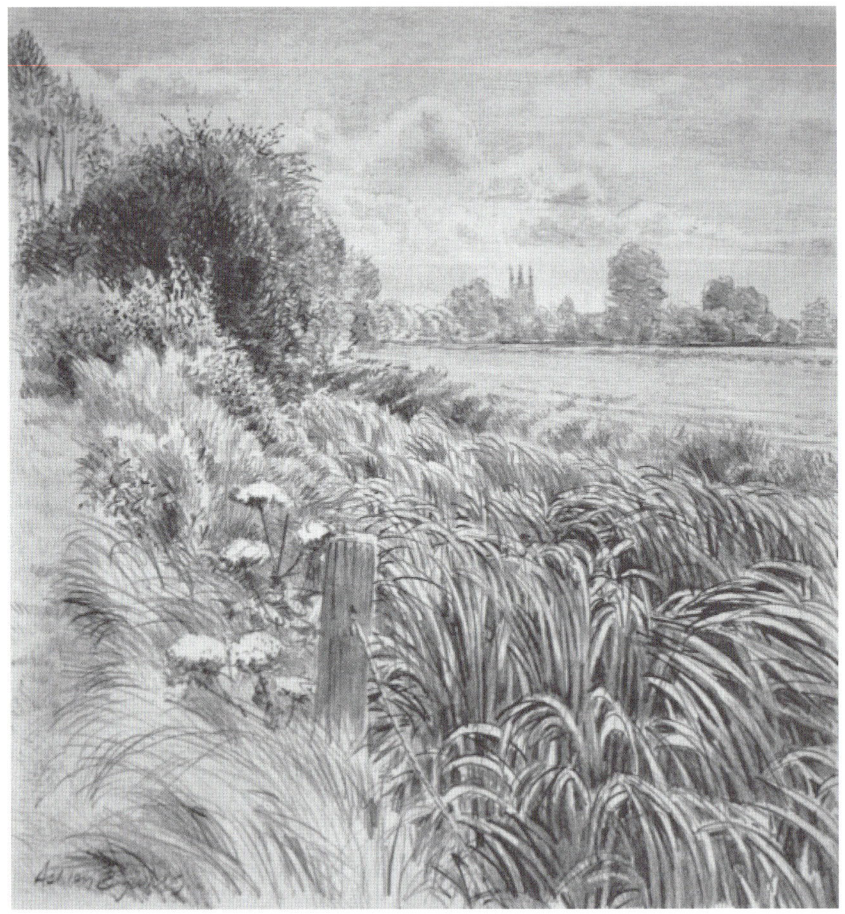

DISTANT VIEW – CRICKLADE CHURCH

The tower of Cricklade Church can just be seen in the distance in this pencil sketch. The foreground shows the river chocked with reeds, a condition not uncommon in these upper reaches of its course.

THE THAMES AT CRICKLADE

(Opposite Page)

I found this ideal viewpoint of one of the small pools on the river which was framed by overhanging willows. It is typical of many delightful pastoral scenes on the upper Thames.

COMMAS AND BRAMBLES

(Left)

Late summer and early autumn are times to collect blackberries that grow in abundance along the overgrown river margins. The fruits attract several species of butterflies, particularly commas. These butterflies always make interesting compositions with their bright orange wings, but once the wings are closed they resemble ragged brown leaves in a wonderful example of camouflage.

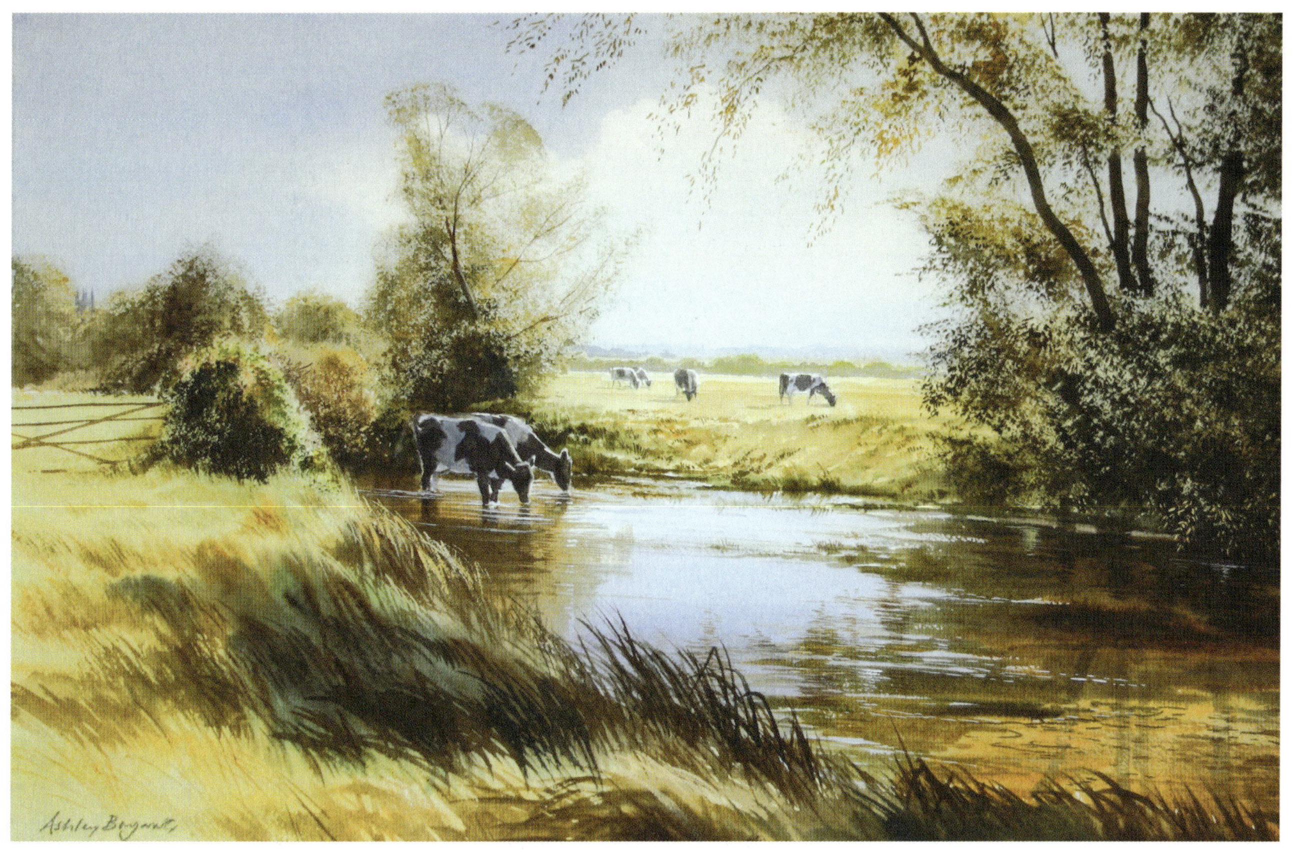

The Thames flows through rich pasture land and wild flower-filled meadows as it sweeps purposefully around Cricklade. In Summer, grassy meadows echo with the sound of grasshoppers, whilst high overhead the skylark's song contributes to sounds that were once commonplace in the countryside. In its upland reaches the river has many characteristics: it occasionally sweeps into a wide sunlit pool as shown in the main painting; it hurries under thickets of bramble and briar intertwined with old-man's beard and greater bindweed; it sparkles around gravel bars and dives into reed-choked channels. Here and there its pace slackens as it slides through darker corridors and deeper pools, shafts of sunlight picking out the shapes of intertwined tree roots and lurking chub. These fish are masters of survival in small rivers, waiting for food to wash down in the current and growing surprisingly large on the proceeds.

The Thames receives contributions from numerous tributaries along its length, but none more controversial than the river Churn, which flows into the river just below Cricklade. By convention the source of the river is determined by its longest tributary. At this point the Churn is the longer of the two rivers by approximately 12 miles, which has lead to a claim that the source of the Thames should be reassigned to the Churn's source, Seven Springs near Cheltenham. The contention will always remain, but ever since Roman times Trewsbury Mead has been the accepted source of the *Tamesis* (the Latin name for the Thames).

CASTLE EATON

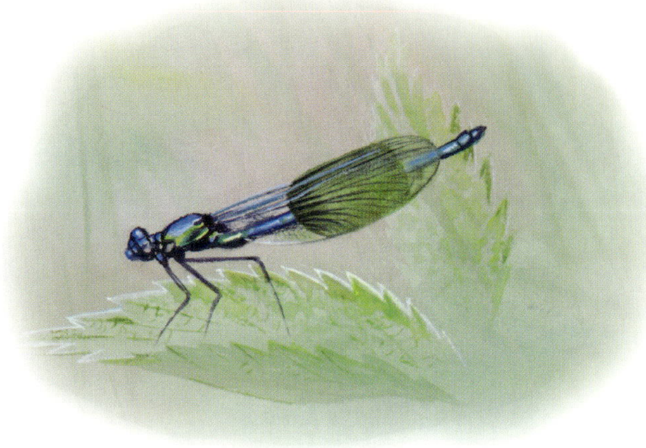

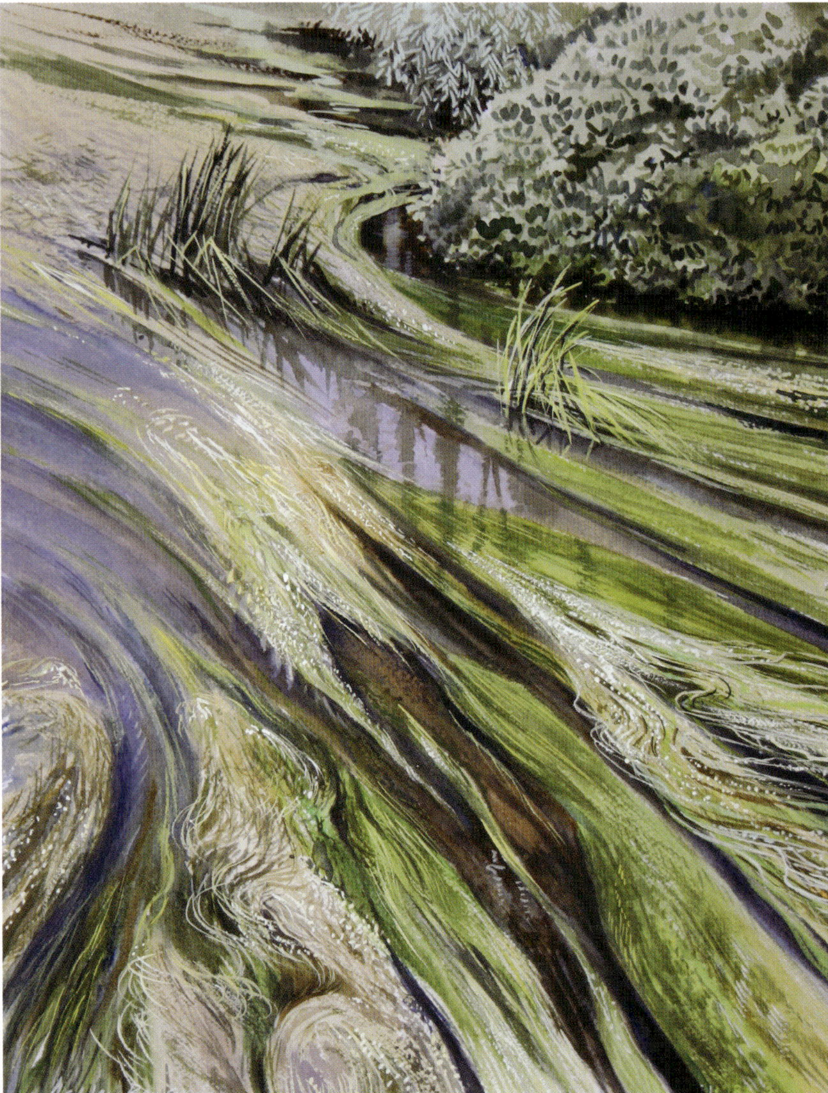

DAMSELFLY
(Above)
During the summer months, July and August in particular, there are several species of damselfly and dragonfly to be seen hawking over the river's surface. One of the most common, and by far the easiest to recognise, is the banded demoiselle, with its dark wing spots and iridescent blue green colouring.

THE THAMES AT CASTLE EATON
(Opposite Page)
One of the best locations to paint at Castle Eaton is from the Red Lion, where the lawn sweeps down to the waterside. A cool beverage on a hot day is an added advantage.

WEEDY WATERS
(Left)
The view from the bridge near the Red Lion provided this amazing arrangement of contorted weeds drifting in the shallows. Natural forms are the inspiration for many modern paintings, and I shall be working on several compositions based on these themes.

The warm, lazy days of summer are the most evocative and memorable along any river. Here the banks are clothed with rich vegetation including stately teasels, maturing spikes of russet docks and spectacular patches of purple loosestrife. The river flows lazily between its banks and huge streams of weed wave hypnotically in the deeper waters and coil into strange twisted whorls in the shallows.

If you sit quietly and watch, you may be rewarded by the sight of a kingfisher as it flies past or perches on a nearby branch where its spectacular plumage can be admired at leisure. The river is well-stocked with fish, and shoals of minnows swim temptingly between streams of weed. The grey wagtail is another delightful bird of the upper Thames that is easy to recognise with its distinctive yellow, white and grey plumage.

It seems inconceivable that barges once made their way past Castle Eaton to a wharf at Cricklade. This required much huffing, pulling and levering but there was only so much that muscle power could achieve. One solution for grounded barges was to build a small dam downstream of the barge to raise the waterlevel. This was achieved by driving wooden stakes into the riverbed, then placing boards against them. An increase of a few inches was normally enough to refloat the barge, which was then hauled upstream to the next obstruction. Competition from roads and railways has since swept away most water-borne transport.

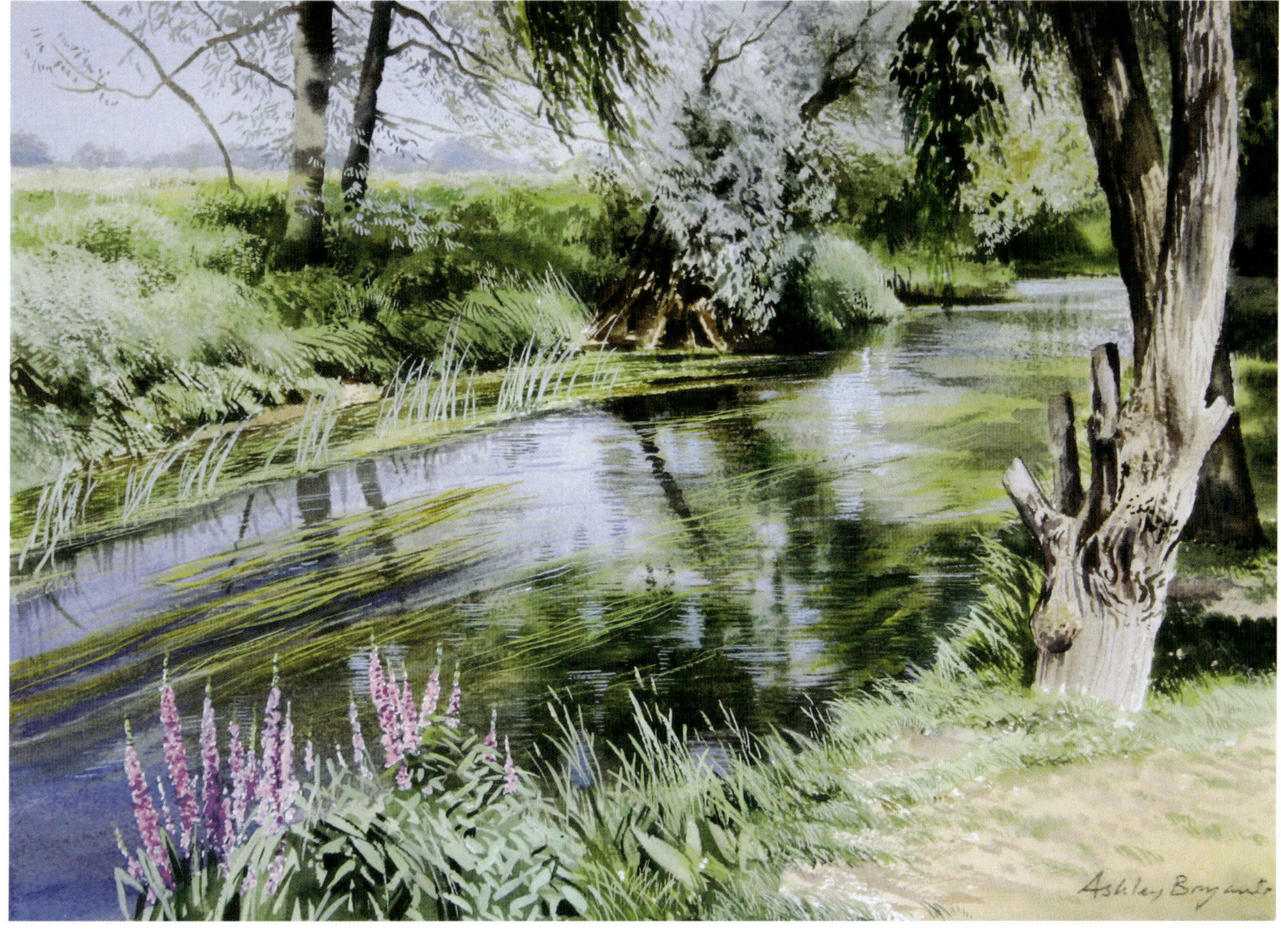

INGLESHAM

At Inglesham the river grows significantly wider, thanks to the influx of the river Coln. In addition, the widening and dredging that was carried out to provide access to the Thames and Severn Canal has allowed for navigation downstream.

This canal provided an important link between Britain's principal rivers as well as creating an east-west link. Barges laden with cheeses and Cotswold stone were joined by carriers of ironware, tinware and earthenware from the west Midlands, coal from south Wales and a host of other materials and products en-route to Oxford and London. The canal provided an important commercial highway, though – like most canals – it faced competition from the railways, and ultimately closed in 1911. During its earlier success it suffered from water shortage (in common with all canals routed over hills); water always flows downhill when locks are operated and there is a limit to the replenishment of water from reservoirs. The need to conserve water even prompted the building of water towers above lock-keeper's cottages which became known as roundhouses. One ivy-covered example is seen in the main painting behind the more modern cottage. The towers collected rainwater for domestic use, but the cocktail of algae and dead birds that must have accumulated in these tanks was no better than drinking canal water.

Inglesham church is the sole survivor of a medieval village and a visit is definitely recommended. It was restored in the late nineteenth century by the Society for the Protection of Ancient Buildings founded by William Morris who lived nearby. Its restoration was so perfect it hardly looks as if anything has been touched – a strange comment to make but we are all so accustomed to the excessive "Victorianisation" of churches. Here, it is easy to imagine a sixteenth-century congregation being completely at home amongst the old box pews, flagstone flooring and uneven walls in this simple country church which exudes a spiritual calm. The village disappeared in the fifteenth century with the decline in the wool trade on which it had depended, but here and there amongst the fields traces of old foundations can still be found.

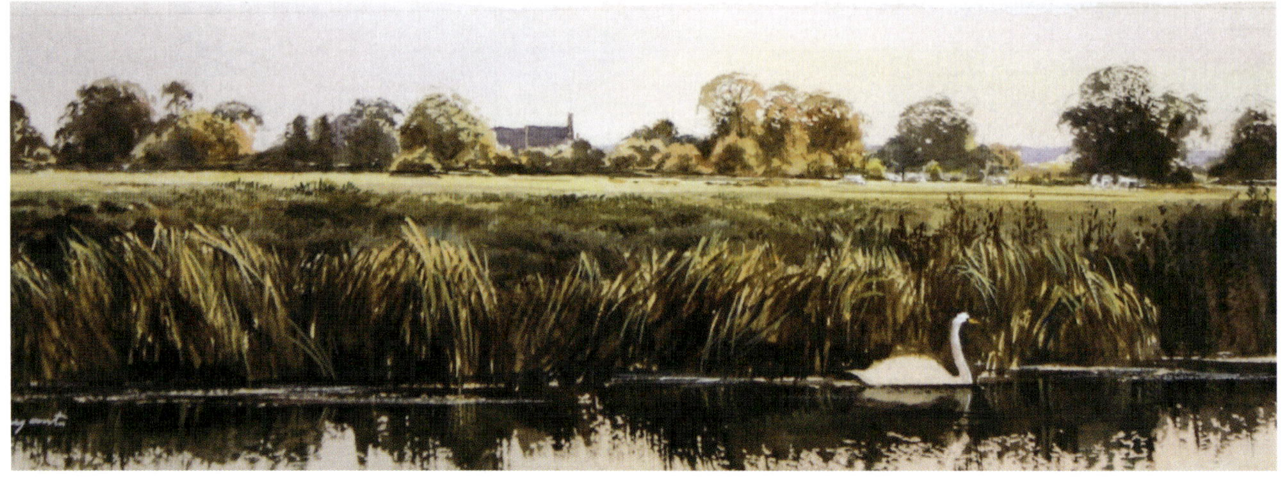

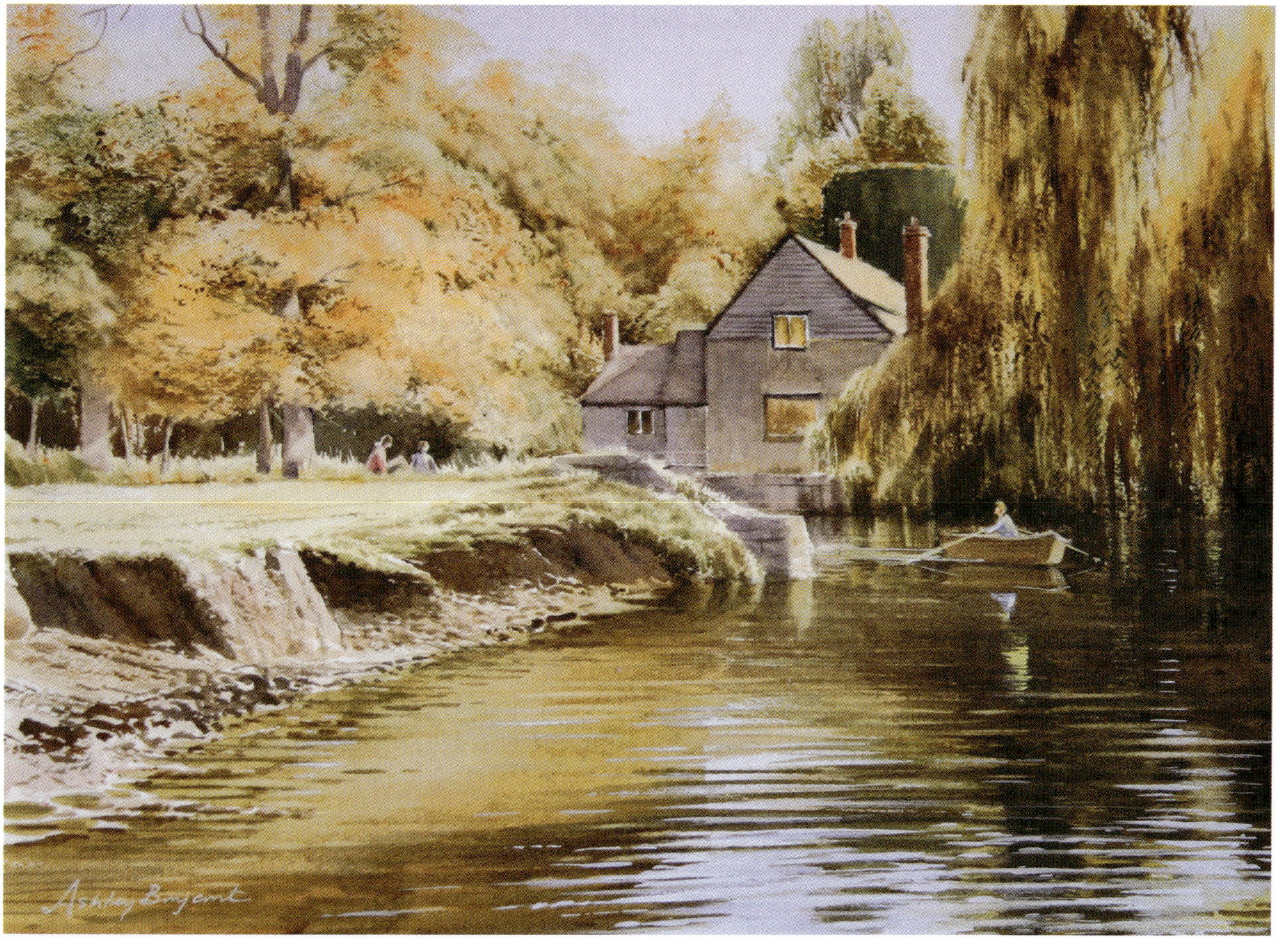

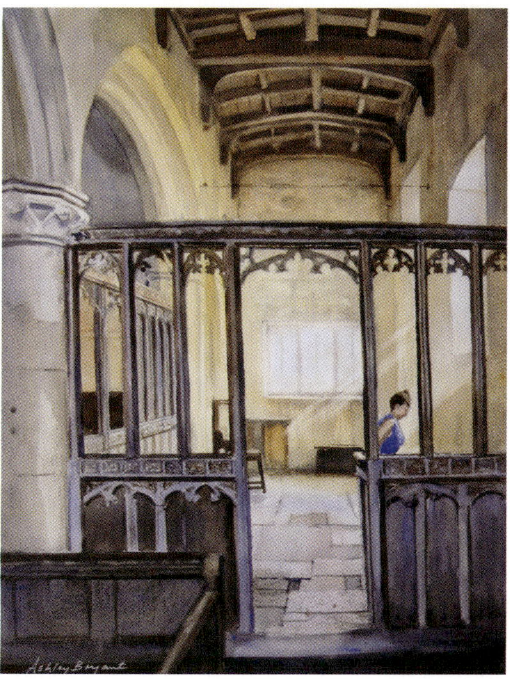

THE THAMES AT INGLESHAM
(Above)
This is a favourite view of artists and photographers which shows the original roundhouse behind the later lock cottage. The Thames flows in from the left and the old entrance to the Thames and Severn Canal is behind the rowing boat, overgrown by tall willows. I completed this painting in 2000, but in 2004, on a return journey, I was surprised to find a big gap in the trees as the canal is being restored!

RIVERBANK – INGLESHAM
(Far left)
From the high banks and calm stretches of the wider Thames we have a distant view over the meadows to Inglesham church.

INGLESHAM CHURCH
(Left)
This church is a little gem and a tribute to its sensitive restoration. In this watercolour I tried to capture some of its timeless qualities.

LECHLADE

Lechlade is the highest town boats can reach on the Thames and provides the boating community and tourists alike with a wide choice of pubs, restaurants and antique and gift shops. This appealing small town on the southern fringes of the Cotswolds was once an inland port, which became one of the busiest in the country when the Thames and Severn Canal was opened in 1789. The riverside wharves were crowded with barges and the quaysides teamed with dock-hands, bargees, merchants and farmers. The present marina occupies the centre of this once thriving activity but almost all vestiges of the port have long been swept away.

One Lechlade attraction for artists and photographers is Halfpenny bridge, built in 1792 during a busy period of bridge construction. This replaced a ferry and, as the name implies, it was a toll bridge. In those days bridges were not financed by central government and their construction was often left to wealthy landowners who naturally required a return on their money. Halfpenny bridge is certainly an elegant structure of glowing Cotswold stone, and the languid Thames provides a complement of boats and swans to complete the setting.

The Thames Path provides a popular riverside walk upstream to nearby Inglesham or downstream to St. John's Lock, the first lock on the river. The areas around each Thames lock are always well maintained with neat lawns, and flowerbeds reminiscent of country railway stations in the 1950s. At St. John's there is the added interest of a stone carving of Old Father Thames, who gazes serenely at passing boats. He too, is an artistic focal point.

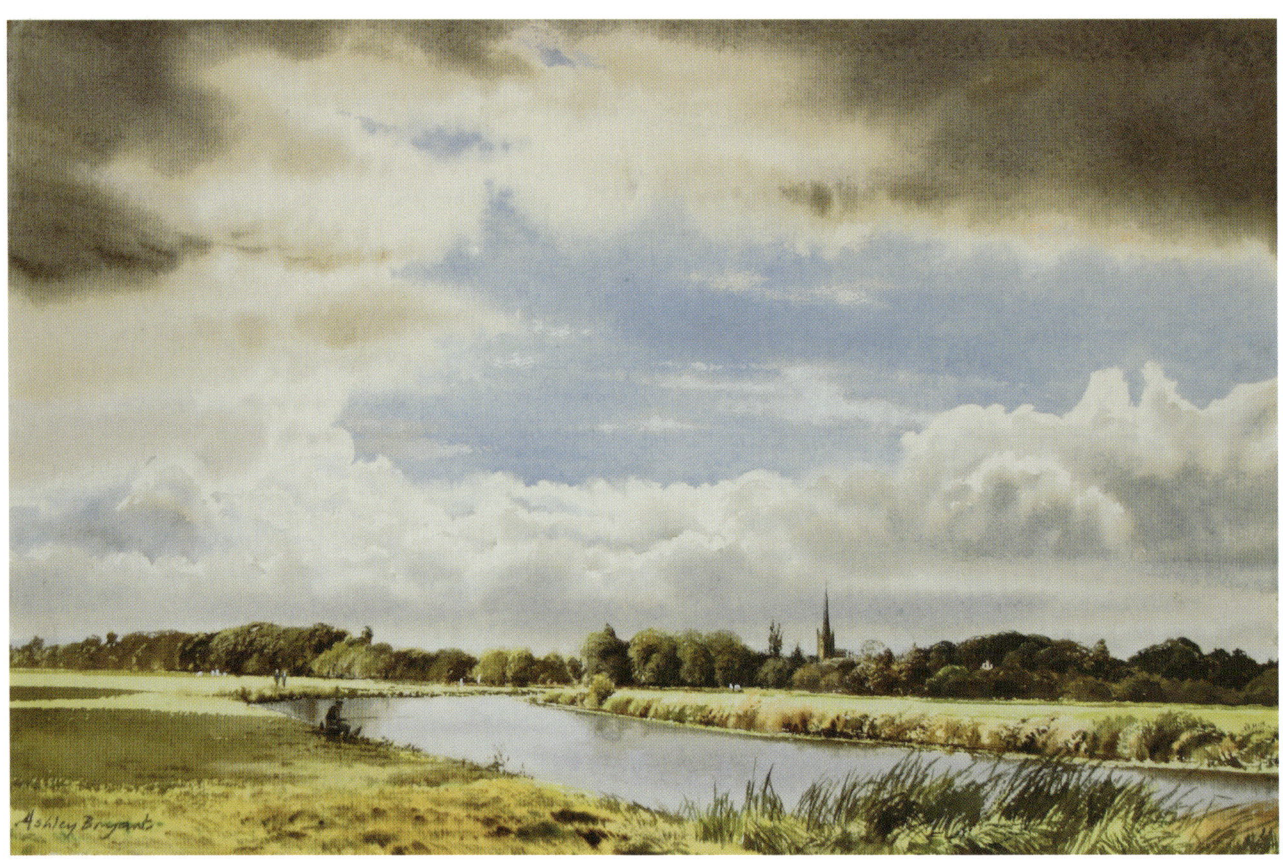

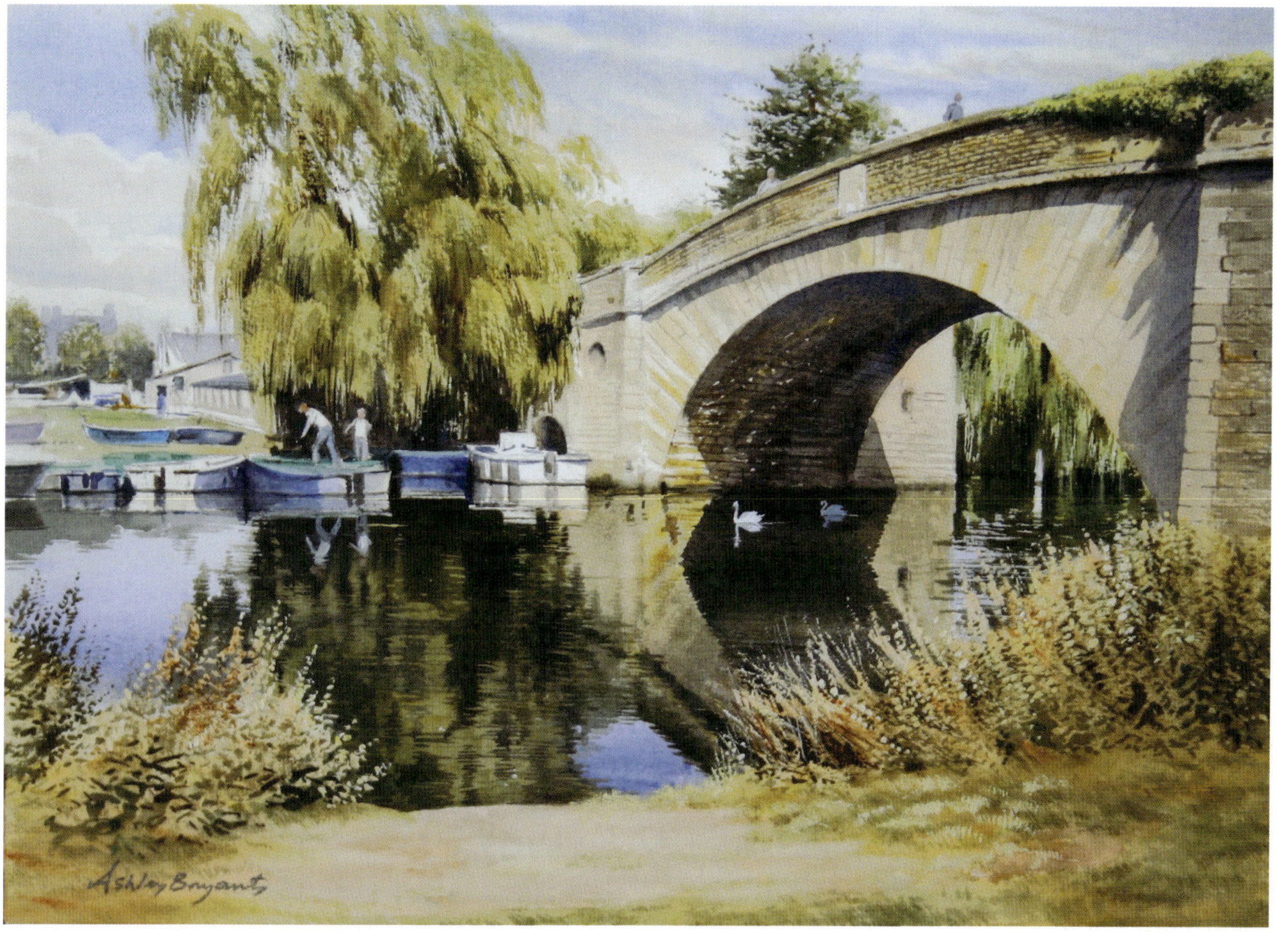

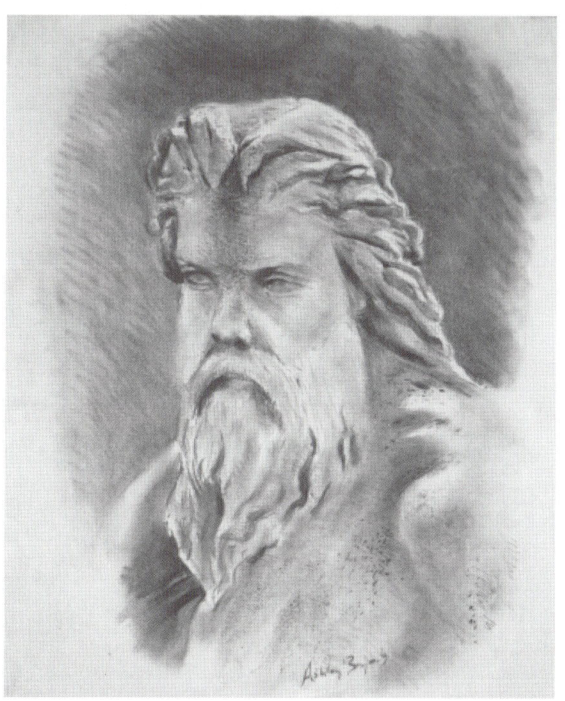

HALFPENNY BRIDGE

(Above)

When I painted this scene it was a late September afternoon and the bridge glowed with light on the upstream side. The view looks towards Lechlade, which is situated entirely on the north side of the river.

THE THAMES AT LECHLADE

(Opposite Page)

The spire of St. Lawrence's church provides a landmark for miles around, whilst the rest of Lechlade is hidden by the trees in the distance. The vantage point for this watercolour was just upstream from St. John's Lock. I considered including a few boats but decided they would have disturbed the tranquillity of the scene. Long periods of time often pass without any boating traffic on these upper reaches.

OLD FATHER THAMES

(Left)

In this charcoal sketch I tried to capture the serene but knowing gaze on the face of Old Father Thames. This statue was shown at the Great Exhibition in 1851, moved to the source of the Thames where he resided for many years, until he was moved to avoid the growing risk of vandalism.

BUSCOT

BUSCOT WEIR
(Below)
High summer as the Thames lazily winds its way to the weir and footbridge.

WATERLILIES
(Right)
These waterlillies caught my eye on a visit to Buscot Park.

FISHERMEN AT BUSCOT
(Opposite Page)
This accommodating angler allowed me to produce this pencil sketch.

SIGNAL CRAYFISH
(Opposite Page Below)
These powerful crayfish, originally introduced from America, are now found in large numbers in the Thames.

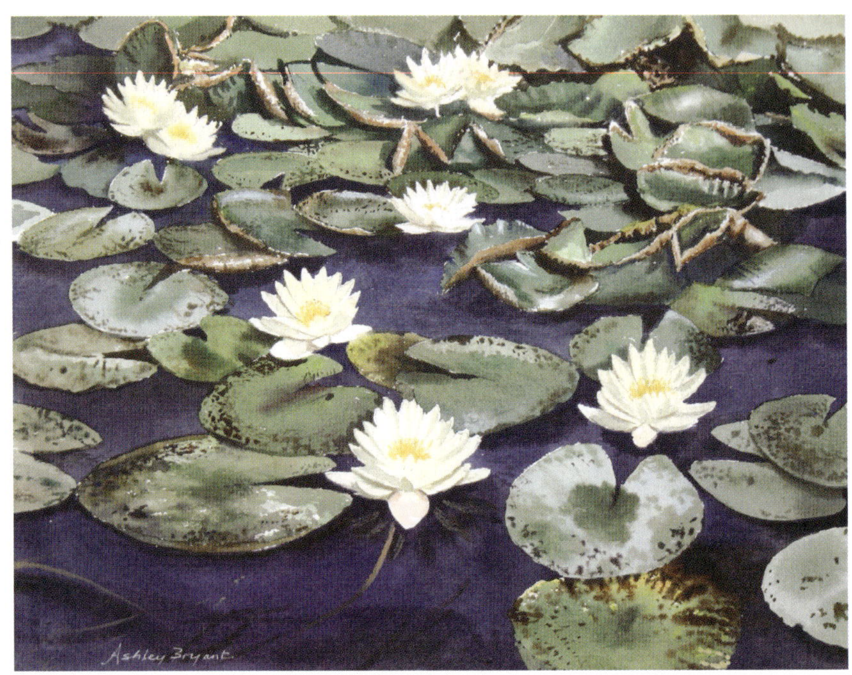

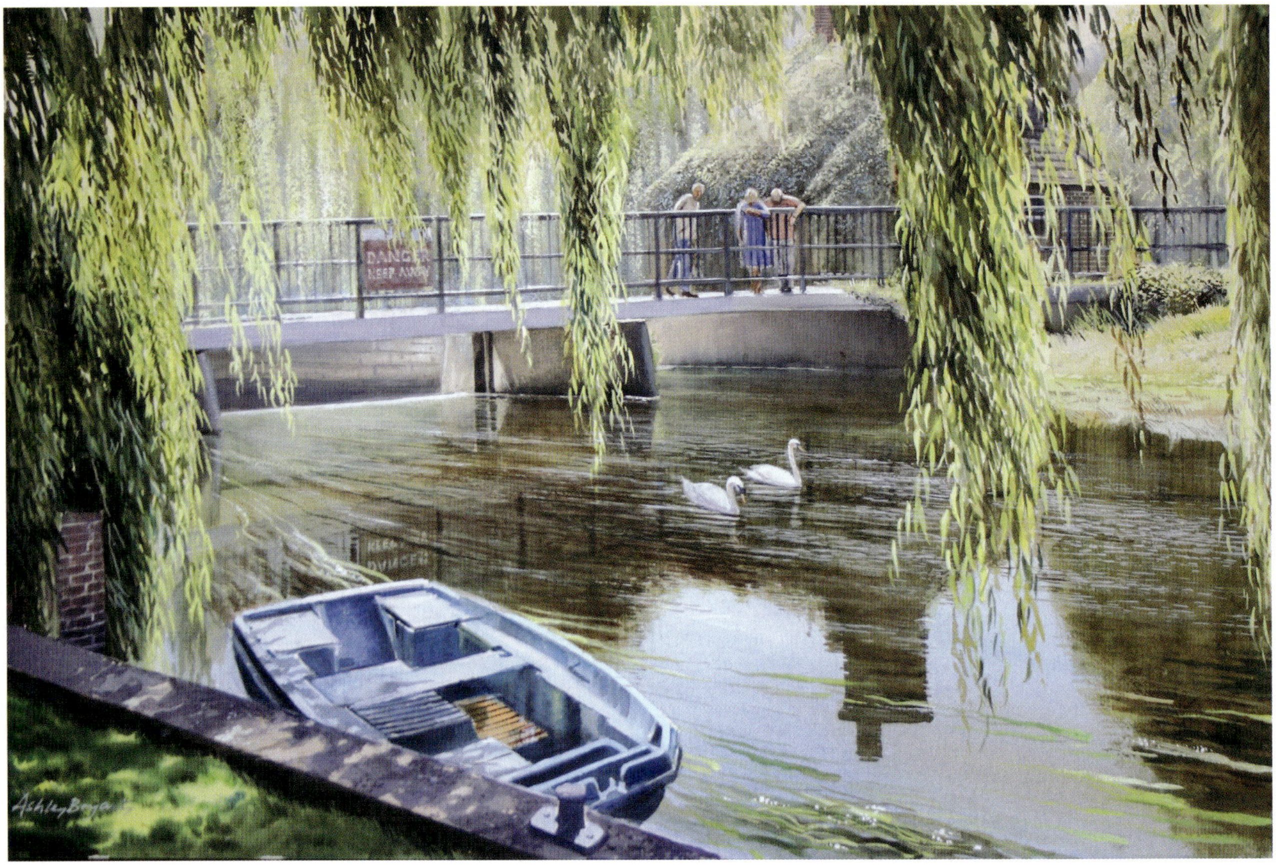

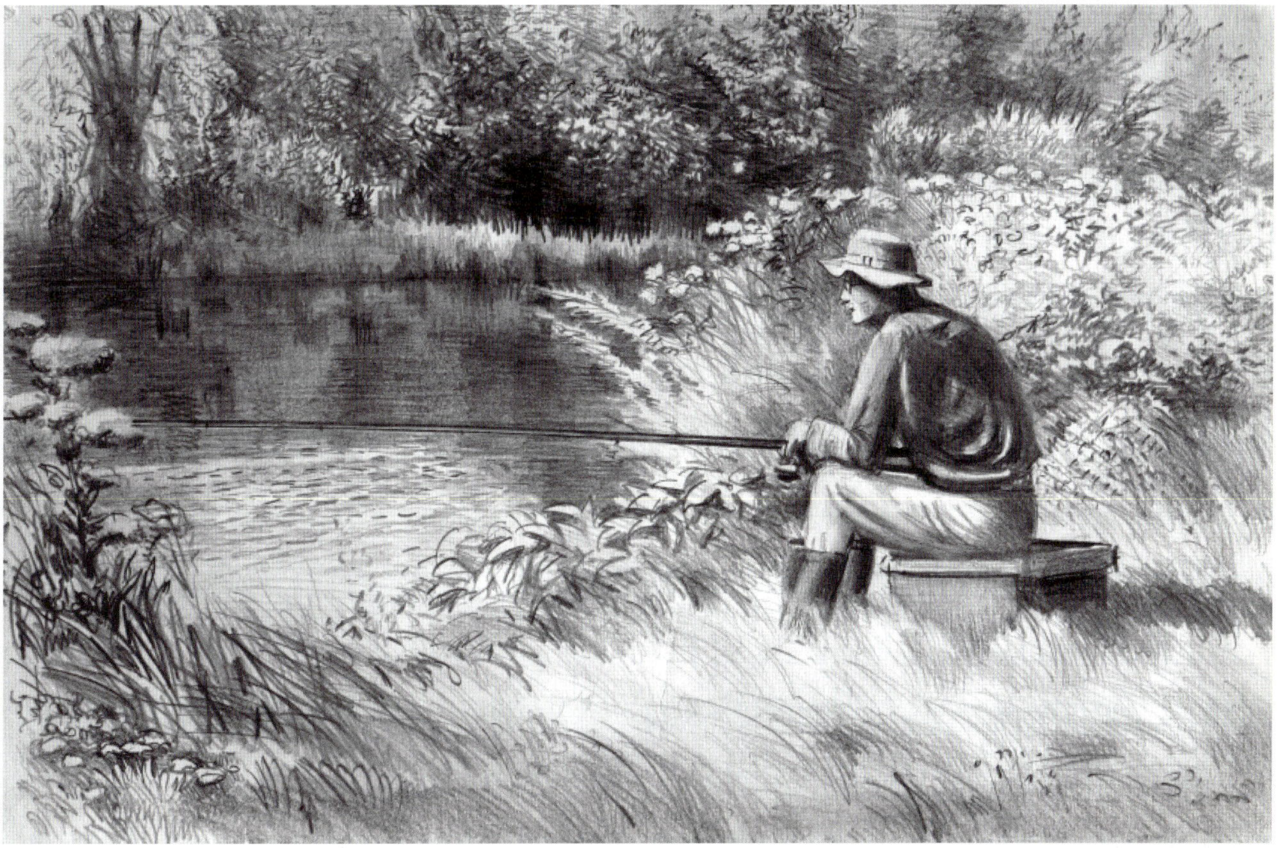

The Thames Path winds its way along the river towards Buscot, the spire of Lechlade church receding into the distance. Not far away stands Buscot House, built in the palladian style in the 1770's. This architectural gem contains an exceptional art collection with paintings by Rembrandt, Murillo, Reynolds and Burne-Jones.

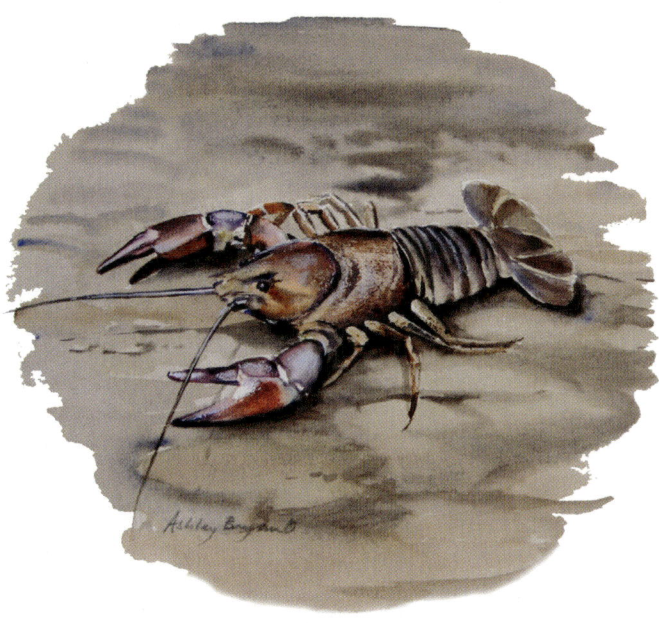

The ever-widening river begins to attract anglers. These are the people who really know about their patch of the Thames and it is useful to chat with them about the river. An unusual creature they catch on rod and line is the American signal crayfish, an introduced species that is voracious in its feeding habits, eating small fish and fish eggs and therefore of concern to anglers. They have spread rapidly and caused the complete demise of the natural crayfish, finding few friends since their irresponsible introduction into British waters.

KELMSCOTT

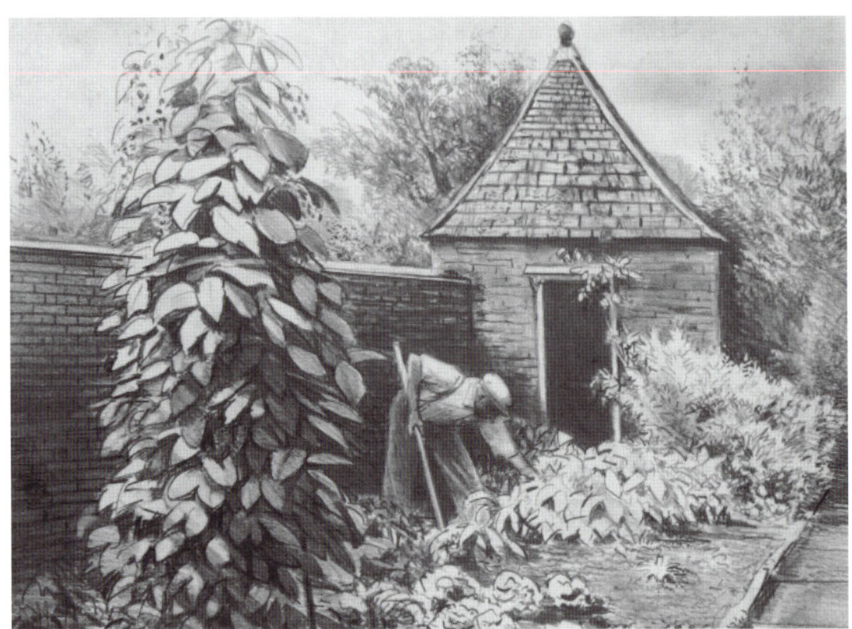

THE VEGETABLE GARDEN
Artists are drawn to Kelmscott Manor for a number of reasons – the association with Morris and the Pre-Raphaelites as well as an opportunity to sketch the delightful Elizabethan building. There are many interesting viewpoints of the manor house and its outbuildings, but this corner of the garden appealed to me.

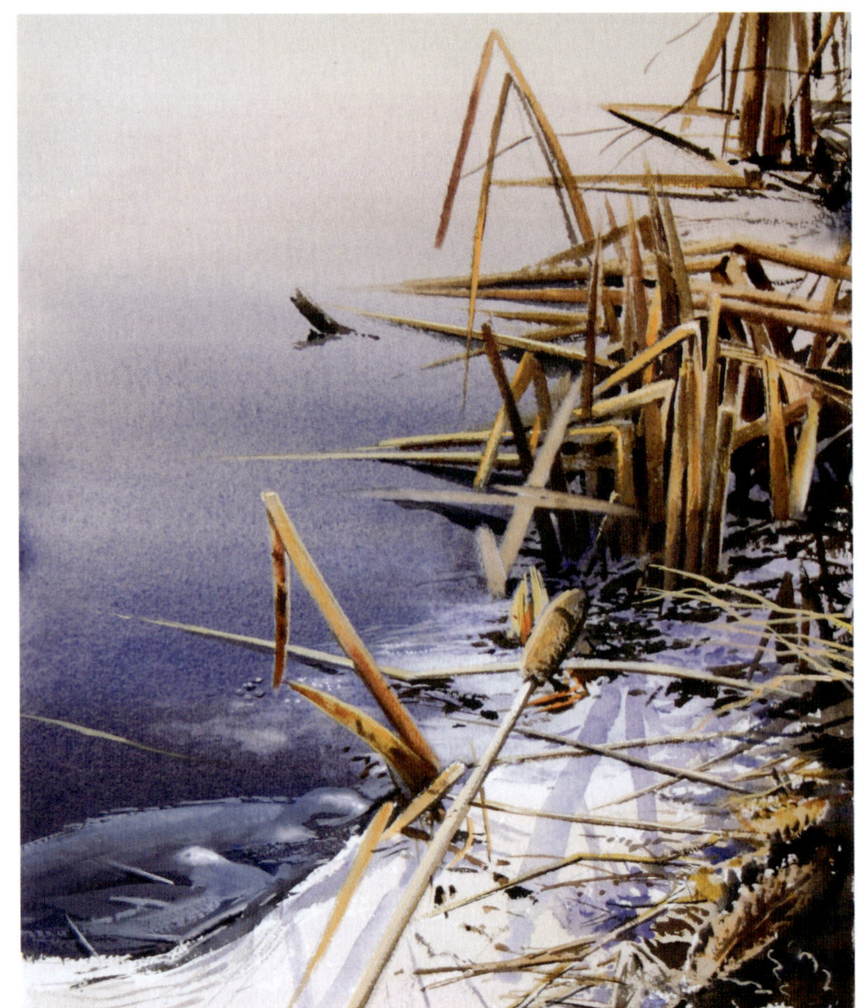

THE THAMES AT KELMSCOTT
(Opposite Page)
This frosty morning provided a blend of interesting colours with subtle shades of pinks, blues and browns which I tried to hold in mind until I later produced this painting in my studio. I had intended to sketch the manor house but this view proved irresistible. However, I plan on a summer visit when I can soak up the atmosphere of William Morris' boating parties and hope that a little of his guests' talents will rub off.

THE RIVER'S EDGE
(Right Below)
A study of the reed-fringed river downstream from Kelmscott on a winter's day.

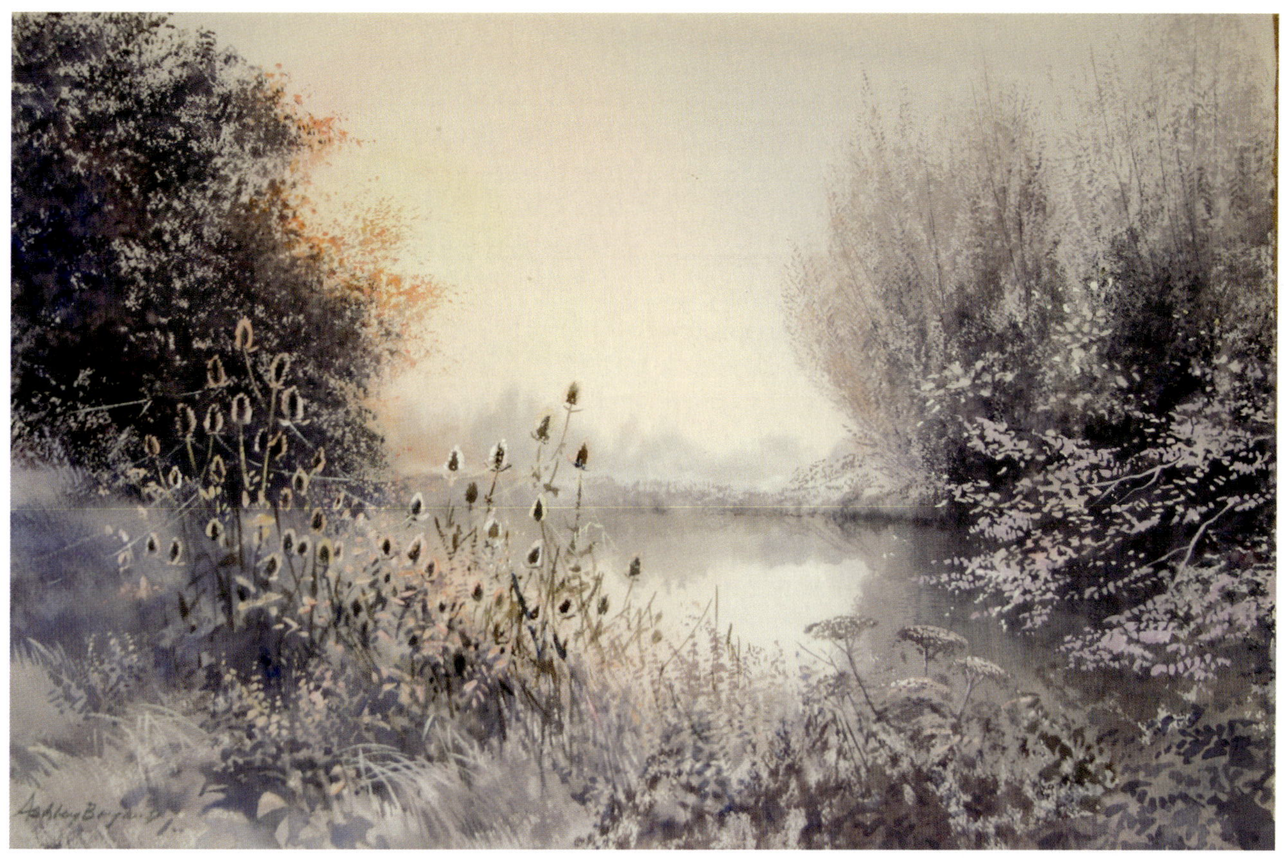

My over-riding attraction in this stretch of the Thames was in visiting Kelmscott Manor, but on this freezing November morning I found it closed to visitors. Nevertheless, as one door literally closed another opened and it provided an opportunity to walk by the river in the footsteps of some notable Victorian artists.

In the late nineteenth century, Kelmscott Manor was the country home of William Morris, the leading light in the Arts and Crafts movement. Using traditionally inspired designs he produced furniture, textiles and wallpapers using the best craftsmanship and materials. It is not surprising that his passion for traditional values and the romance of the past brought him into contact with the art movement of the day that shared these ideals, namely the Pre-Raphaelite Brotherhood. In fact, he shared the lease at Kelmscott from 1871 with Dante Gabriel Rossetti, the most flamboyant of the Pre-Raphaelite artists. Their relationship deteriorated however, partly because Rossetti proved to be an irascible and moody co-tenant, but mainly because of the strain caused by his relationship with Morris' wife.

During the height of their friendship their talents and energies drew like-minded people to Kelmscott. These guests were not just artists and craftsmen, and formed a wider circle of writers, poets and philosophers. The Manor became a focus for inspiration and provided a forum for swapping and developing ideas – a veritable powerhouse of creativity. Throughout this period boating parties were held along the river and with a little imagination one can see the likes of Millais, Holman Hunt and Burne-Jones smoking their after-picnic pipes under the shade of a tree, contentedly enjoying the poetry of Christina Rossetti.

RADCOT

The oldest bridge on the Thames is impossible to ignore, so I made my way downstream to see it at Radcot. The date of construction is unknown and even the century is uncertain, but it is likely to have been built as early as the 12th century. The structure incorporates ecclesiastical features such as ribbed arches and a niche over the central arch that once held a statue of the Virgin Mary. Tolls were originally paid to Beaulieu Abbey, indicating monastic builders. We know nothing of its history before 1312 when a grant of "pontage" was awarded for repairs, presumably quite a long time after it was constructed.

Radcot Bridge provided a key crossing of the Thames between Farringdon in the immediate south and Bampton in the north, but it held strategic importance over a far wider area. For this reason it was fought over in two major battles. The Battle of Radcot was fought here between the forces of the Earl of Oxford and Henry of Lancaster in 1387. It was a bloody battle and the Thames was said to have flowed red. In the second instance the bridge was fought over in 1645 during the Civil War. Some battlefields retain an atmosphere of gloom, but this is not the case at Radcot. My visits have always found this location to be calm and relaxing and I have tried to capture this mood in the paintings.

There were plans in the late eighteenth century to demolish Radcot Bridge, when widening of the river to improve navigation threatened the entire structure. Fortunately it was found to be more practical to construct a new cut with its own wider bridge a short distance to the north, and the original bridge remained to span a backwater, preserving it for posterity.

The Thames valley slopes gently upwards on either side of its flood plain, and the attractive town of Farringdon provides some glorious views over this lovely rural landscape.

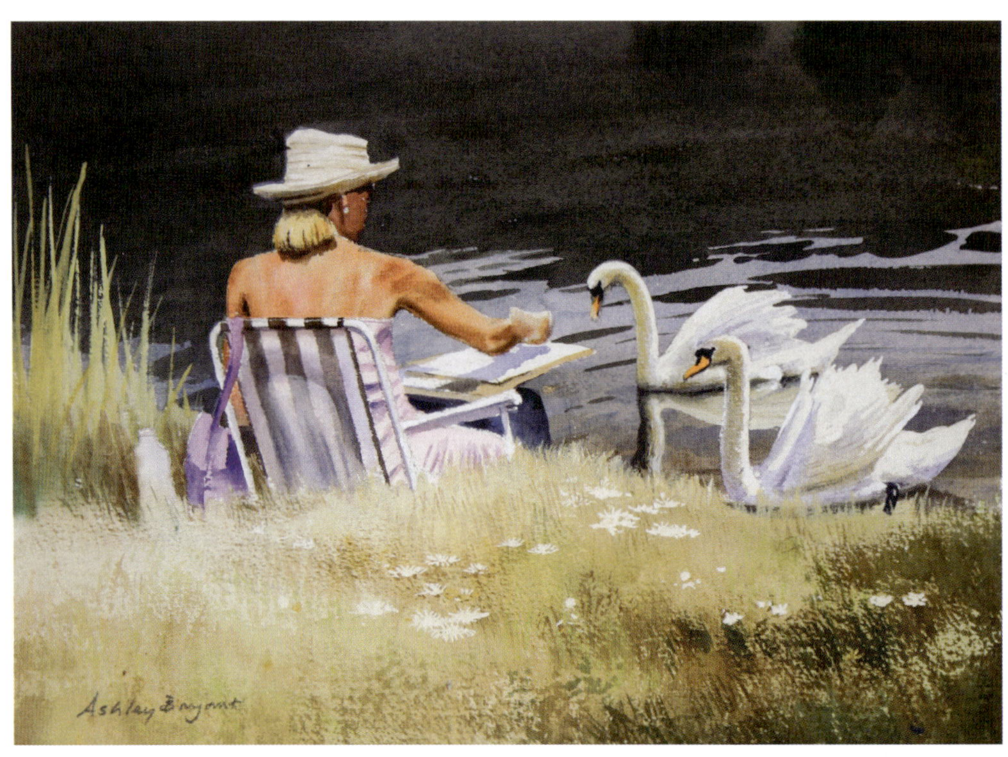

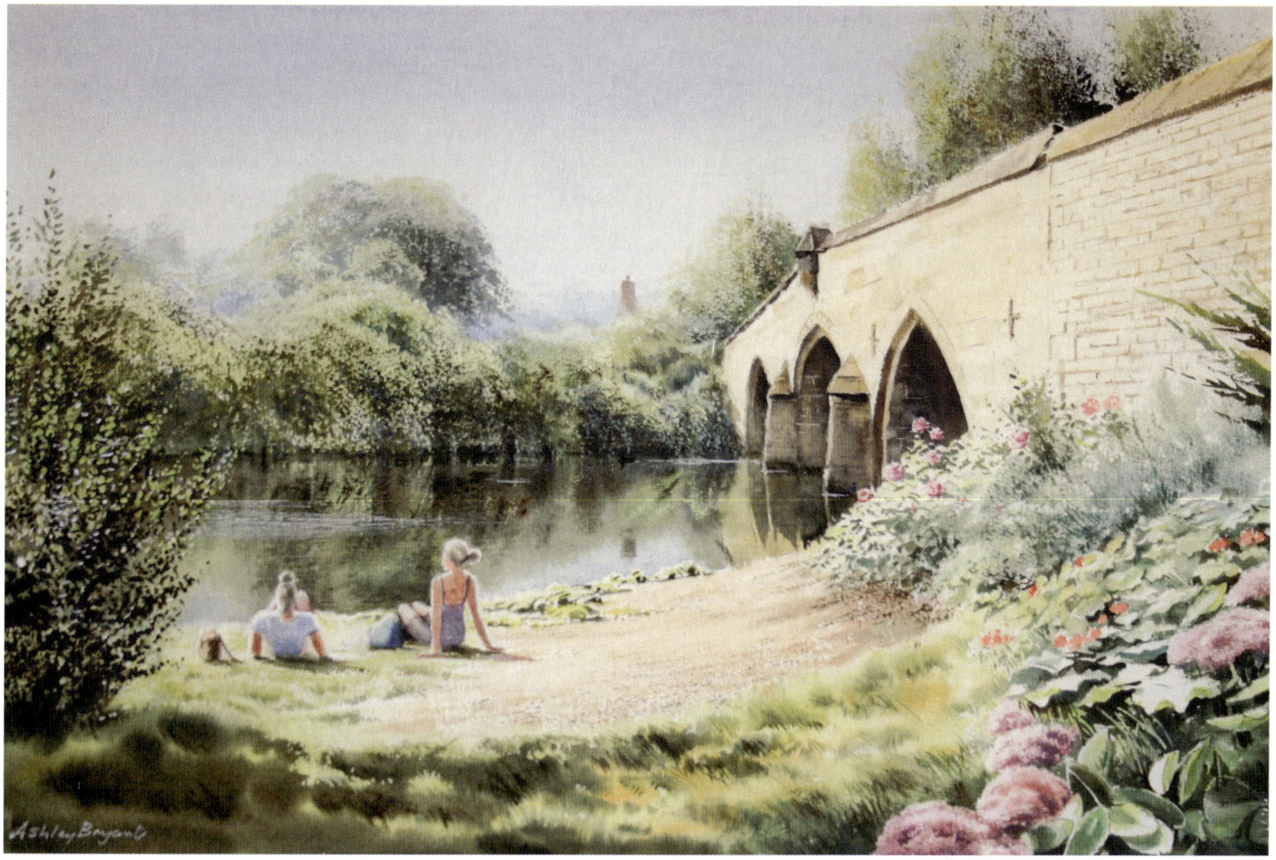

CAPTIVE AUDIENCE
(Opposite page)
I am not sure whether the artist or the swans are the subject of this painting. The artist was totally absorbed in her own watercolour of the swans.

THE THAMES AT RADCOT
(Above)
This mellow scene shows Radcot Bridge and the calm Thames backwater. The pointed arches and style of the bridge indicate an ecclesiastical influence.

THAMES VALLEY FROM FARRINGDON
(Below)
A pencil sketch showing an evening view of the Thames valley from Farringdon looking over to Radcot in the far distance.

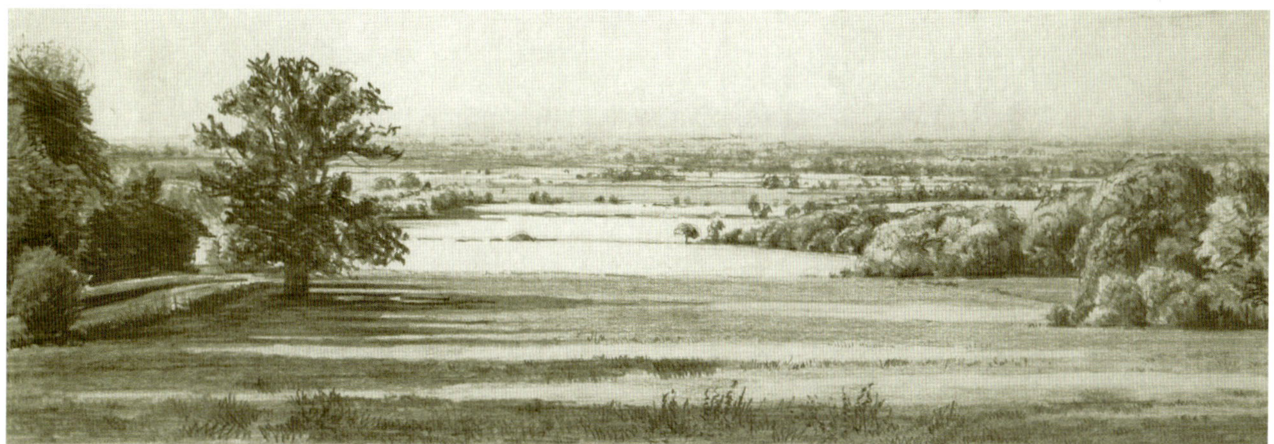

NEWBRIDGE

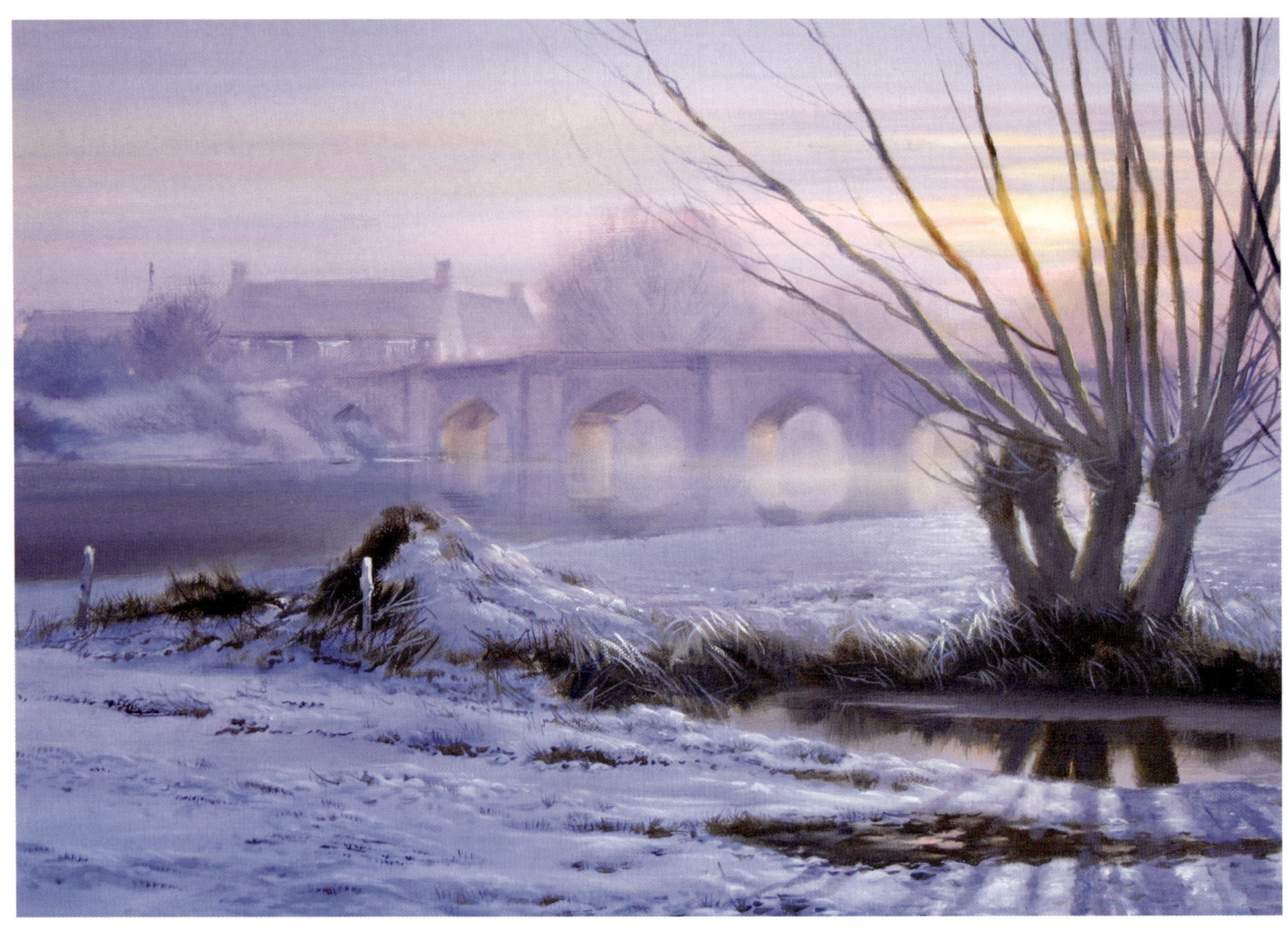

THE THAMES AT NEWBRIDGE
(Above)
A cold January morning greeted me on one of my visits to Newbridge. In order to help with the wintery feel I emphasised the light scattering of snow, as snow scenes are in scarce supply these days. Snow on the ground adds to the difficulties of travelling around the country, so the artist requires imagination for such a painting.

PIKE FISHERMEN
(Opposite Page)
The art of fishing is imbued with a lot of hope and a blank day never seems to defeat the true angler. Perhaps there is always plenty to see and enjoy on the river, but these two anglers were very pleased with their catch and were obviously enjoying a successful day.

The name "Newbridge" is a misnomer since this graceful but sturdy bridge, claimed to be the oldest on the Thames, has stood here since the thirteenth century. Nowadays it takes a large volume of heavy traffic, especially at peak periods. Lorries roar away from the traffic lights disturbing the peace of this isolated crossing of the river, and scrapes on the masonry of the bridge show it is no stranger to traffic accidents. However, the bridge is built of stern stuff, its strong pointed arches and heavy buttresses resisting the awesome power of the river in flood. Two weeks before my first visit here, the Thames had almost reached the top of the central arch and the floodwater had extended to a ¼ mile wide. Anyone who has tried to move a child's paddling pool containing a few inches of water will gain some idea of the incredible force of this wall of water. On the south side of the bridge, the Maybush Inn suffered badly with water lapping half way up the bar. Such is the propensity of the Thames to flood, an occurence which seems likely to increase in regularity with global warming.

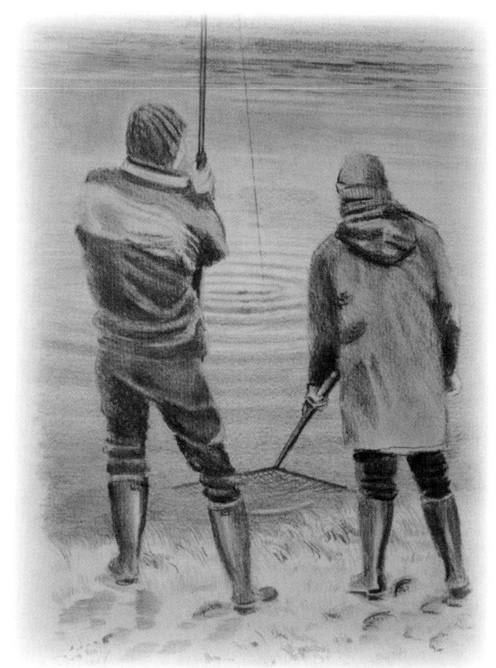

The Windrush is the largest tributary to join the Thames so far, emerging almost unnoticed on the upstream side of the bridge. This clear tributary, rising (35-miles away) from the Cotswolds, is well known for its trout and barbel, but many other species of fish are also caught in the Thames at this point.

On the morning of my visit two anglers caught my attention and I followed their pike-fishing activities with interest. In the surging waters that followed the flood, they ledgered their bait (sprats from the fishmonger) in a deep and quiet channel of water. Once they had placed their rods in rests, the coffee drinking and sandwich eating began. They joked that if they didn't catch anything they could at least take the bait home to eat. Suddenly, a rod started bouncing in its rest, an angler raced forwards and the fight was on. The pike, clearly of some size, raced for the centre of the river where its strength and the strong current took it downstream on its first powerful run. The angler's reel was screaming, the line was stripped off against the pre-set resistance, taking the fish almost fifty yards towards the bridge before it was held in check.

It was drawn back time and time again, slack line wound in quickly. Then, with a bucking of the rod and a whirring of the reel, the fish was off again. After ten minutes of adrenaline overload, the angler eventually drew the fish towards the bank and its white belly could be seen in the depths as it rolled and struggled. The second angler held the landing net as the pike was drawn forwards for the final nerve-wracking seconds of capture. Any fisherman will tell you this is when fish often make a final and successful lunge for freedom. But it was in the net, and hauled triumphantly on to the bank. It tipped the scales at just under 20lbs, and was ceremoniously put back into the river to grow even larger. No doubt the pike will also grow with the telling, and over a pint or two it has probably beome a 30lb monster. Such is the lore of fishing.

SWINFORD

EYNSHAM LOCK
(Opposite Page)
This is one of the few manually operated locks on the Thames, similar to those on most canals.

RIVERSIDE MEADOWS
(Right)
The Thames meanders towards Swinford Bridge through meadows, grazed by cattle and sturdy ponies, which provide several interesting vantage points for paintings.

SWINFORD BRIDGE
(Below)
This bridge was constructed as part of a turnpike system in 1771, and charges are still levied today.

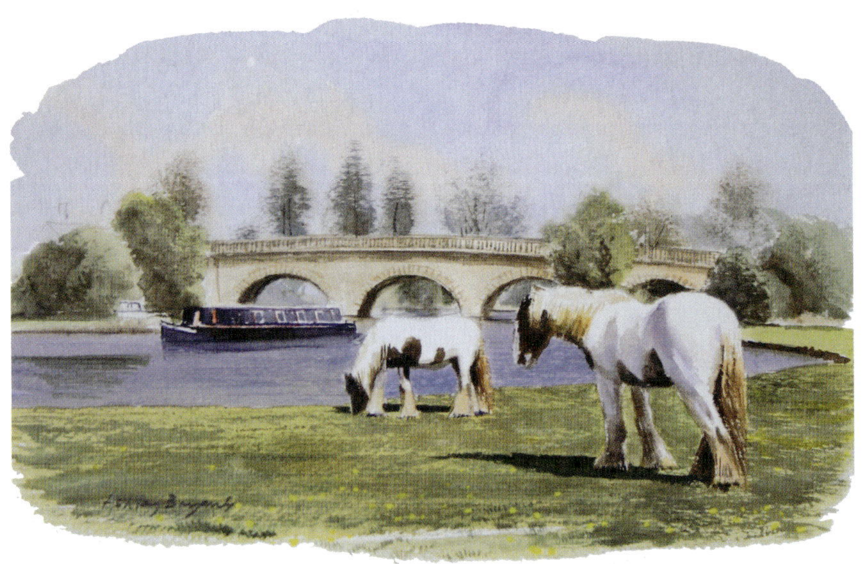

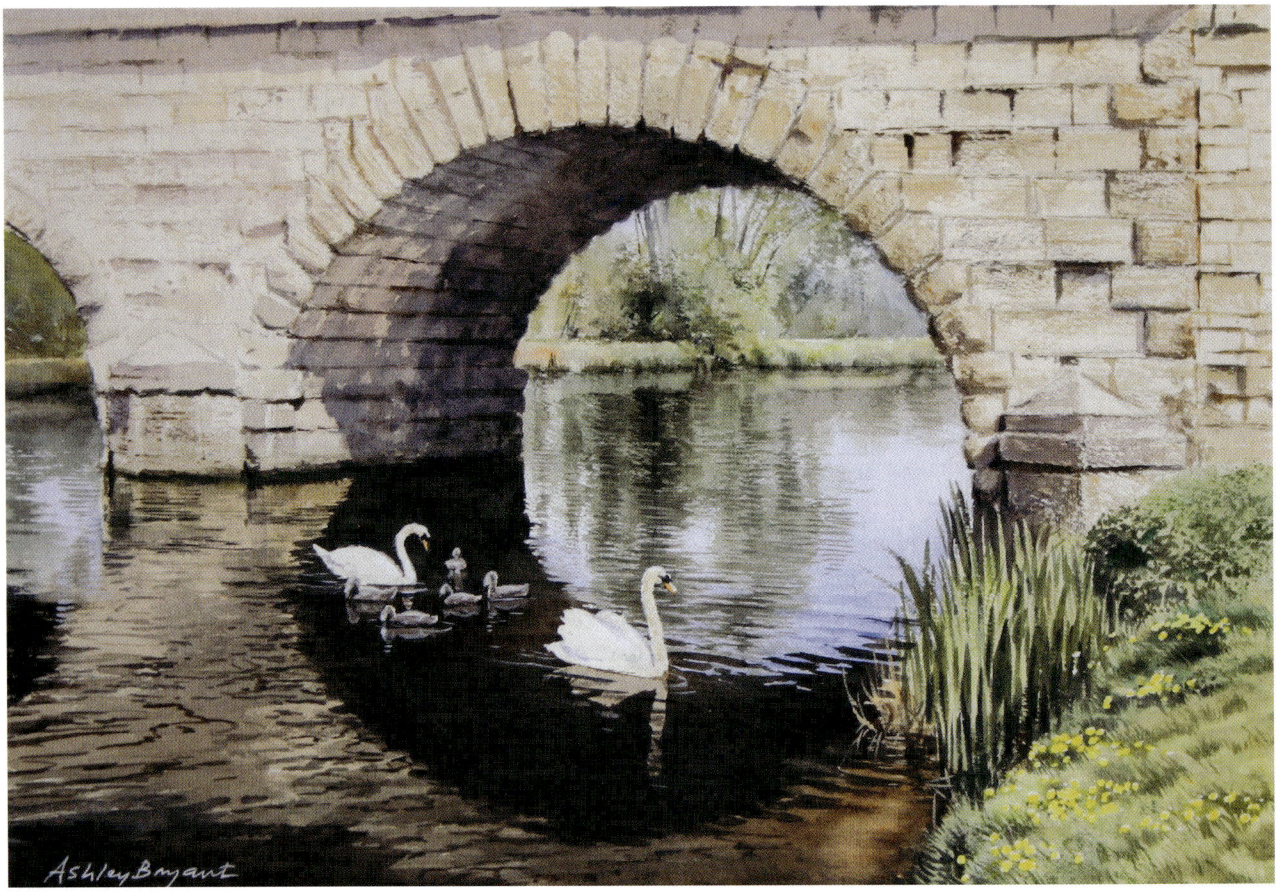

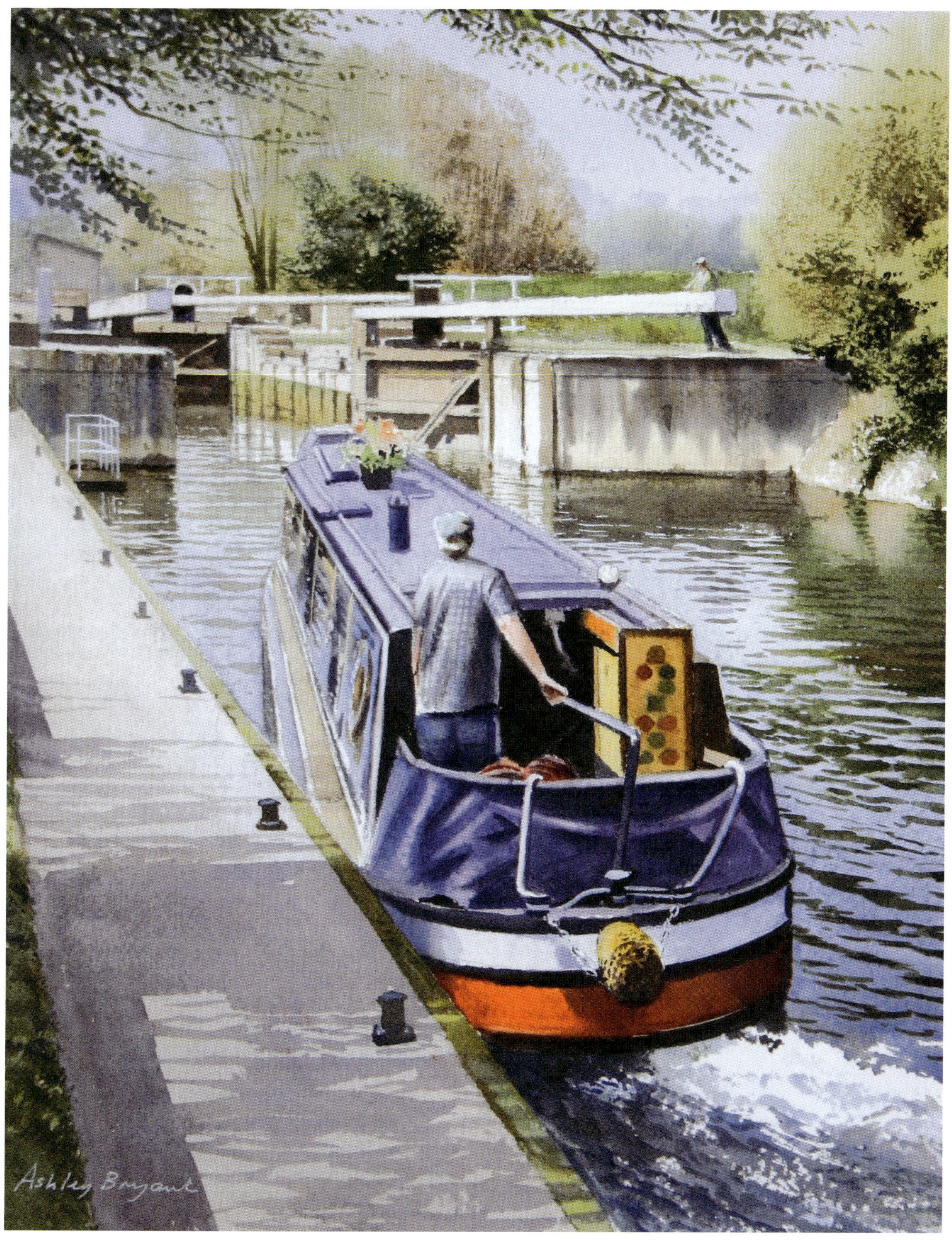
Ashley Bryant

WYTHAM WOODS

A study of local maps showed that part of this 600 acre wood swept down to the banks of the Thames, and I had hoped to produce a painting of a bluebell-filled glade by the river. On exploring the area I soon found this to be unattainable. The view of the river is blocked from the Thames Path by a thicket of thorn trees; in fact any view of the river from the wood is obscured.

This beautiful woodland is owned by Oxford University and includes a field study centre for wildlife and ecological research. The woodland is private and visitors need permission to walk here. The sounds of nightingales, several species of warblers (blackcaps and garden warblers as well as the more common willow warbler) and chiffchaff are heard in spring. There are several badger sets and organised badger-watching evenings are held occasionally. Dragonflies hawk through the woodland glades and butterflies, including the speckled wood, and various species of fritillaries are abundant in summer. It is, in short, a haven for wildlife.

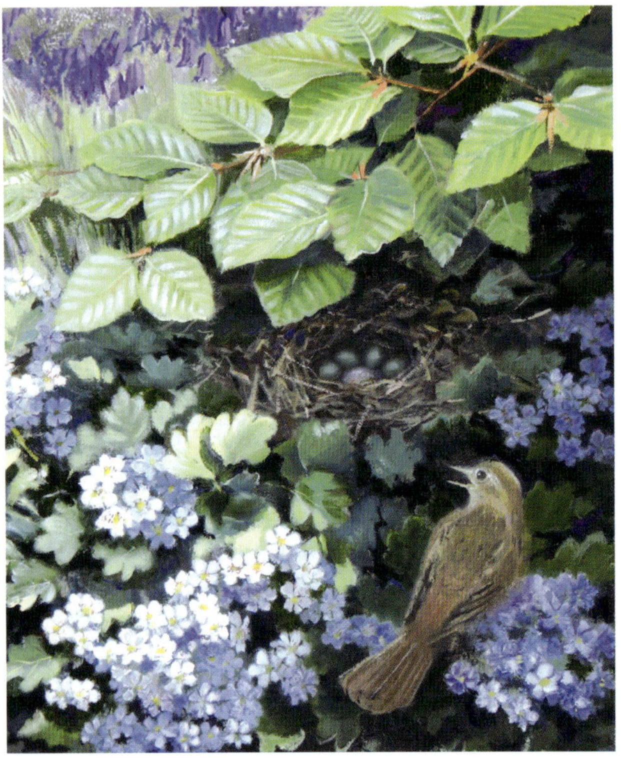

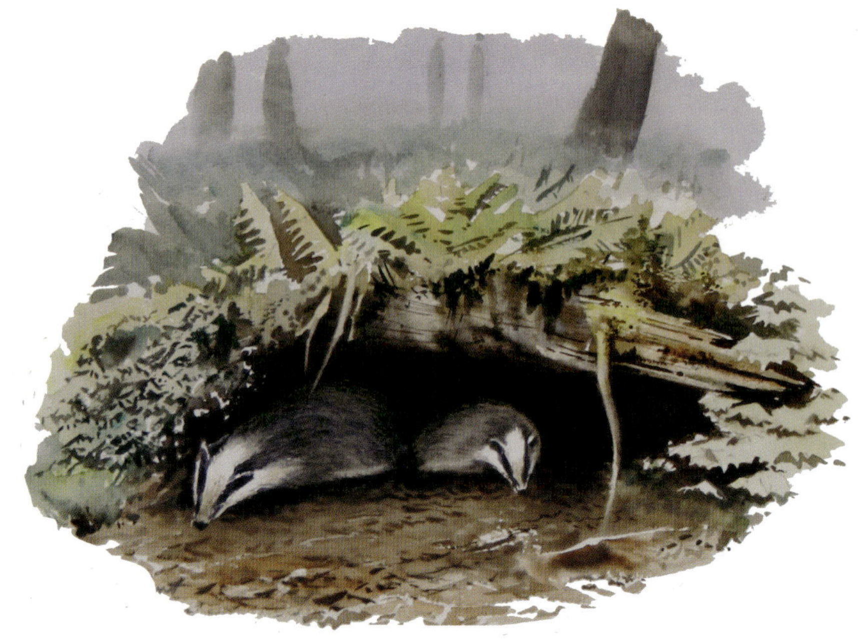

NIGHTINGALE
(Above)
The rich, clear sound of the nightingale is a joy to hear, but the birds themselves are secretive, spending their time in deep thickets. In this painting the nightingale has made a nest of leaves and grasses and has already laid a clutch of four greenish eggs. Sadly for the parent birds, a cuckoo has already paid a visit and left its own egg.

BADGERS
(Right)
This quiet and extensive mixed woodland is home to numerous badgers. On a badger watch these lovely creatures were observed.

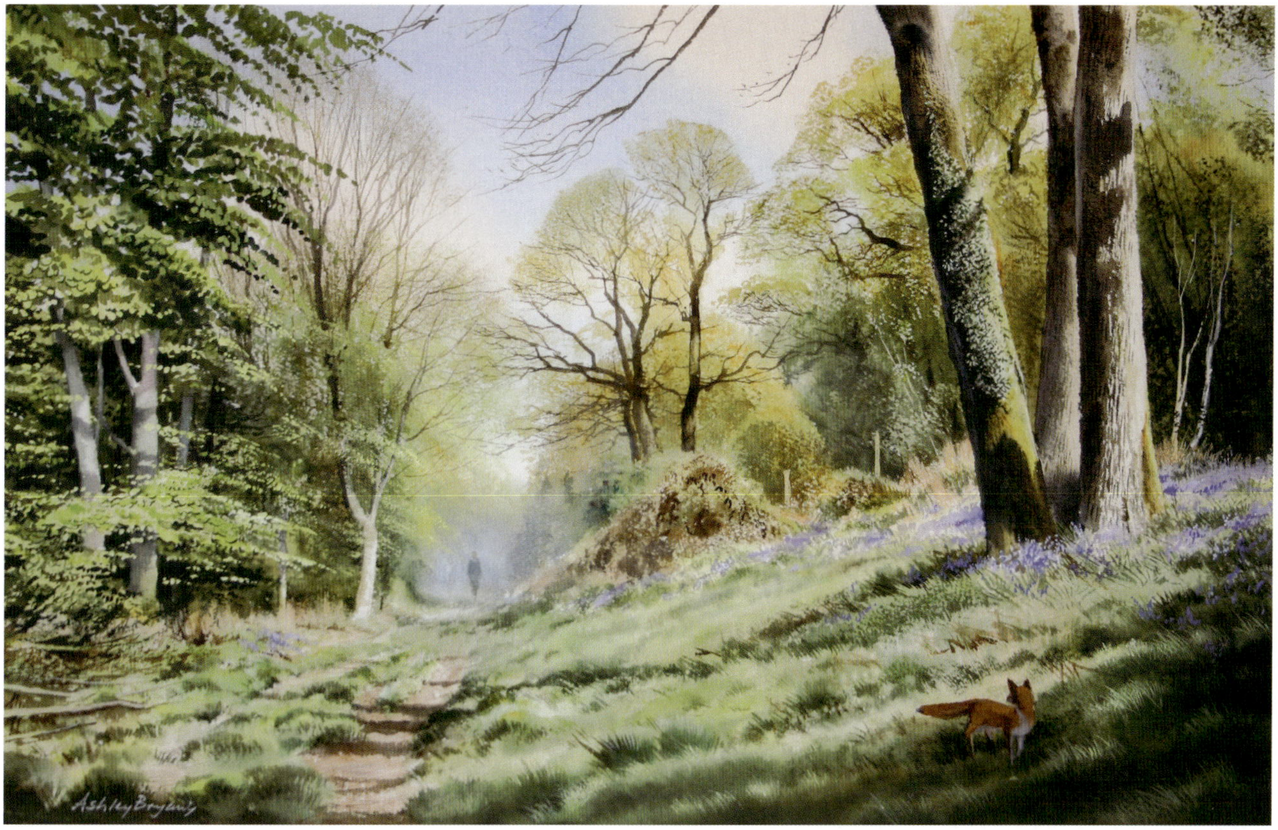

WYTHAM WOODS
(Above)
The lower reaches of the woods are seen here in late April. The Thames is just a few yards from the left hand margin of the painting but is totally obscured from view.

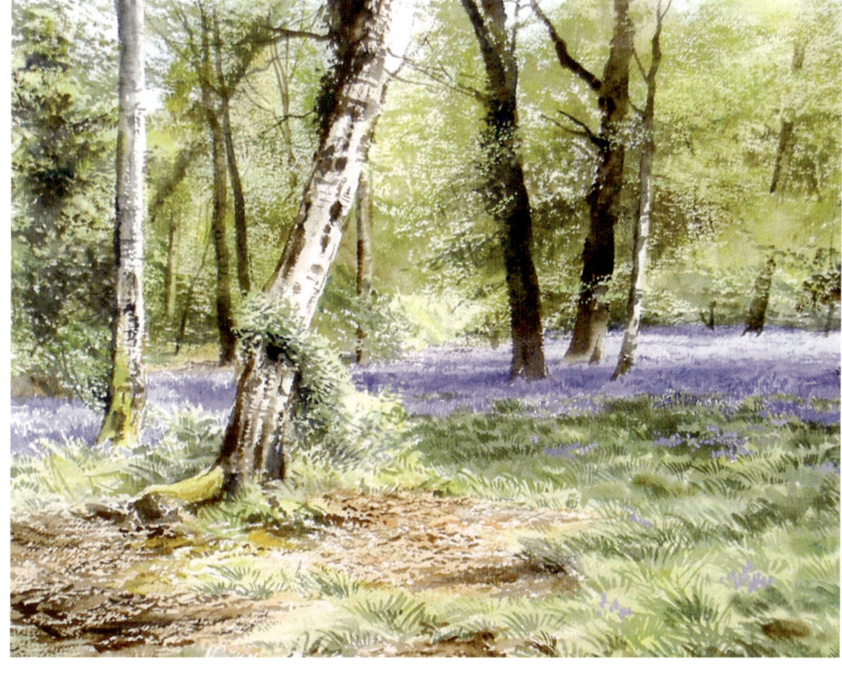

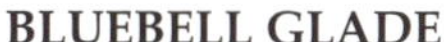

BLUEBELL GLADE
(Right)
This drift of bluebells, which caught my eye, provided a delightful scene against the silver birches.

GODSTOW

THE GHOST
Moonlight on the ruins of Godstow Nunnery brings strange surpises.

THE FAIR ROSAMUND
(Opposite Page)
Rosamund de Clifford, the mistress of Henry II.

THE THAMES AT GODSTOW
(Below)
The Trout Inn is seen behind another ancient bridge.

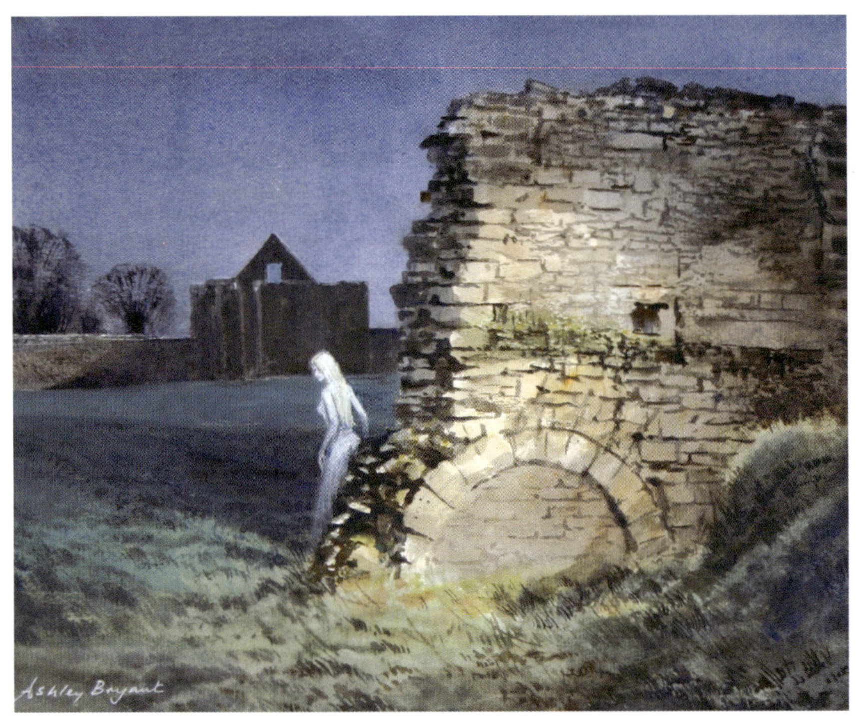

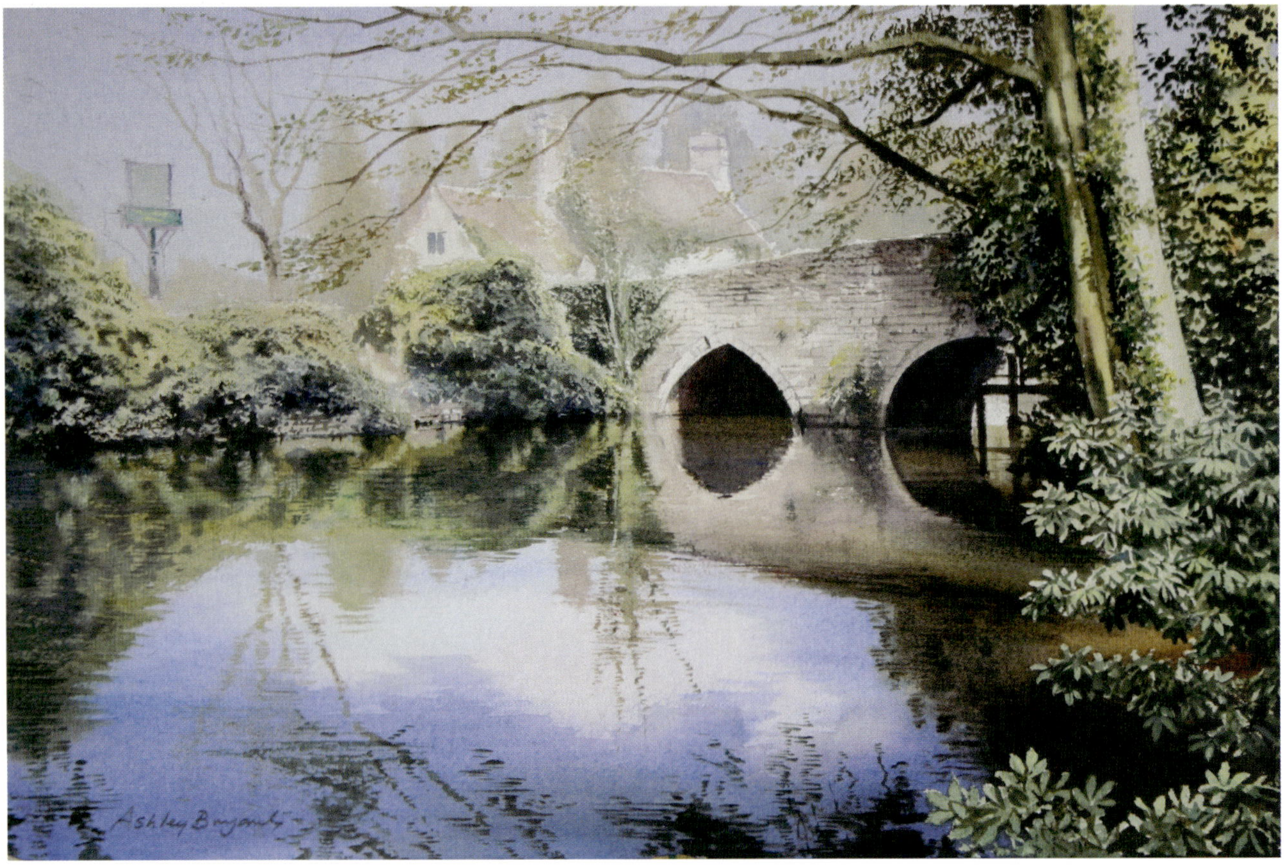

The Trout Inn at Godstow, originally the hospice of Godstow Nunnery, makes a welcome break on route to Oxford. Built in 1138 (conveniently away from the Nunnery), it is a well known location for film and television productions, and students from Oxford call here for breakfast after University balls. Visitors can dine on a terrace by the Thames, and ducks and huge chub compete for food thrown into the river by diners.

It is impossible to pass Godstow without recalling the story of Rosamund de Clifford, one of the most tragic heroines of English history, which unfolded on the far banks of the river at Godstow Nunnery. The fifteen year old Rosamund had been placed here in 1149 by here father, Lord Clifford, to receive a formal education. Strolling by the Thames one day, and by a quirk of fate, she caught the roving eye of King Henry II, and she soon became his mistress. To keep matters private Rosamund was whisked away to the seclusion of Henry's hunting lodge at nearby Woodstock. In an age when queens begrudgingly accepted that kings had mistresses, Henry's queen, the powerful Eleanor of Aquitaine, kept this knowledge as future ammunition. Revenge eventually came.

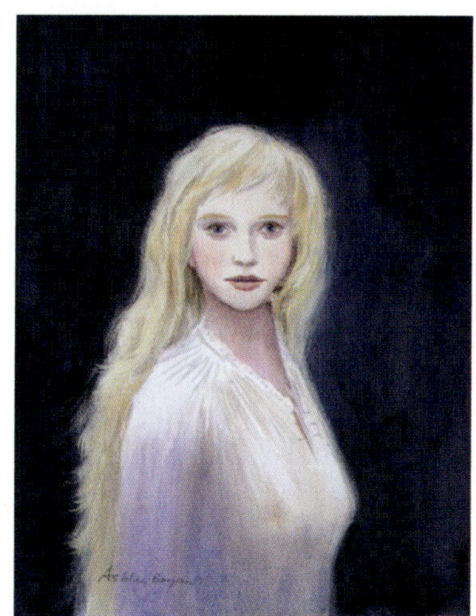

Fact and fiction about Rosamund's story have merged over the centuries. The Victorians embroidered the legend. In one version Rosamund was secreted at Woodstock in a hidden bower at the centre of a labyrinth that could only be reached by those with special knowledge. Queen Eleanor used exceptional cunning to reach the bower, where she presented Rosamund with a choice of death by poisoning or stabbing. Rosamund chose poisoning. Another account has Henry signalling to Rosamund from the Trout Inn, when the coast was clear for midnight trysts. Rosamund arrived at the Inn via a secret underground tunnel, but one night she was intercepted by the queen wielding a dagger.

Eleanor and Henry had a tempestuous relationship and the demise of a mistress must have been sweetly satisfying for the queen.

Rosamund's story however, does not rest here. She was buried at Godstow Nunnery with pomp and ceremony. The Nunnery was endowed by a grieving king, and her tomb became a focus of pilgrimage and veneration. Some years later, Bishop Hugh of Lincoln paid a visit to the Nunnery, and, shocked to see such reverence for Rosamund, immediately instructed that she be buried elsewhere. He considered such adulation for a mistress improper and a bad example to the nuns. Nevertheless, the nuns were fond of their Rosamund and when the bishop's back was turned they gathered her bones and re-buried them in a secret location in the Nunnery.

After such turmoil it is hardly surprising that her ghost is said to haunt the area. After lengthy consideration at the Trout Inn one evening, I decided to see for myself. The Nunnery ruins were cold and silent in the moonlight, and even the traffic on the nearby Oxford by-pass had abated. After several minutes a silvery shape appeared. Was it a sparkle of moonlight on the grass that seemed to move or could it have been Rosamund herself? It might even have been an overactive artist's imagination.

OXFORD

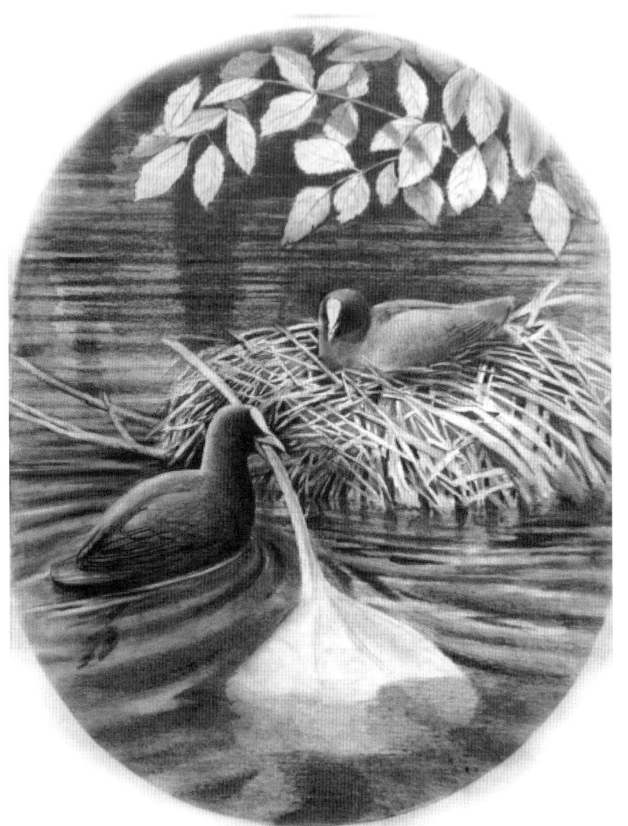

A well-used path winds along the riverside between Godstow and Oxford. On the far side of the wide river lies Port Meadow, given to Oxford by William the Conqueror. This protected grazing land has, over the centuries, prevented the expansion of Oxford in this direction. Some of the "dreaming spires", glimpses of which are few and far between from the Thames Path, can be seen in the distance. Behind us the sweeping vista of Wytham Woods provides an attractive composition for a painting – at least in a painting you cannot hear the constant noise of traffic from the nearby Oxford by-pass.

The Thames Path through Oxford is relatively green and the first buildings appear near Osney Bridge. In this area children often fish with handlines trying to catch crayfish (the American Signal variety) – almost always successfully, since they are abundant on the riverbed here.

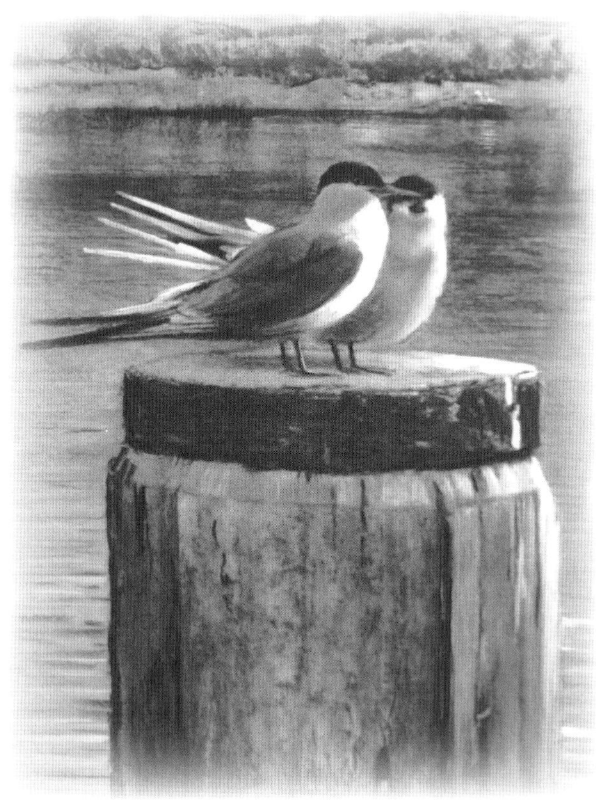

Oxford is about as far away as you can get from the sea in Britain, yet common terns are plentiful on the river. These seabirds find inland waterways to their liking and nest on islands in the river and nearby gravel pits.

Coots are probably the most common birds on the Thames and I noticed one sitting on its nest in a backwater. On the far side of the river, its mate had discovered a huge waterlilly leaf, and had started to drag in across. In mid stream a cruiser appeared and the coot had to swim back again with its precious cargo. The bird repeated its attempt, yet as it neared the centre of the channel, the same situation occurred once again. Finally, after expending considerable effort as the leaf dragged in the water, it reached the nest only to be greeted by its mate with the most disdainful look – "what have you brought that for?"

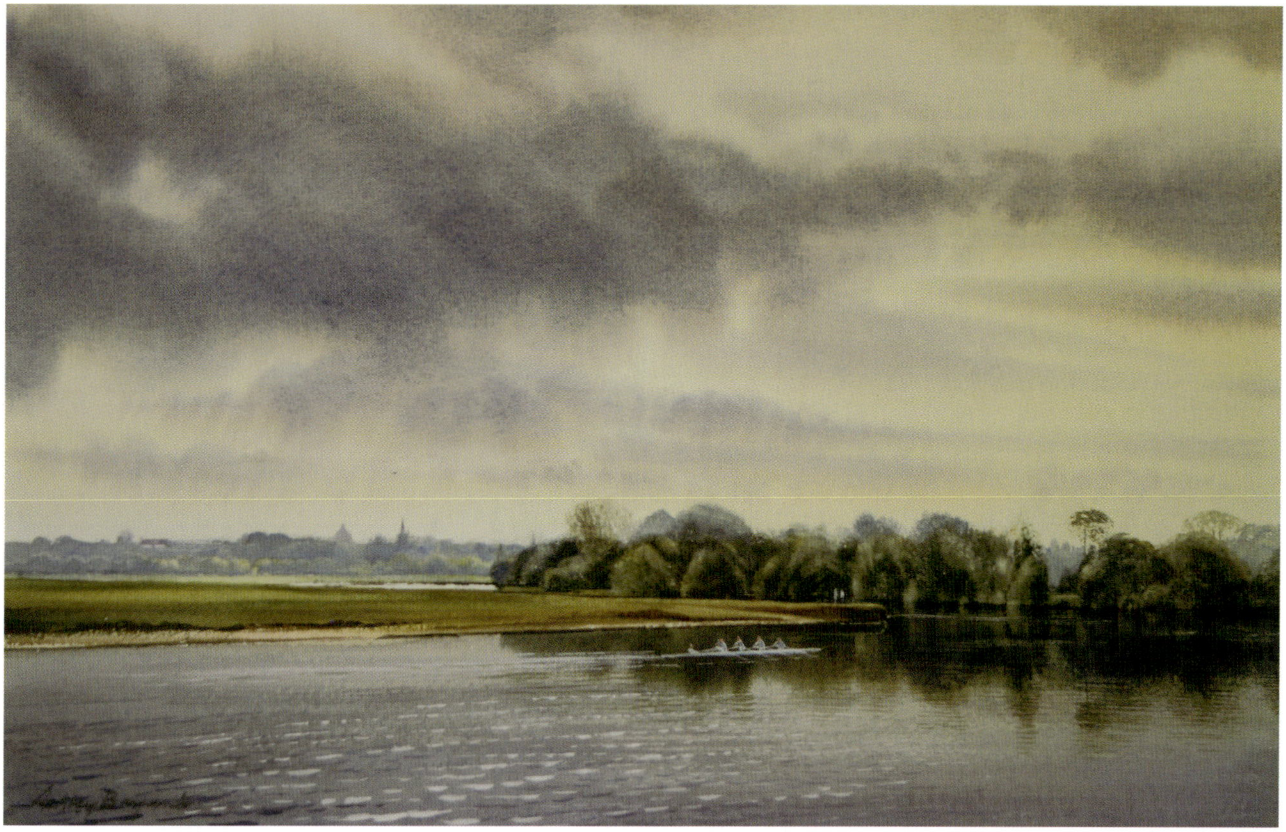

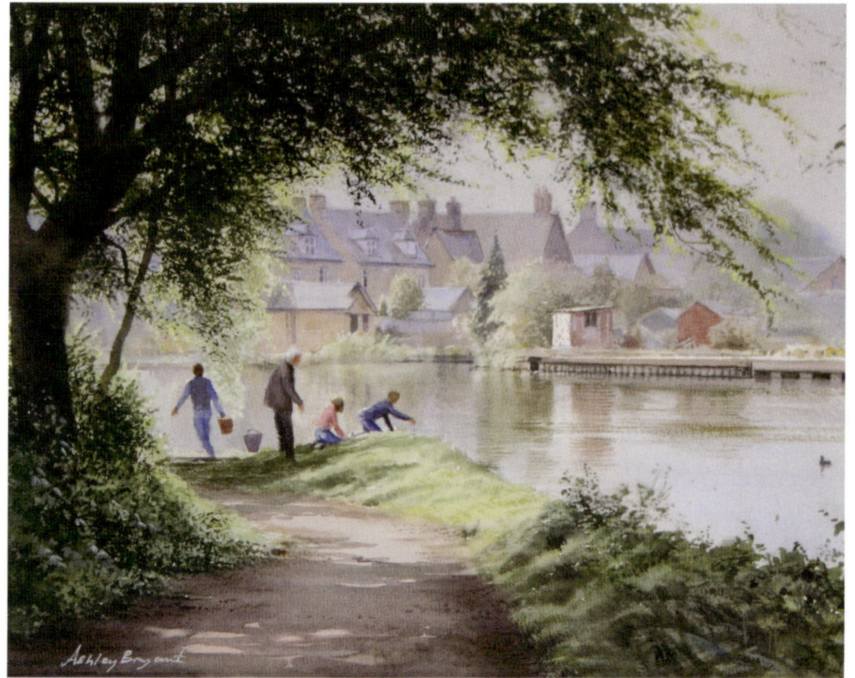

THE THAMES NEAR OXFORD
(Above)
The distant "dreaming spires" seen on route from Godstow. Boat crews are often seen here training.

CATCHING CRAYFISH
(Left)
This family enjoyed catching crayfish for tea.

THE PRESENT
(Opposite Page Above)
This coot made a great deal of effort to bring the present of a large leaf to its mate.

COMMON TERNS
(Opposite Page Below)
These beautiful birds had paired up for breeding nearby.

OXFORD

The watercourses and side streams of the Thames at Oxford have been adapted over the last millennium to suit the needs of mills, navigation and industry, a huge task with only pick, shovel and muscle power. For example, the monks who built Osney Abbey diverted the Thames to power their mill. When Osney Lock was constructed in the eighteenth century the old mill stream was adapted and enlarged into a new navigational cut. An enterprising keeper of Oxford Jail put in a bid for the contract. Since his costs were based on the labour of inmates, his overheads were negligible, and he was able to undercut the competition by a huge margin. The prisoners must have been happy to escape their gloomy cells for sunlight, fresh air and a view of the outside world.

The heart of one of Britain's greatest mediaeval cities lies just a few hundred yards away from the Thames but the riverside has no buildings of any great interest or architectural merit. There is simply no indication of Oxford's greatness, its development as a strategically important town after the Norman Conquest, its pre-eminence as a university town for eight centuries or its leadership in areas of modern business enterprise. Old Father Thames can only look to the future here for some worthy architectural tributes.

The next road crossing is at Folly Bridge, built on the site of Oxford's first Thames bridge of 1085 (the Grand Pont) by Robert D'Oyley, a chief henchman of William the Conqueror. This first bridge replaced a deep and dangerous ford, where people would often hold on to the horns of an ox for safety when crossing. It was this oxen ford which gave the town its name. The name "Folly" is derived from a house which used to stand nearby, occupied at one time by the brilliant thirteenth-century scholar Roger Bacon. It acquired an unusual upper storey in the seventeenth century, coining the name Folly House. Today, a castellated building next to the bridge continues the theme.

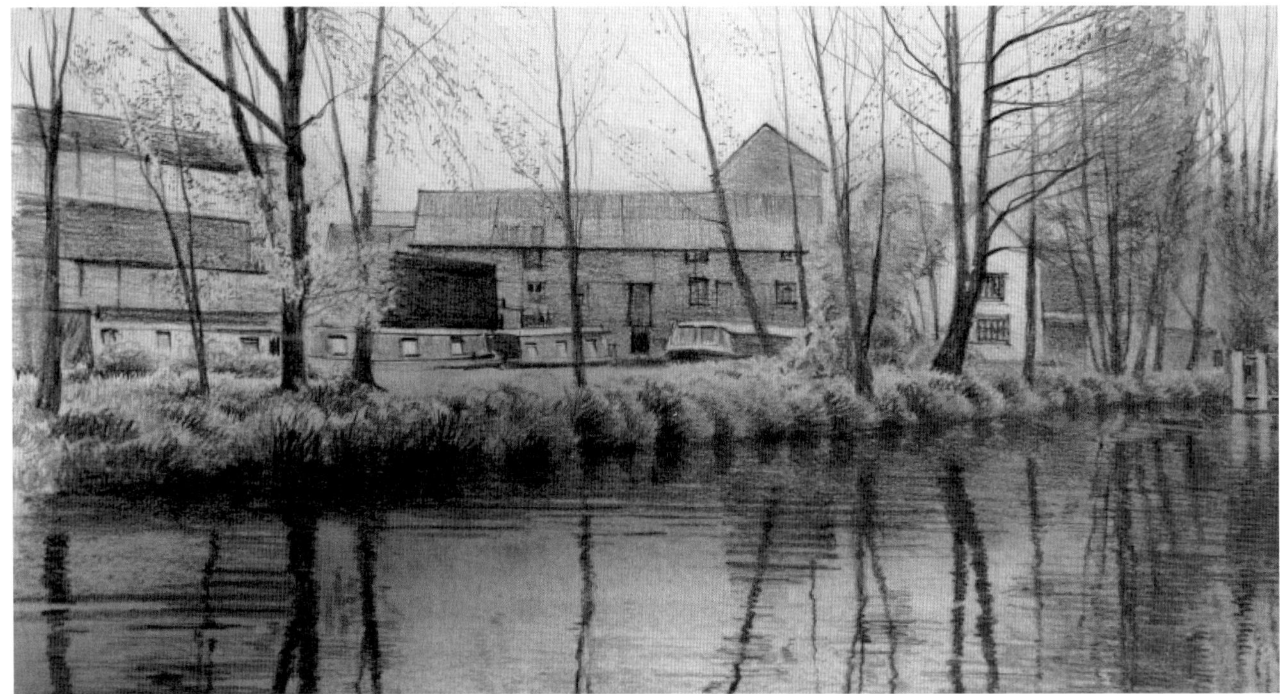

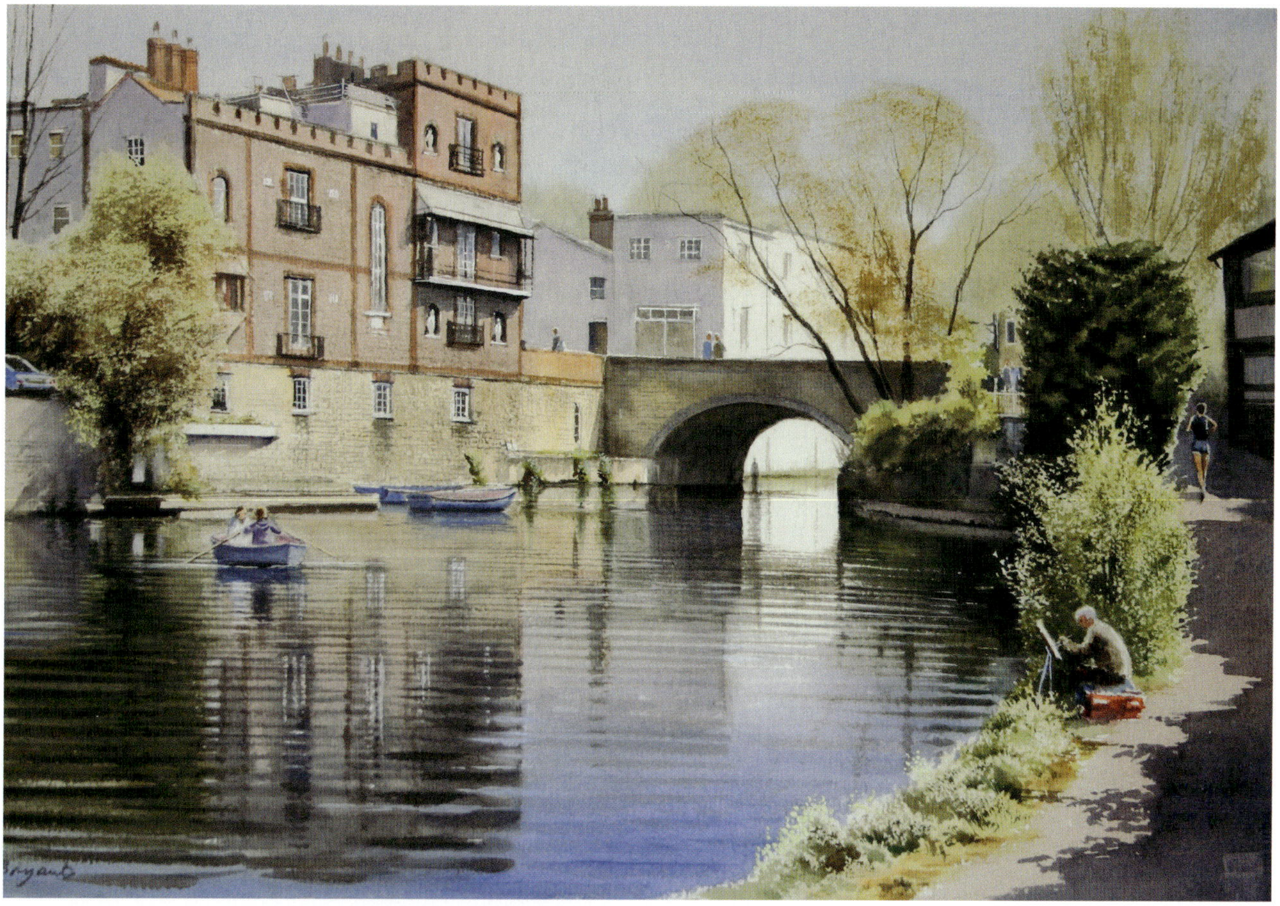

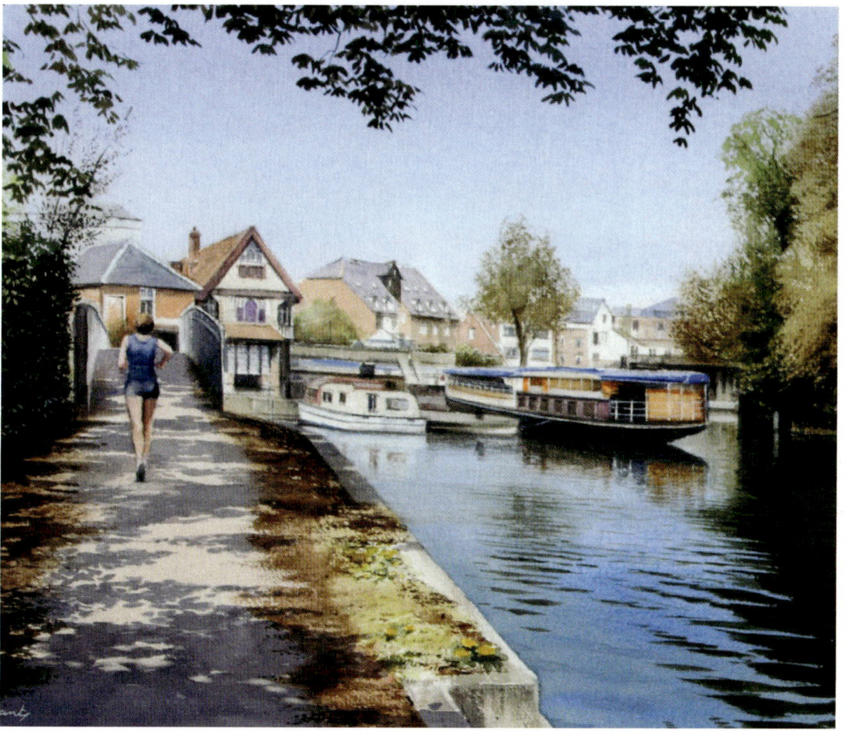

FOLLY BRIDGE
(Above)
A ford once existed here which people crossed at their peril. It was safer to hold on to the horns of an obliging ox, and it was this crossing which gave the town its name.

APPROACHING OSNEY LOCK
(Opposite Page)
A pencil sketch showing the Thames near Osney Lock.

THE TOWPATH
(Left)
This is the terminus for boats from Abingdon and lies to the south of Folly Bridge.

OXFORD

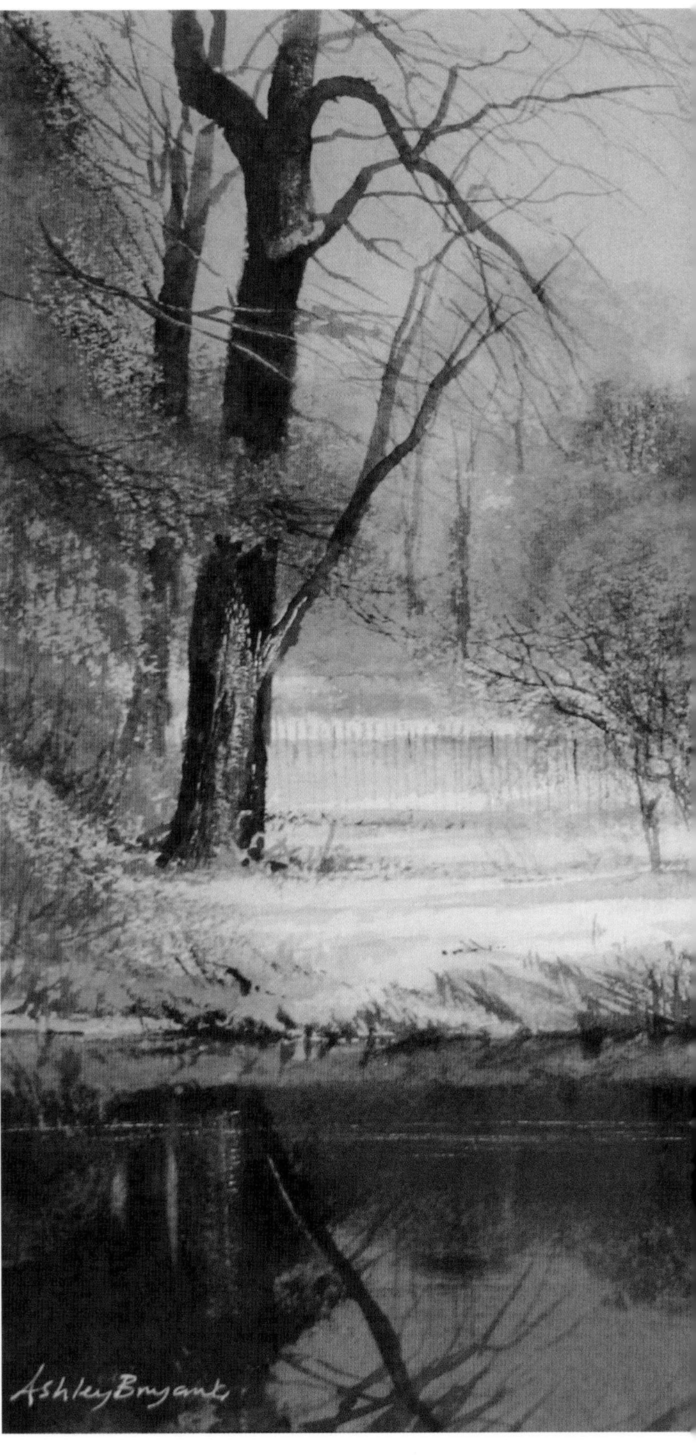

The timeless scenes of punting on the river, ripples reflecting under the arches of mellow stone bridges, familiar college buildings and students relaxing on manicured lawns which sweep down to the waterside, are not those surrounding the Thames but the river Cherwell. The Thames is strictly rationed in these picture-postcard views, but at least there are small glimpses of the old Oxford to be seen across Christchurch Meadows. When the leaves have fallen from the trees in autumn a clearer prospect emerges, and some of the "dreaming spires" can be seen through the branches.

The dome of Ratcliffe Camera is one of the most distinctive of Oxford's buildings. It was built in the Palladian style in 1737-49 to the design of James Gibbs with money bequeathed by Dr. John Radcliffe, the royal physician. It originally held a library of scientific and medical books, but now forms the main reading room of the Bodlian library. In the centre of the painting, and in the centre of Oxford itself, stands the university church of St. Mary's. Its fourteenth-century spire is the tallest of all of Oxford's churches. On the right stands the tower of Merton College, the statutes for which date back to 1264 making it one of the oldest in Oxford.

The walk downstream is punctuated by rowing clubs on the far bank and the spectacle of crews in training. Beware of a lack of concentration, since speeding cyclists on the towpath aim for gaps between pedestrians but not always with precision. The walk from Godstow to the Oxford suburb of Ifley is recommended, providing a great deal to enjoy and, for the artist, a variety of delightful compositions.

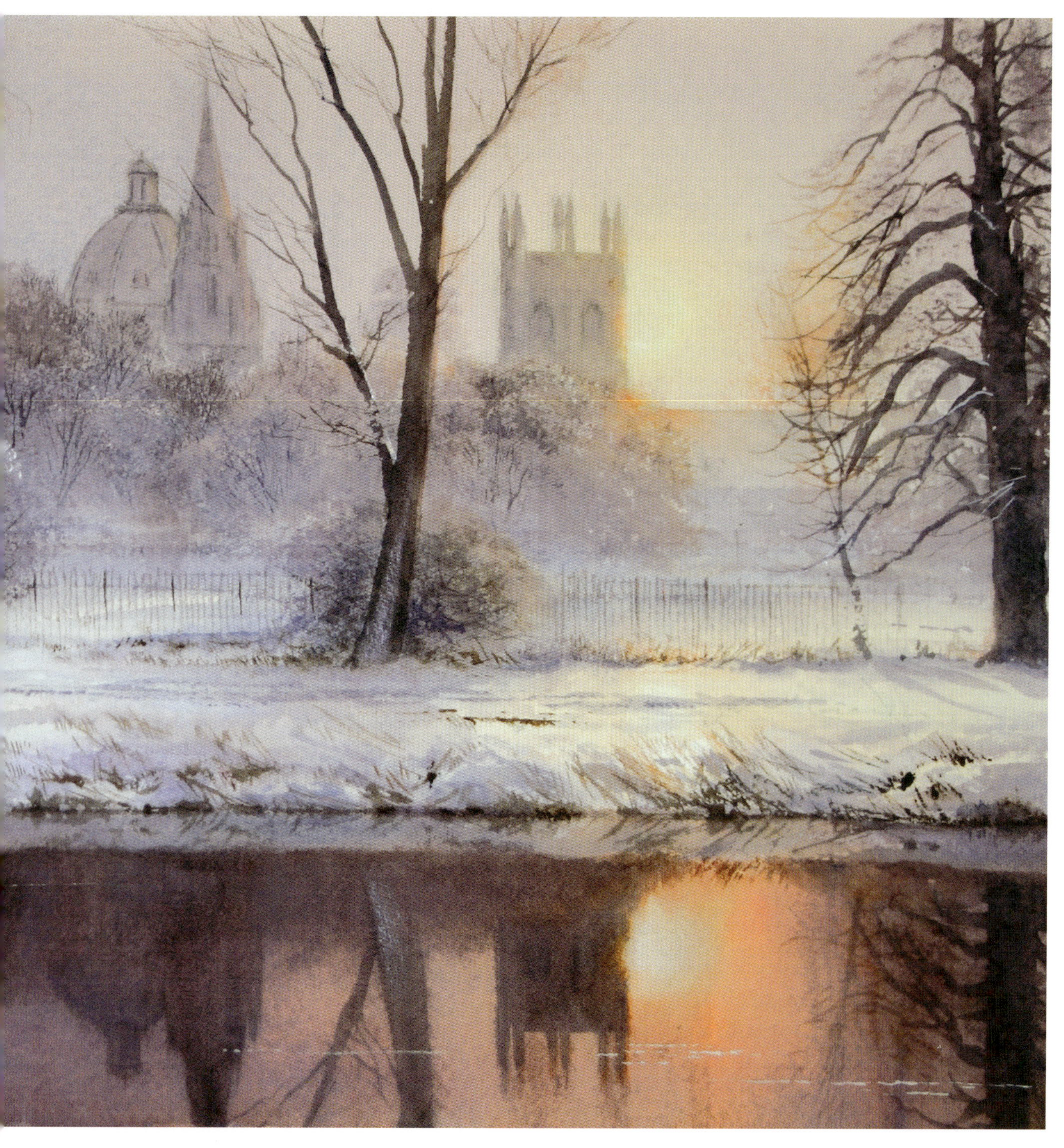

THE DREAMING SPIRES
Across the Thames and Christchurch Meadows are views of the Radcliffe Camera, St. Mary's Church and Merton College.

OTTERS

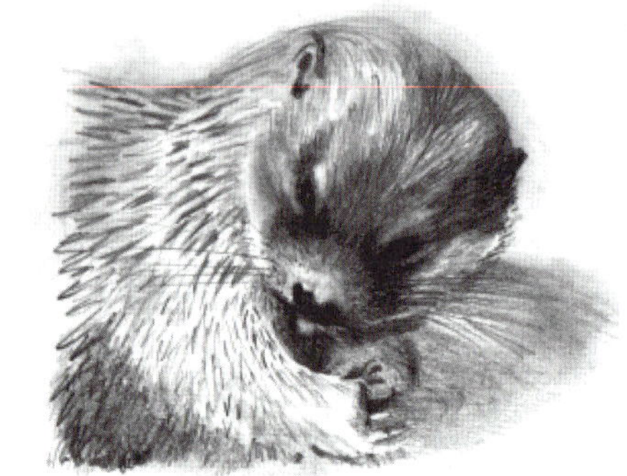

"Near the congested haunts of men . . . otters are occasionally trapped" quoted *The Observer's Book of British Wild Animals* in the early 1950s. Fortunately, our attitude to conservation has improved and otter numbers have increased, although they are still rare and solitary animals. Anyone seeing one is fortunate indeed since they are over-alert and ultra shy and, as with all aquatic mammals, they can disappear without trace in a split second. They are at their most active during dawn and dusk, generally lying low in daylight hours.

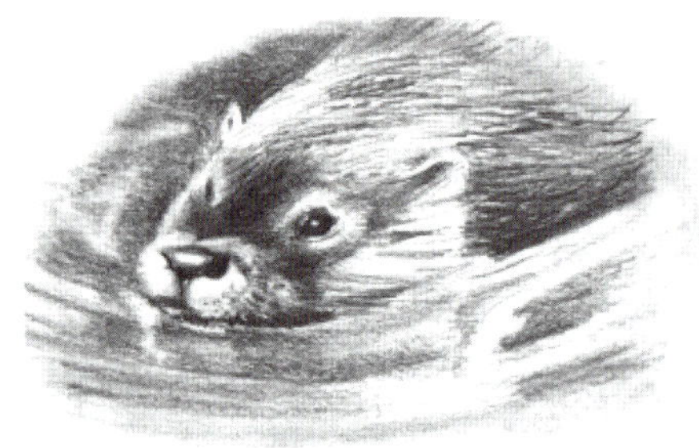

Otters are undoubtedly spreading along the river, but due to the necessity of large territories (a mechanism to aid the spread of the population), they are thinly distributed and hard to find. On some rivers artificial holts (the holes where they shelter and breed) have been created for them, and cleaner and less polluted rivers have improved fish stocks, although eels, one of the otter's favourite foods, have declined. May these delightful creatures continue to thrive.

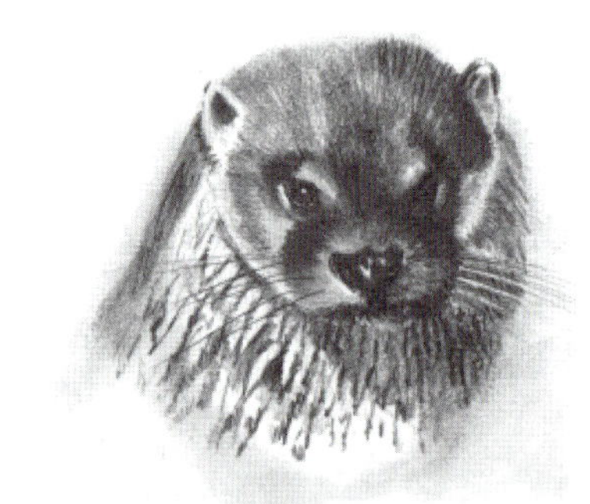

OTTER SKETCHES
(Above right)
Once you have an audience of otters it is impossible to stop sketching these endearing creatures.

PAIR OF OTTERS
(Below Right)
In this oil painting, the male (dog) otter is in front. He stays in the vicinity of the female and cubs in a loose family arrangement, but is ever anxious to drive out the adolescent youngsters from its territory.

IDEAL TERRITORY
(Opposite Page)
Clean waters, rivers undisturbed by people or boats, plenty of fish to eat and riverbanks with tree roots which frame their shelters all contribute to the ideal habitat for otters.

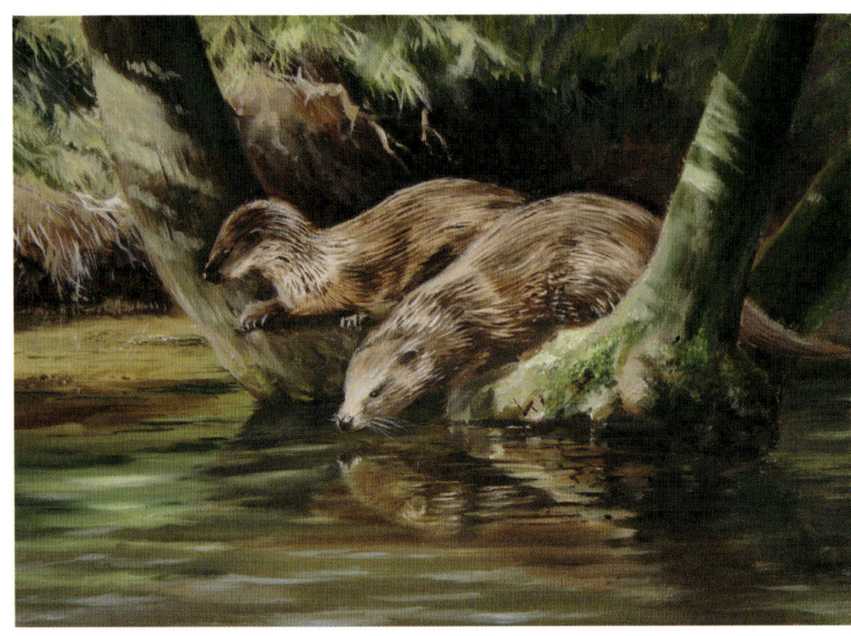

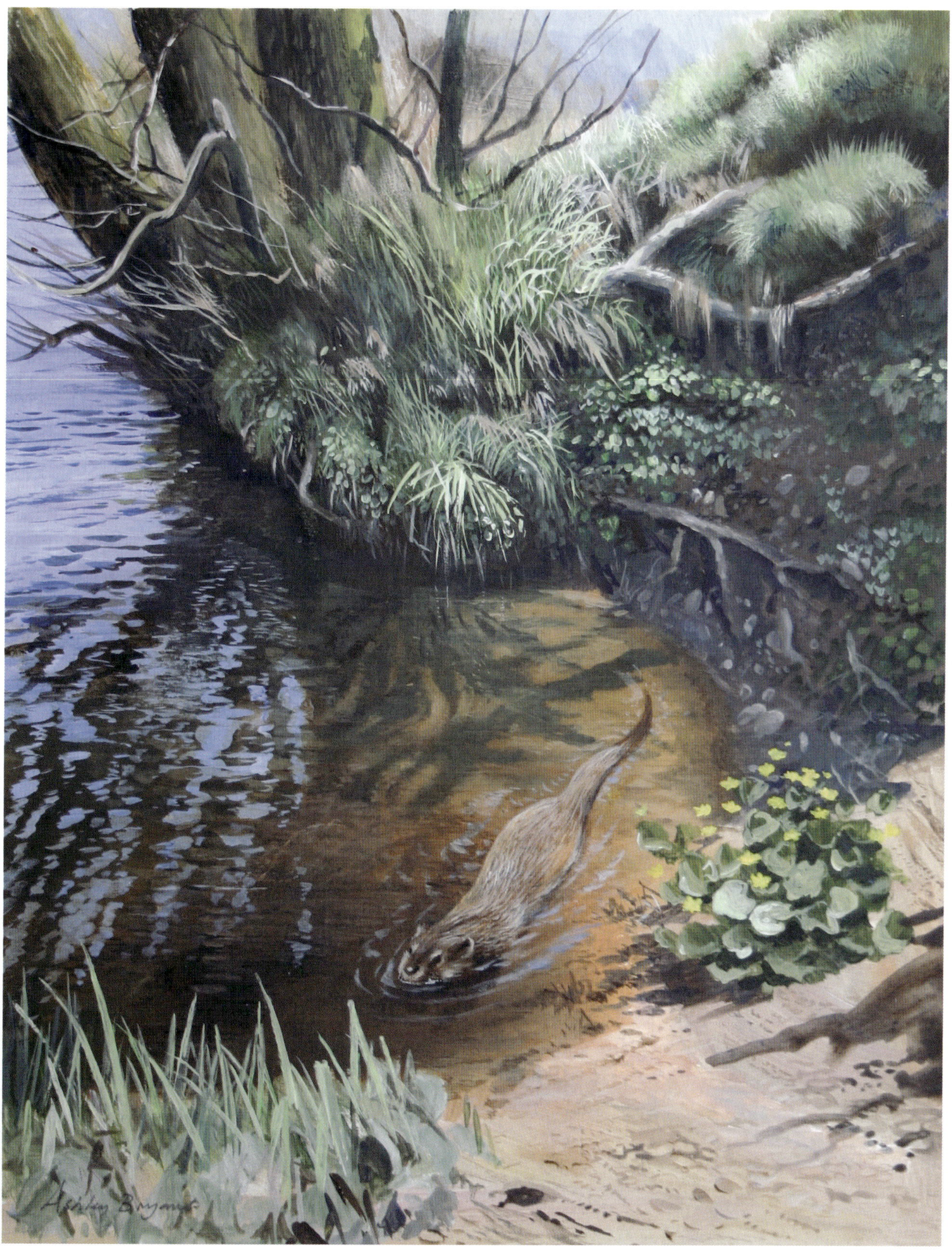

The Thames

NUNEHAM COURTNEY

After Iffley and Sandford, the Thames follows a delightful rural route through rich countryside to Abingdon, equally enjoyable from the Thames Path or from a boat. Salters Steamers provide regular boat trips between Oxford and Abingdon, although since the craft switched to diesel, their "steaming" days are long over. The Thames itself can be considered one great wildlife park. The water and the riverbank provide exceptional habitats and create a corridor for wildlife. The flash of electric blue-green as a kingfisher speeds past give any day a lift, and stately great crested grebes dive with hardly a ripple. In summer these birds sit with sharp alertness on their floating nests which move up and down in the wake of passing boats. Herons stand motionless in the margins and can be approached quite close by boat, so near that you can sometimes see the details of their piercing eyes.

In this lovely wooded and tree-dotted landscape, on a slope above the left bank, stands Nuneham House. The house and estate, including the original village of Nuneham Courtney, were purchased in the early eighteenth-century by Viscount Harcourt, the Lord High Chancellor Of England. By the 1750's he had decided to virtually rebuild the house on a grander scale in the Palladian style. However, the village blocked the views from this grand mansion and invaded the privacy of an increasingly wealthy lifestyle. In a move not uncommon in this era, the tenants were rehoused and the village obliterated. The energetic Capability Brown was engaged to develop a parkland with uninterrupted vistas down to and beyond the Thames. Today, cornfields sweep up to the house from the riverbank where agriculture has claimed the land once more.

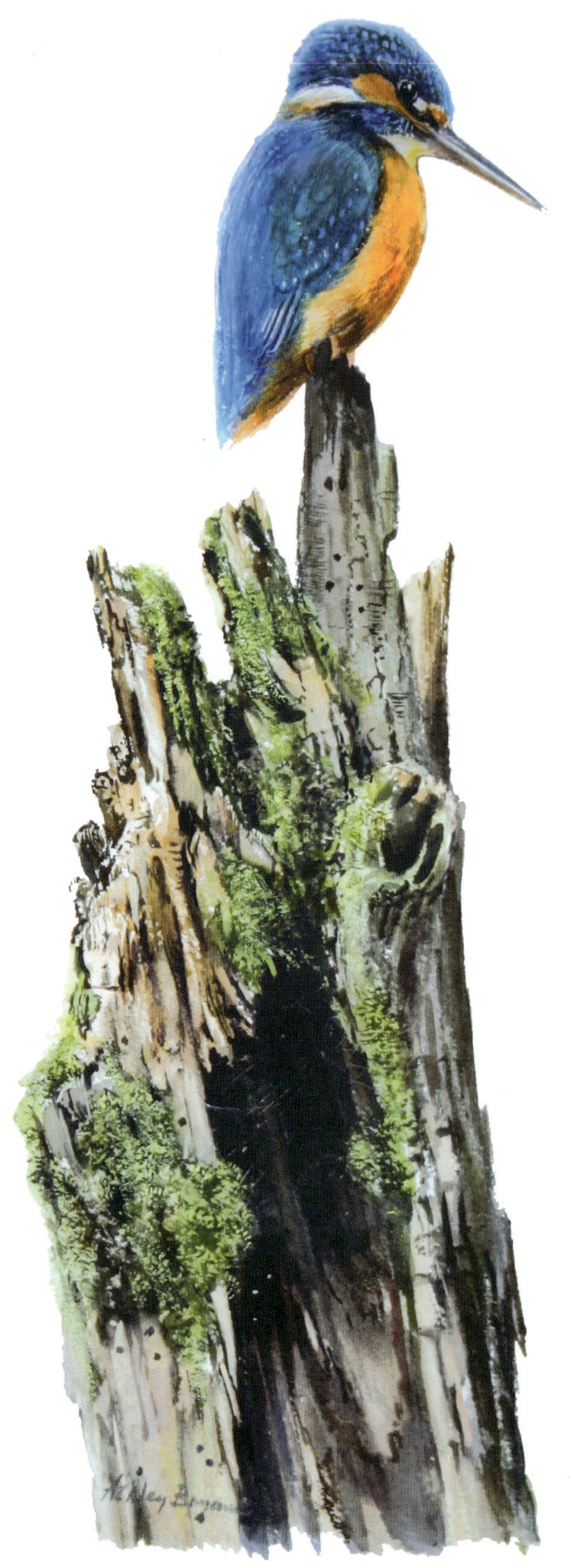

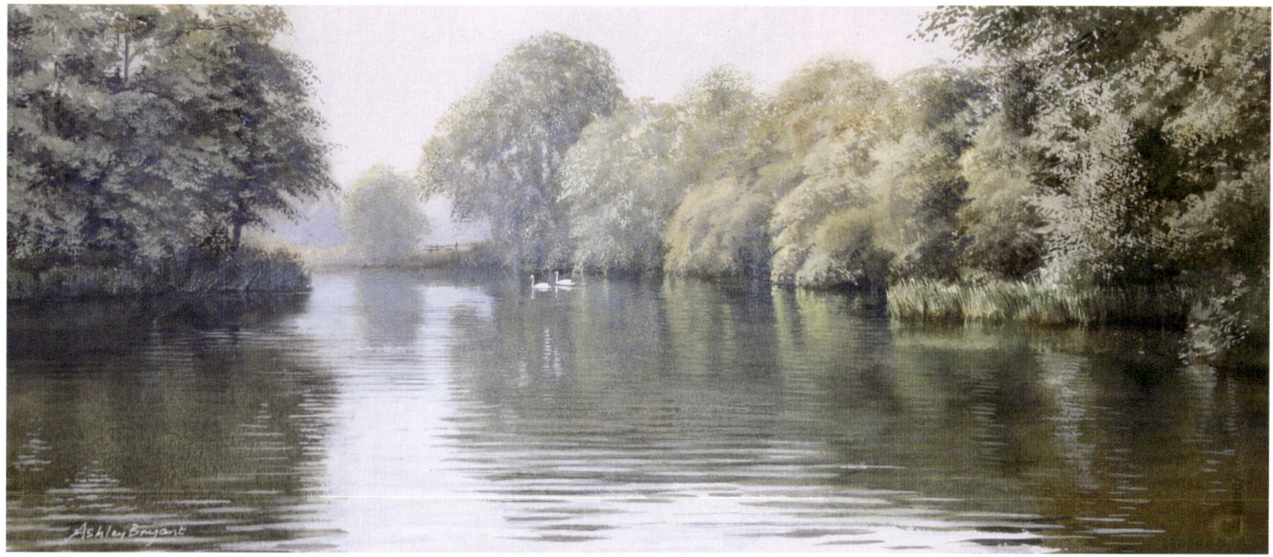

KINGFISHER
(Opposite page)
It is surprising how few people have seen a kingfisher, since these birds are widespread if not particularly common. Once seen, they are never forgotten.

THE THAMES NEAR NUNEHAM COURTNEY
(Above)
A view from a boat in mid-stream on a misty morning between Nuneham Courtney and Abingdon, showing the Thames in a placid mood.

RIVERSIDE FLOWERS
(Below)
A composition of common spring flowers including wood anenomies, primroses and lesser celendines that adorn the banks of the tree-lined river.

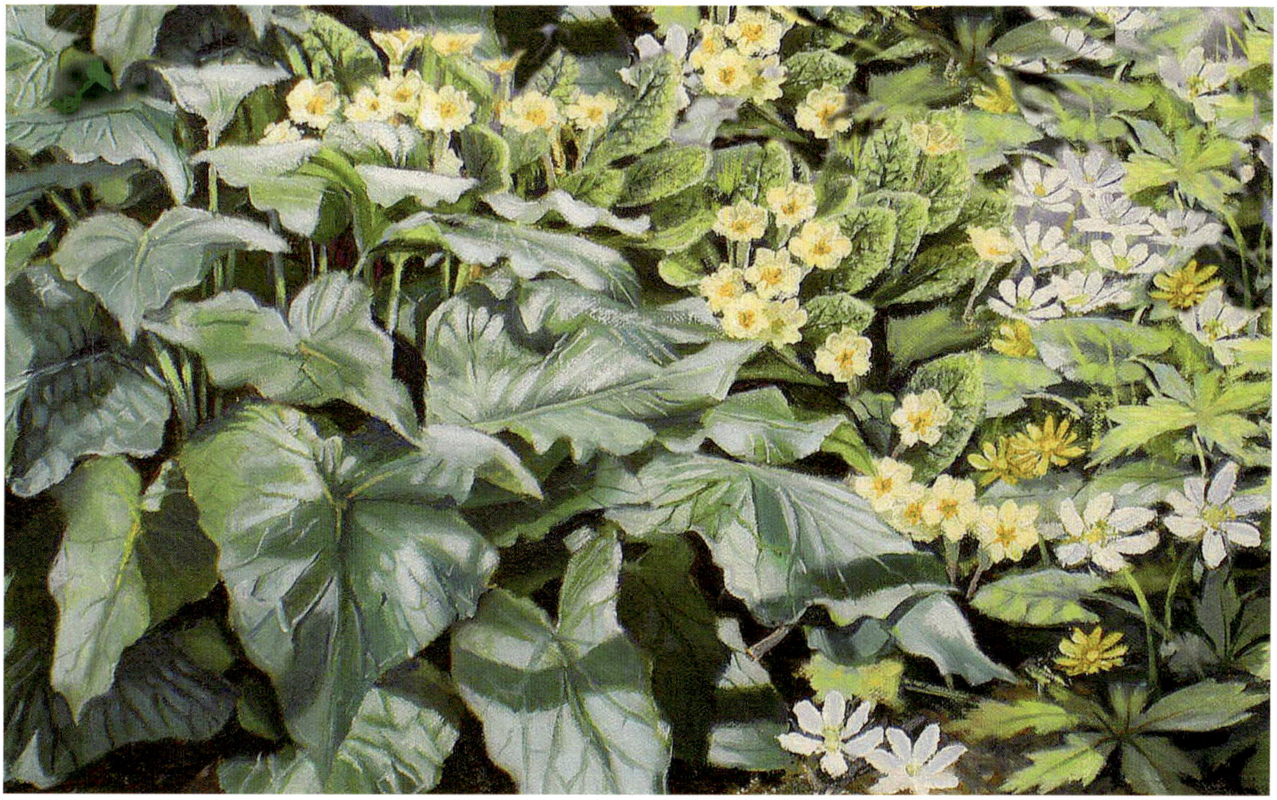

ABINGDON

BRIDGE STREET
(Right)
In this pen and wash sketch Abingdon Bridge leads into Bridge Street and the old part of the town which at one time was the county town of Berkshire.

THE THAMES AT ABINGDON
(Opposite Page)
Abingdon provides some of the most stunning views of the Thames, and this traditional view of St.Helen's Church frames by trees is a perfect example.

ABINGDON APPROACH
(Below)
From Abingdon Lock it is a short walk to the town. The spire of St. Helen's church can be seen in the distance.

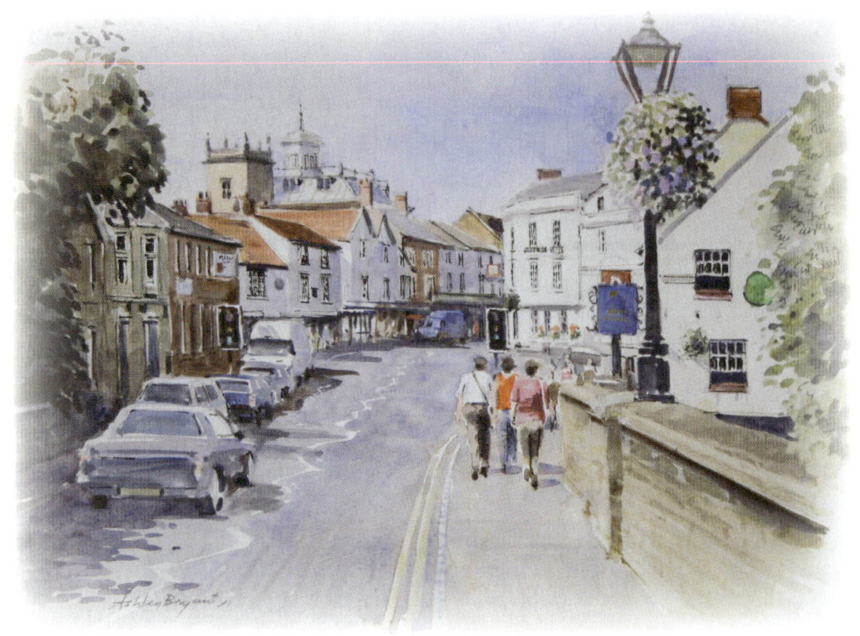

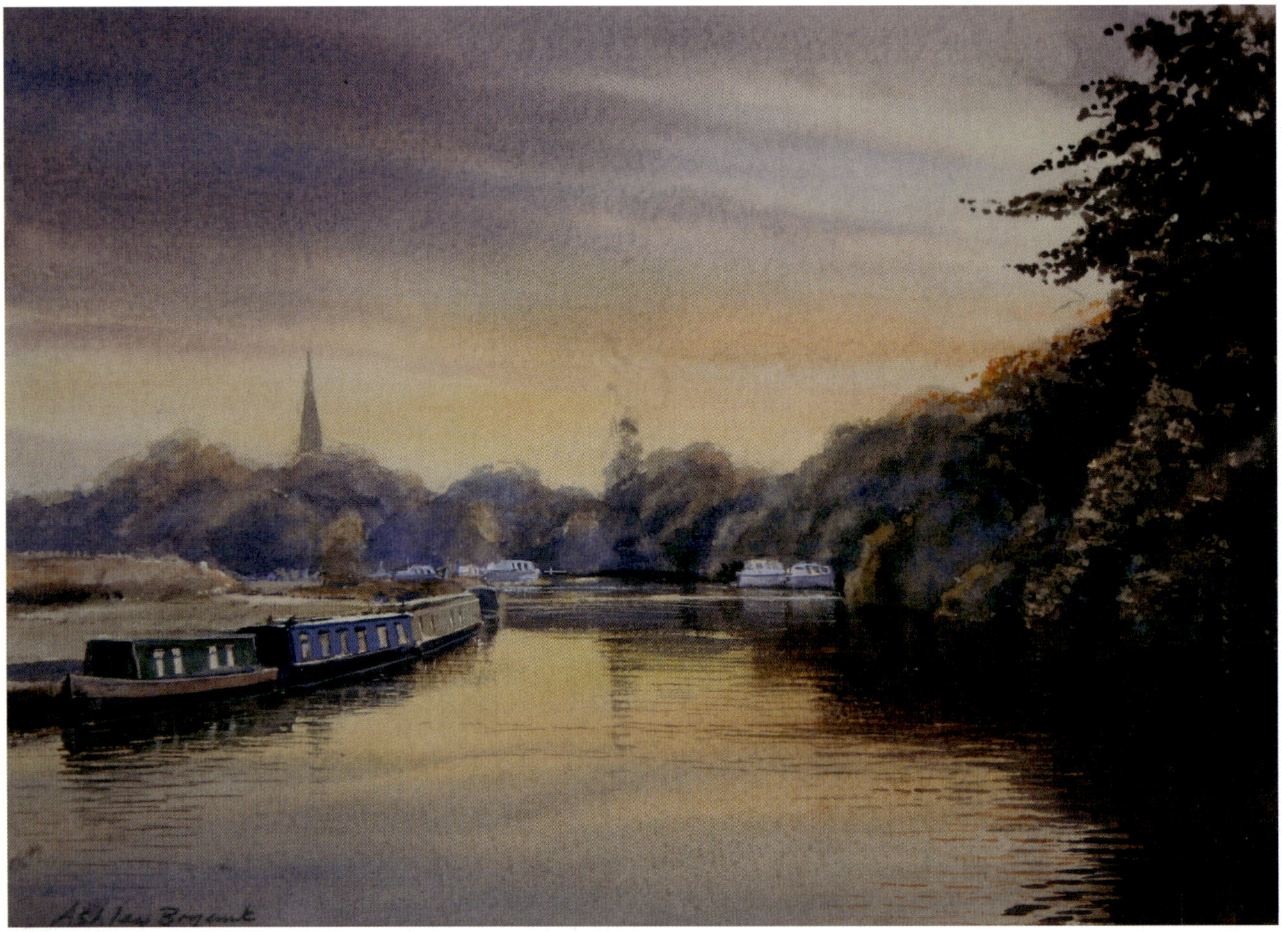

The distant spire of St. Helen's church indicates we are approaching one of the oldest and most interesting towns on the Thames. In fact, the town council claim it to be the oldest town in England. Without question it has seen its share of history – the schoolboy stuff of my youth where Alfred the Great fought the Danes and won. As a frontier town between two kingdoms – those of Wessex and Mercia, it was no stranger to battles.

A key event in shaping Abingdon's history was the building of an abbey as early as A.D. 675. This abbey grew in wealth and influence and, during the middle-ages, it exceeded Westminster Abbey in size, controlling the lives of everyone for miles around. This stranglehold on lifestyles, liberties and trade eventually galvanised the townspeople into forming town guilds in order to protect their interests. The guilds built almshouses, they promoted the building of a bridge in the early 1400's which brought trade to the town and they endowed "their" church of St. Helen. The Reformation brought a sudden change in fortunes; the huge abbey practically disappeared, whilst the guilds and the town flourished.

Abingdon has many nooks and crannies to explore and an artist would never be short of inspiration here, particularly along the Thames with views from the bridge and its collection of moored boats, old almshouses, pubs, Abingdon Lock and, of course, St. Helen's church.

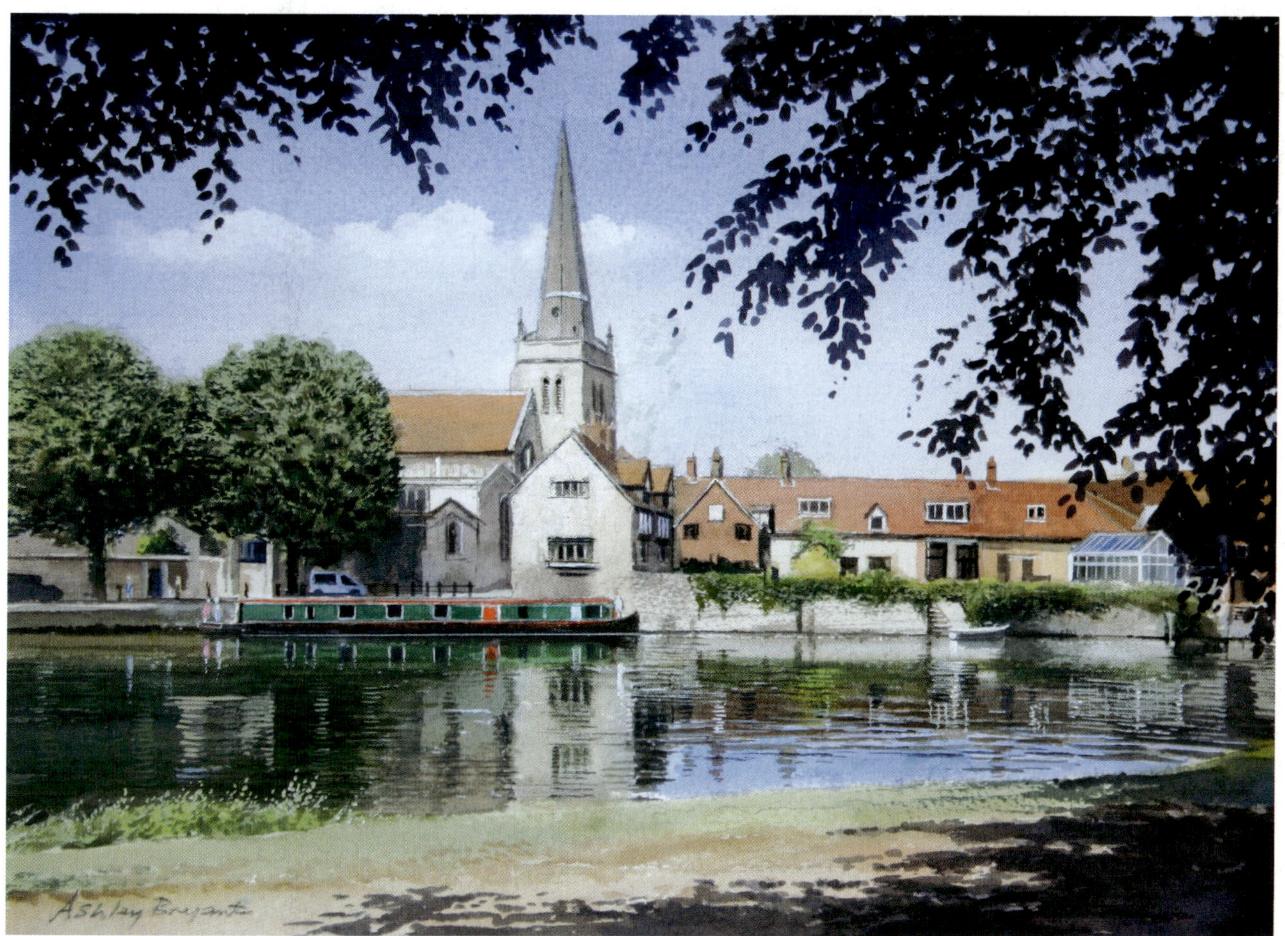

SUTTON COURTNEY

THE OLD CHANNEL
(Opposite Page, above)
The river calmly passes Sutton Courtney and its water-front properties whilst the boating traffic uses the Culham cut.

FRUITS & FLOWERS
(Opposite Page, Below)
A composition showing some of the local summer plants including willowherb, greater bindweed, mature spikes of dock and early blackberries.

SUTTON POOLS
(Below)
The Thames flows over weirs to create lakes, known locally as Sutton Pools. These provide an attractive local amenity.

Approaching Culham the river turns sharply right along a nineteenth-century navigation channel close to the village. The old course of the river continues in an arc around the edge of Sutton Courtney. Dotted with waterlillies, its banks colourful with willowherbs in summer, it gives every appearance of a backwater. Houses lining the far side of the river have an enviable location with lawns sweeping down to the water's edge.

There is no prospect of flooding here, since any increase in the level causes the water to spill over weirs to Sutton Pools below. These local lakes surrounded by wooded margins provide an attractive setting for picnics and for enjoying the wildlife of the area. There are few better places to experience the dawn chorus on a May morning or to relax and enjoy the quiet calm of a summer's evening.

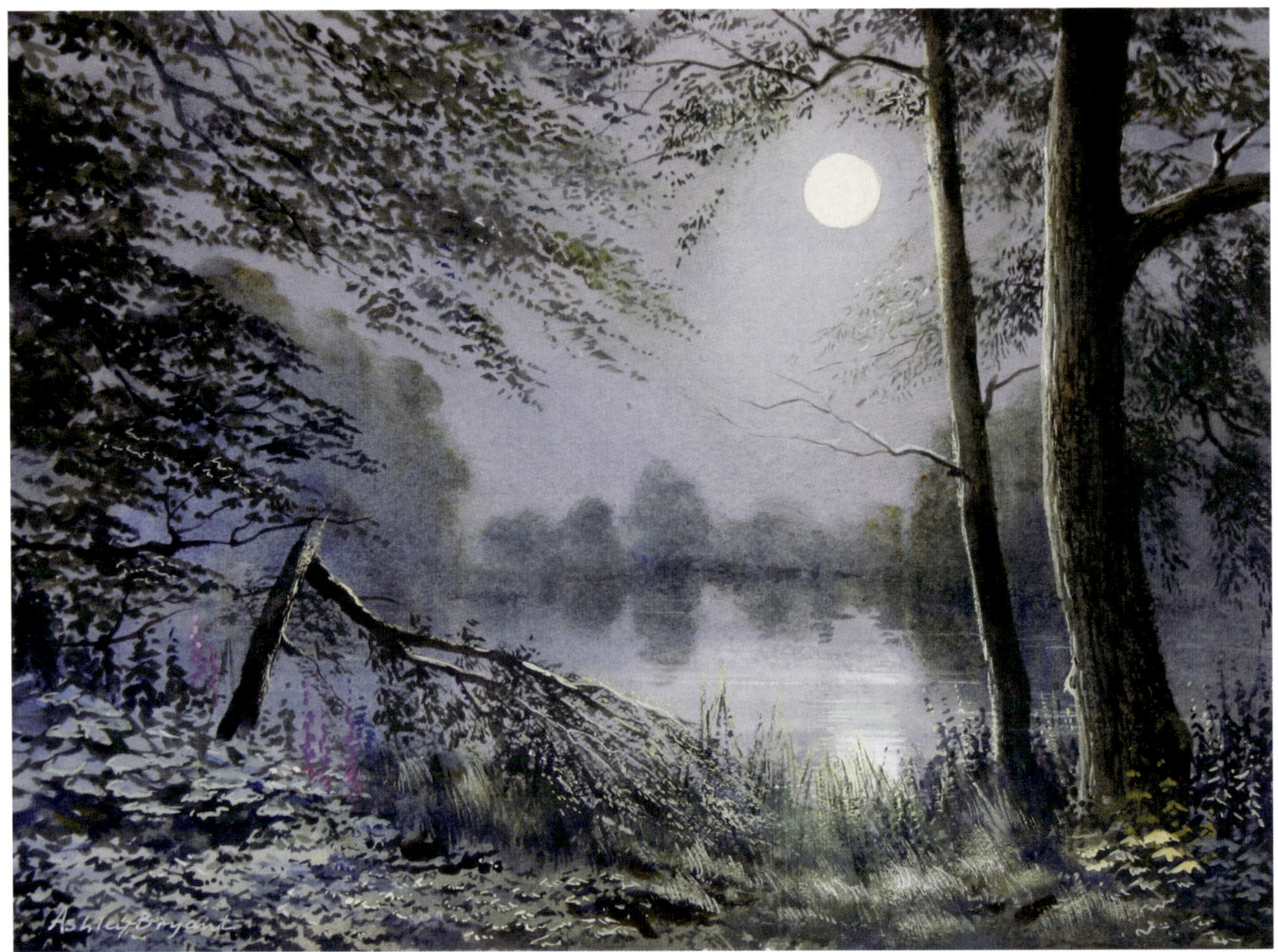

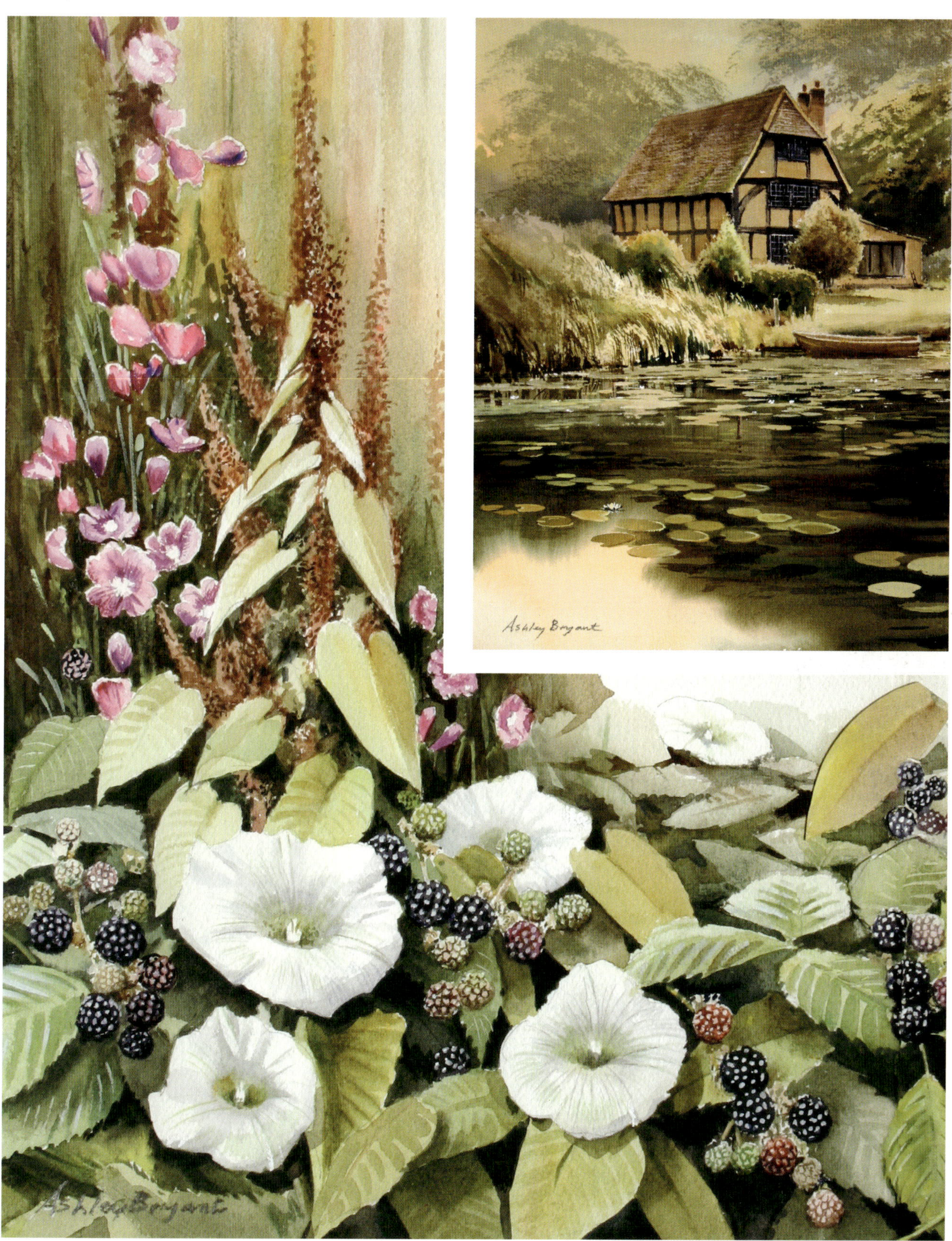
Ashley Bryant
Ashley Bryant

CLIFTON HAMPDEN

The tiny chocolate-box village of Clifton Hampden stands in a charming riverside setting with its beautiful church and collection of pink cottages. The church stands on a small cliff at an elevated position, allowing it to be seen above the trees which obscure the rest of the village. Like many churches it was heavily restored in Victorian times, but its structure dates from the twelfth century, when it was a chapel of Dorchester Abbey.

On the south bank of the river stands the Barley Mow, an ancient pub. Old books tell of its quaint ways – low beams, oak panelling, windows as small as the doors on rabbit hutches and locals who speak in broad Berkshire accents and enjoy tankards of strong cider. Before the bridge was built, a ferry operated and the ferryman would sit by a window in the pub, cider in hand, watching for customers. Charles Dickens loved its garden, Jerome K Jermone's *Three Men in a Boat* called at the Inn and it was here that John Ruskin was "wrapt in a poetic dream while standing by the river". Since then the pub has been rebuilt, creating more space for large crowds of diners; in 1864 a bridge was built by Sir Gilbert Scott, rendering the ferryman redundant.

The two-mile walk downstream to Day's Lock is idyllic and one of the most enjoyable short walks along the river. It passes through Clifton Meadows where wildflowers proliferate amongst a sea of waving grasses in spring and early summer – a paradise for the botanist.

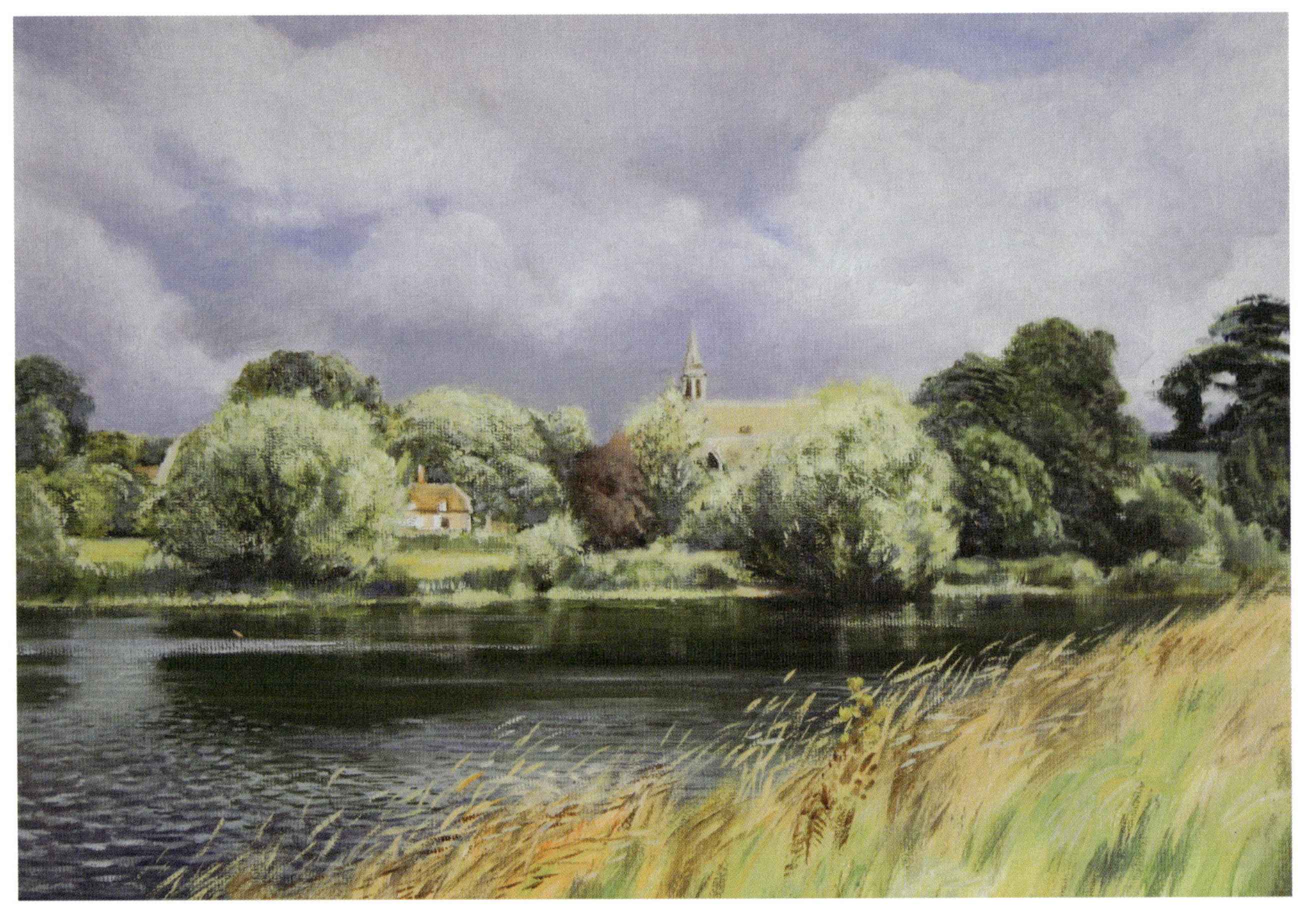

THE BRIDGE AT CLIFTON HAMPDEN
(Right)
Two swans preen on the riverbank in front of Sir Gilbert Scott's brick bridge.

THE THAMES AT CLIFTON HAMPDEN
(Opposite Page)
In this small oil painting, the church spire rises above the trees against a cloudy midsummer sky.

RIVERSIDE – CLIFTON HAMPDEN
(Below)
When the grass is cut and the hay harvested at Clifton Meadows a variety of cattle enjoy the pasture.

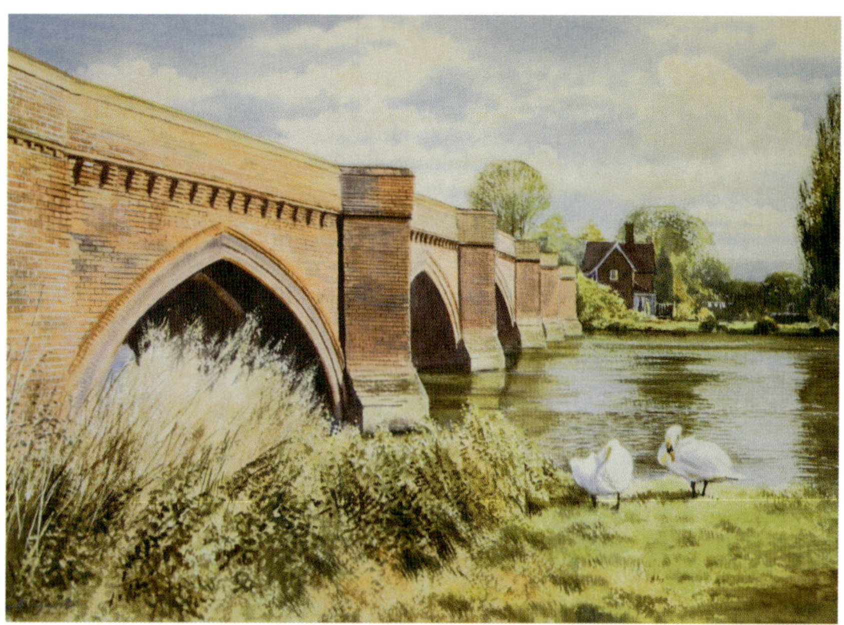

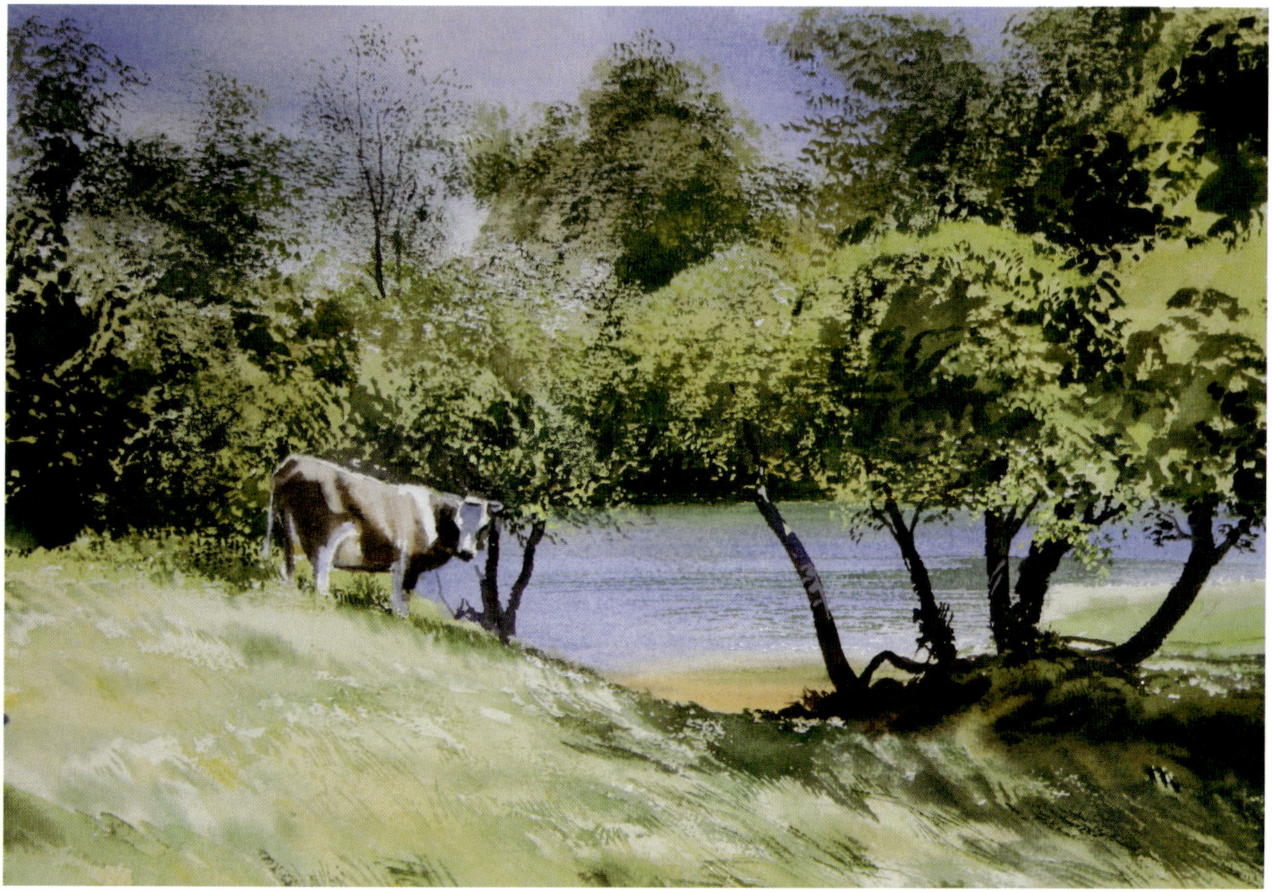

LITTLE WITTENHAM

LITTLE WITTENHAM CHURCH
(Right)

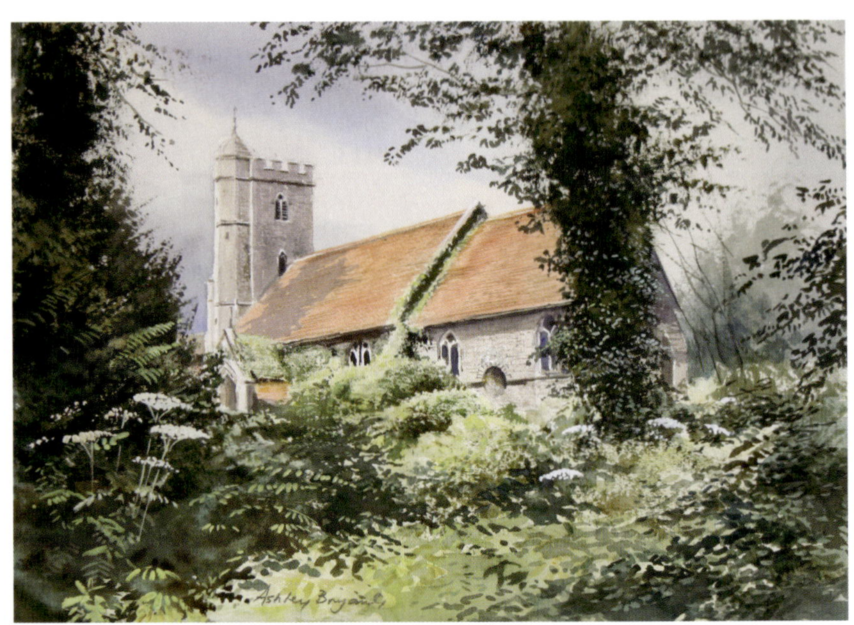

BARN OWL
(Opposite Page Left)
A barn owl hunts at dawn between Little Wittenham and Clifton Hampden. The Sinodun Hills are seen in the distance.

MALLARD
(Opposite Page Right)
It is easy to over look the most common bird on the river yet the mallard drake makes a fine subject to paint.

THE THAMES AT LITTLE WITTENHAM
(Below)
A view from the footbridge near Day's Lock looking downstream.

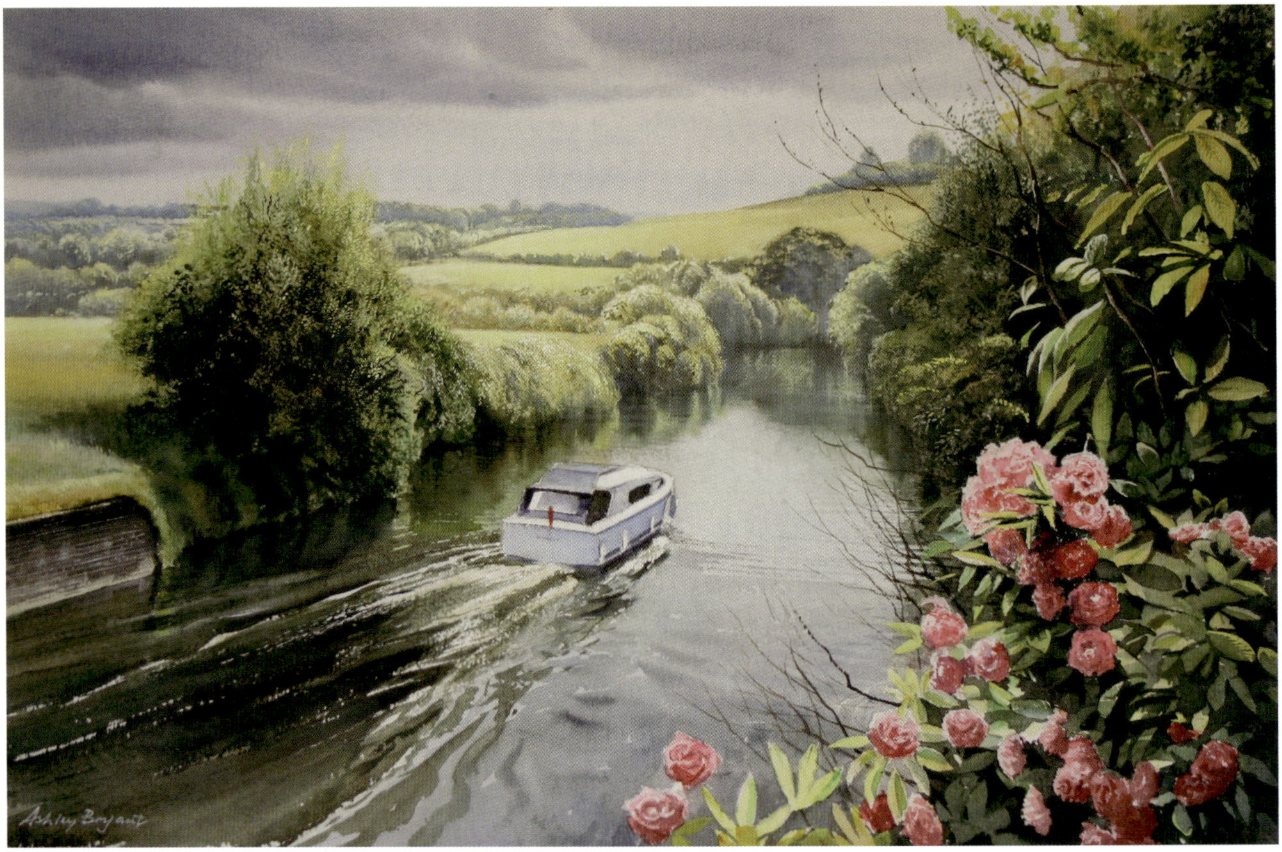

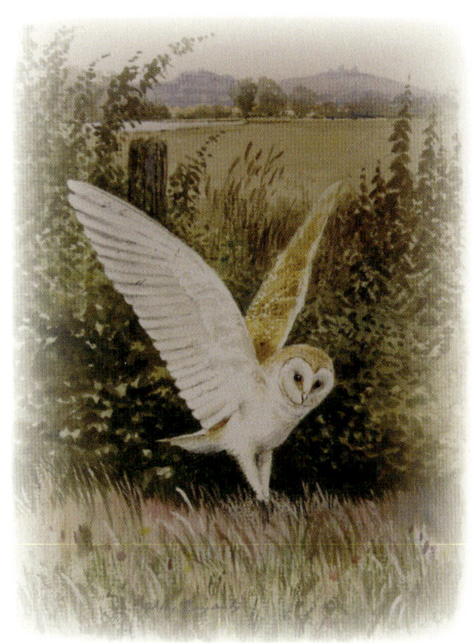

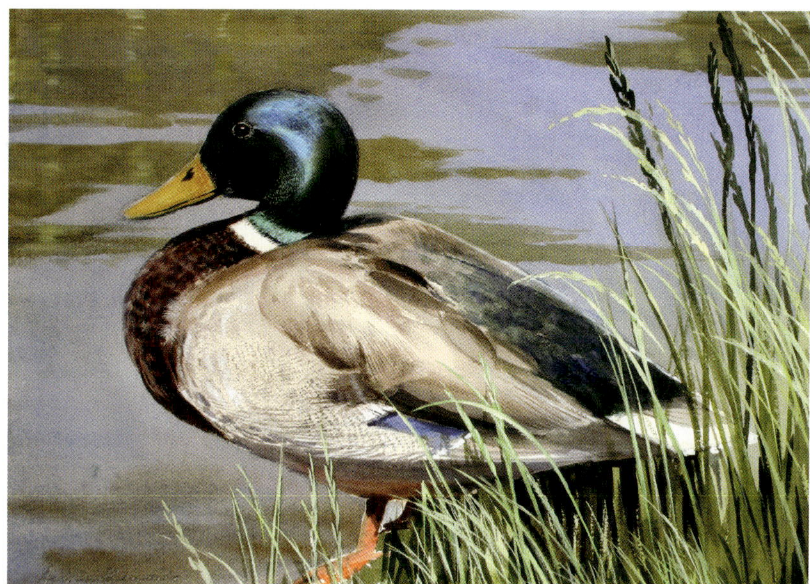

As the river sweeps in a wide bend towards Little Wittenham the outline of the Sinodun Hills start to rise in the landscape. The nearer of these rises, Round Hill, is a nature reserve, whilst the other, Castle Hill, is ringed by the embankments and ditches of an Iron Age fort. Earlier activity is now indicated by recent excavations whilst the Romans later used the site, for this was an area dominated by Roman occupation.

The clusters of trees on the summit give rise to the name Wittenham Clumps and the shape of the two hills to the term Mother Dunch's Buttocks. The Dunches were local wealthy landowners and their splendid tombs of the Tudor period are found in Little Wittenham church. One of the larger matriarchs of the family must have deserved this dedication, but her comments have not been passed down for posterity.

The views from Round Hill are well worth the climb from the tiny, well manicured village of Little Wittenham, as the Thames valley unfolds into a splendid panorama.

Down below, on the left, are the church and Day's Lock. Across the river on its tributary the Thame lies the ancient Roman town of Dorchester, once the Saxon capital of Wessex and a cathedral city in its heyday. It is now little more than a village in size, yet it oozes with charm. To the south the distant Goring Gap encroaches on the river and the far off Vale of the White Horse lies behind us to the west.

Yet again we find an area rich in wildlife. The overhanging vegetation along the side stream at Day's Lock is home to various warblers and reed buntings. Barn owls hunt along the grassy river's margins and kingfishers are a daily delight; but it is the great crested newts that make it a site of special interest to naturalists.

SHILLINGFORD

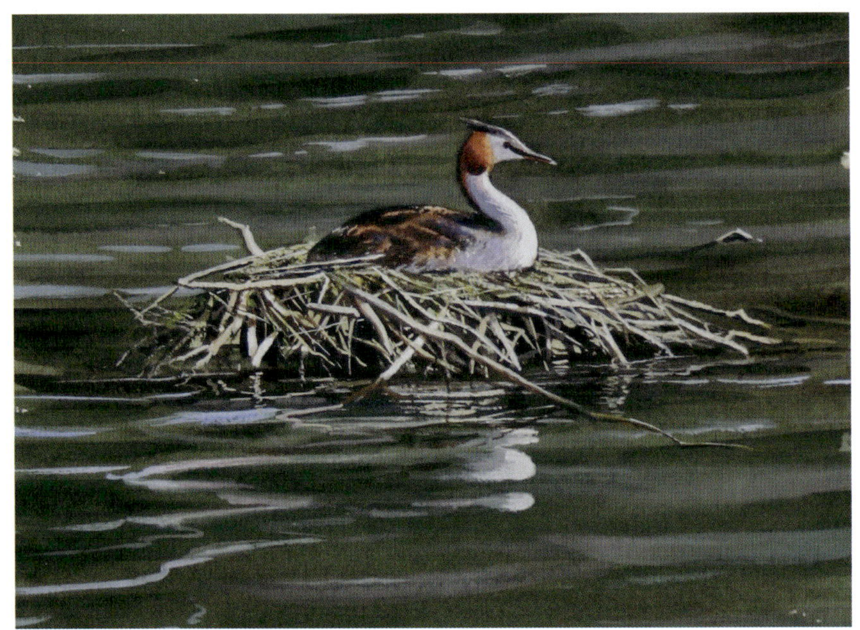

GREAT CRESTED GREBE
(Right)
It is difficult to resist painting these graceful birds when they keep still on their nests.

OLD BOAT HOUSE
(Opposite Page)
This unusual thatched boat house is situated near to Shillingford Court.

IDEAL RETREAT
(Below)
This mock-Tudor boat house cum pavilion near Shillingford Bridge was a welcome retreat in the heyday of rowing on the river.

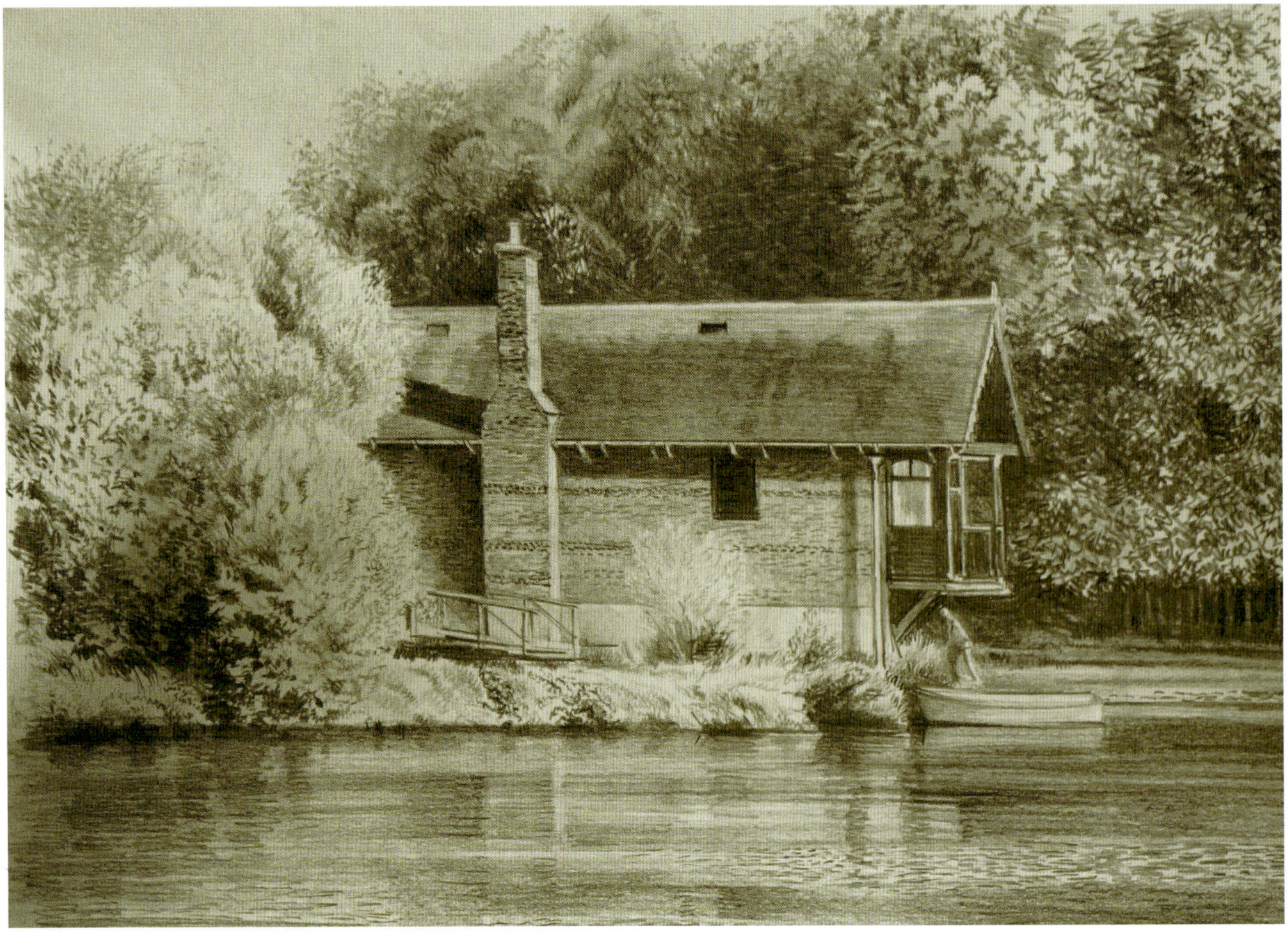

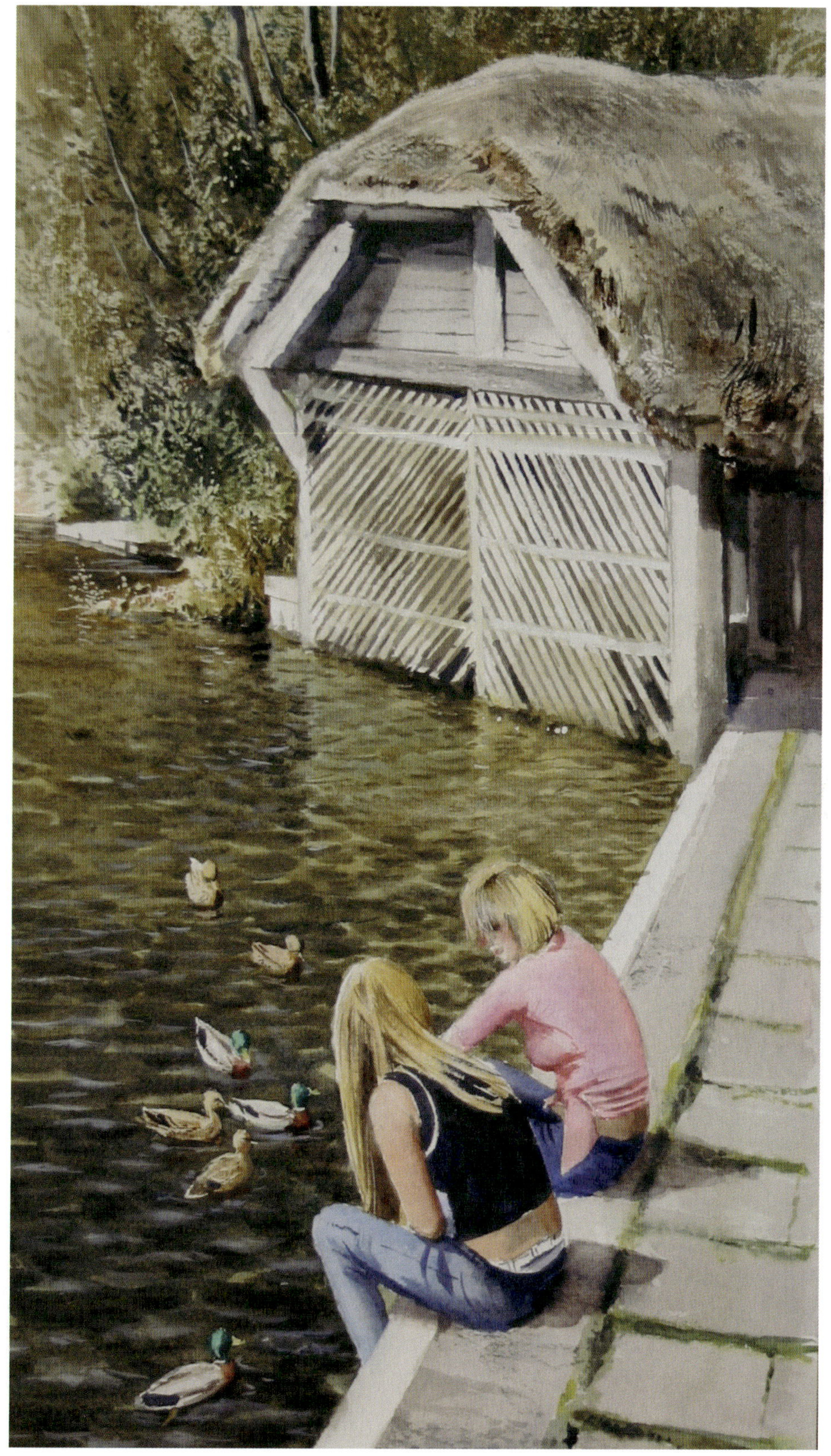

The Thames

WALLINGFORD

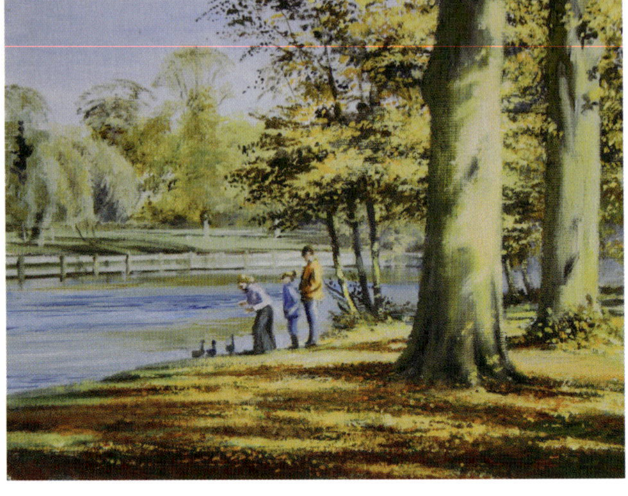

Wallingford is another ancient and charming riverside town. Its rich history surpasses even that of Abingdon. Wallingford developed as a settlement by a ford and was reckoned to be the lowest point downstream where the river could be forded throughout the year, although this claim was probably shared by nearby Shillingford, Moulsford and Goring. A bridge has existed here since Saxon times, and the latest is essentially a widened thirteenth-century structure.

Looking into the depths of the water from the bridge, one questions whether the river could ever have been forded here. The answer is straightforward – the Thames has become deeper. The building of locks has created deeper and calmer stretches of water to help the passage of boats. The Neolithic traveller would have set his toe in here knowing the crossing would be on a firm, stoney bed, and although wide and swift flowing, the river would be little more than knee deep. Fording points such as these made excellent sites for bridges in later years.

Chance played a part in Wallingford's development when William the Conqueror came here to cross the river fresh from the Battle of Hastings. Sympathy for the Norman cause amongst the local Saxon elite helped to promote the town's interests, increasing its privileges and its growth, and barely a year after the Conquest the walls of a great Norman castle were rising above the town. The castle witnessed many battles and significant episodes in English history, but was never taken by opposing forces. After its Royalist cause was lost during the Civil War it surrendered, and Cromwell eventually blew it up as it was considered too much of a risk in this staunchly Royalist area. Today, amongst the mounds and ruined walls it is difficult to imagine its former dominance and impregnability.

The riverside meadows provide an ideal vantage point for painting or sketching the bridge, with the slim spire of St Peter's church peeping through the trees. A short distance downstream, the rowing club generates a good deal of energy, and at weekends in particular the calm reflections on the water are disturbed by the young and fit.

FEEDING THE DUCKS
(Above)
Wherever you are it is always enjoyable to feed the ducks.

THE THAMES AT WALLINGFORD
(Opposite Page Above)
One of the traditional views from the water meadows looking towards the bridge. The slim spire of St. Peter's church is seen above the bridge and behind the trees, with the rowing club in the foreground.

BY WALLINGFORD BRIDGE
(Opposite Page Below)
Equipped with just four coloured pencils this view upstream from the bridge was a laborious task, as each element of the picture required overlays of different colours.

HARD TRAINING SESSION
(Below)
A charcoal sketch of an exhausted rower.

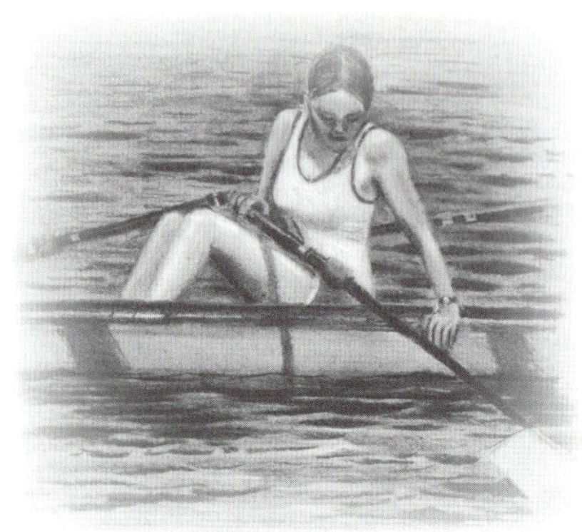

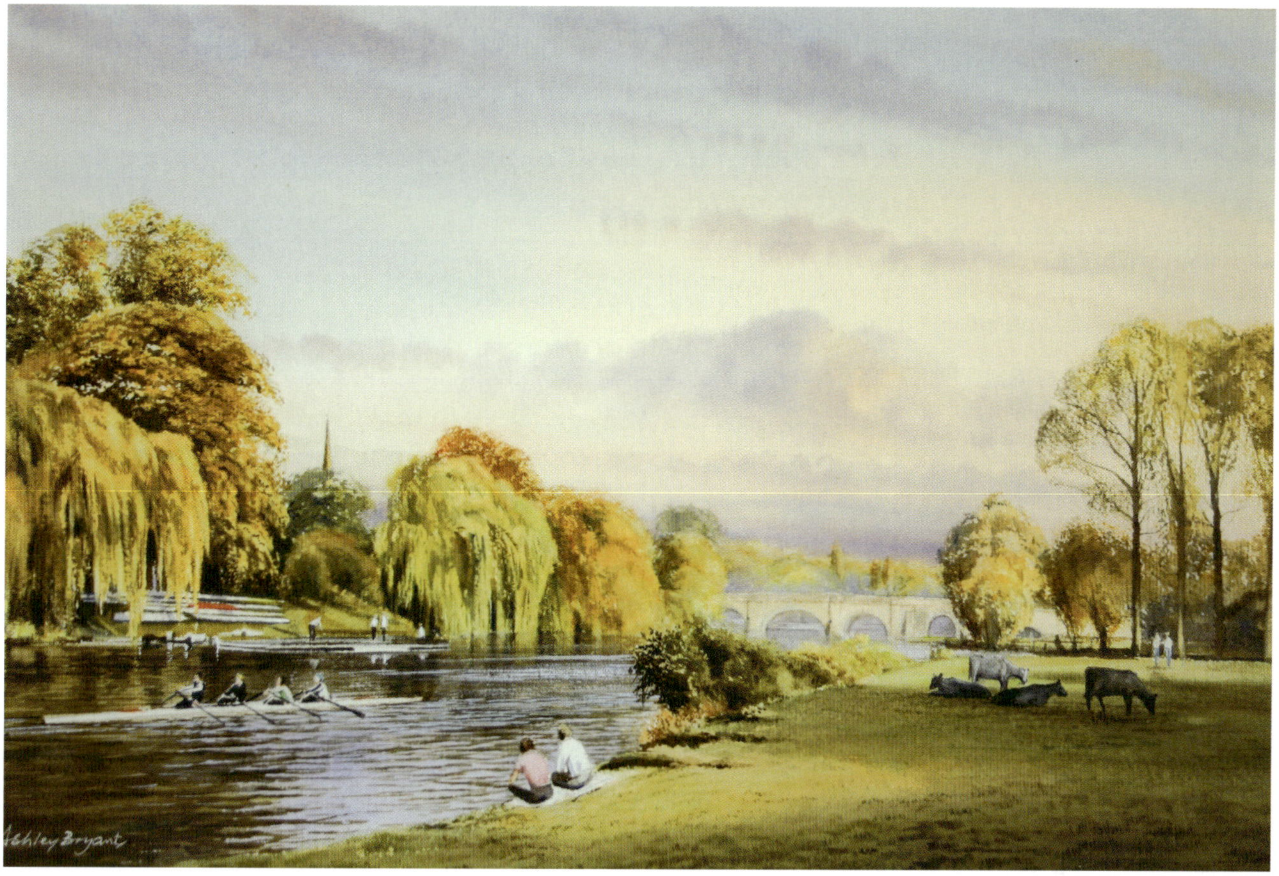

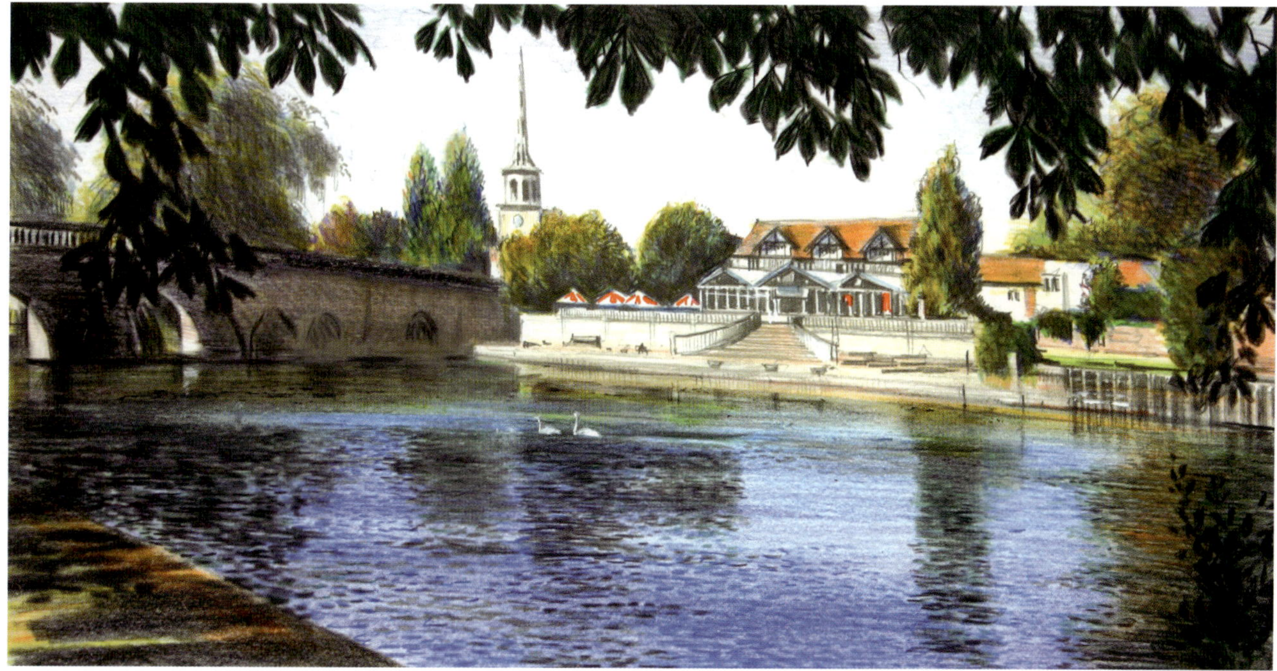

STREATLEY

WALKING THE DOG
(Opposite Page Above)
To the north and towards Moulsford the valley is shallower and wider.

THE THAMES VALLEY FROM THE BERKSHIRE DOWNS
(Below)
Lardon Chase offers a splendid view of the Thames valley, seen overlooking Goring in late summer. Every season has special attractions. Although spectacular, the widest Thames panorama is seen from Langdon Hills in Essex.

As the river flows south from Wallingford, the land progressively rises on either side with the Chilterns on the east and the Berkshire Downs on the west, converging to form a valley known as the Goring Gap. Down below, the villages of Goring and Streatley nestle on their respective banks, flanked by steep hills.

This area enjoys some of the best scenery on the Thames, so it is hardly surprising that the river is crowded on summer weekends with cruisers and narrow-boats queuing to pass through Goring Lock. Tourists flock to the area and those walking the Ridgeway National Trail cross the Thames here and pause to look down from the bridge – a significant milestone on their journey.

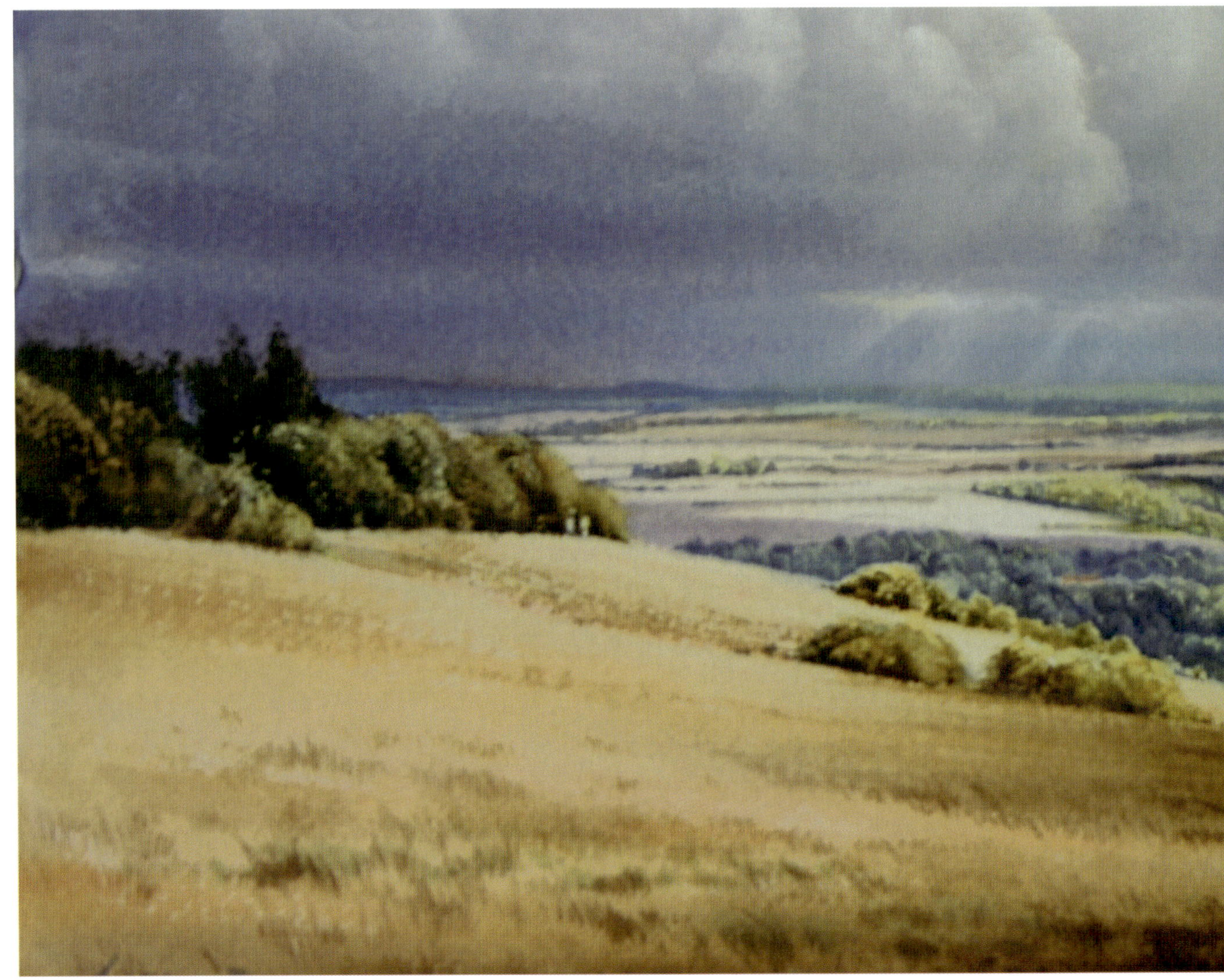

There are many subjects to paint; Goring Lock and its bustling activity, the old mill, the church and numerous attractive riverside settings. There are interesting compositions to be found in smaller Streatley, and some outstanding views from the National Trust's open land of Lardon Chase at the top of Streatley Hill. Viewed from the car park, the Thames Valley makes a spectacular distant cleft, framed on either side by foreground trees. As you walk onwards the views progressively extend up and down the valley with the Sinodun Hills visible to the north and the Berkshire Downs disappearing to the south.

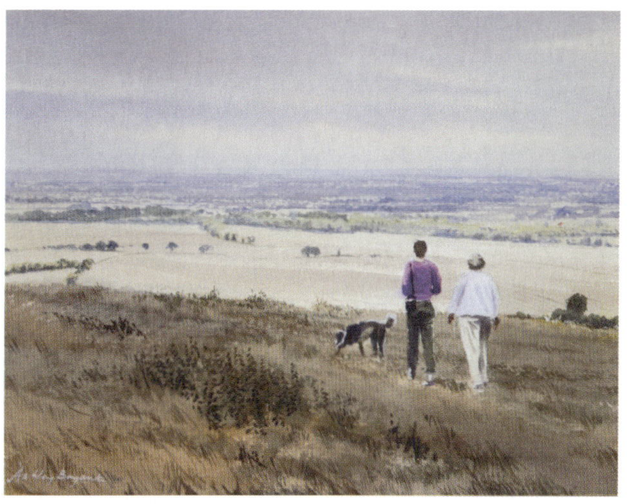

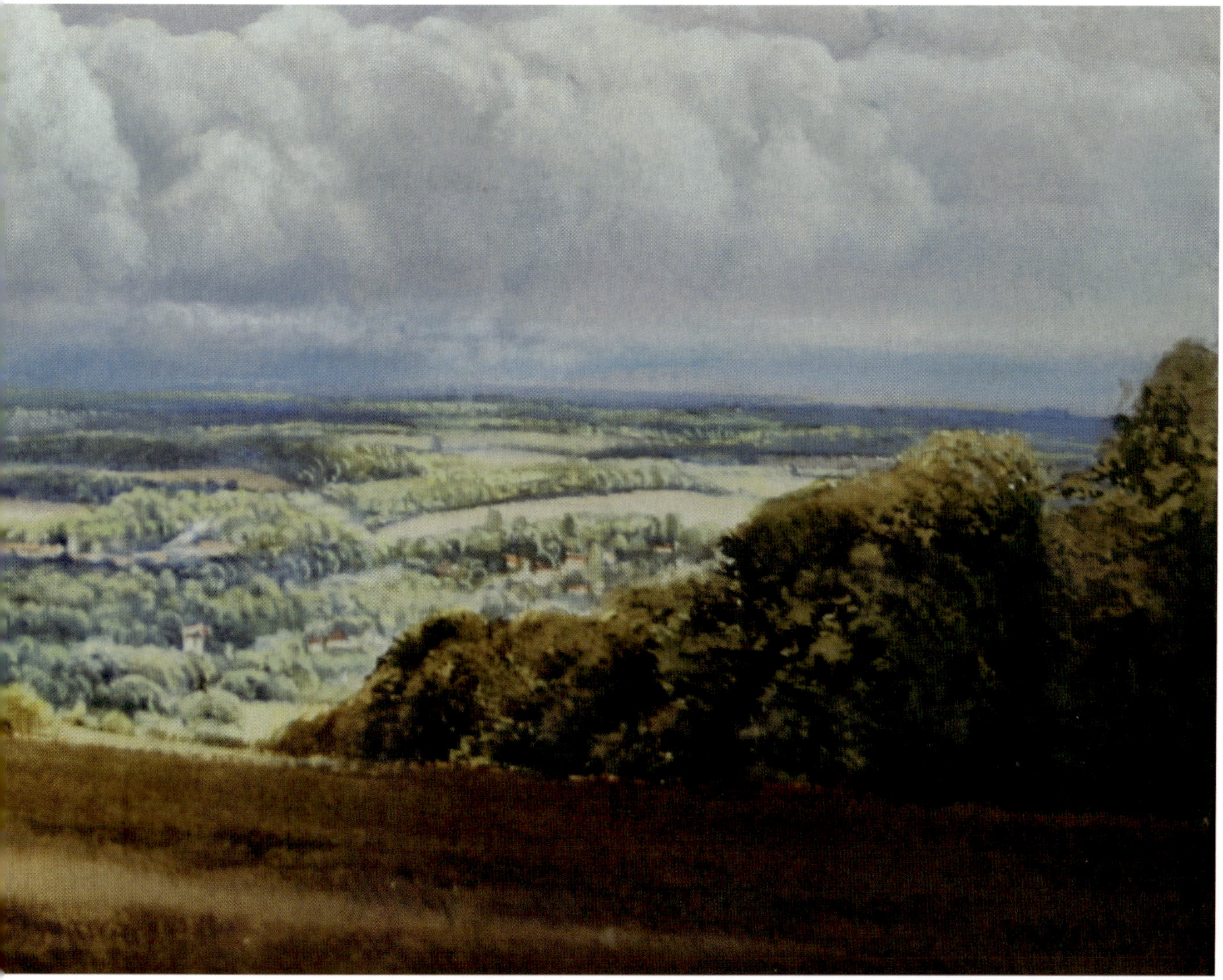

GORING GAP

RIVERSIDE WALK – GORING
(Right)
The attractive riverside along the Thames Path at Goring.

THE THAMES NEAR GORING
(Below)
Seen in the light of a November's afternoon, the river sweeps around the edge of the Chilterns between Goring and Whitchurch.

THROUGH THE CHILTERNS
(Opposite Page)
The Thames Path leaves the riverside to cut through a corner of the Chilterns.

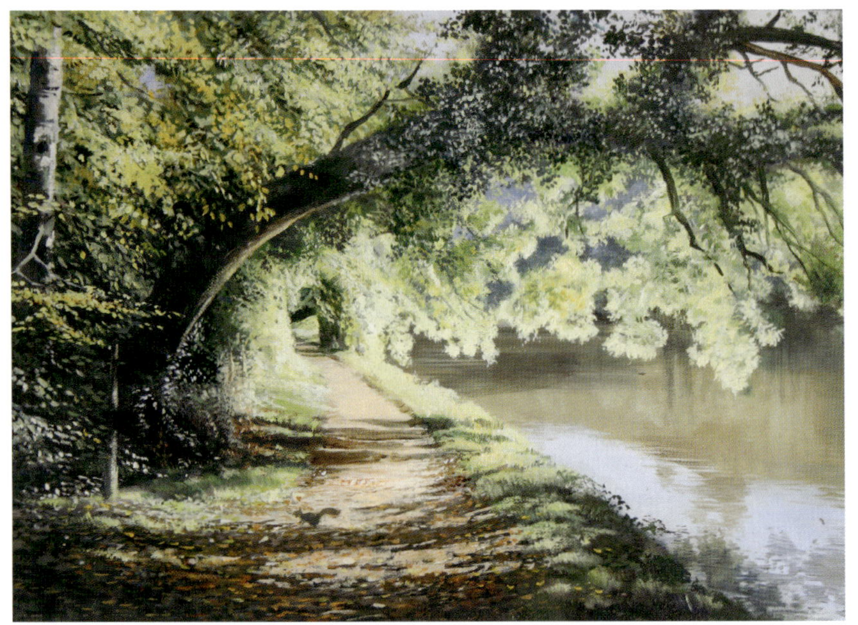

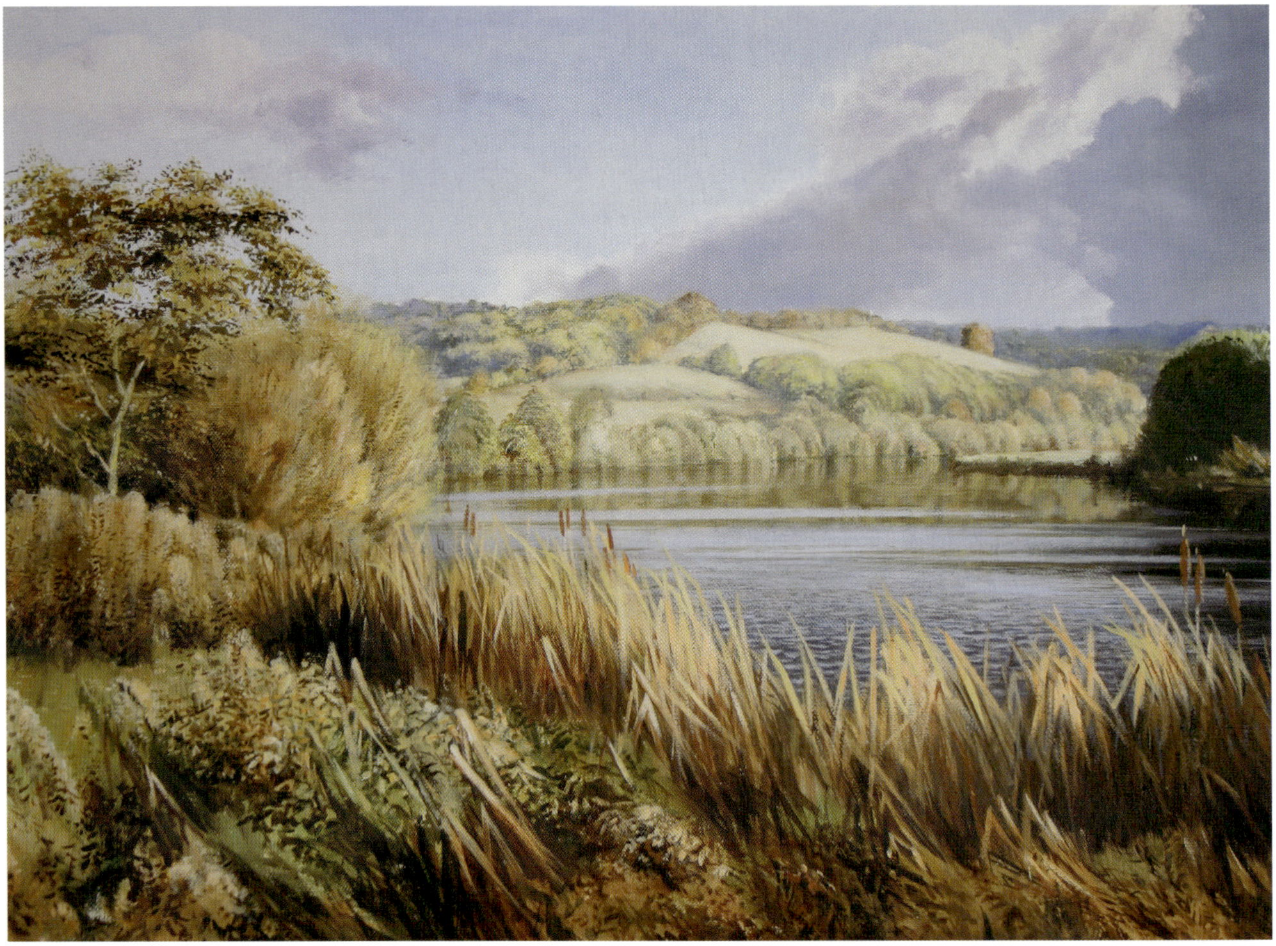

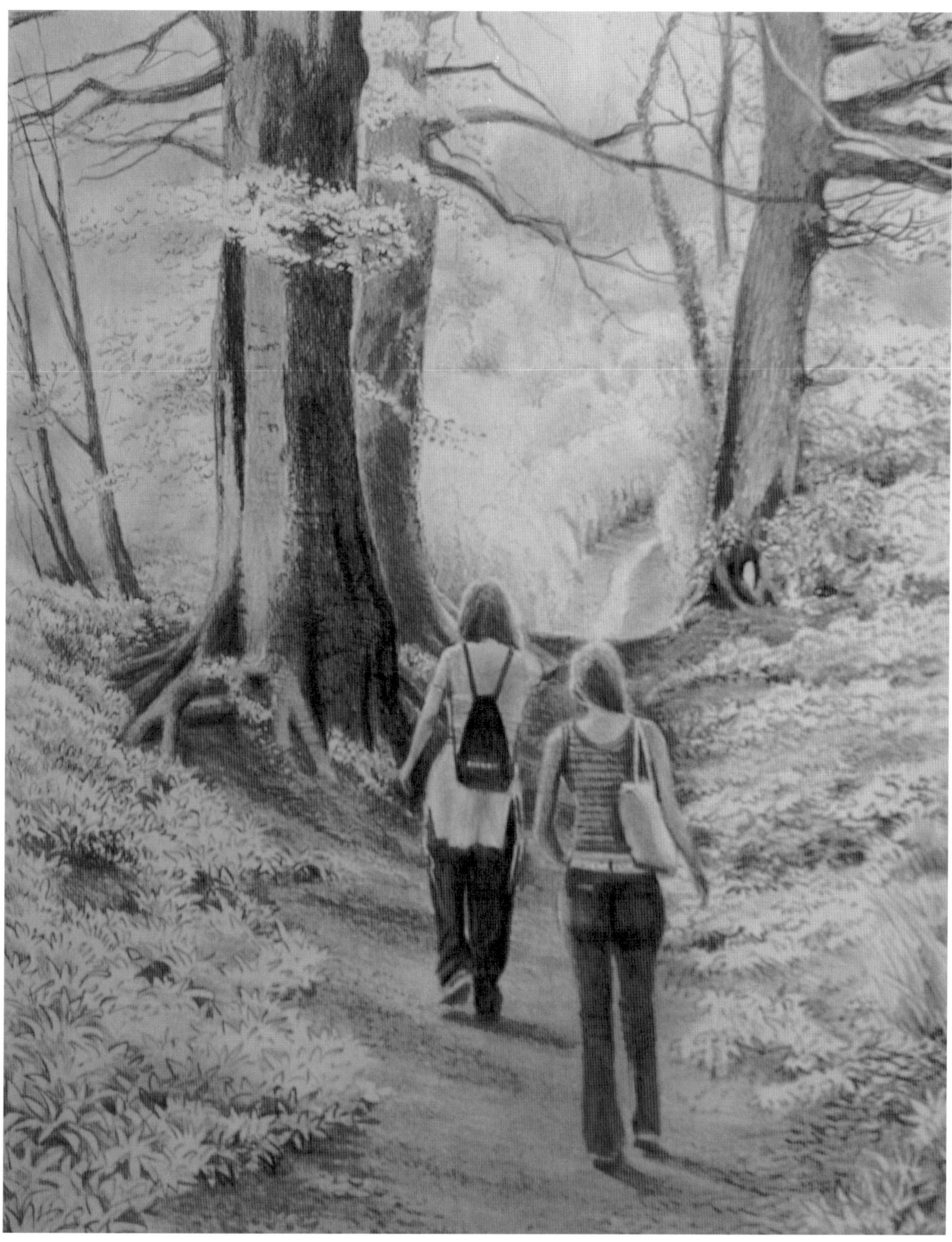

WHITCHURCH

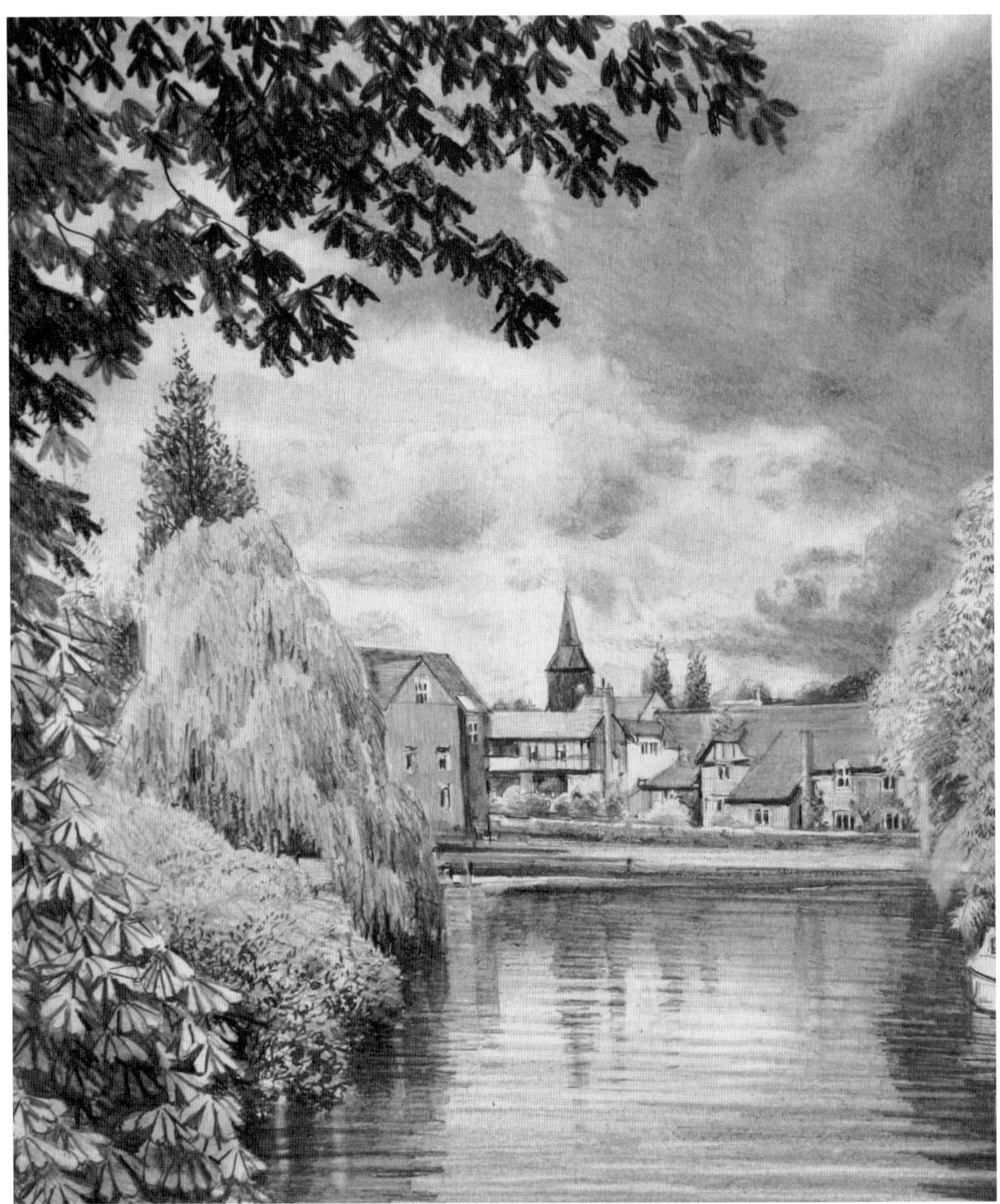

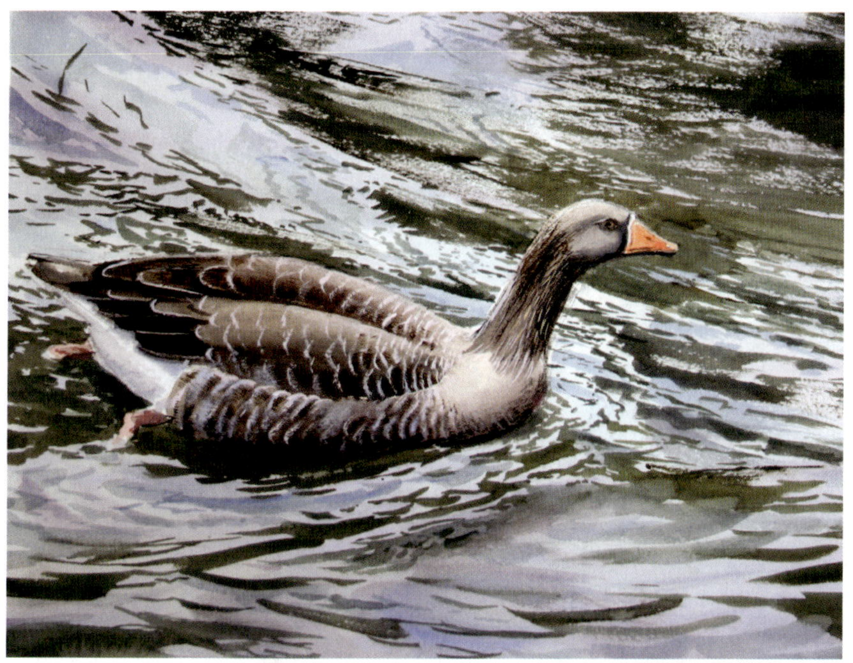

GREYLAG GOOSE
(Left)
The Greylag, one of the more unusual species of goose on the Thames, was once the most common goose of "old England". The age of archery relied on these birds for the fletchings of arrows.

THE THAMES AT WHITCHURCH
(Opposite Page)
This pencil sketch of the "calendar" view of Whitchurch as seen from the toll-bridge shows the mill pool and attractive riverside buildings. The mill stands on the left behind the trees and the church of Norman origin was rebuilt in 1858.

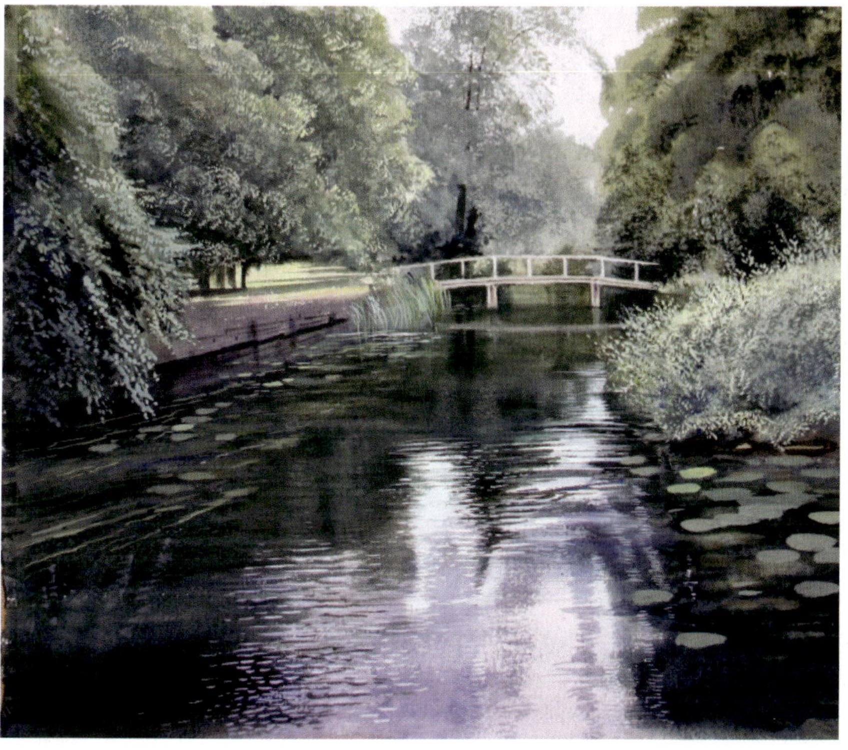

THE MILL STREAM
(Left)
The owner of the mill kindly showed me the mill stream at the rear of his property. Whilst the footbridge was not quite as elegant as Monet's at Giverny, the scene and the overcast day made an interesting composition in greens, blues and greys.

PANGBOURNE

STEAM BARGES
(Right)
Very few of these narrow boats, powered by steam from coal boilers, remain in use today. Most of them were scrapped in the 1950's or converted to diesel engines.

THE THAMES NEAR PANGBOURNE
(Opposite Page)
Even in July on a warm but overcast day this stretch of the river between Pangbourne and Mapledurham was very quiet.

NARROW BOATS AT PANGBOURNE
(Below)
A line-up of canal boats at Child Beale Park for an enthusiasts' get-together.

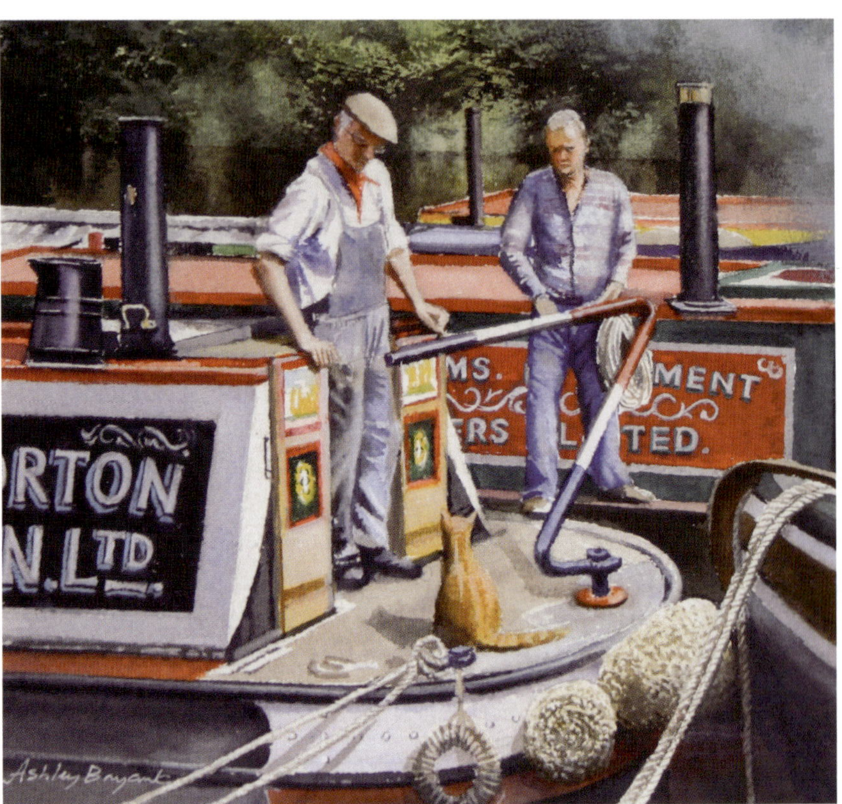

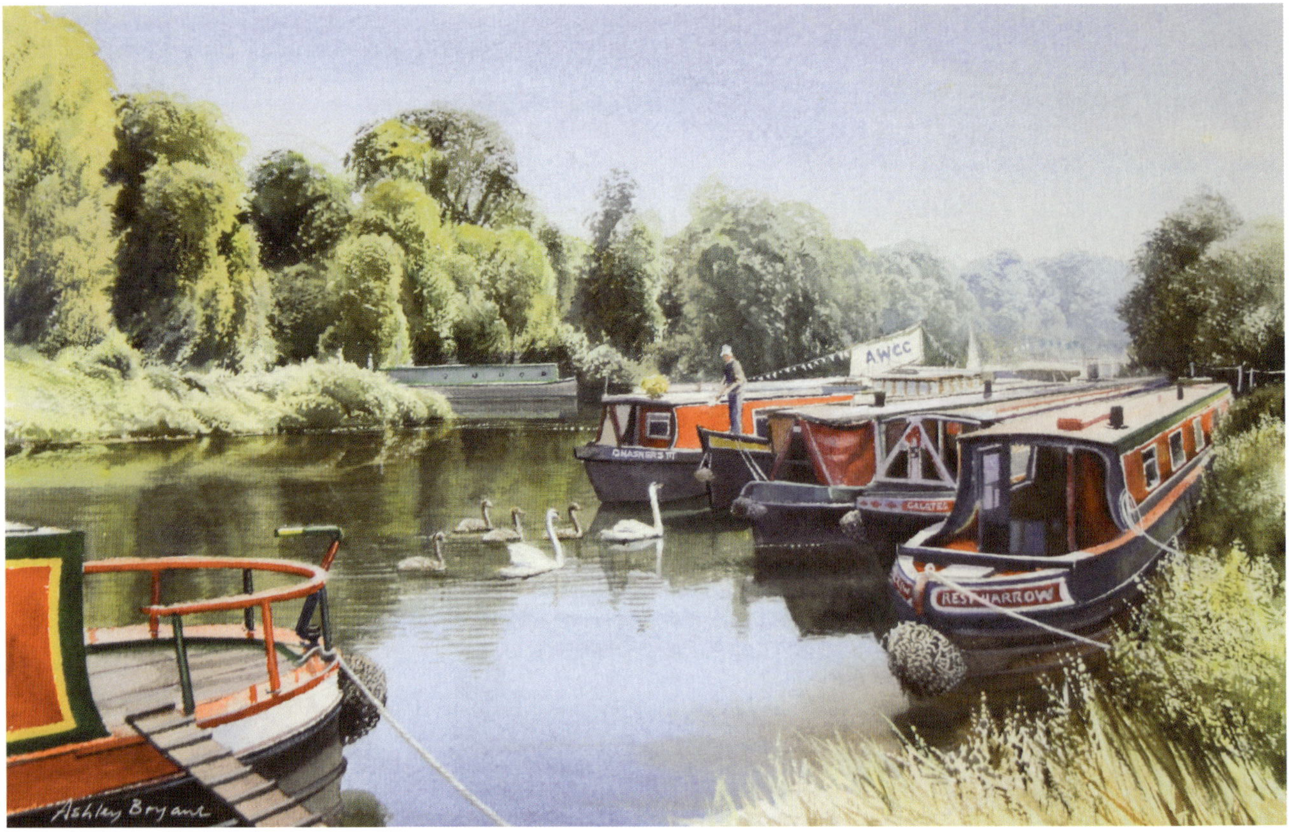

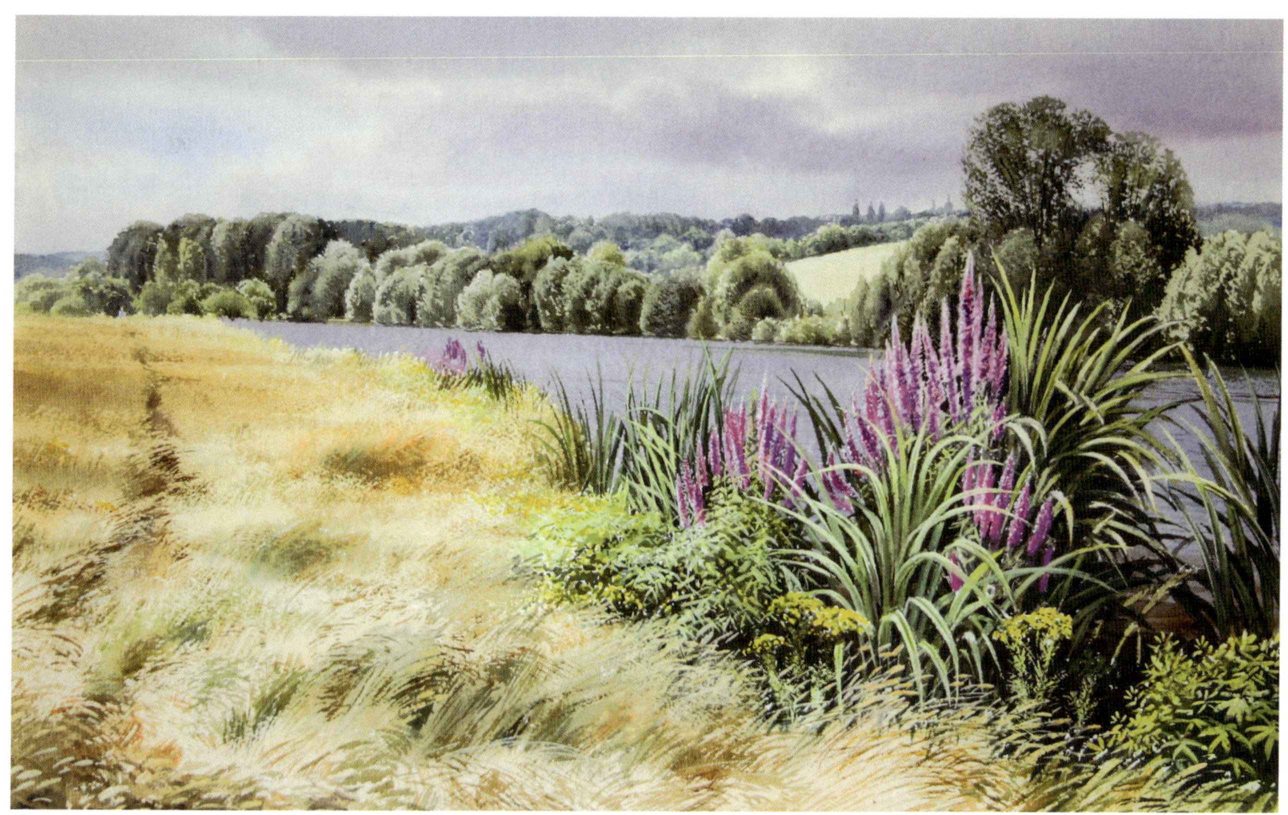

The Toll-bridge crosses from Whitchurch to its larger neighbour Pangbourne, where the small river Pang joins the Thames. A short distance upstream lies Child Beale Park, a popular venue for various outdoor activities. On one of my visits, I saw a gathering of narrow boats. This provides an opportunity for the boating community to swap stories, visit each other's galleys for drinks and to discuss the merits of different engines, compare mooring fees, maintenance and fuel charges and other matters close to their hearts and minds. Their passion is always infectious and after exposure to romantic stories of life on the water the landlubber is in danger of being hooked. To help matters, boat manufacturers were on hand with their latest models, ushering you onboard to view their beautifully appointed craft, and keen to take your particulars as you disembark. Some boats were so luxurious that visitors have to remove their shoes before walking on the plush carpets, yet the lengthy queues showed no lack of interest.

Pangbourne is associated with Kenneth Grahame, author of *The Wind in the Willows*, who was inspired by the Thames in the creation of this children's classic. On publication, a critic from the *Times* pronounced it would never sell, but after dozens of editions its appeal is as strong as ever. On the walk downstream to Mapledurham it is easy to understand his inspiration. Even the Elizabethan Hardwick House on the far bank was used as a model for Toad Hall. This stretch of river has also appealed to many notable artists through the ages. Robert Giddings, writing in 1939, considered the banks so crowded with views they "may have dropped from the gold frames of the Royal Academy".

MAPLEDURHAM

THE LOCK-KEEPER'S COTTAGE
(Right)
Thames locks are famous for their neat and attractive gardens and on the south bank of the river a cottage garden theme is used to give Mapledurham some individuality.

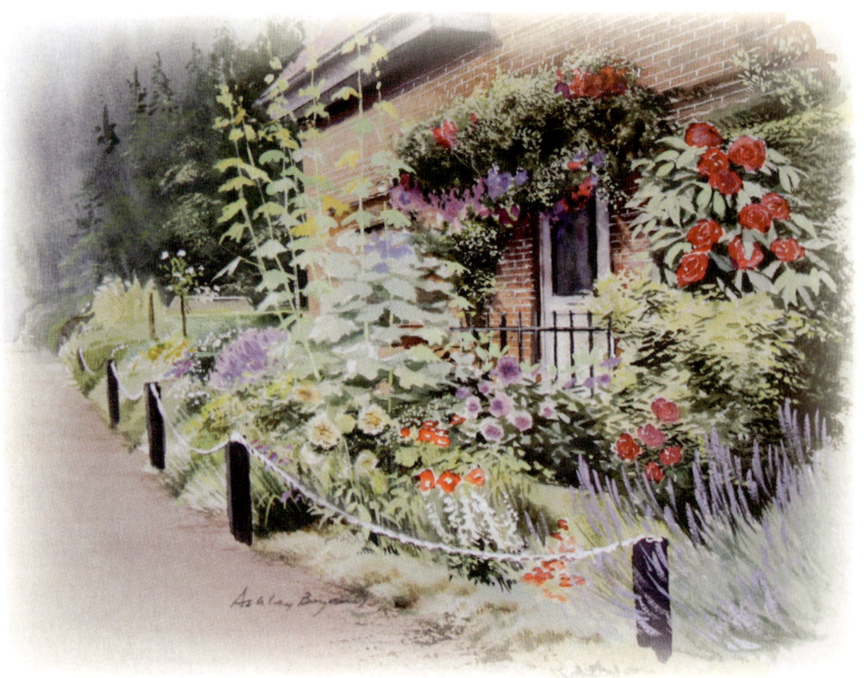

THE THAMES AT MAPLEDURHAM
(Opposite Page)
The perfect picnic spot is found in the shade of the willows at Mapledurham. Since the Thames is so clear it is also a favourite place for swimming. The grounds are private and belong to Mapledurham House, rebuilt as an Elizabethan Manor in 1581 and recently restored by its present owners.

MAPLEDURHAM MILL
(Below)
This old mill is surrounded by trees and lawns and, reflected in the clear mill pond, makes an ideal composition.

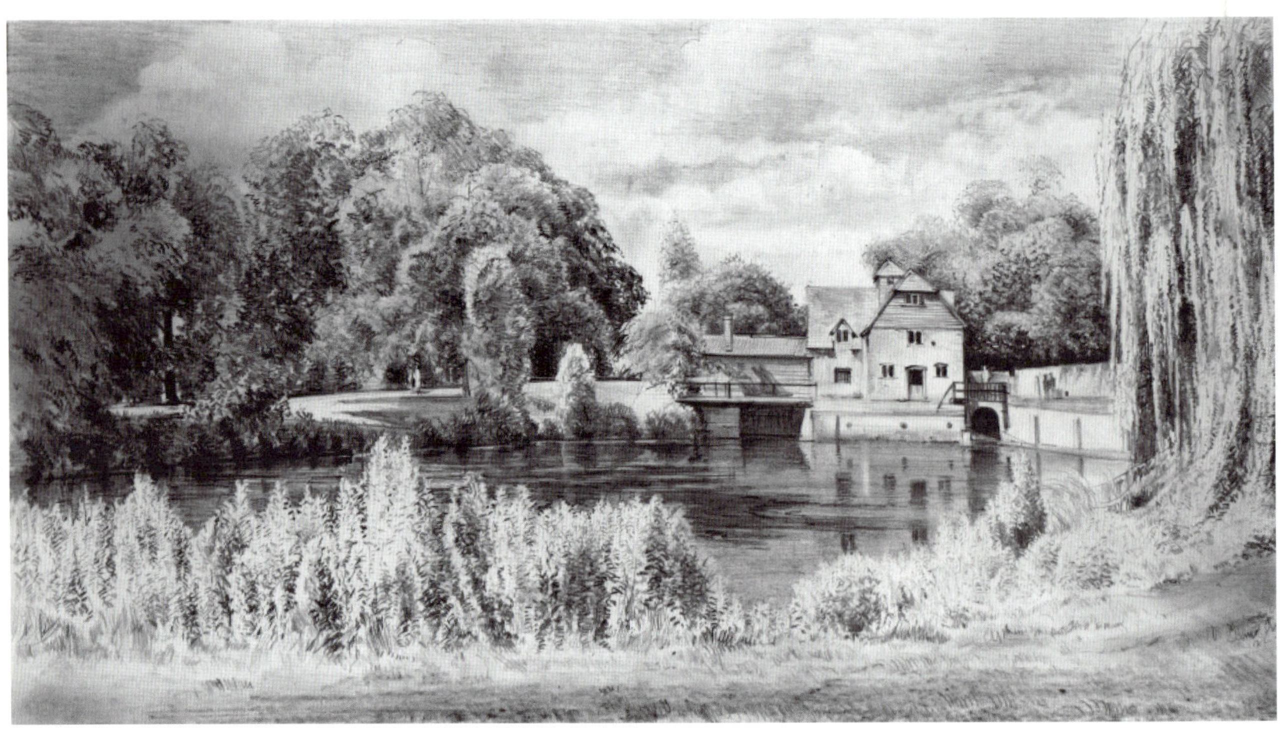

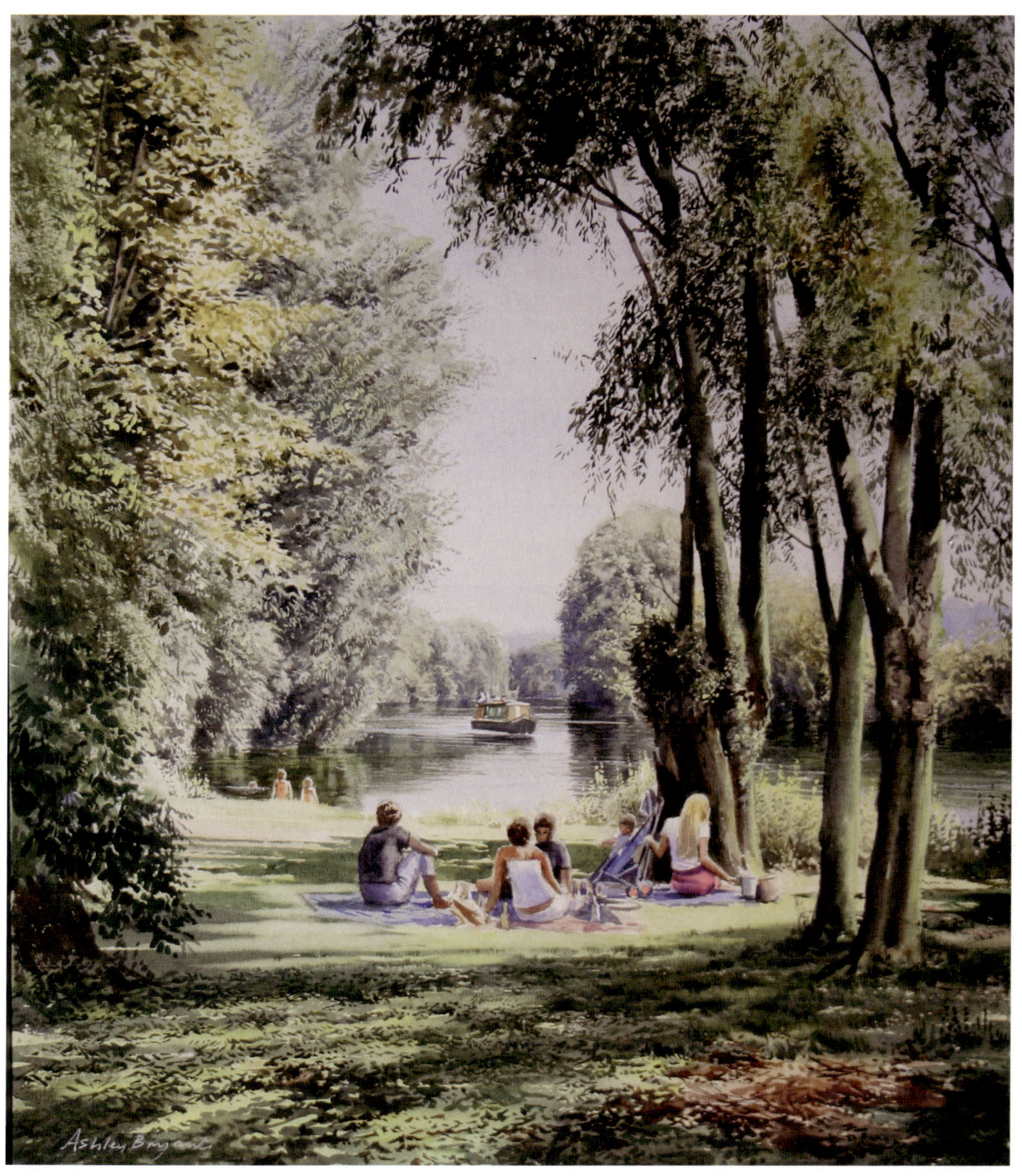

The Thames

READING

SWAN CITY
(Below)
A small proportion of the swans that congregate around Caversham Bridge. These are joined by ducks, coots and seagulls in their quest for scraps of bread.

DUCKLINGS
(Opposite Page Above)
This young brood of ducklings provided an engaging subject for a pastel.

FOREVER HOPEFUL
(Opposite Page Below)
This angler was trying his luck at Tilehurst along the Thames Path en-route to Reading.

Reading, the county town of Berkshire, is situated on the river Kennet, one of the main tributaries of the Thames, but has spread up to the Thames and across the north side in the shape of Caversham, one of its residential districts. This concrete bridge of the 1920s replaced a latticed iron bridge, which itself replaced an earlier structure, complete with bridge chapel.

I must confess that Reading gave me a problem since I could not decide on a composition even after several visits. Perhaps the weather had been gloomy on these occasions, which never helps as everything looks better in sunshine. Finally, I noticed a particular feature of the river here – its huge number of swans. Whether it is because people feed them or because a large gathering of swans simply attracts these gregarious birds, I do not know. Without doubt there are more swans here than anywhere else on the river.

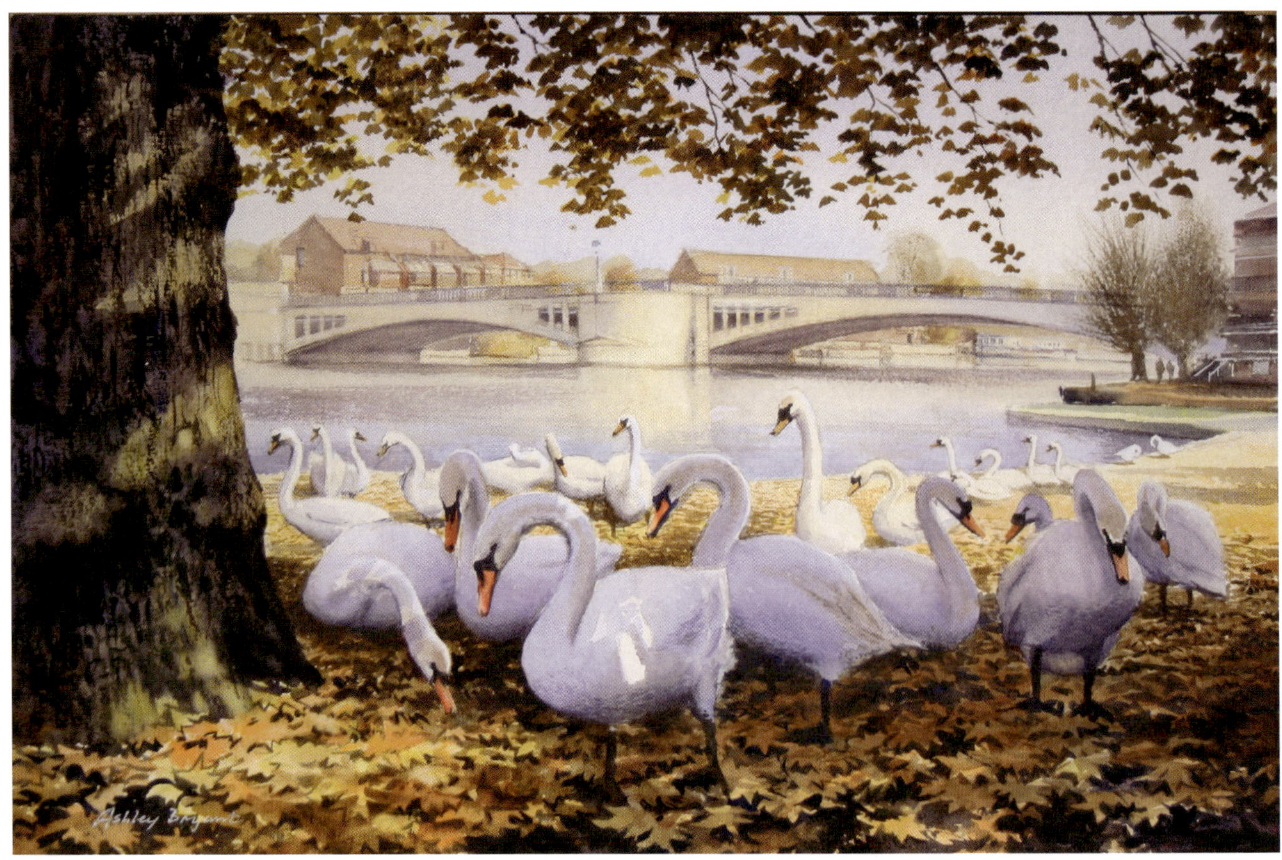

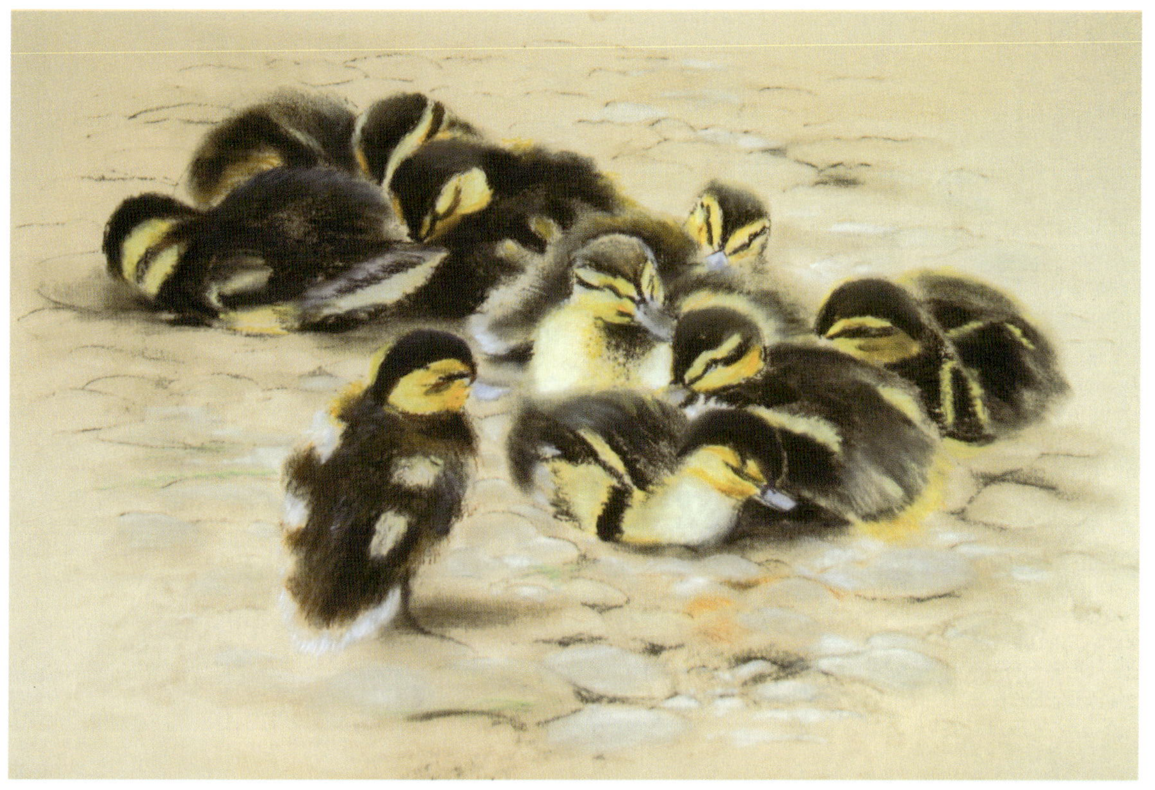

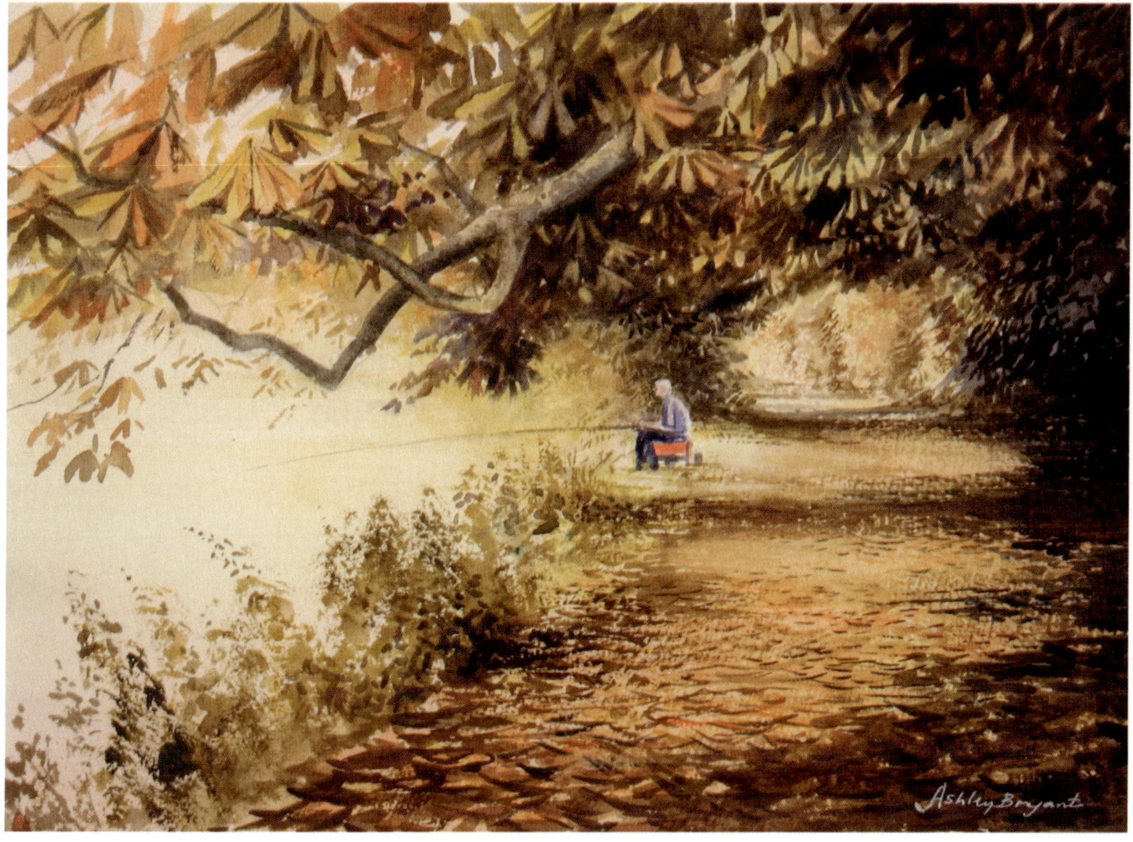
Ashley Bryant

SONNING

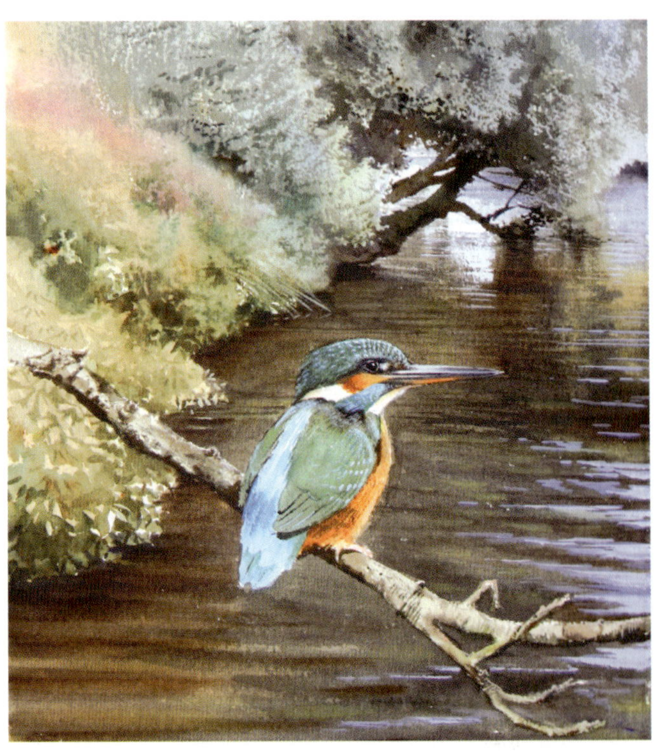

KINGFISHER
It is always difficult to resist a painting of a kingfisher. Whilst I was admiring the view one flew under the central arch of the bridge. I saw another just a short distance downstream.

THE THAMES AT SONNING
(Opposite Page)
In this watercolour, produced in mid-November, the light was so low it almost shone through the arches. The bridge continues with another section of arches over the mill stream which joins the Thames to form this lake-like bay.

SONNING RIVERSIDE
(Below)
This pencil sketch shows the Thames Path en-route to Shiplake.

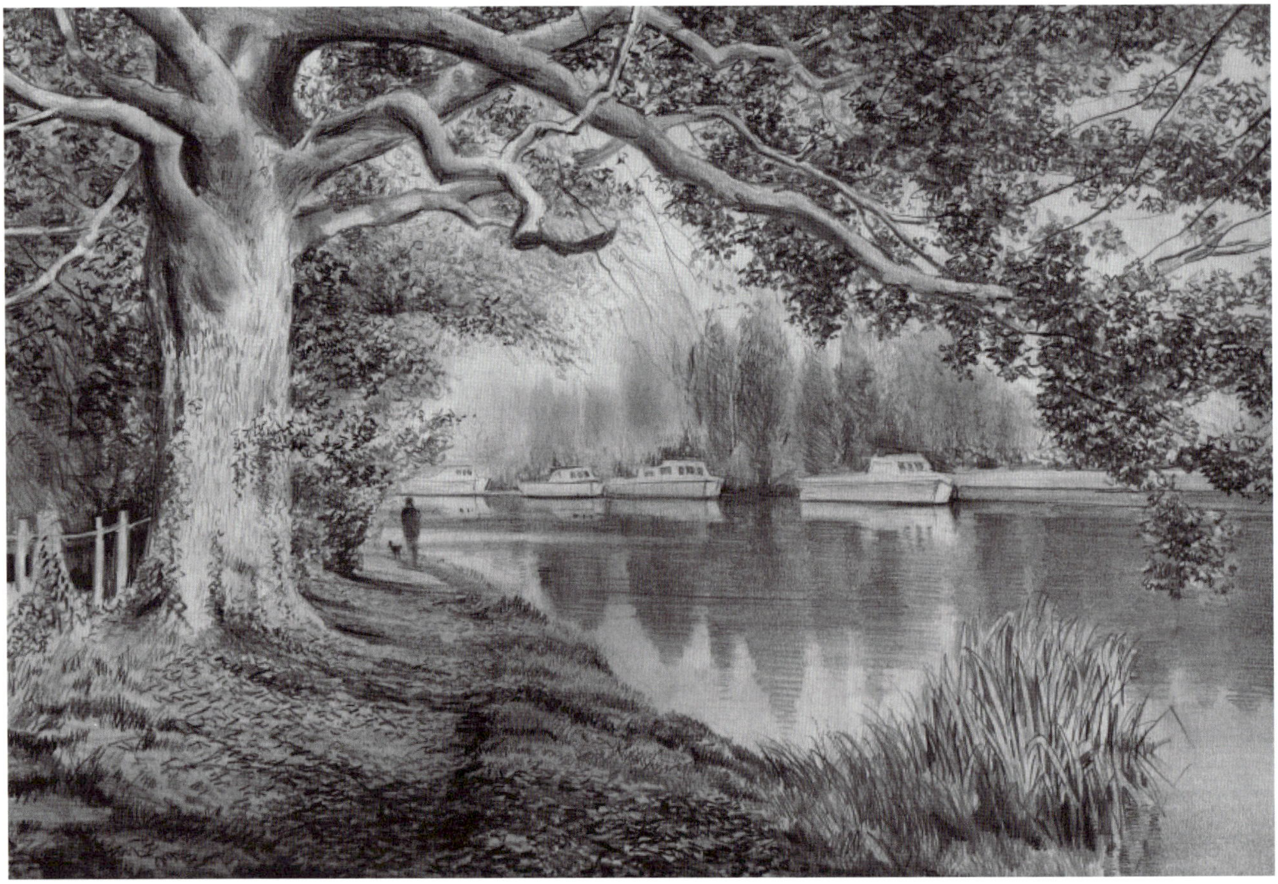

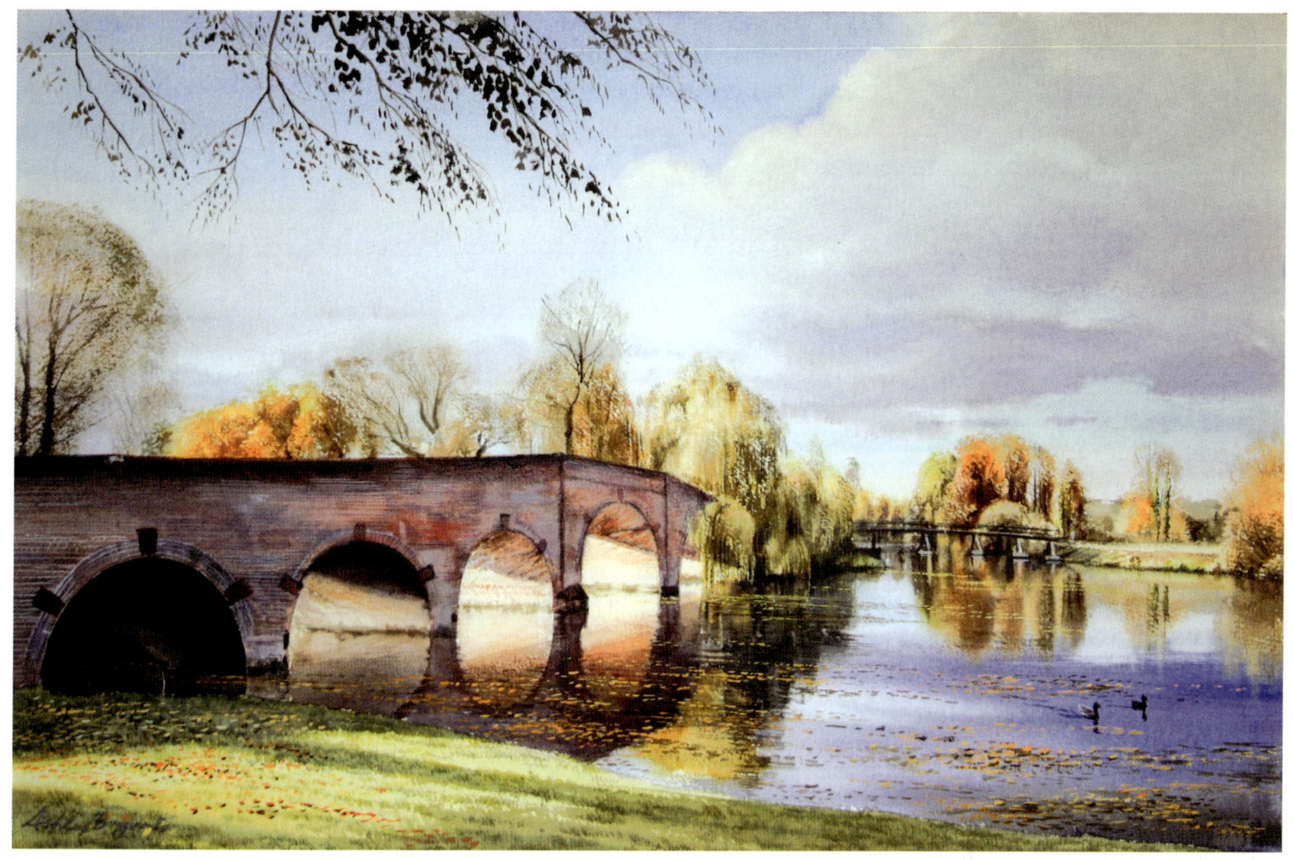

Are the villages becoming more charming on this journey downstream? It would appear that way when Sonning is reached. Oak-framed buildings, mellow orange-red brickwork and rose-covered walls delight the eye, whilst ancient inns of great character tempt you to step inside and enjoy real ales and excellent food. The multi-arched bridge of mellow brick is very much in sympathy with its surroundings. Its single eighteenth-century carriageway causes havoc with modern traffic especially at rush hour, but it would be a brave resident who suggested a modern concrete replacement.

One of the traditional views of Sonning often seen in old engravings takes its viewpoint from the north bank of the river where it overlooks the lake-like pool of the Thames, with the bridge on the right and the squat tower of St Andrew's Church between the trees. Old brick buttresses in the churchyard are all that remain of a bishop's palace. Those who believe in ghosts maybe interested to hear that the spectral form of a girl walks forlornly by the riverside, said to be the child-bride of Richard II.

Sonning mill, now converted into a theatre and restaurant, stands on the upstream side of the bridge, where it provides some further opportunities for riverside compositions. A footbridge takes the Thames Path from the main bridge over to the north bank of the river for an interesting walk to Shiplake, but before continuing it is well worth looking back to take full advantage of this timeless scene.

SHIPLAKE

Whether it is a crisp winter's day or high summer the walk downstream from Sonning is always enjoyable. A chalk ridge on the left shows you are approaching Shiplake. There are many delightful vistas between Sonning and Wargrave as the Thames twists across its flood plain. Enormous trees along the river bank near the College invite artistic studies, with their twisted trunks, vast spreading branches, and the interplay of dappled light between them.

The College boathouse, Shiplake Lock, the river's varied and interesting margins, and the abundant wildlife of the area, offer a wide choice of subjects for the artist.

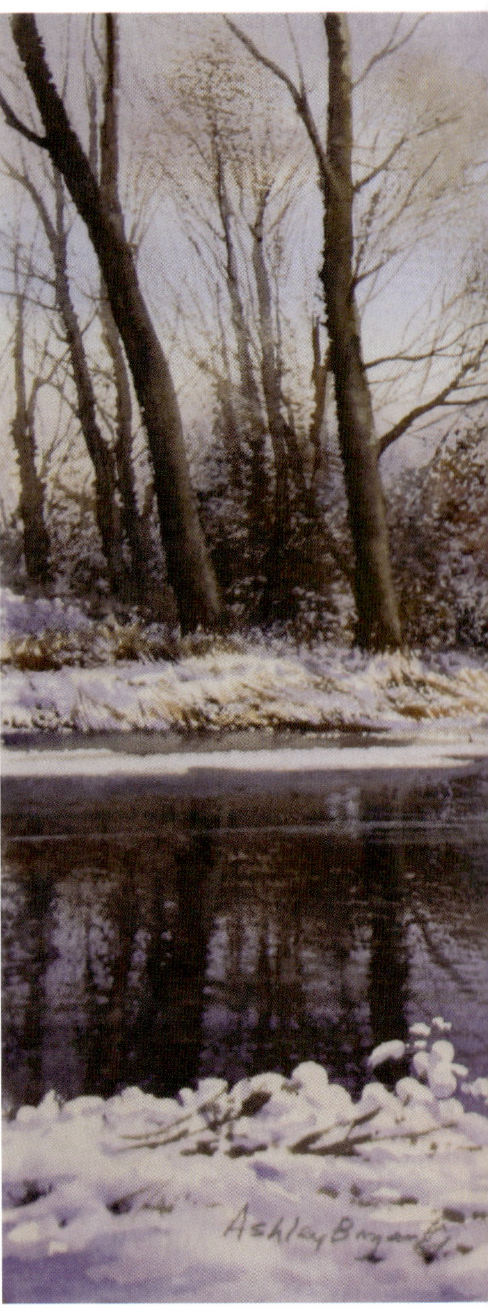

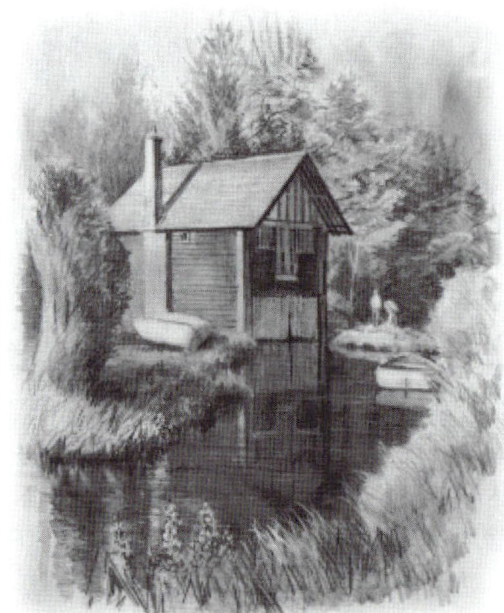

THE COLLEGE BOATHOUSE, SHIPLAKE
(Right)
On the flood plain the boys of Shiplake College enjoy their cricket and rugby, as well as cross-country running along the Thames Path and rowing on the river. School days could really be the best days of your life in this idyllic setting.

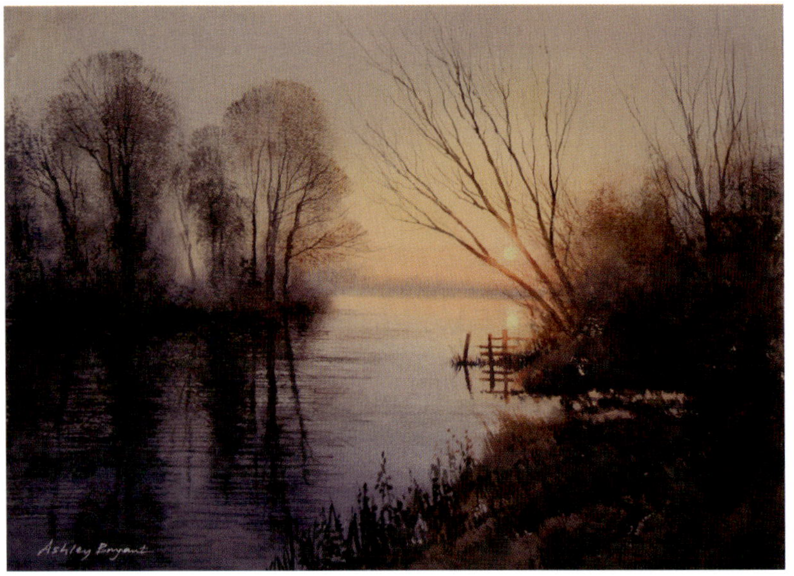

EVENING AT SHIPLAKE
(Left)
The winter trees by the Thames are silhouetted against a darkening sky between Shiplake Lock and the College. In this instance, the breezes during the day had subsided and the evening was calm and cold, but with delightful warm lighting.

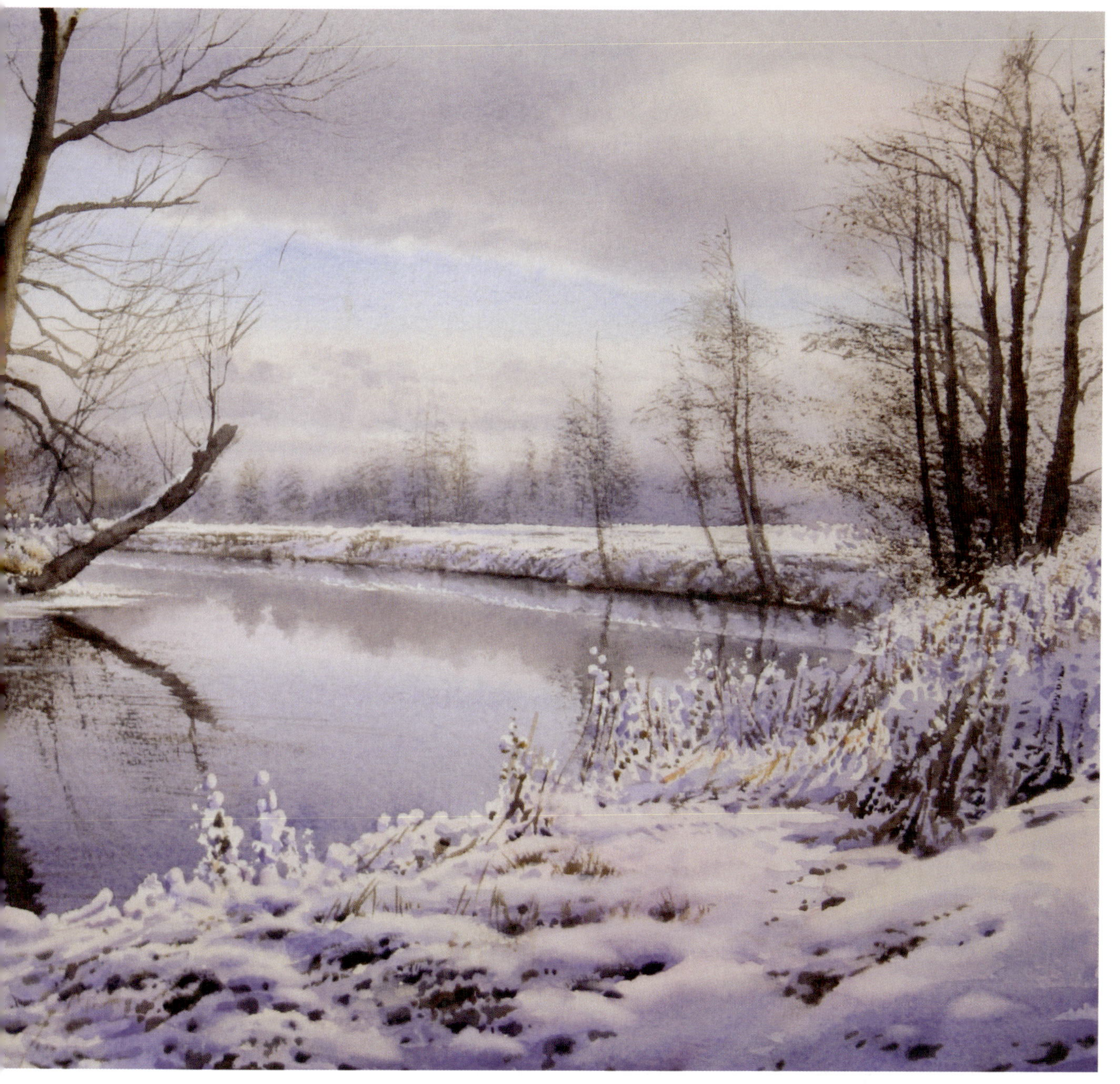

THE THAMES AT SHIPLAKE
(Above)
The Thames sweeps around the playing fields of Shiplake College on a winter's afternoon. These days it is unusual to get a good fall of snow and unless you are on the spot it has normally melted by the time you get there. The answer is to add the snow using a little artist's imagination.

HENLEY

THE TOWPATH AT HENLEY
(Opposite Page)
The towpath provides a delightful walk that can be completed as part of a round trip from Henley to Hambledon Lock, Aston, Remenham and back to Henley. The towpath is popular and the pedestrian is advised to develop eyes in the back of the head to detect cyclists – especially those training rowing crews, their attention focused on the boats.

THE THAMES AT HENLEY
(Below)
During summer boats pass under the arches of the lovely stone bridge in quick succession. The River and Rowing Museum is a short distance upstream, along the far bank.

With its attractive riverside frontage and collection of moored boats, this old market town has a broad appeal for artists, photographers and tourists alike. To quote Charles Dickens "it is the Mecca of the Rowing Man" – and of course the rowing woman. It is the geography of the area that enabled Henley to assert itself as the principal rowing town on the Thames since it sits alongside the longest straight stretch of river. The rowing theme is interactively presented at the River and Rowing Museum along with the story of Henley itself and the Thames. The museum reminds us that the Thames was a great commercial highway and a painting of Henley in 1698 by J. Siberechts shows the waterfront packed with barges.

For those who can steal themselves away from Henley's interesting streets and seductive inns, a walk along the Regatta course downstream to Temple Island is recommended. Its "temple" was built as a classical focal point in the landscape for nearby Fawley Court. The original manor house of Fawley was sacked in the civil war to the dismay of the owner – a Mr Bulstrode Whitelock. His splendid name alone entitles him to a footnote in history.

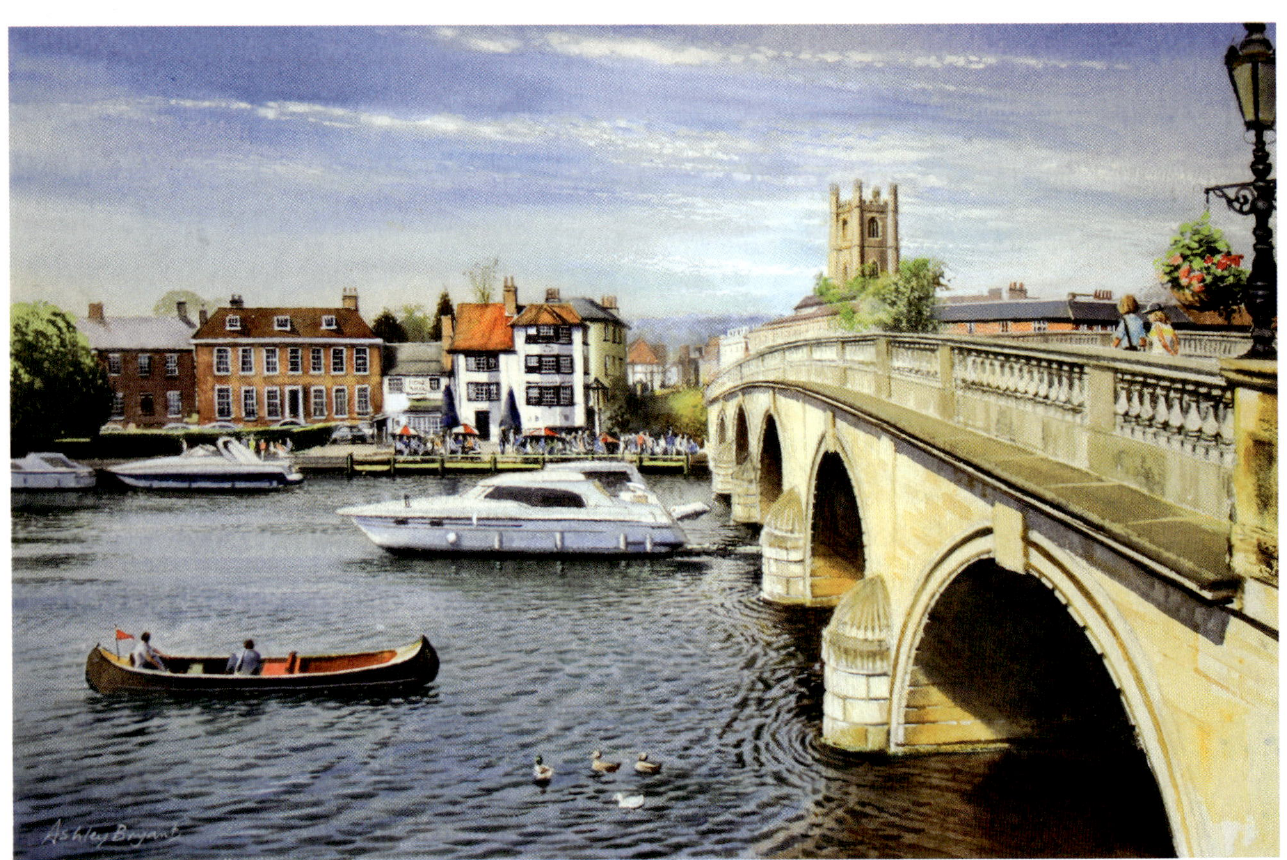

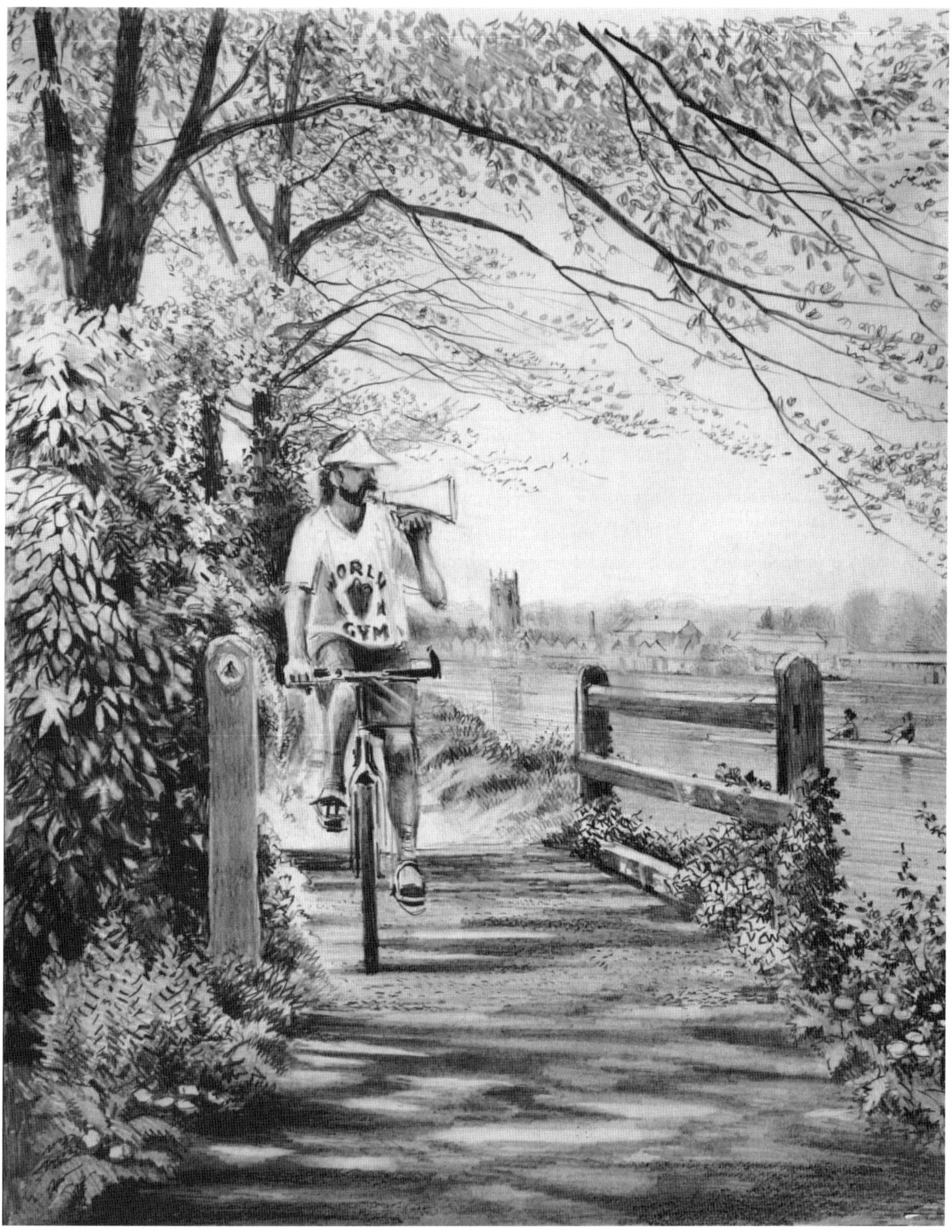
GYM

HENLEY ROYAL REGATTA

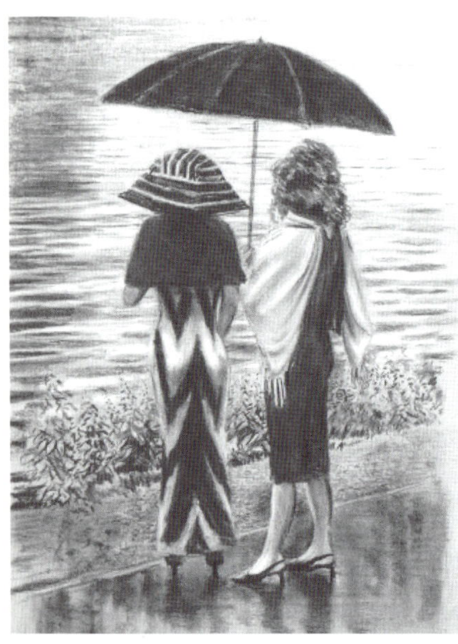

POSH FROCKS
(Left)
A little rain cannot dampen the spirits at Henley.

THE OLD SUPPORTER
(Right)
This lovely old gentleman was a boating enthusiast and rowing supporter as well as one of my mature students.

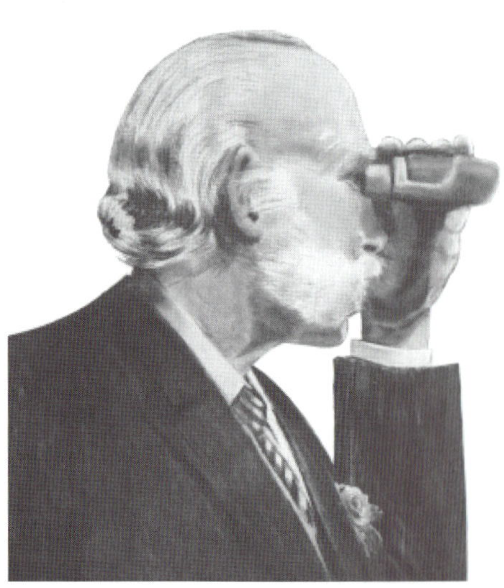

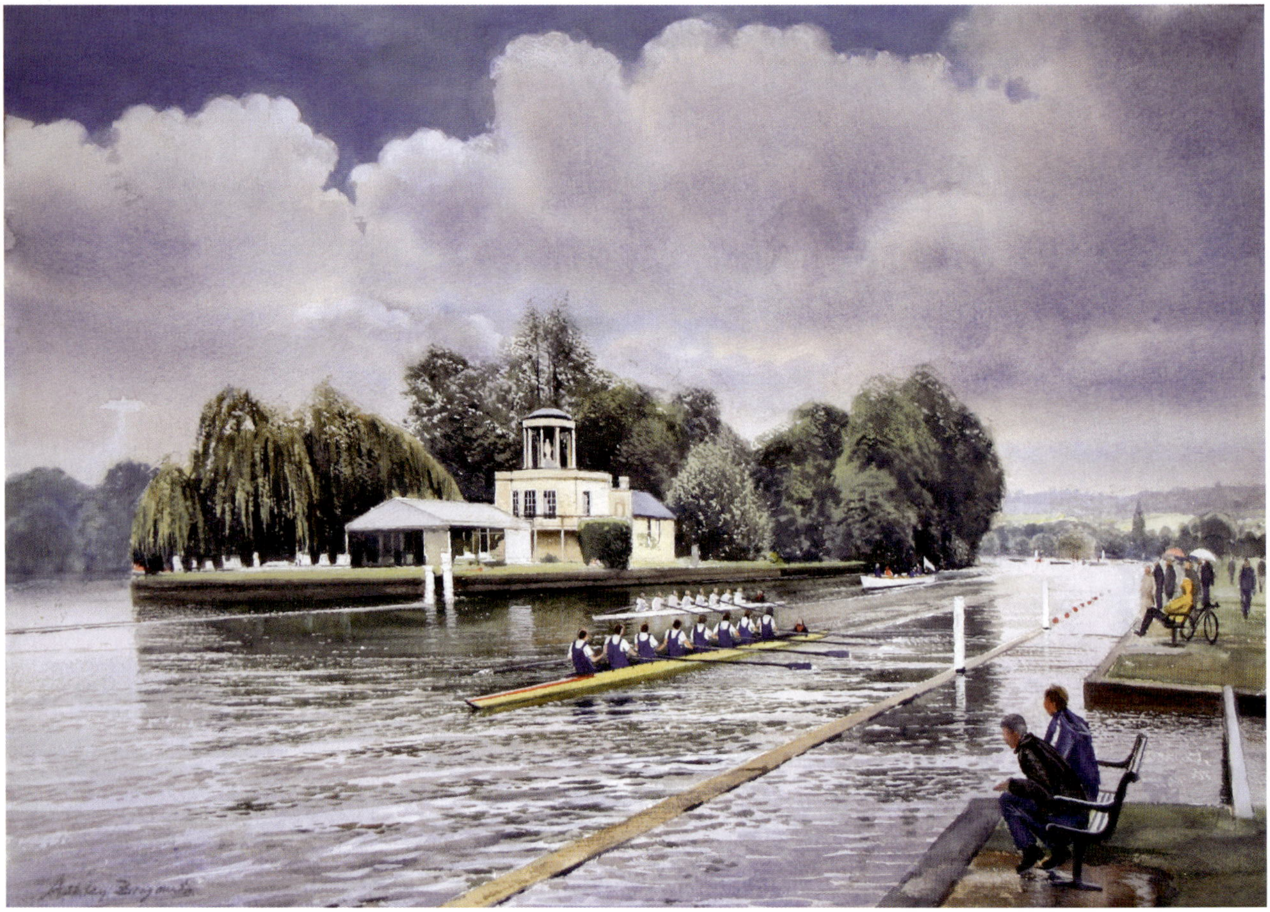

SPECTATORS
(Right)
On the same gloomy day a group of spectators and rowing club members cheer on their colleagues.

HENLEY ROYAL REGATTA
(Opposite page Below)
Under grey skies on a damp and cool July day, two crews pass Temple Island near the start of the race. At this stage, it is unusual to see one boat more than a length ahead.

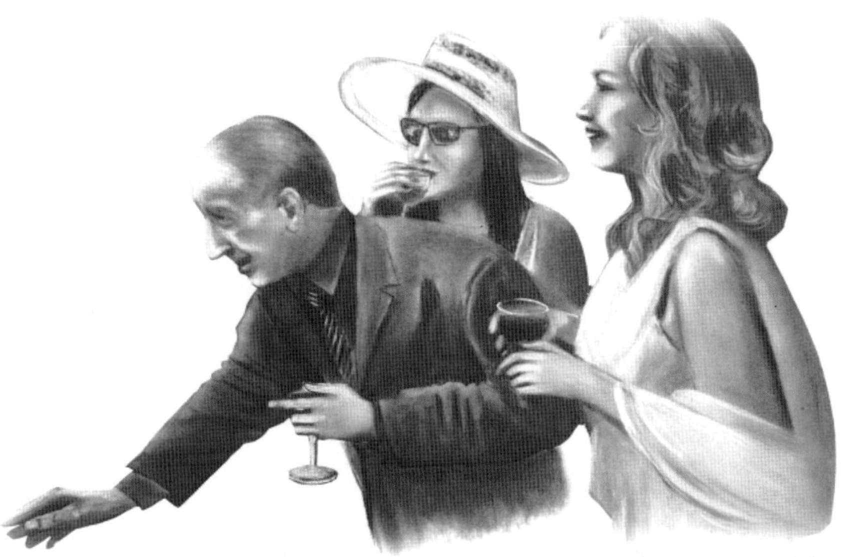

For five days each June, Henley hosts the world's most famous regatta, an experience everyone should enjoy at least once. It is both a sporting and a social event, and for the spectators, an interest in rowing is certainly not essential. During the preceding weeks, a marquee city springs up along both sides of the river, a dead straight rowing channel is anchored in position, and for those attending, hotel accommodation is impossible to find, as Henley braces itself for the highlight of the social calender.

From its early beginnings in 1839 Henley regatta grew in stature gaining the cachet "Royal Regatta" in 1851 and with it a gilded future, but it was not until the early twentieth century that it gained wide recognition and international importance. Today, competitive rowing is increasingly popular, and hopes for Olympic gold medals in rowing are high. Henley has the advantage of the longest straight section of the Thames with a course of 1 mile 450 yards. Unlike the Olympics, the course can only accommodate two boats at a time, extending the number of heats and the time for socialising.

Along the waterside ladies in big hats and posh frocks cheer on their offspring, whilst know-it-alls provide a braying commentary to all those within earshot. Eccentric characters in striped caps and blazers, and sporting walrus moustaches, sit perched on their shooting sticks and share their hip-flasks as they reminisce about the good old days. Elsewhere, the young and beautiful wait at ferry points to cross the river to attend company jollies where tens of thousands of bottles of champagne and millions of strawberries are consumed. For many people the rowing is secondary, merely an excuse for a good day out. Overhead, the frequent whirr of helicopters announces the arrival of the rich and famous, a sensible option since the roads around Henley are solid with traffic.

In complete contrast to the excellent commentary on the public address system are the unintelligible commands of the coxes as they urge on their strapping crew members in the powerhouse departments. The crowds are enthusiastic in their response, their excitement apparent in the crescendo of cheers that accompanies the rowers to the finishing post. Reminiscent of *My Fair Lady* an occasional Eliza Doolittle adds here own words of encouragement. Without doubt there is no better place for people watching.

HAMBLEDON MILL

THE GREBE FAMILY
(Right)
This great crested grebe at Hambledon Lock was encouraging its brood to take to the water, although one insisted on a ride.

THE THAMES AT HAMBLEDON MILL
(Opposite Page Above)
A traditional view of the mill set against the rising Chilterns.

CONVERSATION PIECE
(Opposite Page Below)
Official matters are discussed at Hambledon Lock in this charcoal sketch.

GREBE SKETCH
(Below)
It is difficult to sketch these birds since they are always diving underwater.

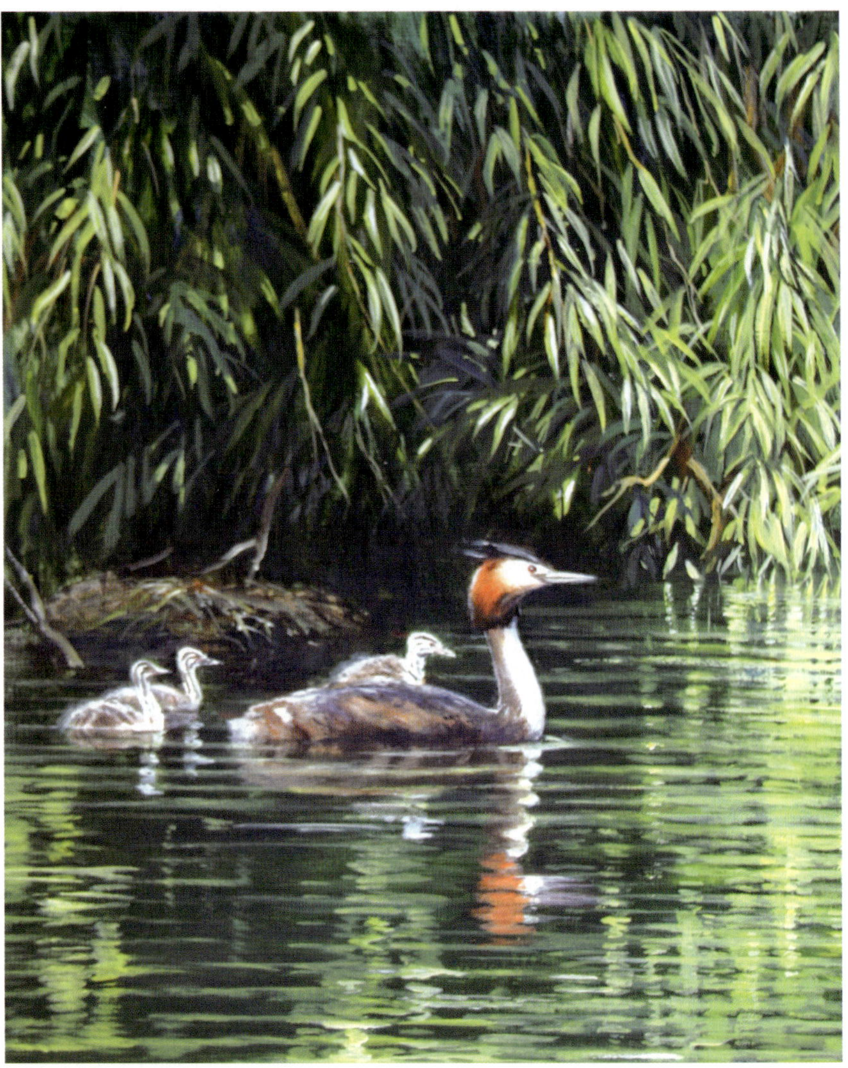

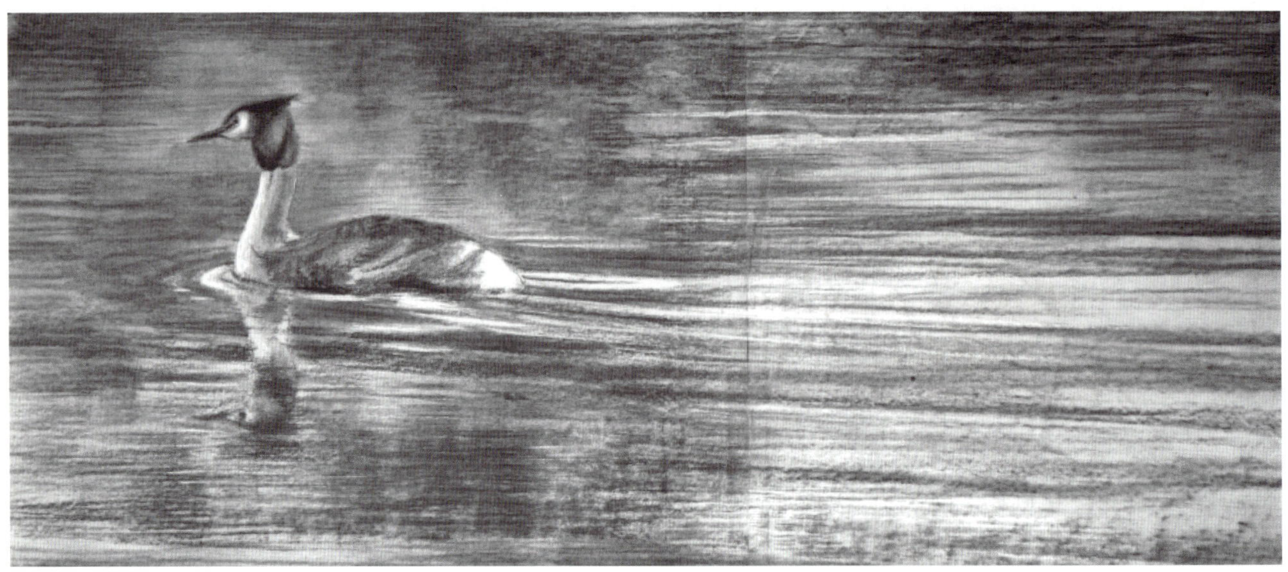

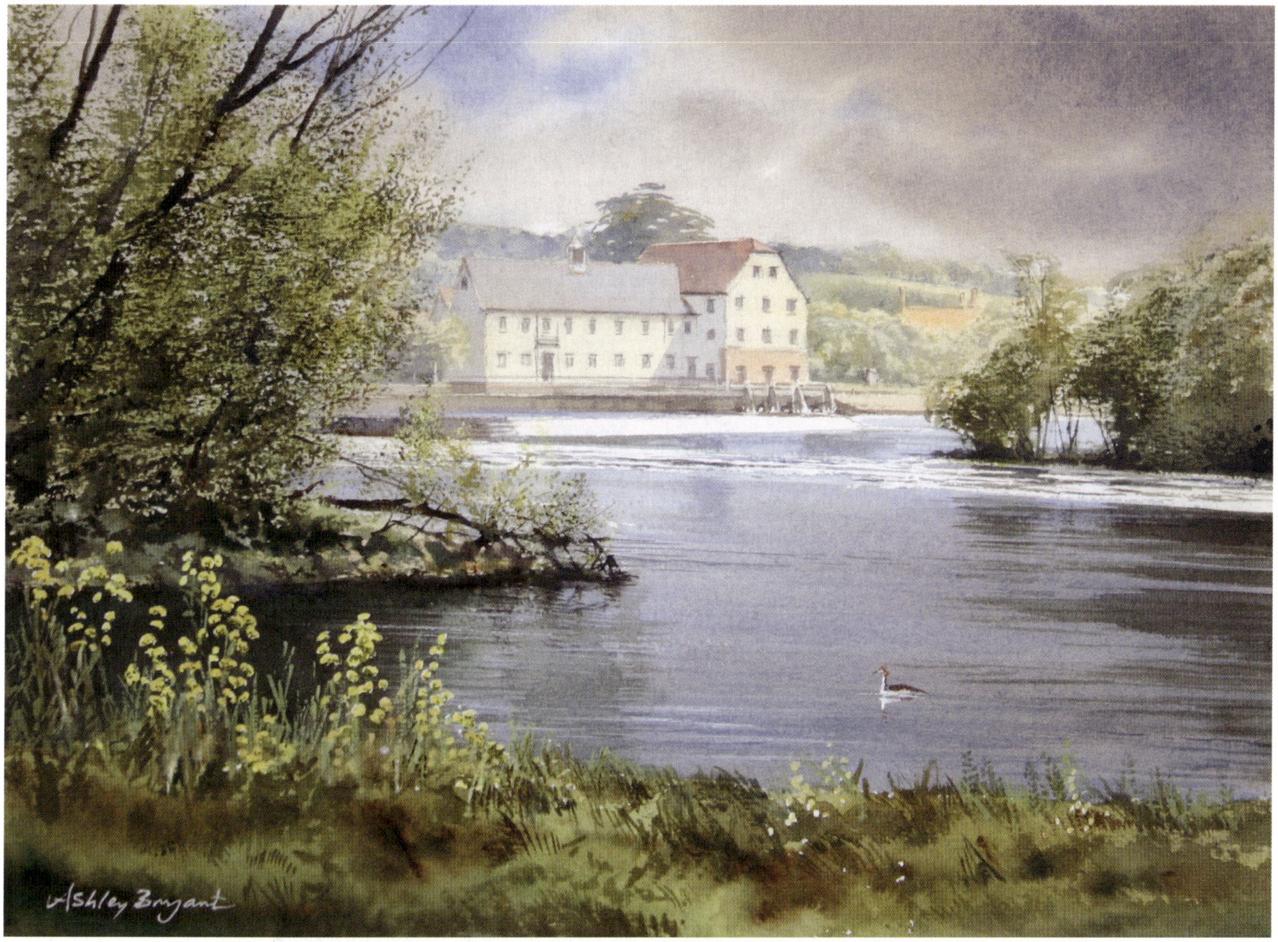

A short distance downstream from the regatta course, the river sweeps in a wide bend to Hambledon Mill. This large weather-boarded building, now converted to flats, makes a fine scene on the far bank behind the weir – another calendar view of the Thames. It is a good place to relax for a while on a recommended circular walk from Henley via Hambledon Mill and Aston, then returning across country via Remenham church. William Haywood, the builder of the splendid bridge at Henley, died before the construction was completed in 1787, and was ultimately buried here. He was so taken with his masterpiece he asked for his body to be incorporated into the structure, a request the town's authorities were unable to grant.

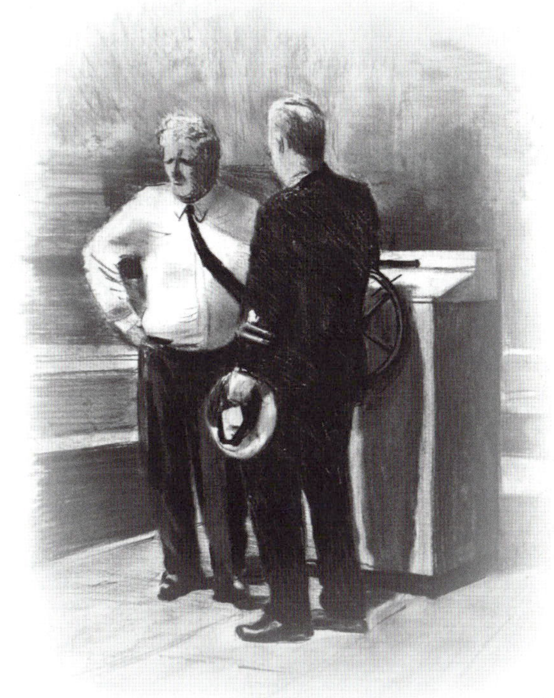

HURLEY / BISHAM

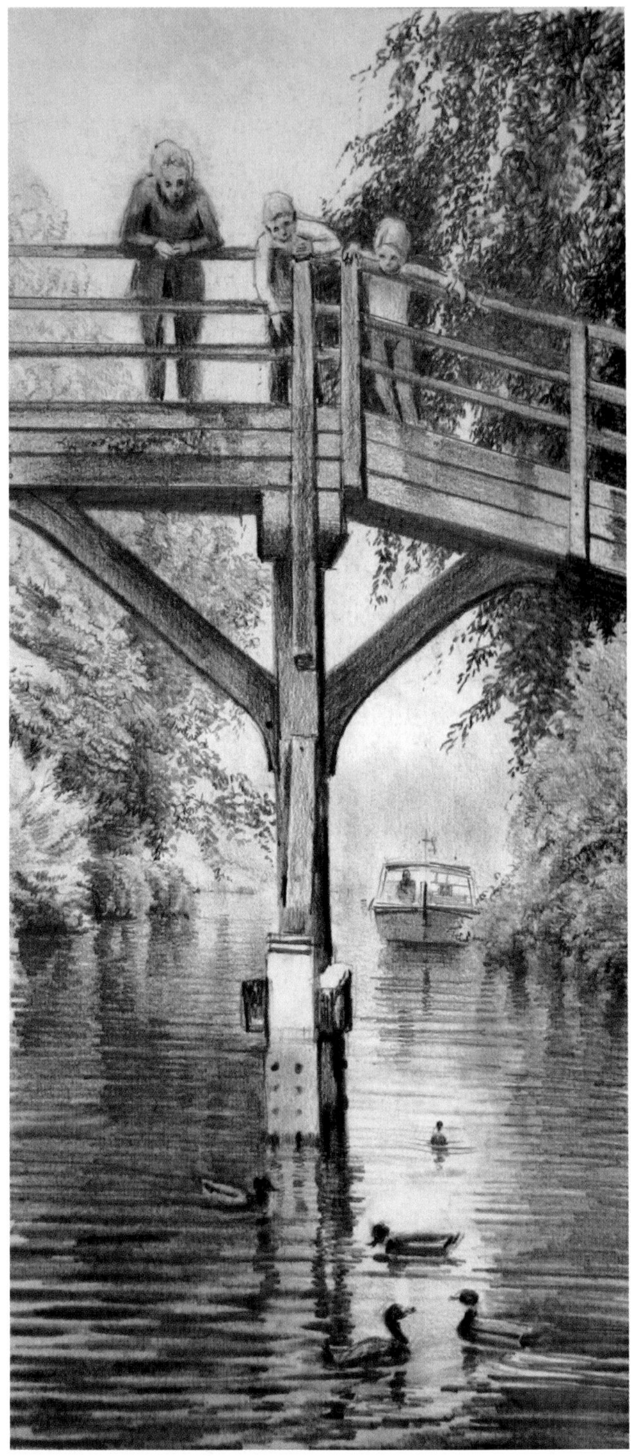

For most of the year Hurley is a green place with overhanging trees and rich riverside vegetation. The river splits into channels between islands giving the Thames a more enclosed feeling, the shady places popular as picnic sites away from the heat of a summer's day. Near Temple footbridge the north bank is crowded with moored cruisers, a "millionaire's row" of expensive toys that are seldom used. It is easy to become enthusiastic about boats when one has a long pocket.

Hurley has an ancient if undramatic history. Its Benedictine Priory, of which hardly a trace remains, was founded in 1087. The Olde Bell is still serving drinks and, claiming to date from 1135, is one of the oldest pubs in the country. At Hurley, the Thames Path crosses to the north bank and before long another religious institution is seen through the trees on the south side. Bisham Abbey met with better fortune than Hurley Priory. Originally a preceptory of the Knights Templar before becoming an Augustinian Priory, it was confiscated by Henry VIII who presented it to Anne of Cleves, as part of a divorce settlement – a gift which cost him nothing. The unhappy Anne soon left and later the young princess Elizebeth was "imprisoned" here in the Abbey House for part of the reign of her sister, "Bloody" Mary. The buildings latest incarnation is as the National Sports Centre where training facilities are available for a wide range of sports and athletics, the culture of self-improvement, competition and teamwork mirroring some of the old Knights' ideals.

The much-painted Bisham church stands a short distance downstream perched almost on the river's edge. It makes an attractive scene especially with the mist rising over the water on a summer's morning or in winter when it is lit by evening sunlight.

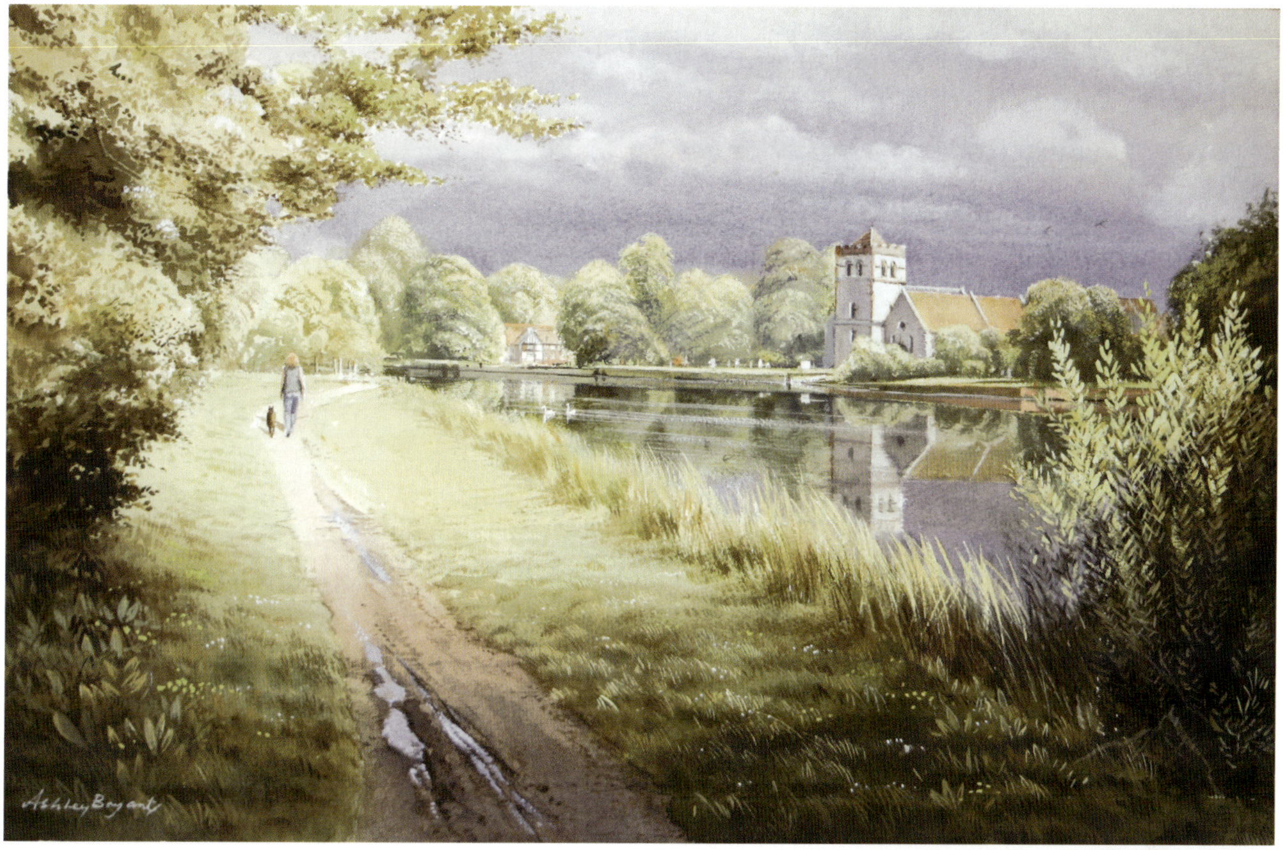

THE THAMES AT BISHAM
(Above)
The church stands close to the river in the wooded setting of Bisham. A storm is approaching and the sky is leaden but bright sunlight illuminated the scene.

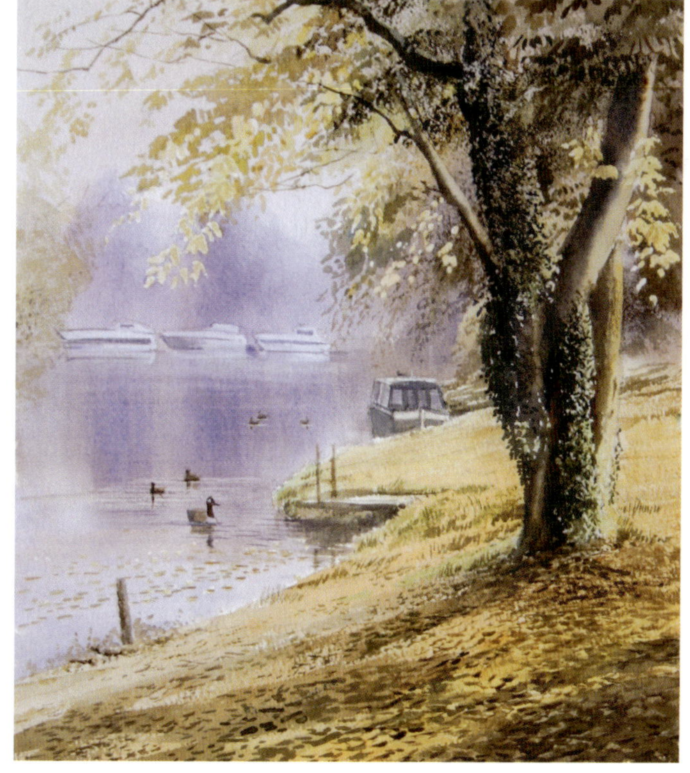

THE THAMES AT HURLEY
(Right)
A line of moored cruisers on the far bank is seen through soft, hazy autumn light.

FEEDING THE DUCKS
(Opposite page)
A quite different view is seen from the footbridge and most people pause to enjoy the views up and downstream. This group feed the ducks at Hurley.

MARLOW

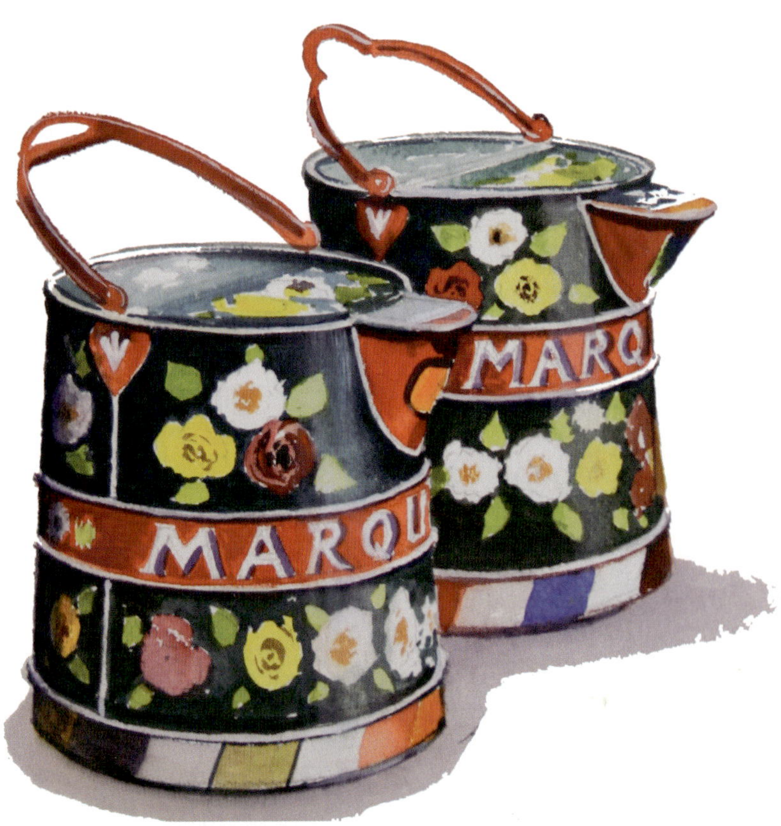

FOLK ART
(Right)
Boat, or folk, art is very popular with owners of narrow boats and takes the form of decoration on containers of all descriptions.

BELOW THE LOCK
(Opposite Page)
A temporary mooring on this picturesque approach to the lock. This watercolour was painted in sepia

THE THAMES AT MARLOW
(Below)
A popular view of Marlow upstream from the lock and looking towards the weir and church.

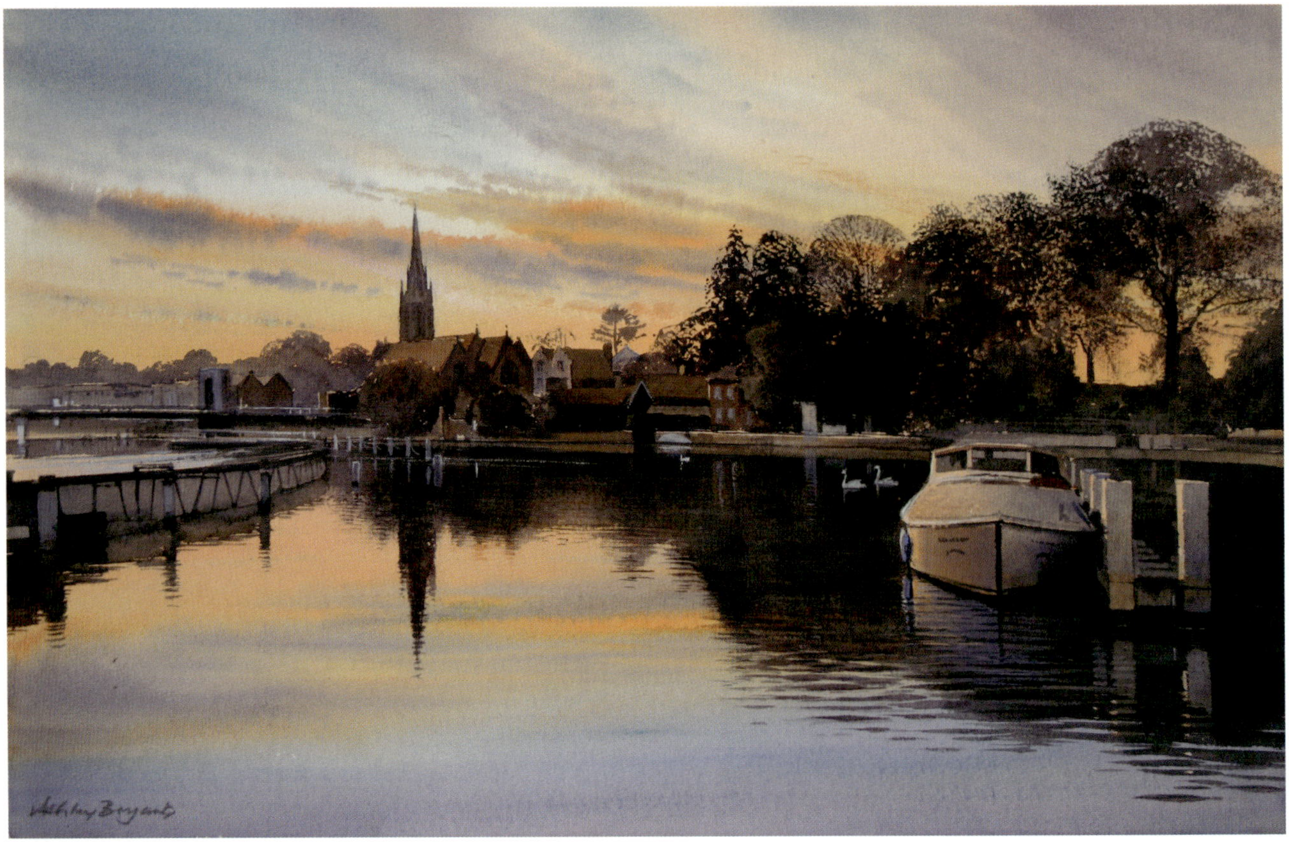

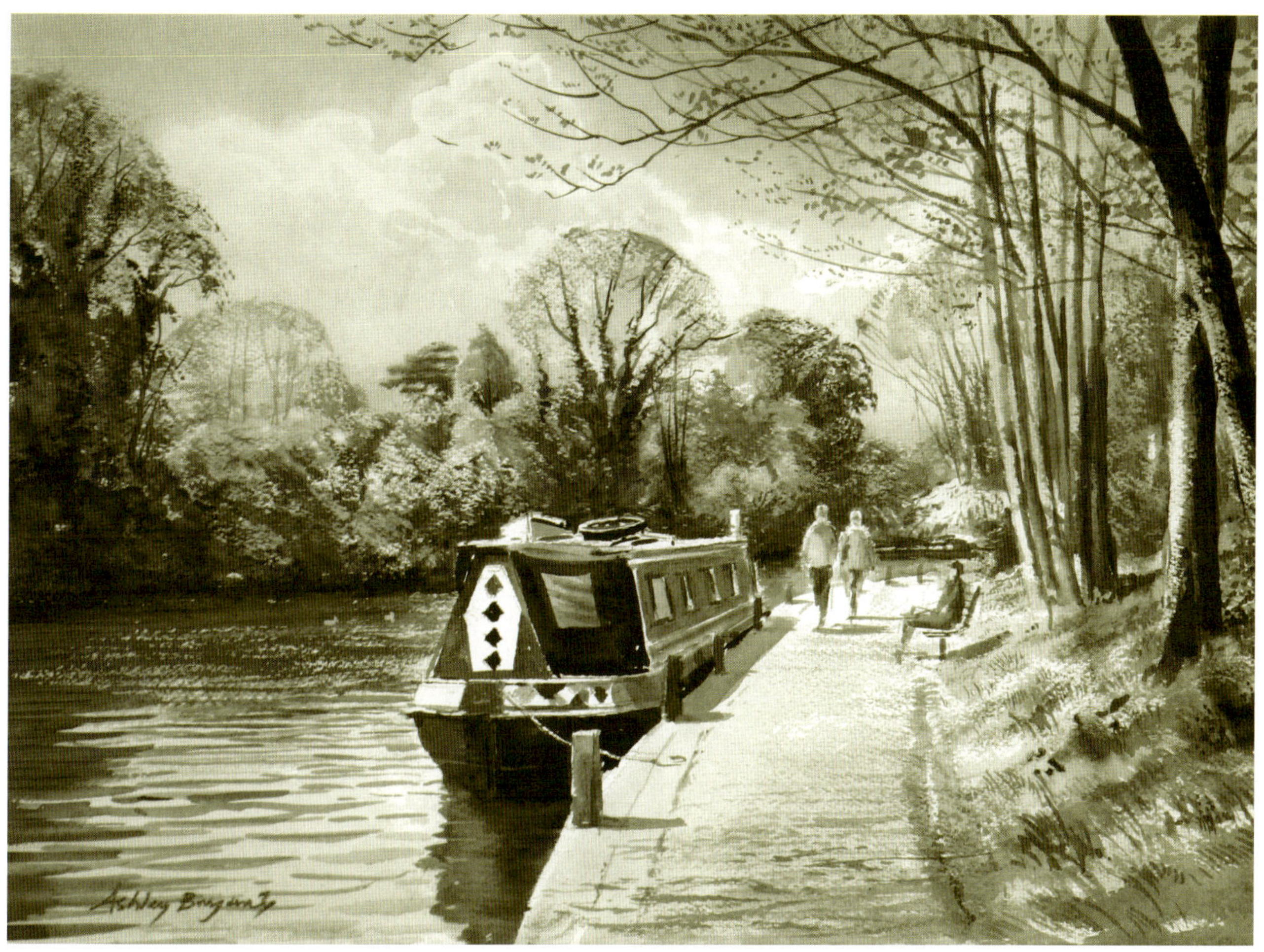

The tall spire of the gothic-style church and the graceful suspension bridge create an immediate impact when approaching Marlow. Moored boats by the busy towpath and swans on the water add interest and character to this attractive riverside town. On the south bank the rowing club generates plenty of youthful activity and the town stages its annual regatta in mid June. The Compleat Angler, once an old inn and now a smart hotel, provides a link with angling which has always been popular here, and its lawns offer an excellent place to relax by the waterside and watch the boating world pass by. A short distance downstream, the lock and weir provide further inspirational settings for the artist.

Marlow (previously known as Great Marlow) was often depicted from Quarry Wood, a favoured location which rises on the south bank of the Thames. Victorian engravings show the river winding across its floodplain towards a surprisingly small town swamped by tall trees against the backdrop of the Chilterns. Today it is not so easy to get a good vantage point from Quarry Wood (interestingly the model for the wild wood in Kenneth Grahame's *The Wind in the Willows*), but a continuation eastwards to Winter Hill brings a wide prospect of the Thames Valley into view. Marlow is now a sizeable town, popular and expensive, confirmed by a peek in any estate agents window.

CLIVEDEN

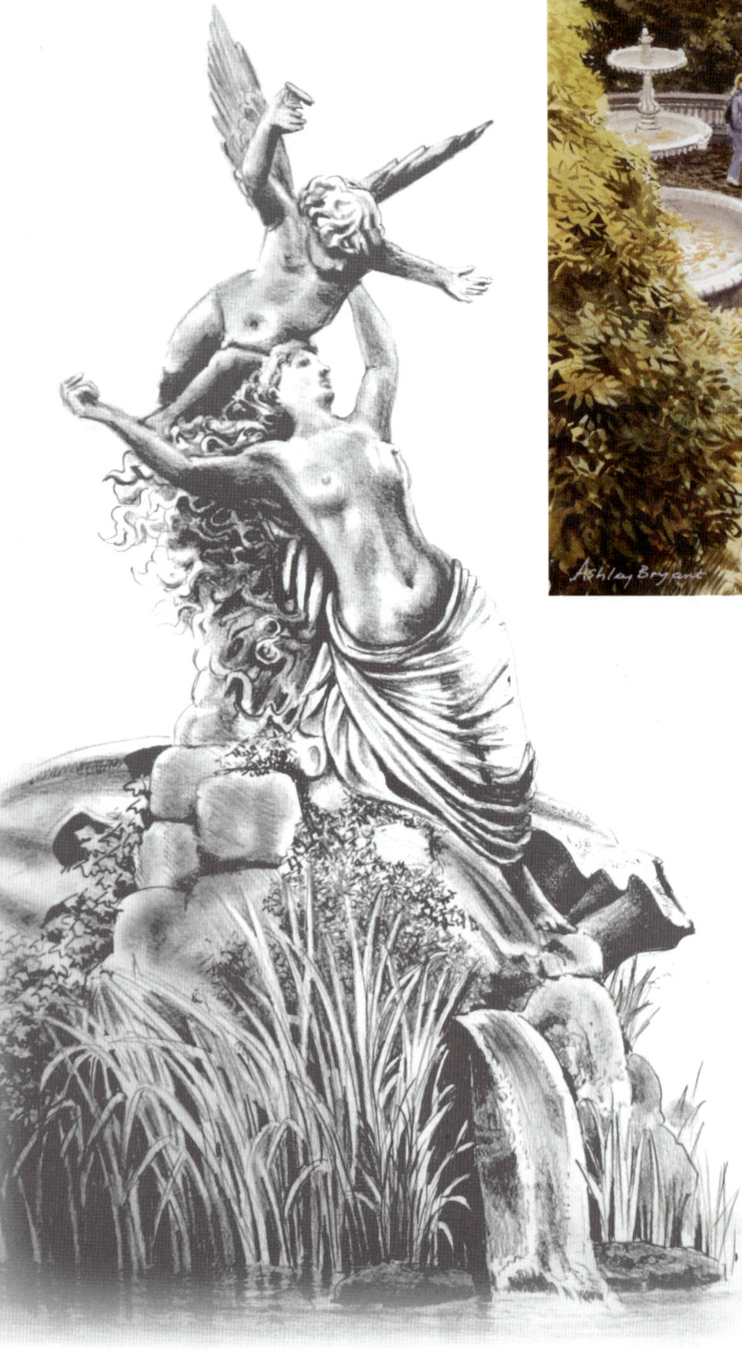

VIEWING PLATFORM
(Above)
Boating pageants on the Thames would have been enjoyed from these vantage points along Clivedon Reach.

FROM THE TERRACE AT CLIVEDEN
(Opposite Page)
This is a well known view from the terrace across the parterred lawns and woods to the distant Thames, a prospect which influenced the siting of the original house.

THE FOUNTAIN OF LOVE
(Left)
Cliveden's owners spared no expense in ornamentation and this sketch shows a small section of this spectacular sculpture.

The Thames Path between Cookham and Maidenhead passes a steeply wooded hillside across the far bank, a majestic sight in autumn when the oaks and chestnuts are in full glory. This is Cliveden Reach, beyond which sits Cliveden House, one of the most famous, or infamous, of the great houses in the Thames valley. The house's notoriety began with its first owner, the 2nd Duke of Buckingham, who killed the Earl of Shewsbury in a duel, a drastic solution to secure the Earl's wife for himself. The house was burnt down twice, the second time by a maid reading in bed by candle light. It was rebuilt in 1850 in an Italianate style by Charles Barry, and in 1893 was purchased by the Astors, an enormously wealthy and influential American family. The house soon became a centre for British society, a lavish home from home for the movers and shakers of the land, with politics at the centre of their discussions. Nancy Astor became the first woman M. P. in 1919.

Scandal descended again on Cliveden in the early 1960's when John Profumo, the Minister for Defence, met Christine Keeler here and developed a 'relationship'. This could have gone unnoticed in the pages of history, but it transpired that another of her 'clients' was a Russian Military Attaché, and this was the height of the "Cold War". The scandal not only ended Profumo's career but brought down the Macmillan government.

From Cliveden's famous terrace there is a distant view of the Thames and from the steeply wooded hillside by the river the views are equally impressive. Numerous tracks wind their way along the hill, meeting at formal viewing platforms from which wealthy guests would have watched boating events on the Thames in Cliveden's heyday. The artist, Stanley Spencer, who lived at nearby Cookham, was so in awe of this breathtaking scenery he said it made him believe in God.

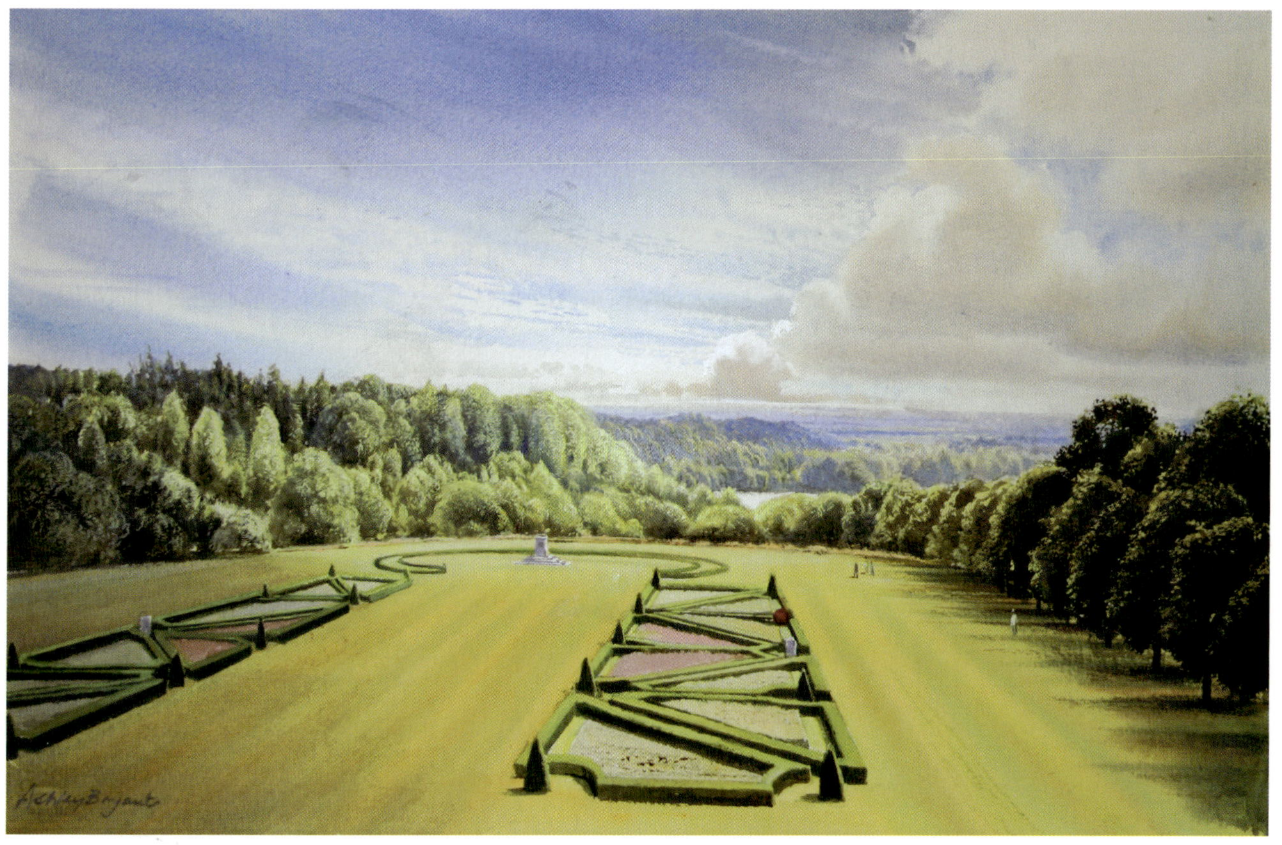

RAY MILL ISLAND

En-route to Maidenhead the river splits into several channels, forming numerous islands, including Ray Mill Island. The original mill from which the island is named is now a hotel offering its patrons superb views of the river. The island is landscaped as a park and botanical garden, and is full of interesting views at every turn. At its northern end, a wide weir provides a venue for canoeists to practise various manoeuvres such as rolls and turns. Turns are made after paddling rapidly to the fastest flow of the weir and then twisting in the waterfall itself to land more-or-less upright – a feat of human endeavour that looks easier than it is. Cries of conern are heard from onlookers when those attempting "eskimo rolls" remain struggling upside down in the turbulent waters. Fortunately, there are always experienced canoeists on hand to help those in need.

A narrow channel takes the boating world to Boulter's Lock, immortalised in Edward John Gregory's evocative painting entitled Boulter's Lock – Sunday Afternoon 1895. Beautifully painted, full of interest and subtle in its colouring, it is a window into the romantic and bygone age of the heyday of boating. The painting is as popular as ever today in prints and greetings cards. This was the age of mahogany skiffs, launches and craft of all descriptions, and people clearly made an effort to dress appropriately in striped blazers, elegant dresses and parasols.

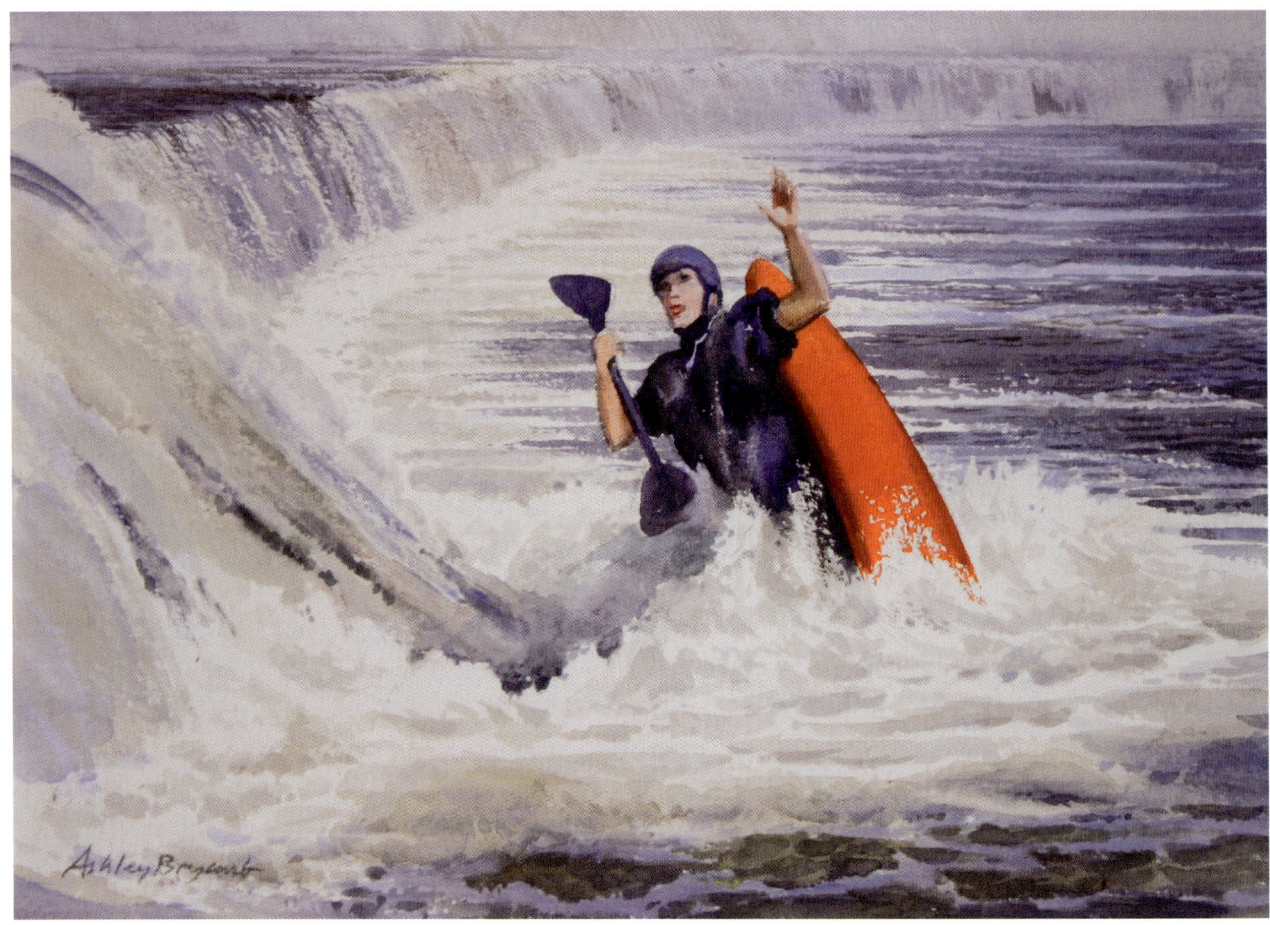

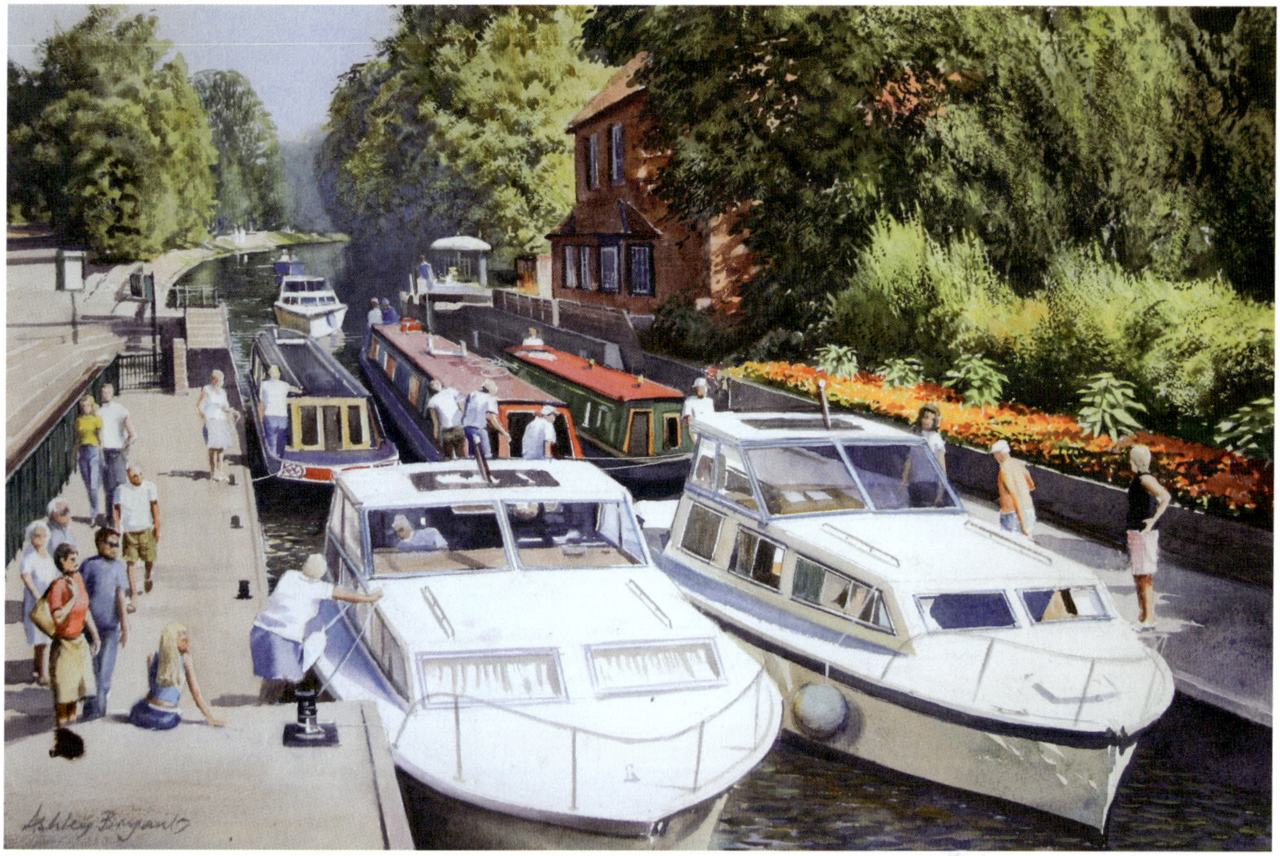

BOULTER'S LOCK
(Above)
A summer Saturday as cruisers and narrow boats squeeze into the lock.

RAY MILL ISLAND
(Right)
Overhanging willows provide shade on a summer's day.

CANOE CAPERS
(Opposite Page)
The weir to the north of Ray Mill Island provides an ideal place for canoeists to perform stunts.

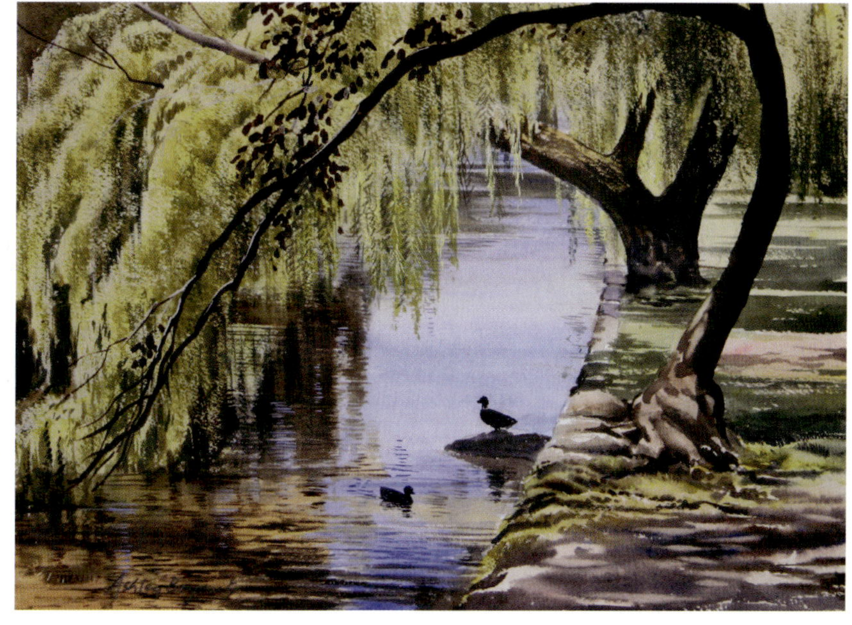

MAIDENHEAD

TUFTED DUCKS
(Right)
Waterfowl are used to disturbances on the river. This pair of tufted ducks treated the regatta as an everyday occurrence.

MAIDENDHEAD REGATTA
(Opposite Page)
A close race on a scorching August day excites the crowd at the finishing post, a view framed by Brunel's single span railway bridge.

TWO OF FOUR
(Below)
Two members of a rowing four – a painting that gives a sense of energy and movement.

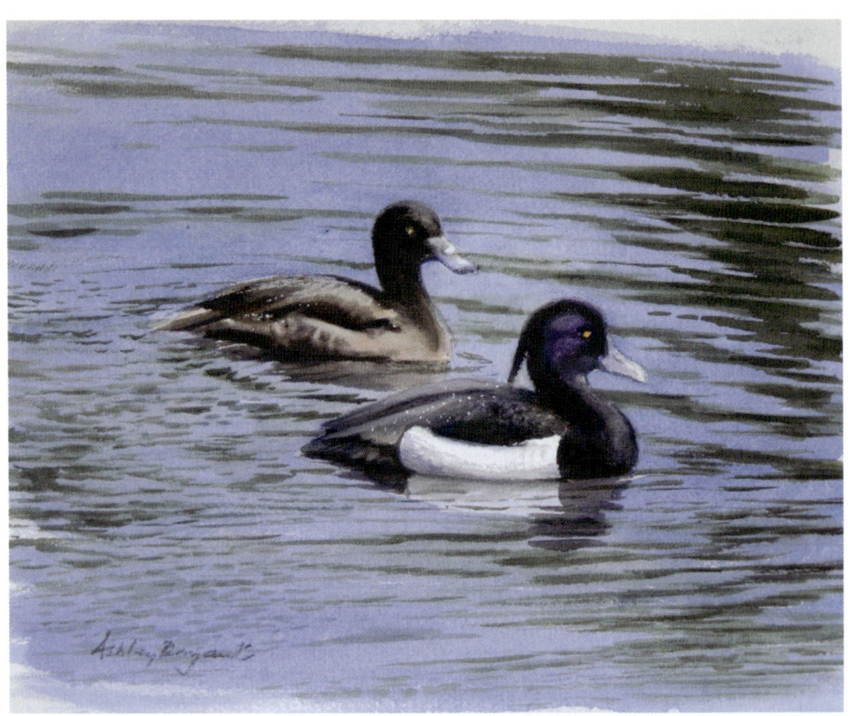

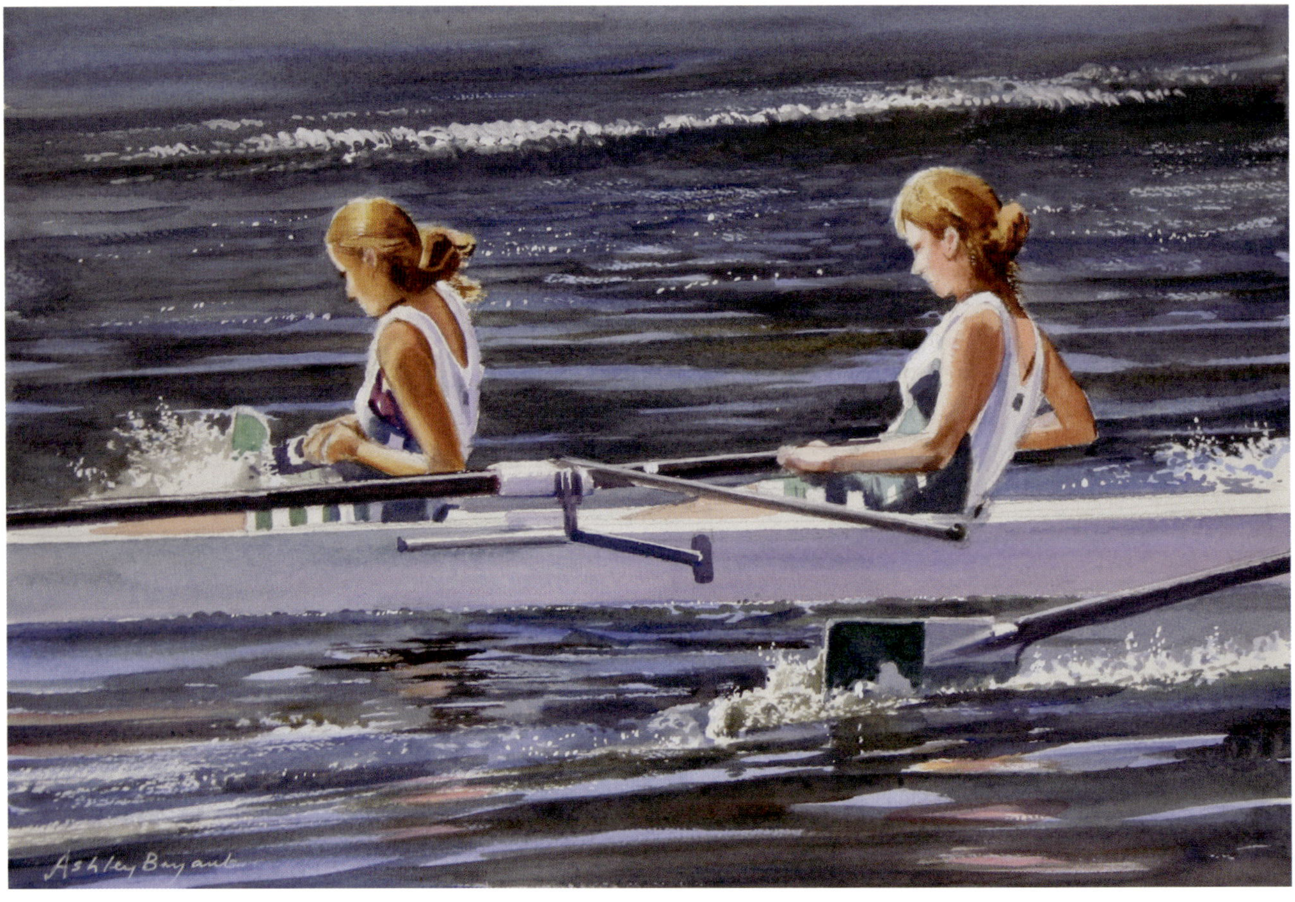

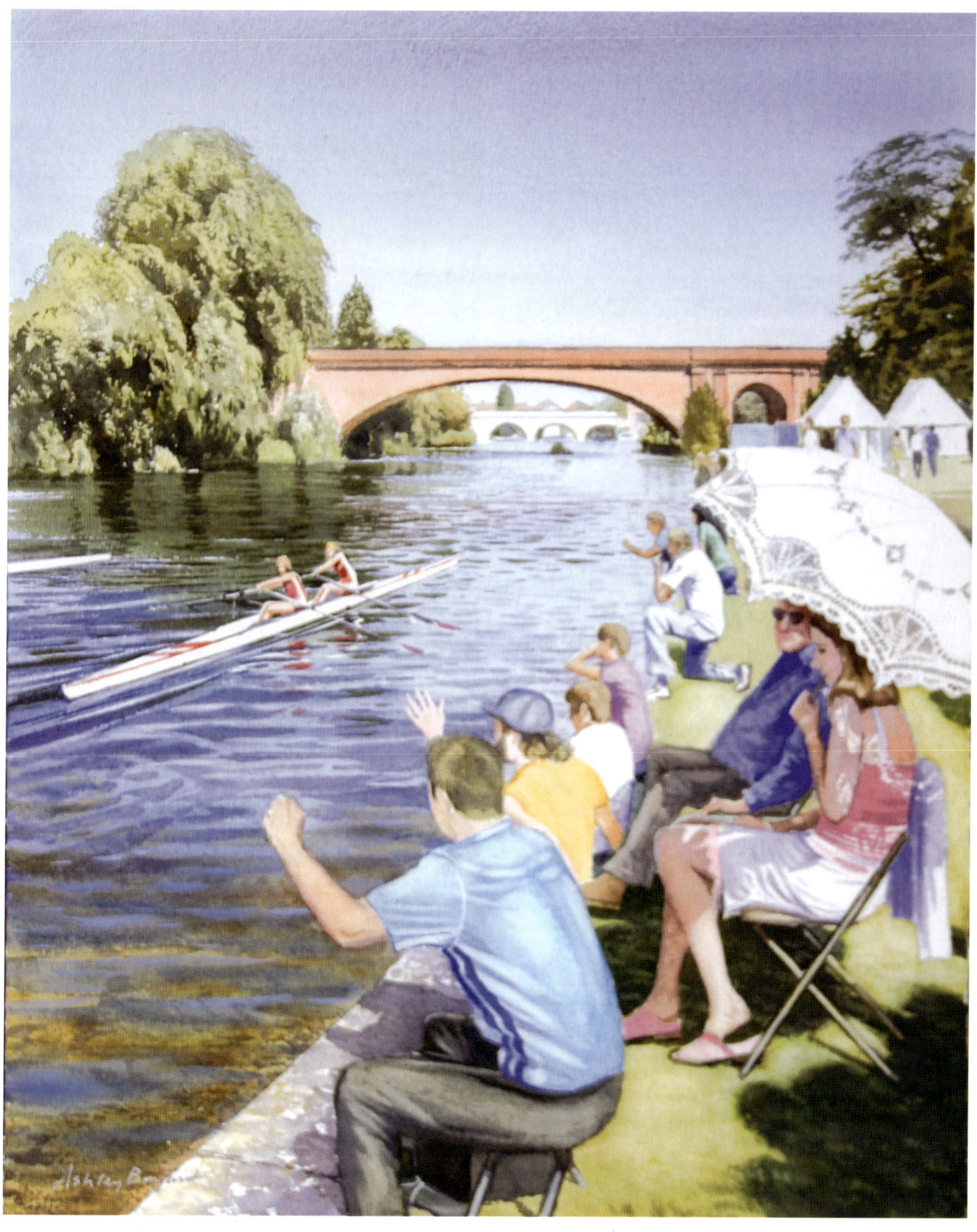

WINDSOR

Over the past few centuries the greatest of the Thames artists have focused their attentions on London, but Windsor did not escape their attention. The huge castle towers over the river and has been incorporated into numerous paintings over the ages.

The high platform of land first caught the eye of William the Conqueror, who quickly recognised its suitability for a fortress in order to control this part of the Thames valley. For the next eight centuries Windsor Castle was enlarged and modified by successive monarchs to satisfy their defensive needs and personal tastes, along with their desire for sheer exhibitionism. The most stunningly beautiful part of the castle is St George's Chapel, its superb, perpendicular architecture even surpassing King's College Chapel at Cambridge in its majesty.

In 1992 a fire broke out in the state apartments causing untold damage to the structure and its priceless contents. Over a period of several years it was eventually restored using traditional materials and the best craftsmanship of modern times. Viewing this superb workmanship gives a visitor an added interest, and it is reassuring to see that the skills are still available to match the great achievements of the past.

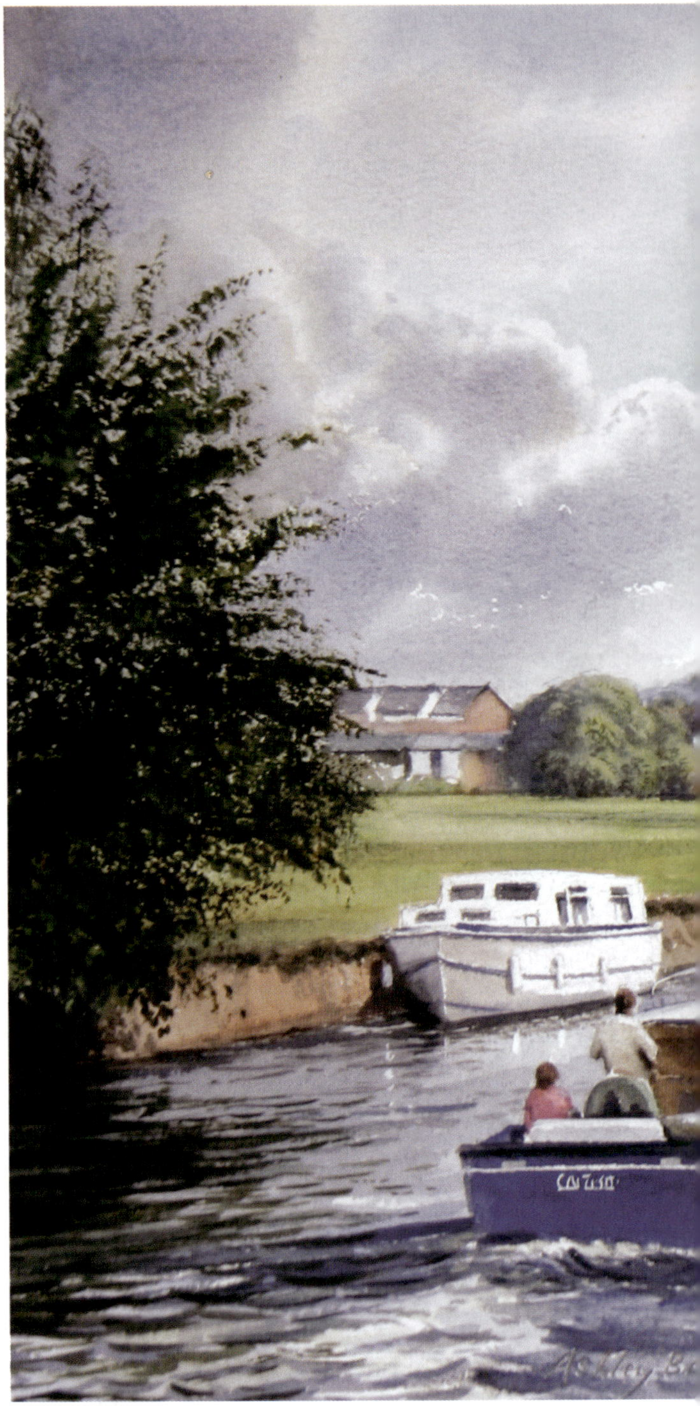

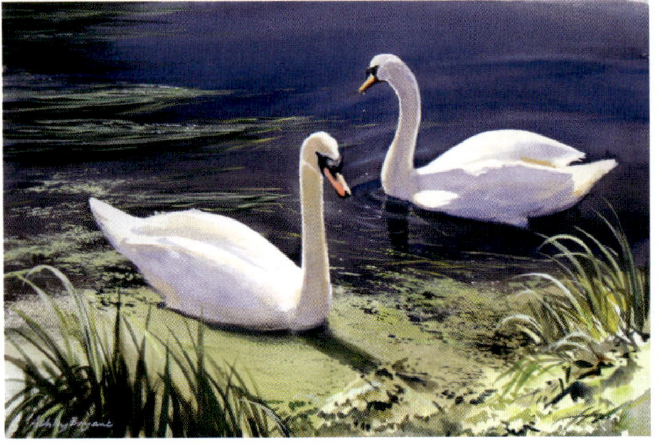

SWANS

(Left)

Swans are seen in great numbers at Windsor, possibly attracted by food-wielding tourists. As always, they make a charming subject.

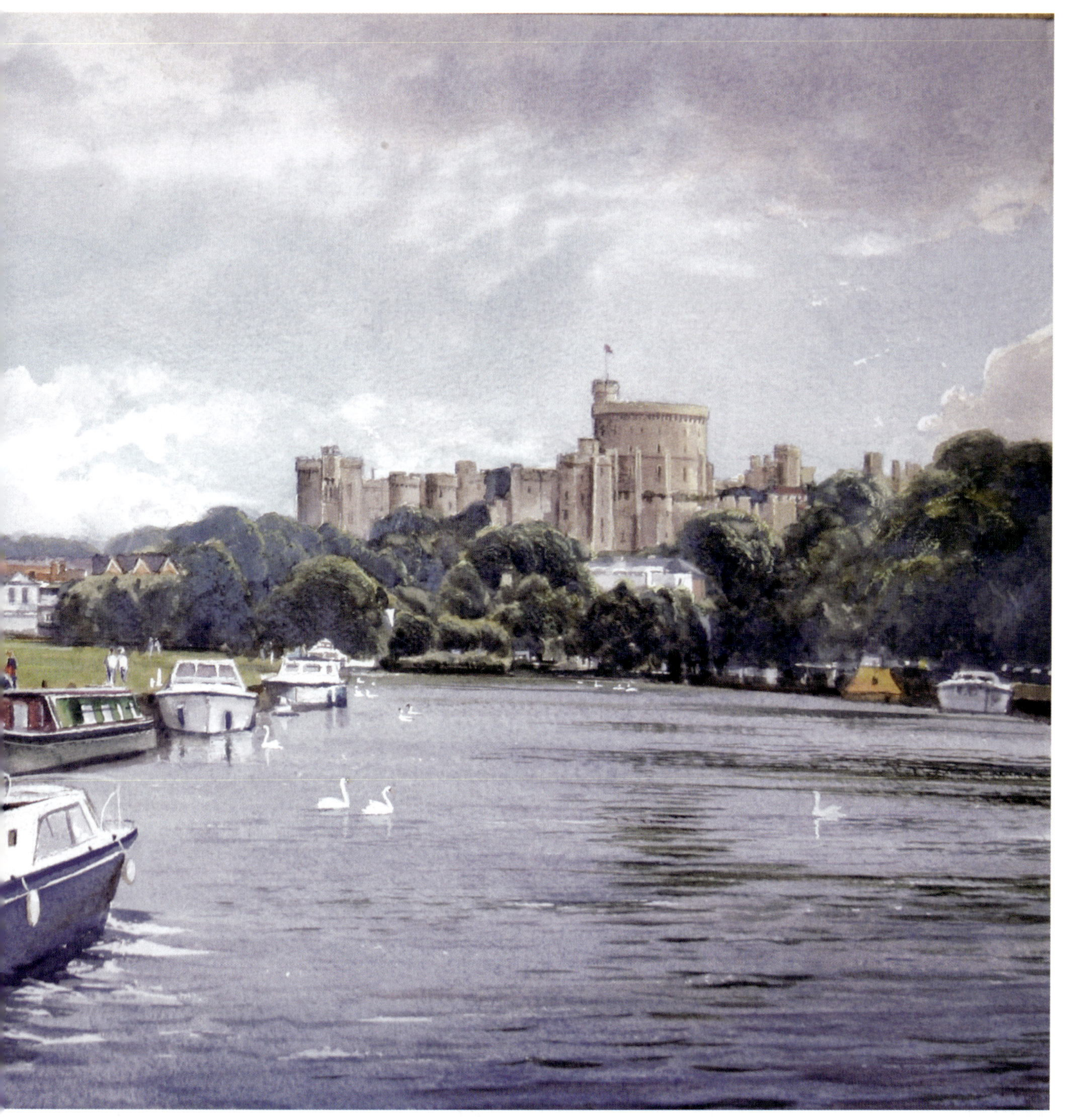

THE THAMES AT WINDSOR
(Above)
A vantage point from a boat is slightly unusual, otherwise this is just another of thousands of views of Windsor Castle.

ETON

THE THAMES AT ETON
(Below)
On a sultry August day, where the Thames sweeps into a calm bay, hardly a ripple disturbs the surface. This view is from the Eton College cricket ground, and the river at this point has undoubtedly received many a well struck six.

ETON COLLEGE
(Opposite Page)
The famous chapel and some of the college buildings are seen between the trees. Writers, poets, numerous prime ministers, scientists, bishops and captains of industry have wiled away their school days here at Britain's most famous school.

Eton College and its famous chapel are often pictured from across the Thames in old paintings and engravings, and I was keen to find these locations for myself. Romney island blocks the view from the Windsor bank and crossing over from the lock along a path marked "Fisherman Only" I found that even here the desired view of Eton College was blocked by a thicket of riverside vegetation. Where this thinned out, the view was obstructed by trees on the far bank.

The resulting painting was a compromise after some imaginative pruning. Looking in detail at some of the paintings of Eton by old masters I now see that they too used a little artistic licence. Fortunately, when I crossed to the Eton side of the river for my next painting there was no such difficulty, and the view of the Thames from the Eton Cricket ground was stunning. A trawl of the river would recover countless cricket balls, lost over many happy summers.

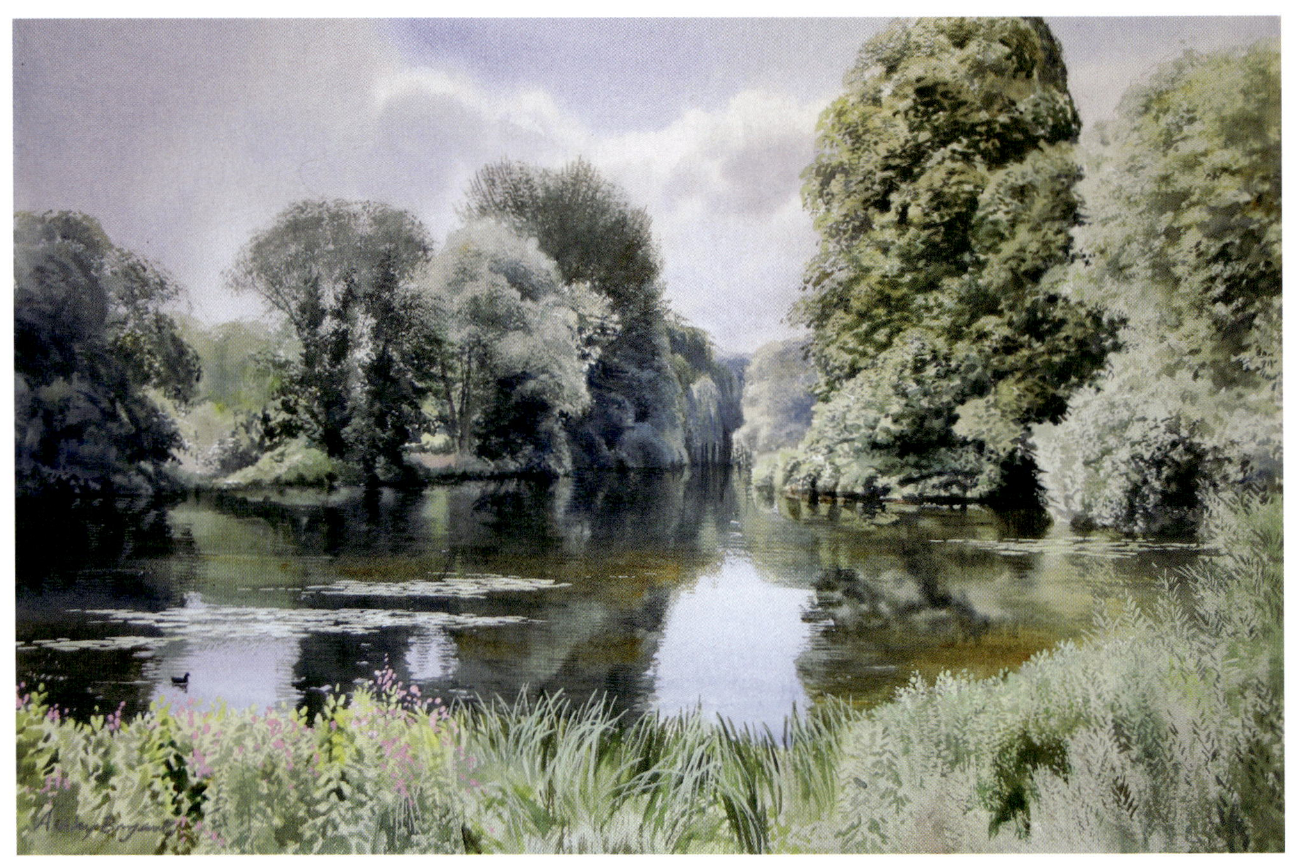

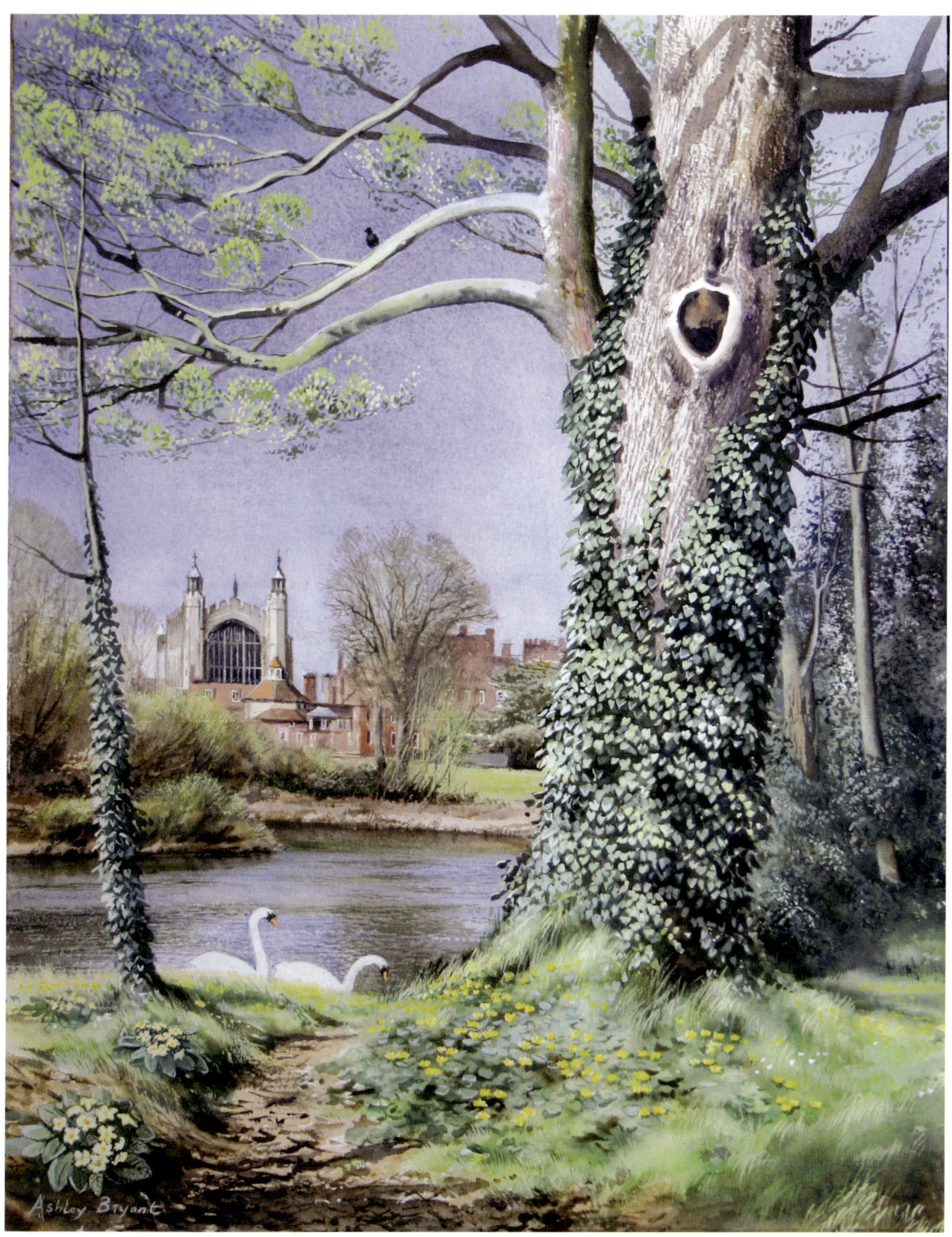

The Thames

RUNNYMEAD

BELOW COOPER'S HILL
(Opposite)
This is a view over the rich countryside at the foot of Cooper's Hill from the American Bar Association memorial to Magna Carta.

RUNNYMEAD FROM COOPER'S HILL
(Below)
Immediately below the memorial rhododendrons produce a magnificent view of colour in May, whilst the wooded slopes of Cooper's Hill provide a glorious autumn display.

The meads along the Thames are associated with one of the key events in English history – the signing of Magna Carta. This "great charter" was forced upon a reluctant King John by the increasingly powerful barons in 1215, and was intended to endorse their powers even further and reduce those of the King. Its lasting importance, however, lay in the establishment of rights for everyone (at least for free men), and lawful judgement by equals and by the law of the land – an early charter for human rights. It made little difference to the majority at the bottom of the pile, but it was a foundation to build on. The signing of the charter has been captured many times by the imagination of artists and I have my own vision to set to canvas one day.

Runnymead is home to three memorials; the Kennedy Memorial to the assassinated American president, a second

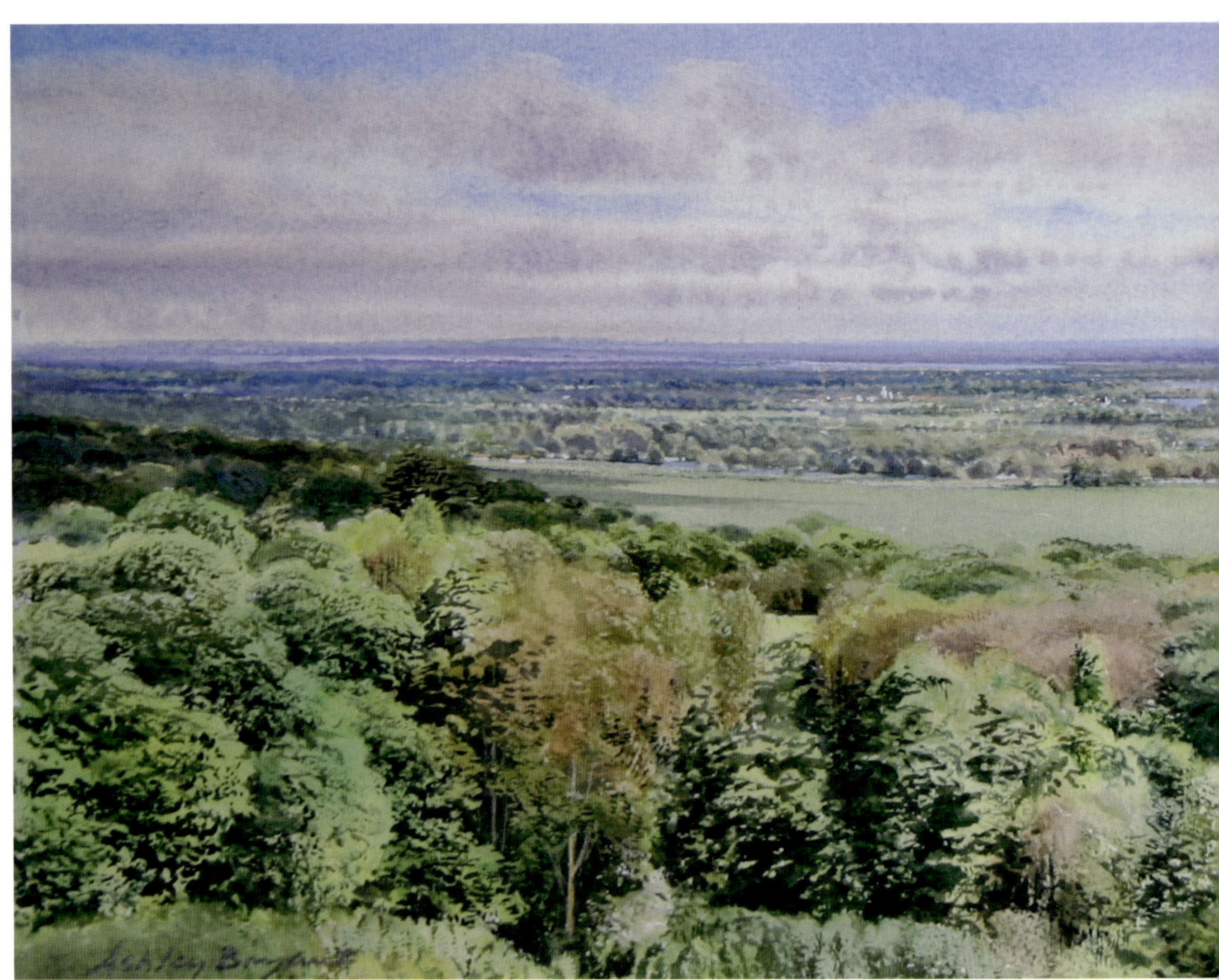

commemorating freedom under the law by the American Bar Association, and the third and most significant is the Commonwealth Air Forces Memorial in memory of those airmen that lost their lives in warfare. This fitting tribute sits on the brink of Cooper's Hill overlooking Runnymead and a huge swathe of the Thames valley. Here, amongst well-tended gardens, the vast quadrangle of the building is lined with the names of thousands upon thousands of airmen. It is a sad place, but beautiful, dignified and thought provoking, whilst its lofty position overlooking Runnymead could not be more appropriate.

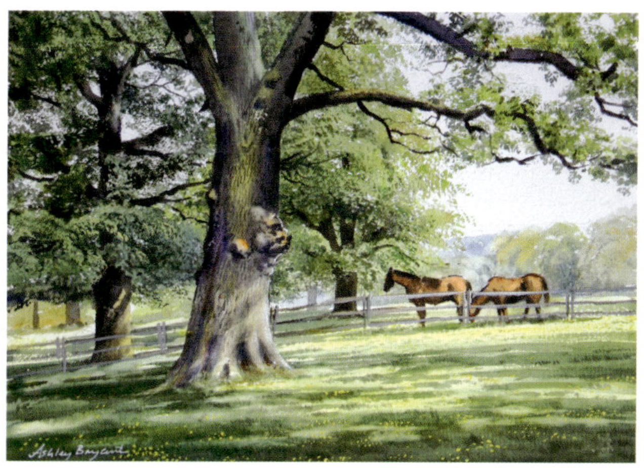

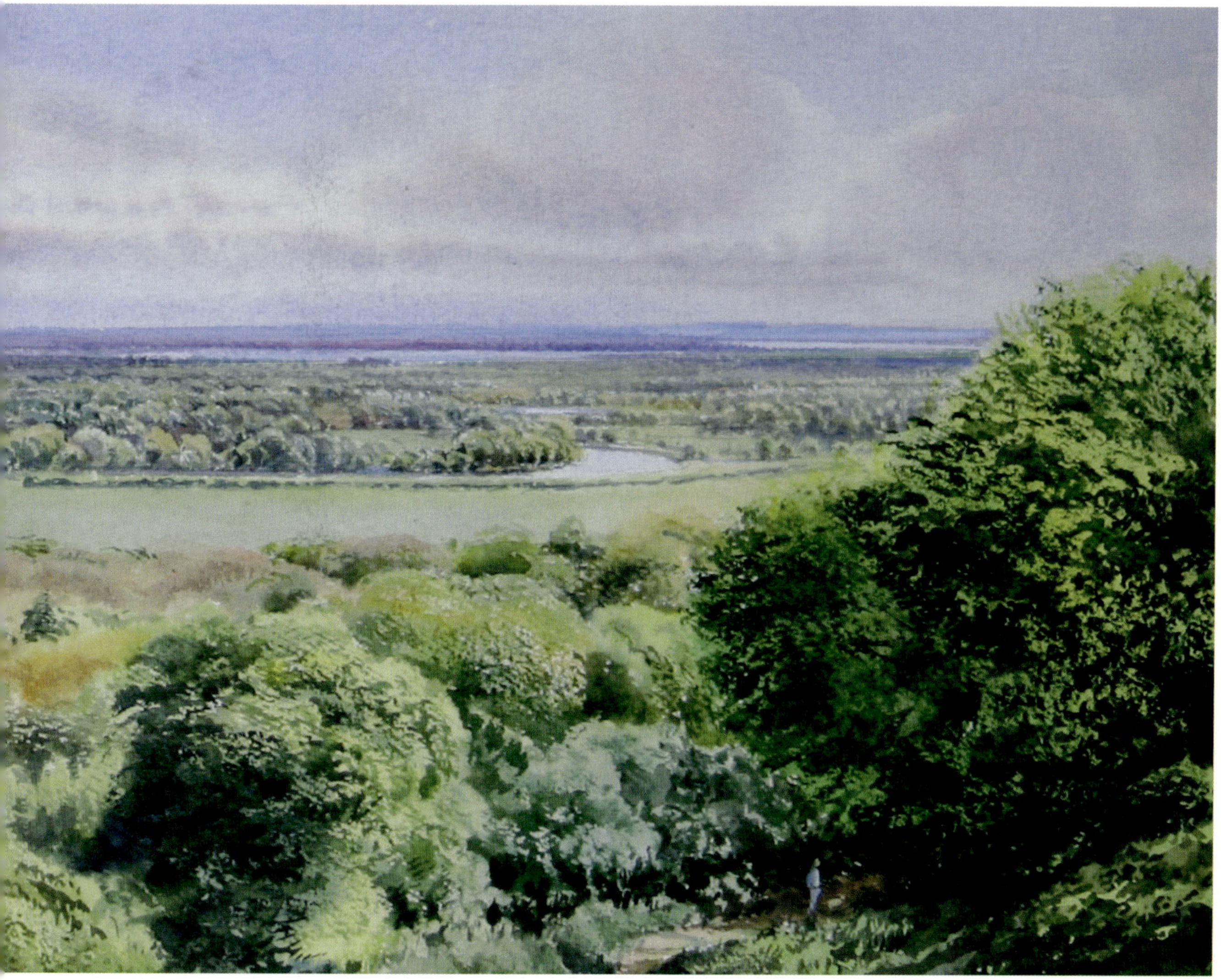

STAINES

THE THAMES AT STAINES
(Below)
Apart from the buildings near the bridge this view has changed little since Victorian times.

THE SWAN HOTEL
(Opposite Page Above)
A collection of boats outside the Swan Hotel provided an interesting composition for this watercolour wash.

GOSLINGS
(Opposite Page Below)
There is no need for a lawn mower when young Canada geese are on the prowl.

By the time Staines Bridge had been completed in 1832, the skills and practices of bridge building had moved on considerably. In comparison with bridges built forty or fifty years earler, the spans of arches are greater and carriageways wider. The focus was on practicality and John Rennie, who built Staines bridge, was a busy engineer and not one to be side-tracked by ostentation.

In the eighteenth and nineteenth centuries some companies paid employees in tokens that could only be spent at company shops, an unfair practice that was made illegal. Nevertheless, tokens continued to be used as change for purchases which ensured people would return. One such place that issued such tokens was the Swan Inn (now the Swan Hotel) near Staines Bridge, which kept the bargees well and truly hooked.

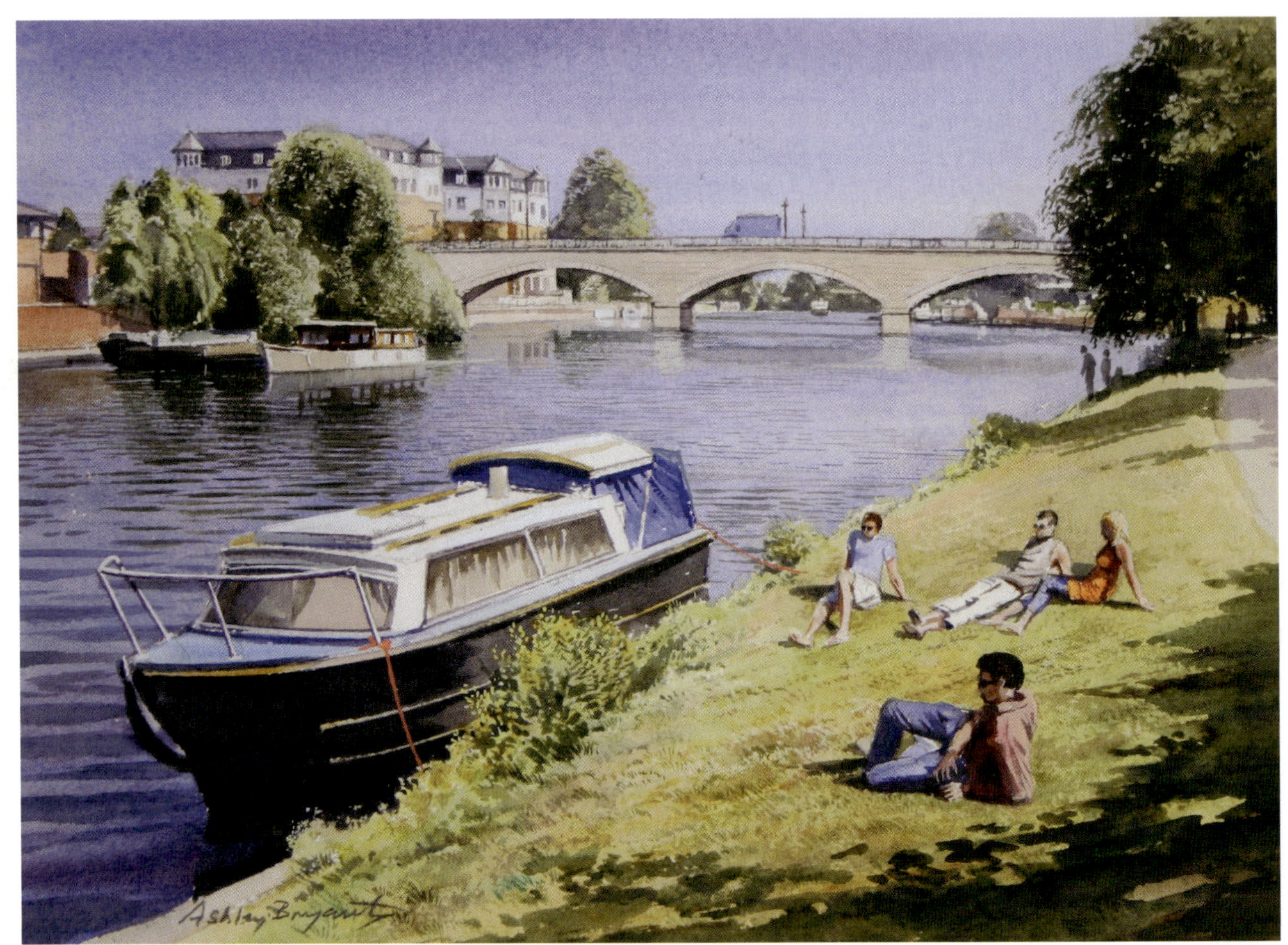

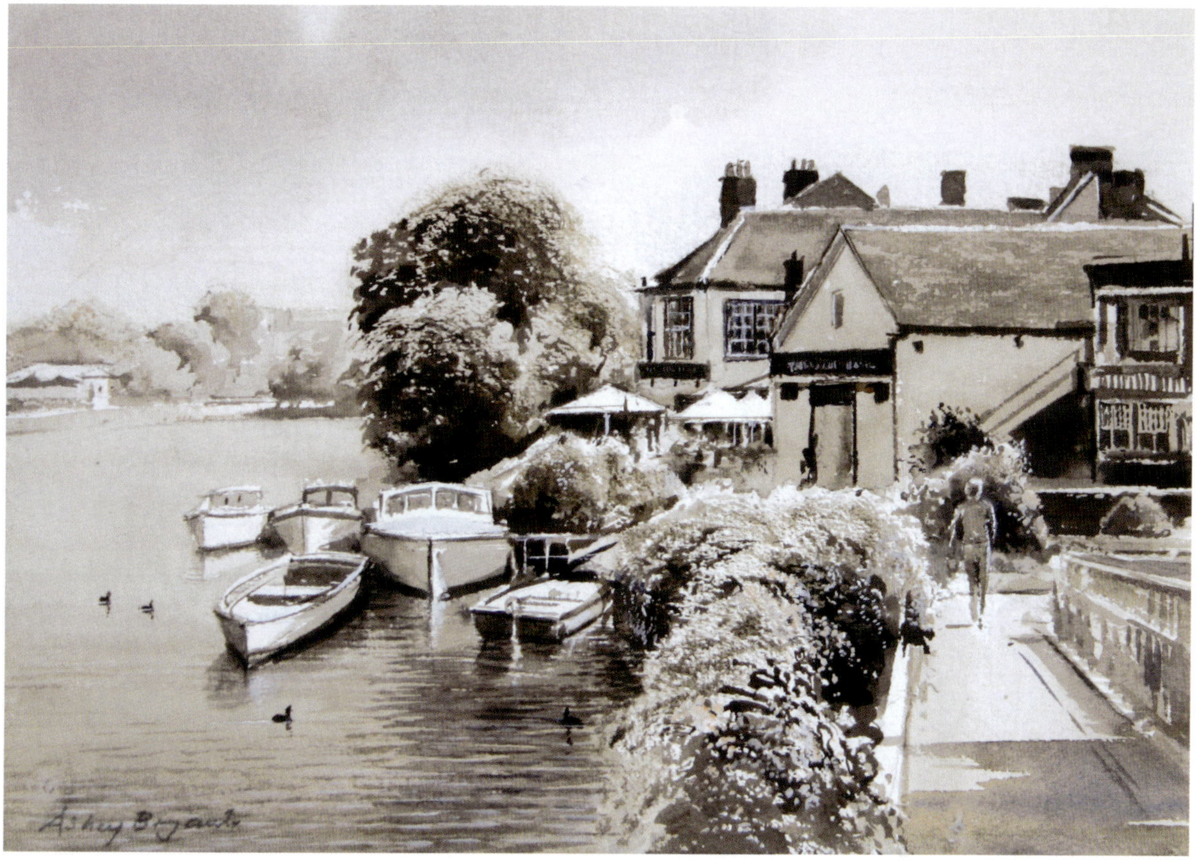

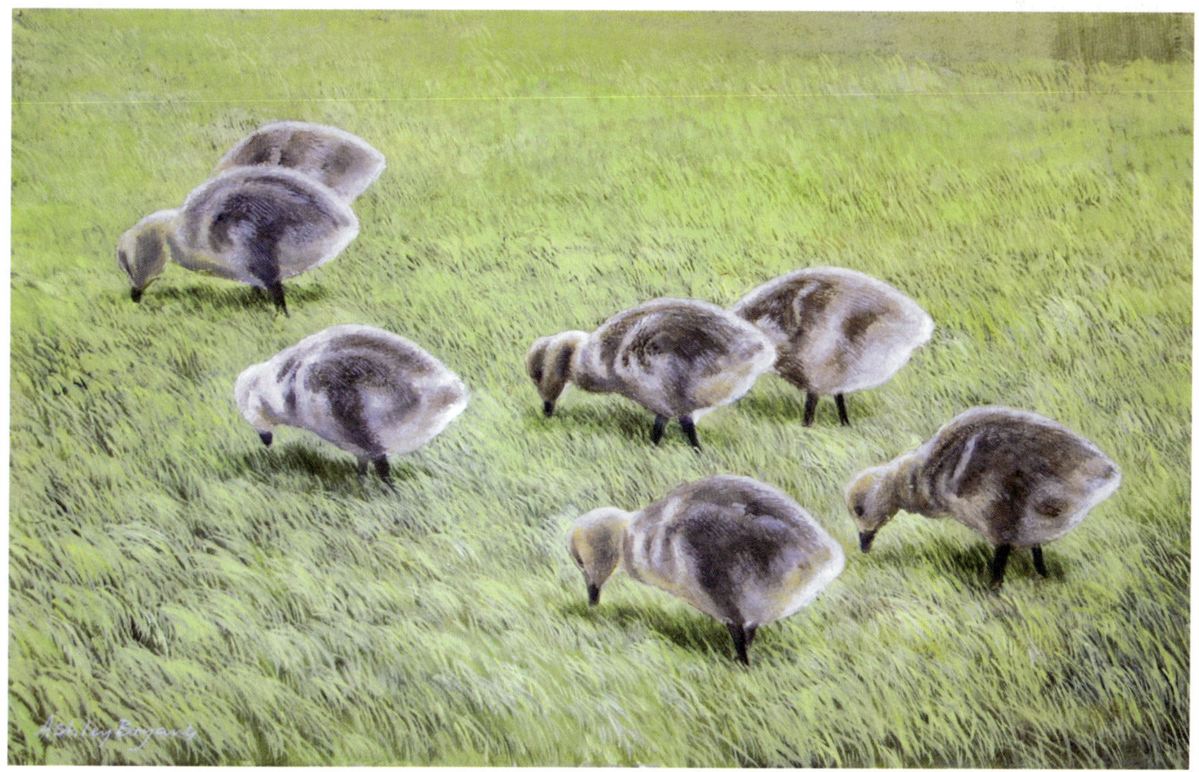

CHERTSEY

THE THAMES AT CHERTSEY
(Opposite Page)
A cloudy day in high summer at Chertsey Bridge. The journey along the Thames path feels relatively rural here since the main part of the town lies away from the river.

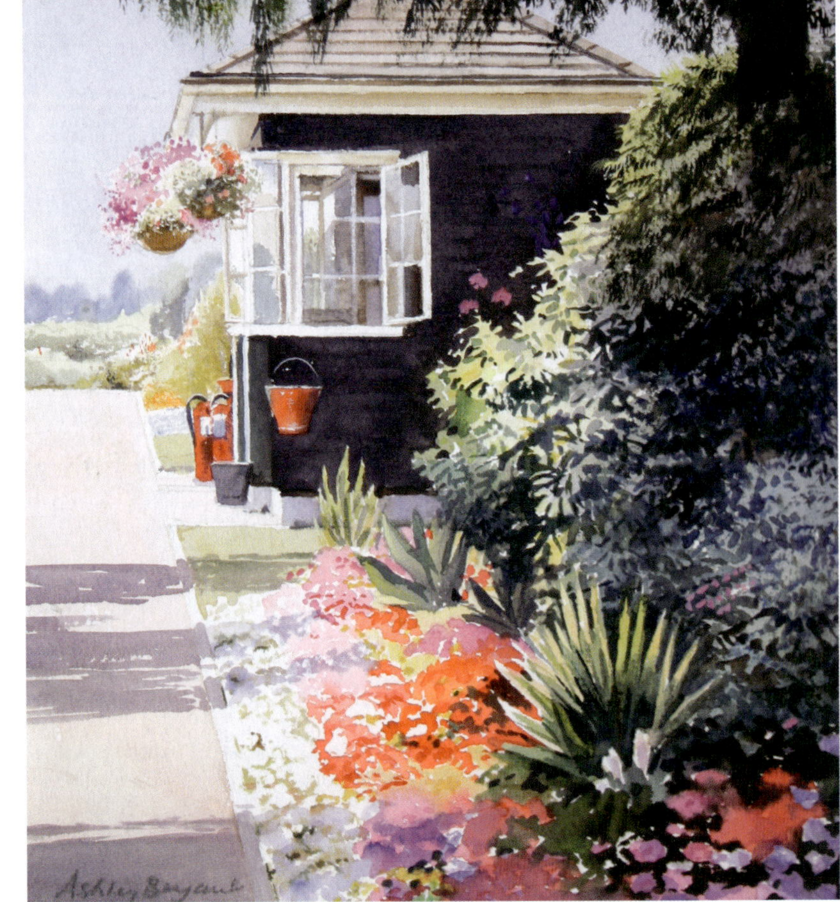

THE LOCK OFFICE
(Above)
The lock at Chertsey is renowned for its colourful gardens and this quickly produced watercolour captures some of the display around the lock keeper's office.

CHERTSEY LOCK
(Left)
Most of the artwork in this book is from the bank-side, but this charcoal sketch was produced quickly from a boat in Chertsey Lock.

Thames locks are strategic points along the river, providing ideal places to take a rest and reflect on the journey. In the upper, lonely reaches of the Thames they are particularly welcome milestones along the route. Here, you can watch the boating world pass by and chat with the lock-keepers who know everything about their patch of the river.

One noticeable aspect of Thames locks is their beautifully maintained gardens with neat edged lawns and perfect rose beds. Some have attractive arrangements of bedding plants, shrubs and clipped hedges, but the lock at Chertsey would surely take first prize for its gardens if ever a competition existed. Summer brings a magnificent display of colour; standard roses tower over arrangements of bedding plants, climbers form a backdrop on trellises and even the lock office is festooned with hanging baskets.

Abbeys, monasteries and priories were often sited conveniently close to the Thames, and in the course of my journey along the river I have found the remains of a number of them. Many, once large and powerful institutions, are now little more than foundation stones or crumbling walls. To read of their histories and see their ruins brings home the full impact and destructive force of the Reformation. Chertsey Abbey suffered accordingly. Built as early as A.D.666, not far from where the lock was later constructed, it grew to a huge size in early mediaeval England, breathing life into the area for nearly nine hundred years before its stones were scattered far and wide.

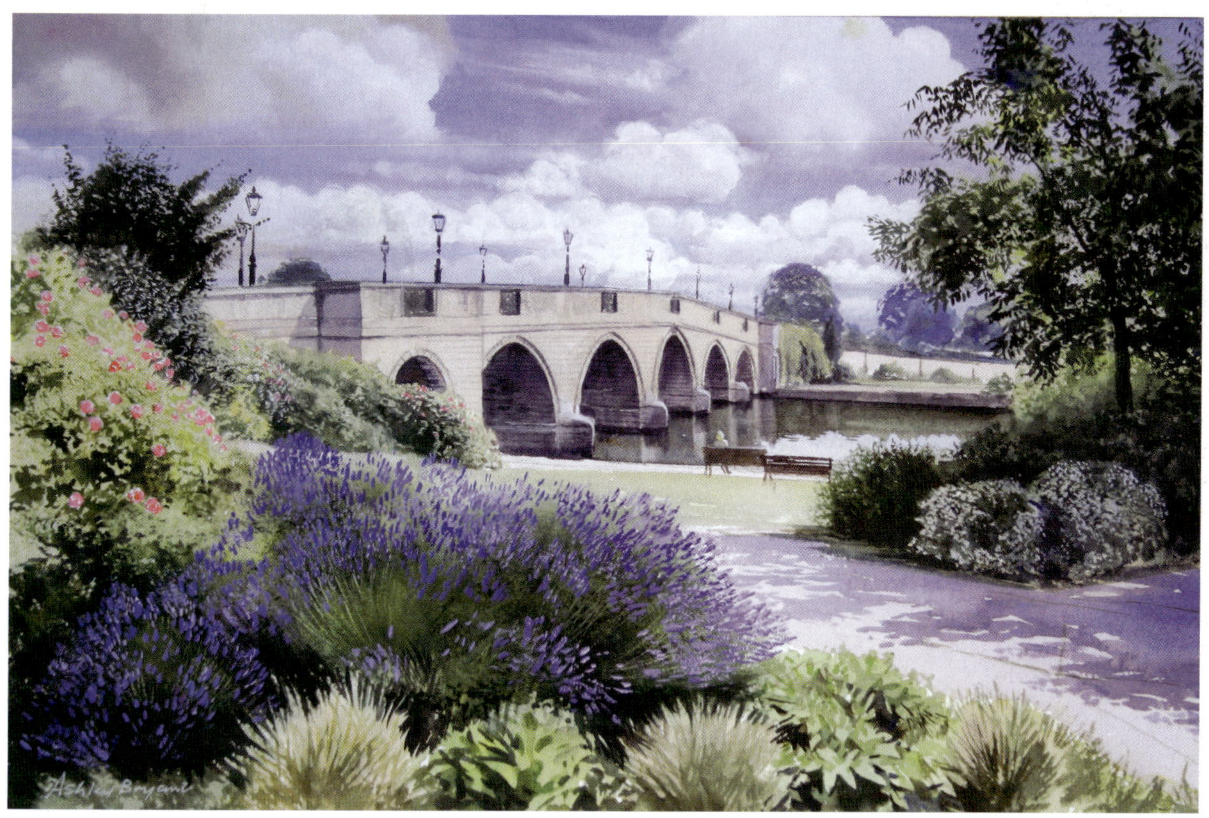

WALTON-ON-THAMES

THE LUNCH BREAK
(Opposite Page Above)
Many people live on boats on the Thames in craft of all kinds. Between Walton and Hampton Court are numerous backwaters and islands where these boats are moored. Some seem to have settled there permanently, whilst others take the occasional trip. This couple enjoy a leisurely lunch on their "floating garden" near Walton-on-Thames.

DABBLING SWANS
(Opposite Page Below)
Swans make an irresistible subject and this group are also focusing on their lunch.

THE THAMES AT WALTON
(Below)
On this overcast March day new growth was appearing along the riverside next to the marina.

Some ex-colleagues once mentioned that they were proud of their home town of Walton-on-Thames, and my hopes were high as I made my approach along the Thames path. A riverside town to be proud of would likely have a bridge to be proud of – a worthy successor to the one in Turner's paintings. Turner produced a number of delightful watercolours here, showing a multi-arched, hump-backed bridge, with the usual collection of people and animals in the foreground.

Unfortunately, the riverside proved to be less interesting than it had been in Turner's day; there was no view that shouted "paint me" and the dismal bridge appeared to have been widened in the 1950s by some boys with a Meccano set. Undaunted, I walked on in the early spring sunshine to find an acceptable view of the river. It was pleasant enough, and the spring growth in the reed beds as the new shoots appeared, and the dancing yellow catkins on the willows made the day seem much better.

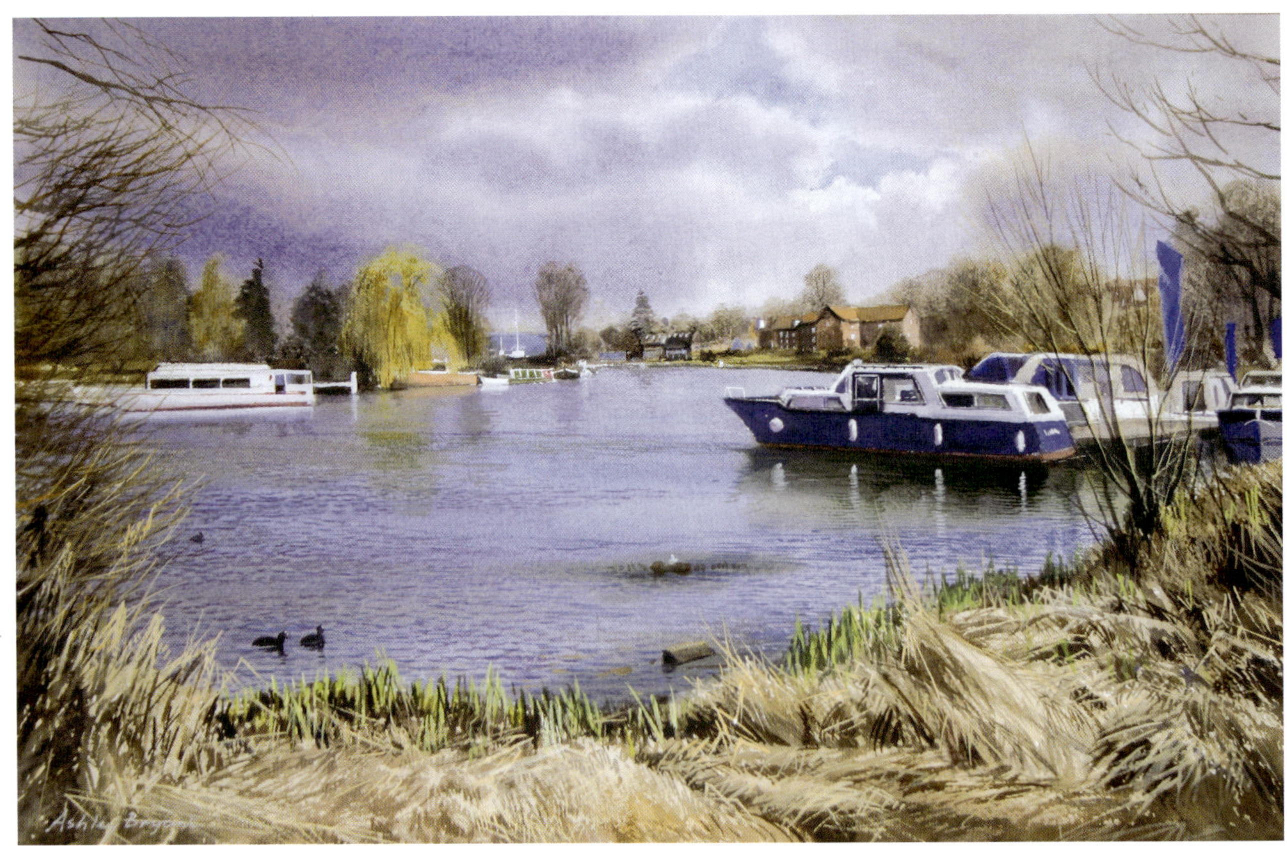

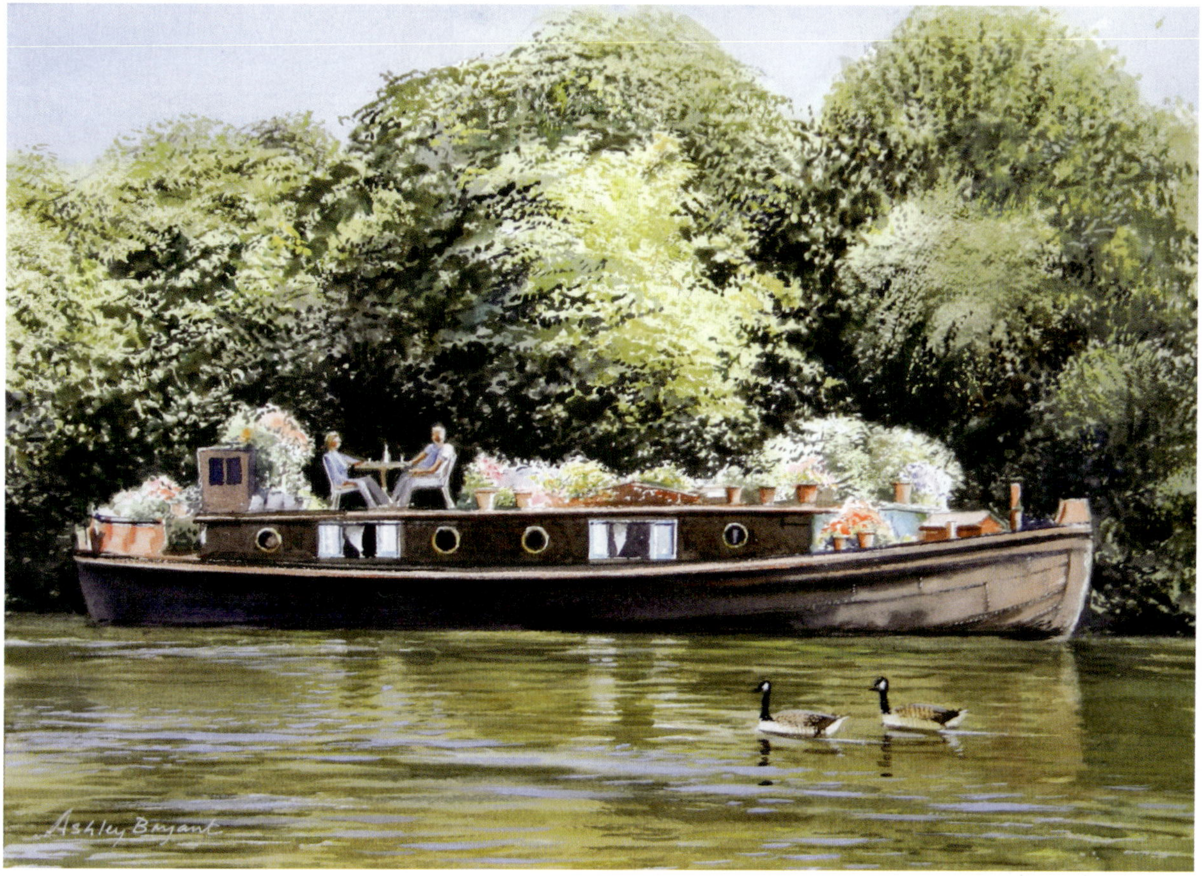

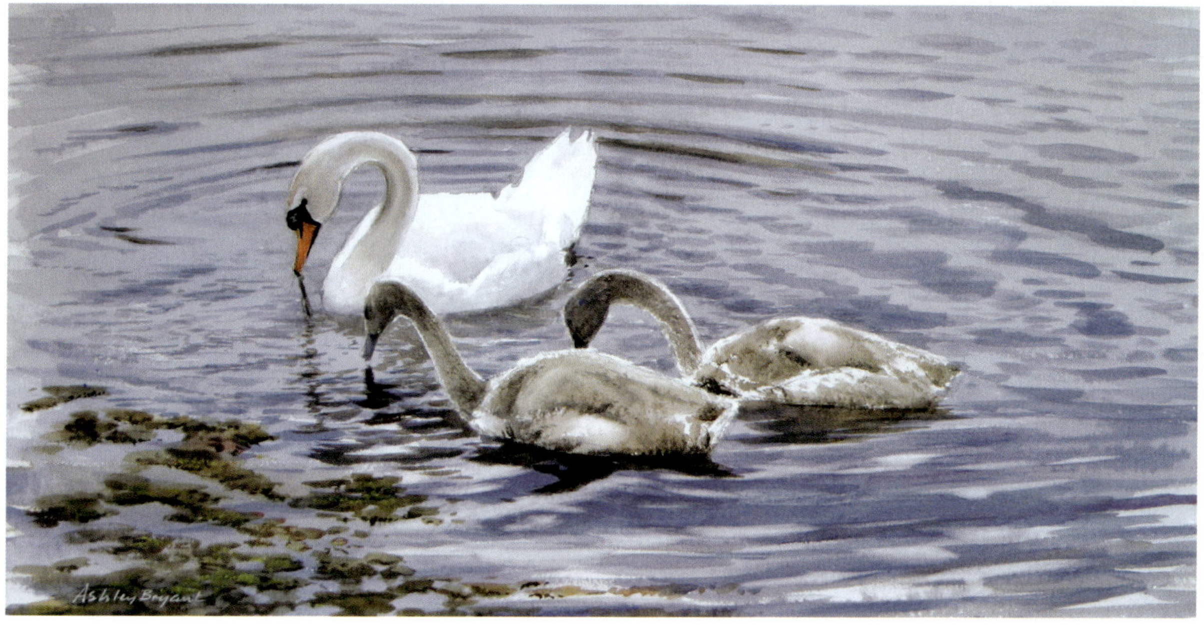
Ashley Bryant

SWAN UPPING

SEARCHING FOR SWANS
(Opposite Page)
The Chief Swan Marker and his crew keep their eyes peeled for swans near Shepperton.

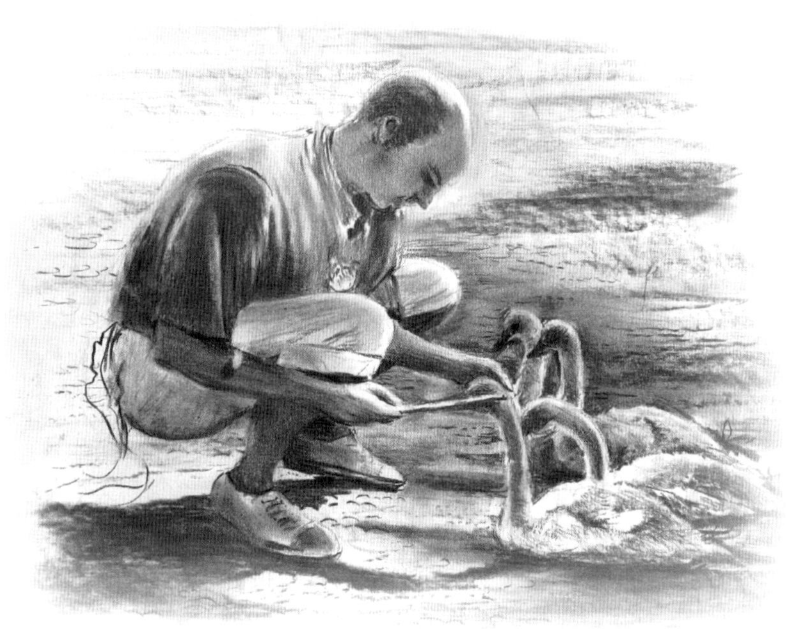

CHARCOAL SKETCHES OF SWAN UPPING
(Right and Clockwise)
Measuring the cygnets, Concerned parents, Trussing the adults, The weigh-in, A flurry of feathers on release.

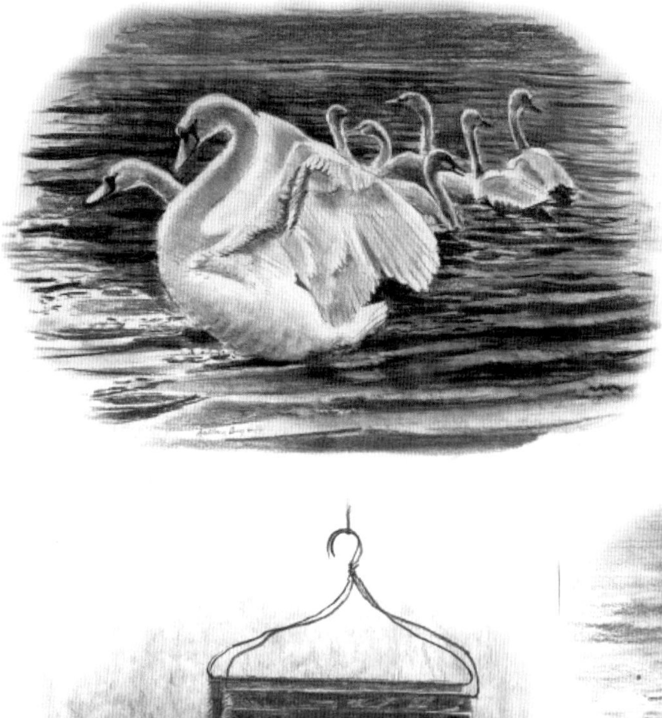

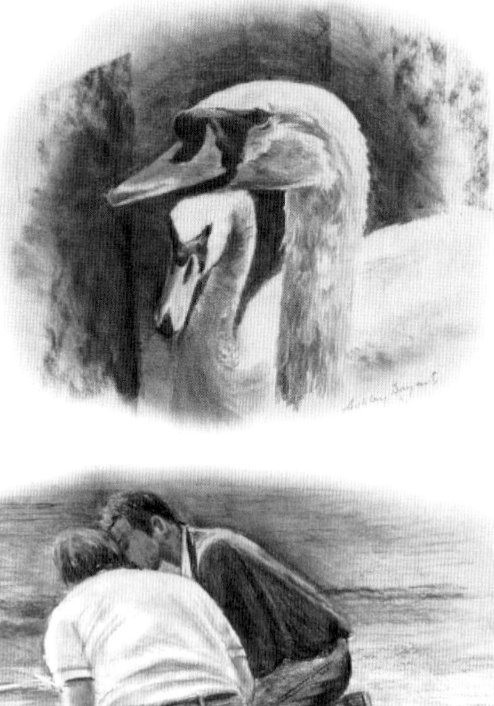

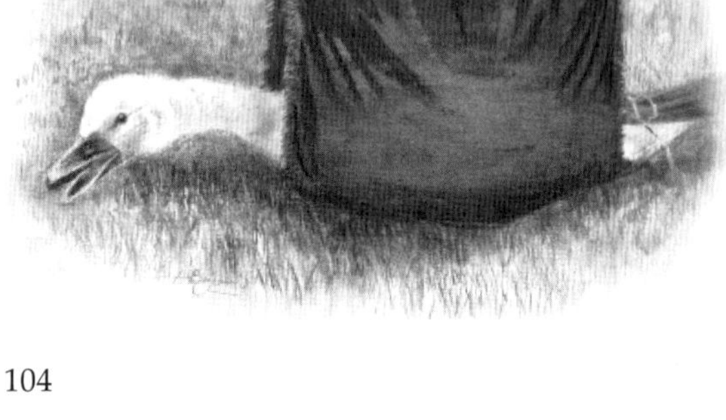

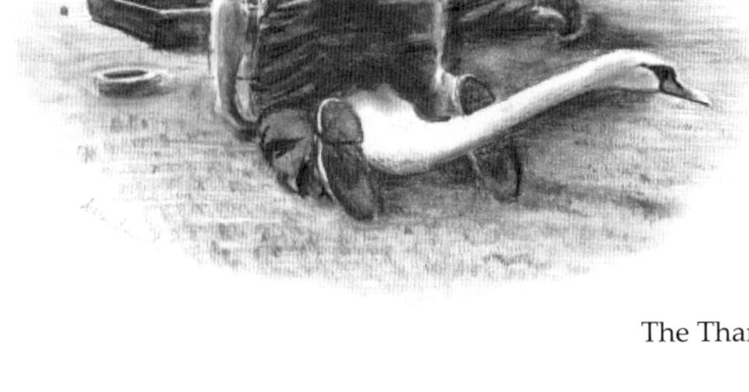

The medieval custom of swan upping continues to this day and I was pleased to take my place on the press boat to accompany the proceedings. The process involves a round up of swans in July each year, principally to mark the current year's cygnets. To capture them the Queen's Swan Marker and the Swan Uppers row upstream in their skiffs, from Sunbury to Abingdon, surrounding each swan family with their traditional boats. The adults and their offspring are hauled aboard. The cygnets cannot yet fly and the parents remain protectively with them. The whole family is given a quick medical check, details are logged and the cygnets weighed, measured and ringed. Specialist organisations then help injured or unhealthy swans.

In medieval times the swan was an important and up-market food for banquets, and in common with anything of value swans were regulated by the crown, which claimed ownership. Swan Upping, the process of marking swans for ownership, started in the 12th century, but since the 15th century the crown has shared ownership with the Vintners' and the Dyers' Companies, but it is only on the Thames that ownership rights are exercised. The tradition of Swan Upping continues with colourful pageantry, but its original purpose of regulating swans for the table is defunct. It now fulfils a more valuable role in children's education and in conserving swans. In conjuction, Oxford University is carrying out a long-term survey on swan populations.

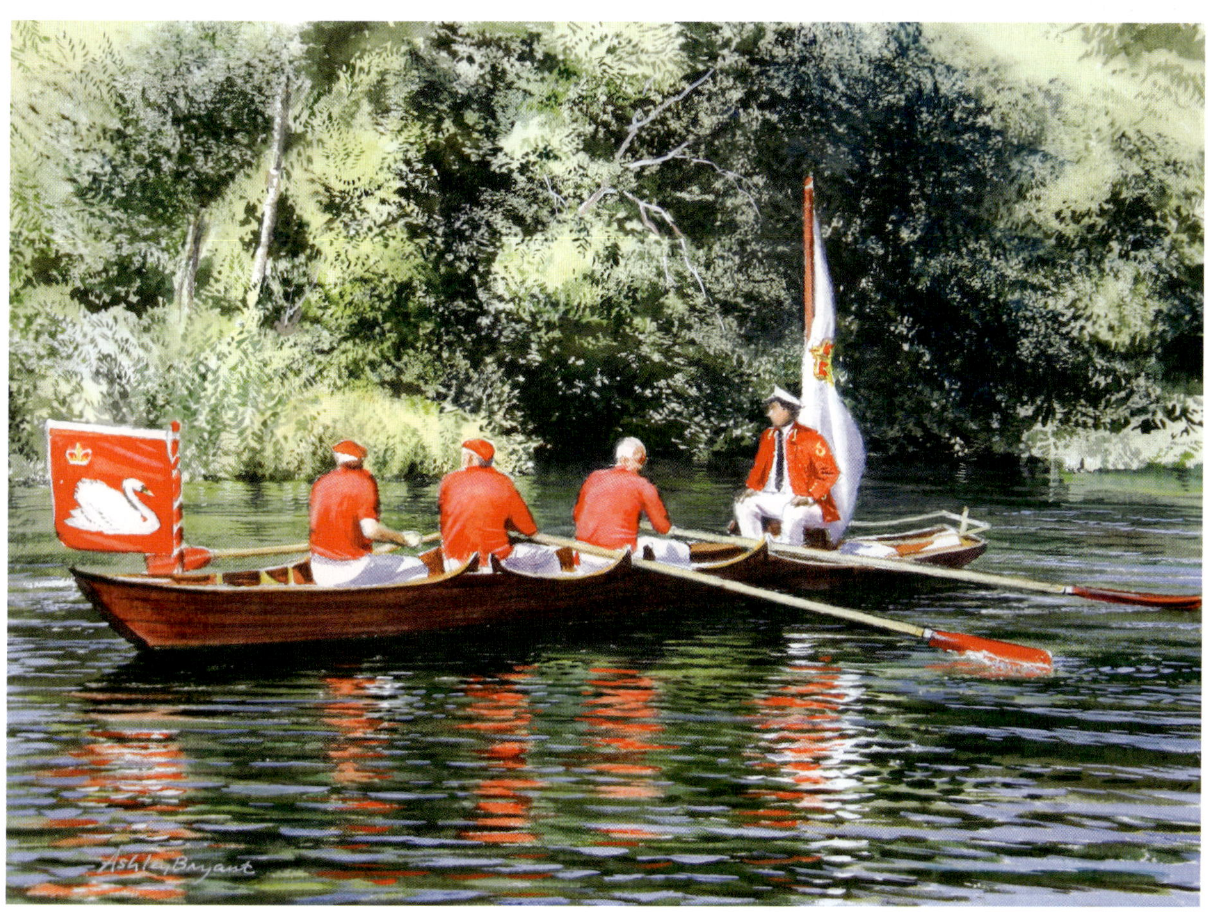

HAMPTON COURT

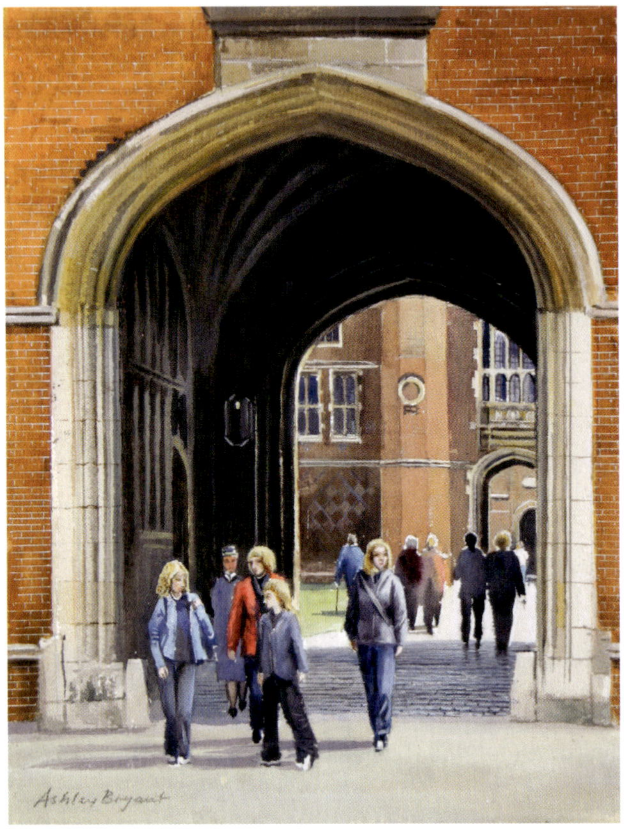

THE GATEWAY
Wolsey's impressive gateway with its vaulted ceiling looks through into the first palace courtyard.

THE THAMES AT HAMPTON COURT
(Opposite Page above)
An October view of part of the palace from the south bank.

CONKERS
(Opposite page below)
Schoolboys are in their element here with so many prize conkers. Life for Cardinal Wolsey was like a game of conkers; he gradually built up his asset at Hampton Court, only to have it taken by somebody else.

During a visit here some years ago I convinced myself to produce this book on the Thames. The palace and the gardens had so much appeal on that warm summer's day and the walk along the Thames path to Richmond appeared so full of interest that I was hooked. Years later this remains one of my favourite stretches of the river and I return whenever I can.

In the early sixteenth century Hampton Court was the centre of Cardinal Wolsey's empire. Wielding the greatest power in the land apart from the king, he used his vast fortune accumulated from position and privilege, to create this spectacular palace. It was built to impress, and royalty, visiting cardinals and statesmen, must have fallen under the spell of Hampton Court and its lavish hospitality. The man certainly had taste and a penchant for the high life. Waiting and watching was the powerful and ruthless King Henry VIII, and when Wolsey's disgrace and demise had been engineered, the palace became his.

To get the most from a visit a guided tour gives a flavour of the high life from the heady days of the Tudors through the additions created by successive monarchs to the 18th century when it was last used by George II. The Tudor kitchens, where 1200 people could be fed per day, are astounding. They are laid out as if in preparation for a feast with a menu including peacock and marzipan deserts decorated with real gold.

The gardens are a great feature, and if you have the stamina, there are sixty acres waiting to be explored. If time is limited, the "wild" gardens are recommended and are free of charge. In spring there are drifts of bluebells and majestic horse chestnuts in blossom; you could imagine you were deep in the English countryside if it were not for the squawk of ring-necked parakeets, now common in the area.

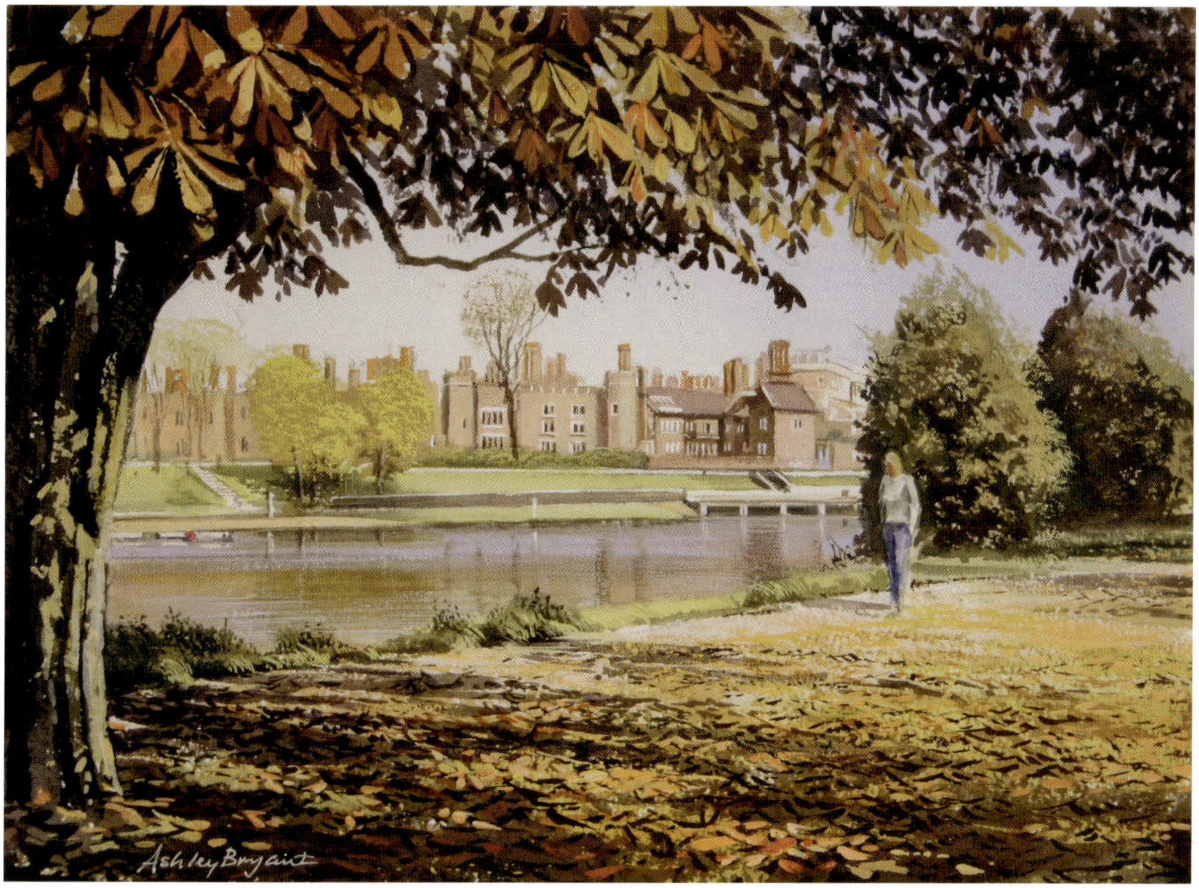

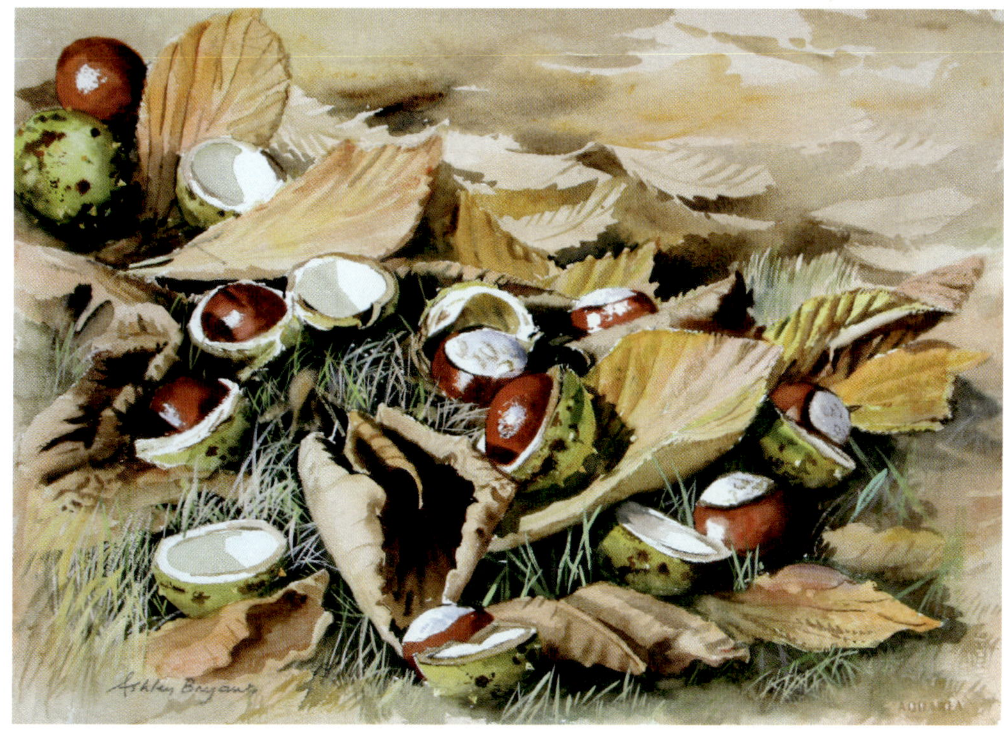
Ashley Bryant

KINGSTON UPON THAMES

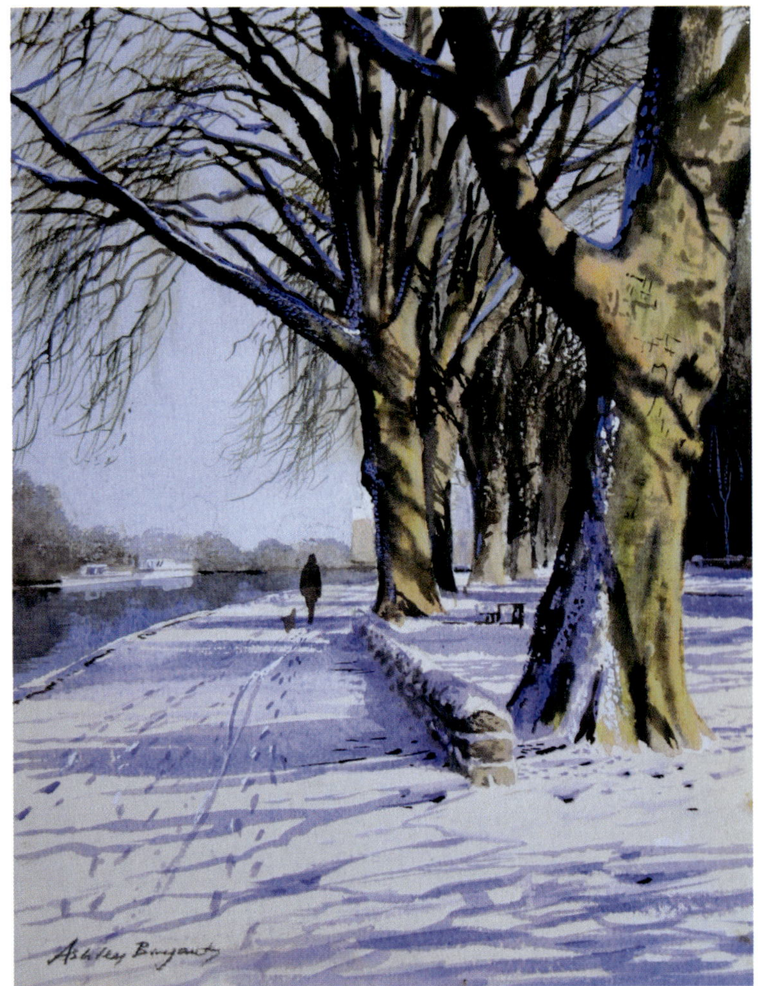

On its approach to Kingston, the Thames path follows an avenue of horse chestnut trees and from this vantage point I found the best view of the bridge. This bridge is the latest in a series dating back to Saxon times and for several centuries Kingston provided the first crossing of the Thames upstream from London. The Thames has naturally been a formidable river to cross and for this reason towns usually developed only on one side of the river, with communications and transport restricted to boat.

Kingston has an old heritage, and one of its proudest assets is the Coronation Stone, reputedly the place where seven Saxon kings were crowned. The name of this royal borough was derived from the stone itself. Kingston has many modern developments, including shopping centres and glass fronted, minimalist restaurants – architecture that is likely to have a short life before its replacement by something marginally better. Fortunately, the classical architectural gems live on. It is well worth strolling to the market place where you find yourself surrounded by lovely old buildings with a harmonious mixture of ages and styles. Here in the summer you can take tea in the open air, watch the interesting world of Kingston pass by and feed the starlings that hover like hummingbirds to take the food from your fingertips. Simple pleasures indeed.

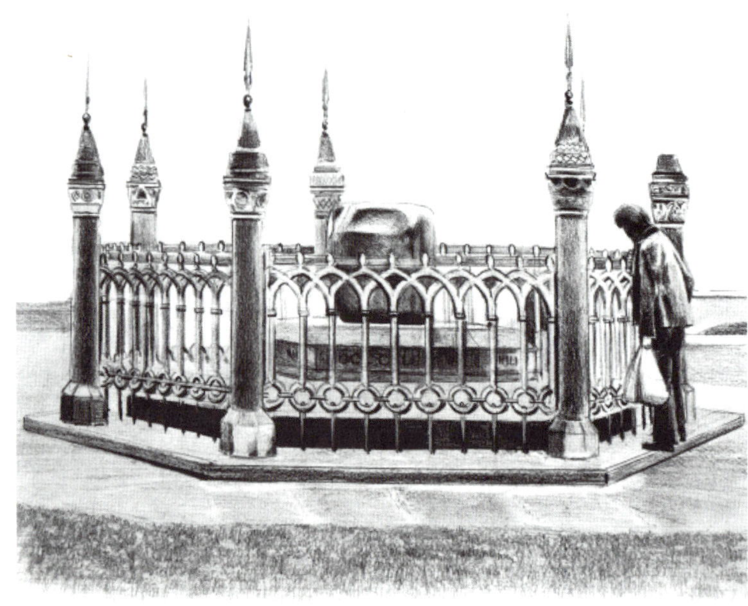

CLATTERN BRIDGE

(Left)

This ancient bridge spans a small tributary of the Thames at Kingston and its name is derived from the clatter of horse's hooves on the cobbles.

THE KINGSTON RIVERSIDE

(Opposite above)

THE CORONATION STONE

(Opposite below)

This stone, Kingston's pride and job, was where seven kings were crowned in the tenth century.

THE THAMES AT KINGSTON

(Below)

The view of the bridge from the tree-lined approach from the Thames path.

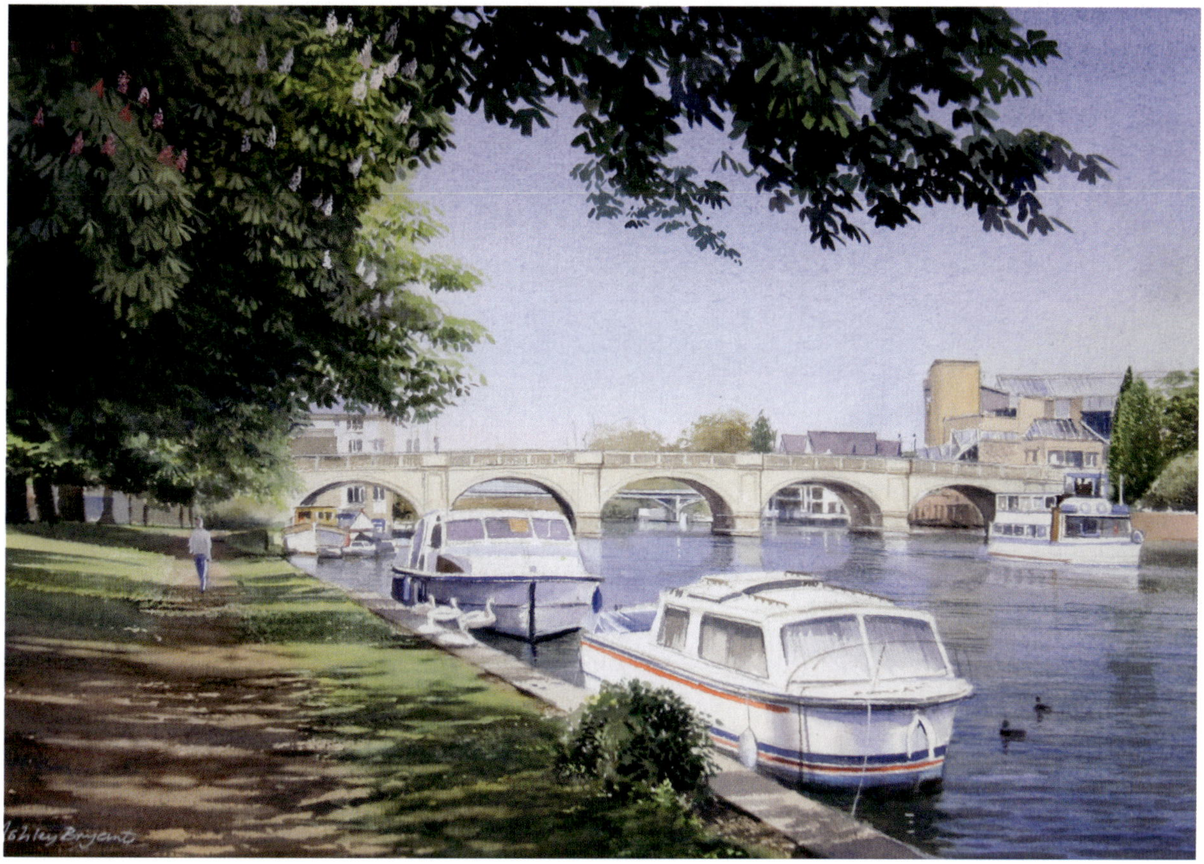

RICHMOND

THE THAMES FROM RICHMOND HILL
(Opposite Page)
A timeless view from the terrace.

OLD FATHER THAMES
(Right)
This splendid fellow relaxes in front of Ham House.

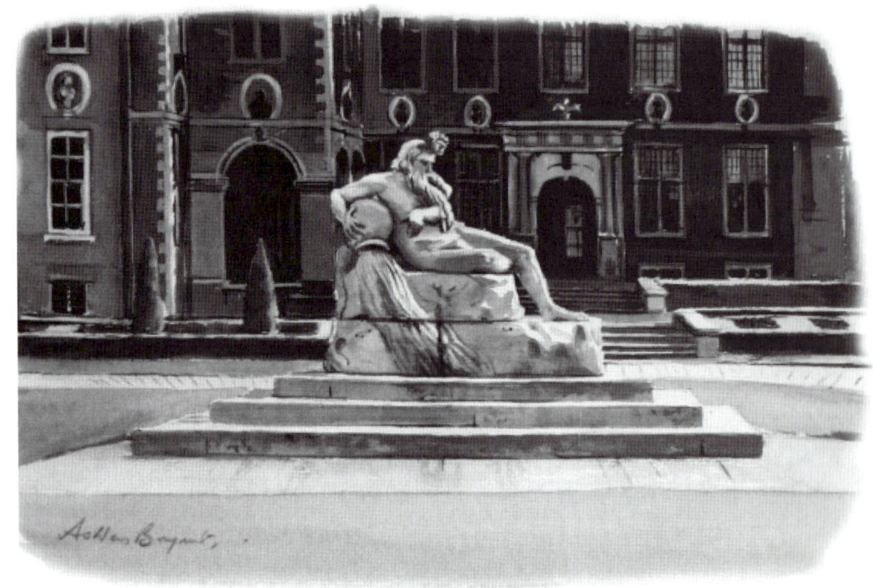

RICHMOND APPROACH
(Below)
These two figures catch the eye as they walk towards Petersham Meadows and Richmond Hill.

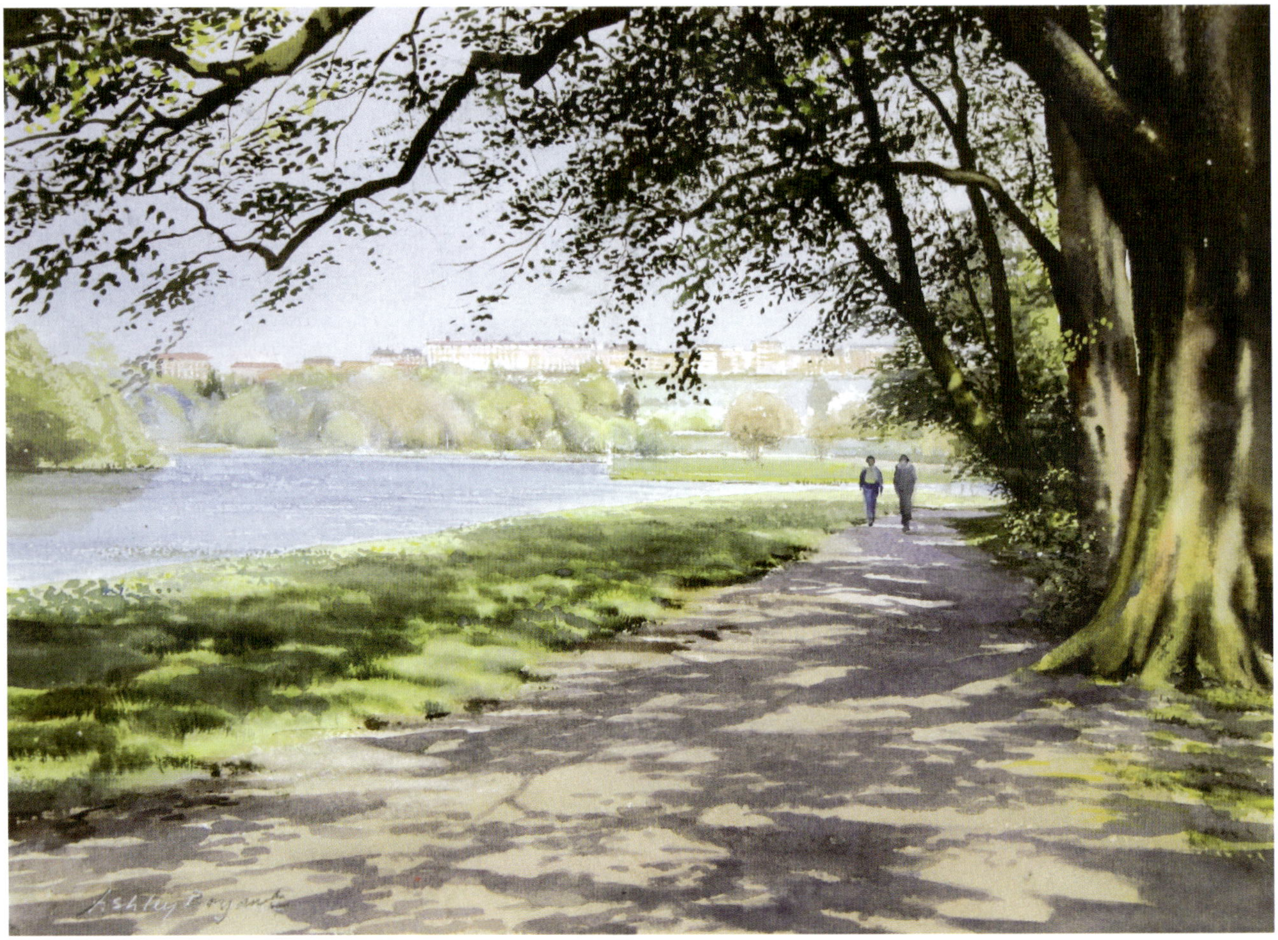

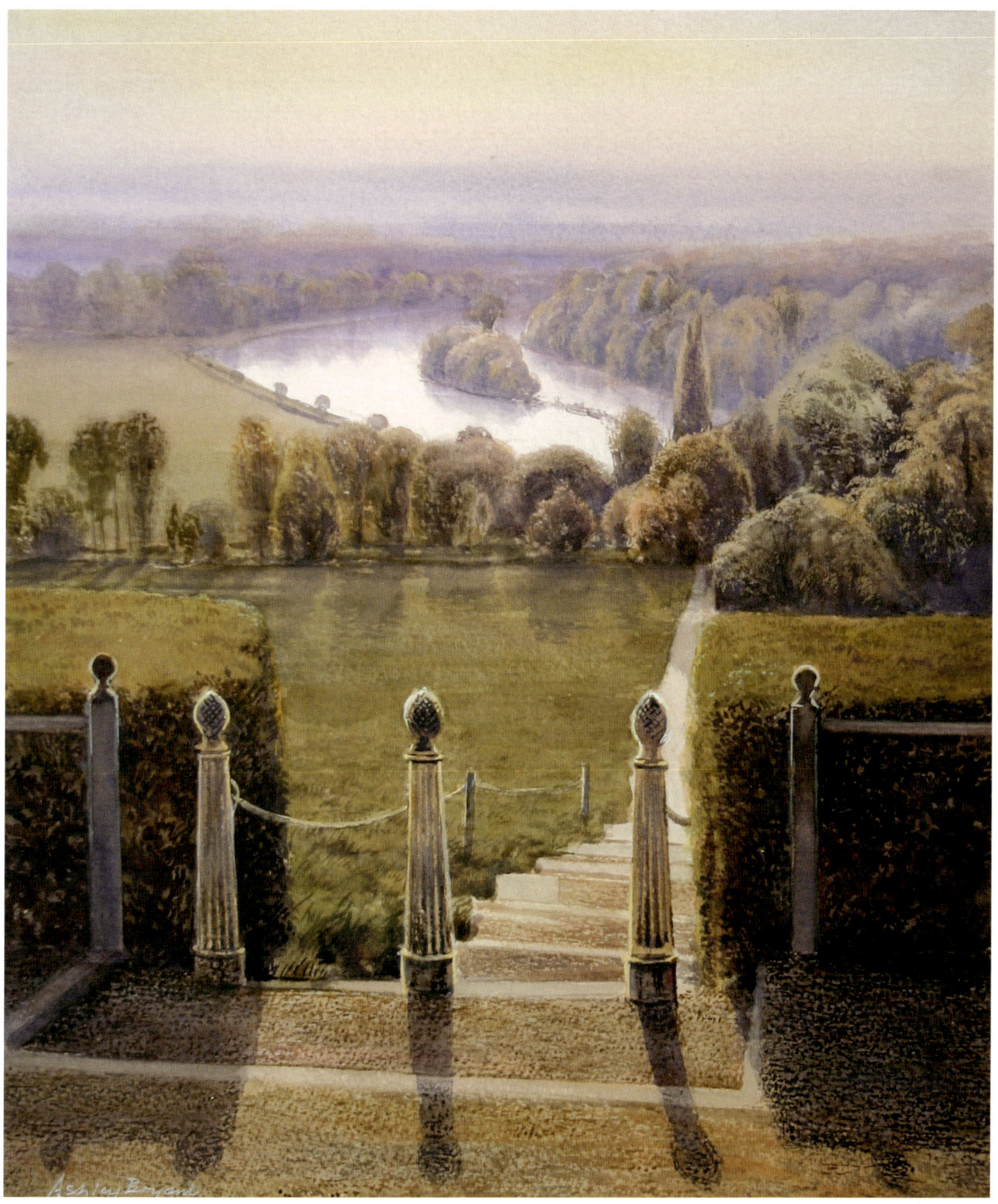
Ashley Bryant

RICHMOND

A firm favourite is the walk downstream to Richmond through the last area of "wilderness" before London sets in. In spring, in this rich countryside, you can almost see the vegetation growing and feel the energy of life. Swathes of wild flowers, such as lady's smock, carpet the sunlit glades by the water's edge and bluebells and red campion drift into the shade. Boats on the river flicker past the curtains of weeping willows that droop to the water's surface, and on the far bank glimpses of old boat houses offer engaging subjects.

Ham House provides an interesting interlude, where Old Father Thames looks out from the gardens. A ferry crosses the river to Marble Hill Park, near to Eel Pie Island – the haunt of 1960's rock groups. Soon Petersham Meadows appear, an area of ancient grazing land below Richmond Hill. The view from the summit of the hill looking back along the winding river is one of the most classic views of the Thames, and has inspired some of our greatest artists and celebrated composers including Purcell and Britten. This short journey from Kingston could take weeks since there is so much to enjoy. At Richmond itself, the bridge and busy landing stages, moored boats and interesting buildings invite me to linger with my sketchbook.

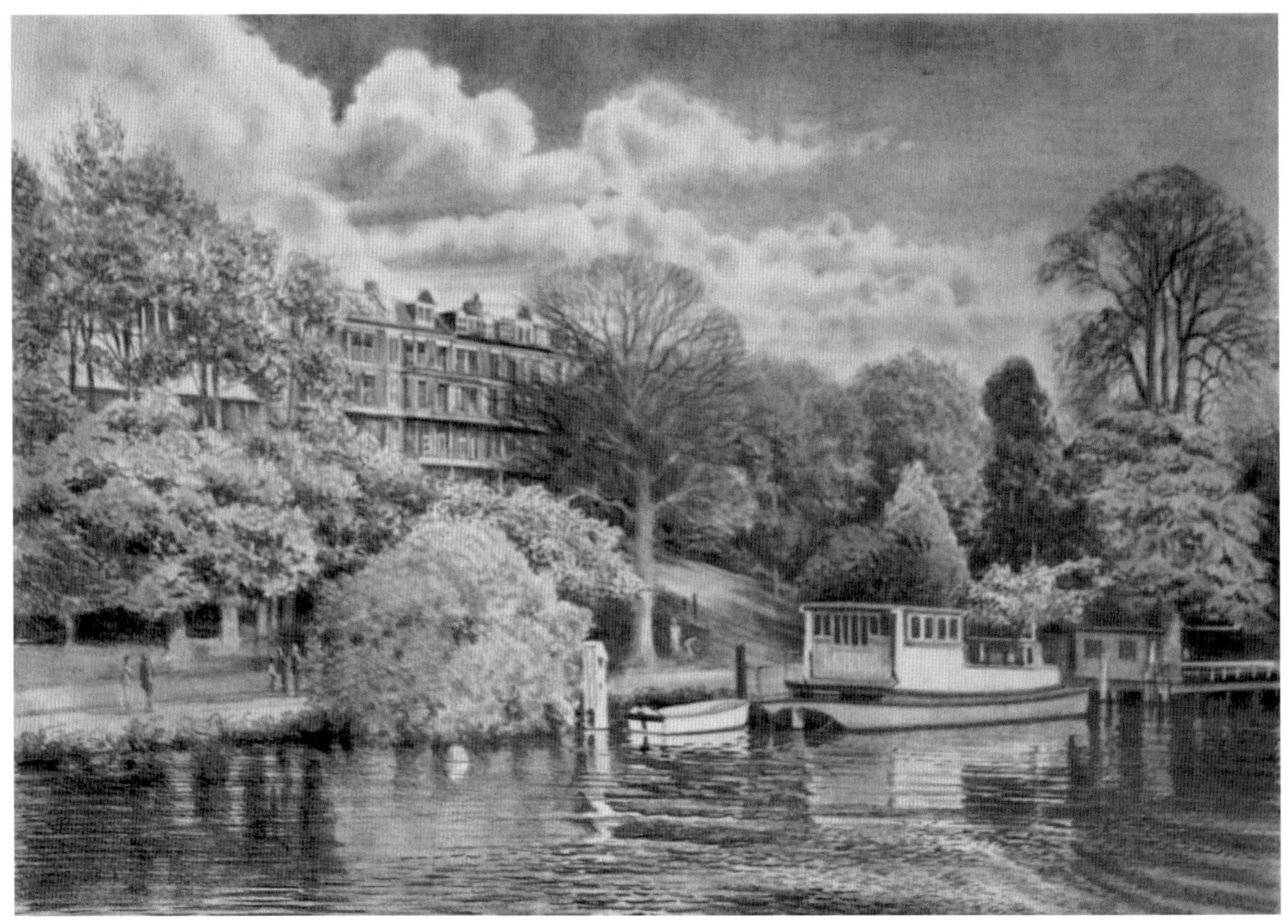

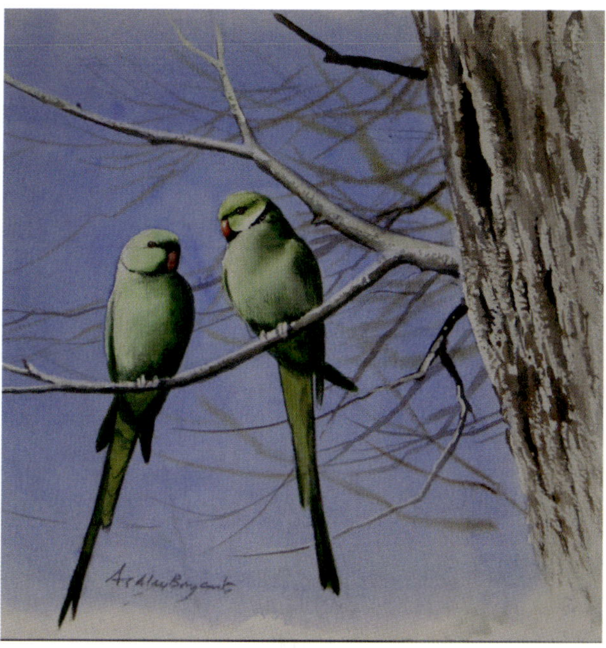

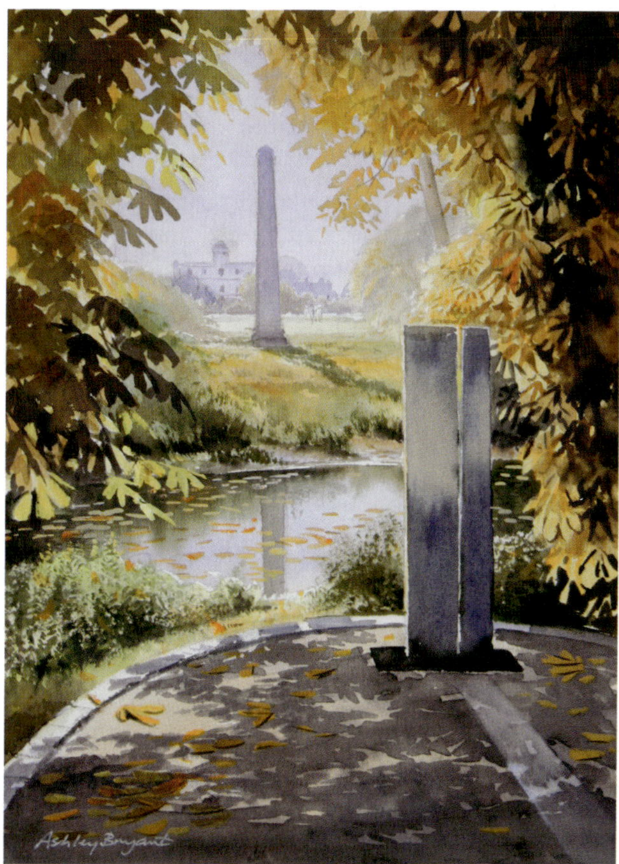

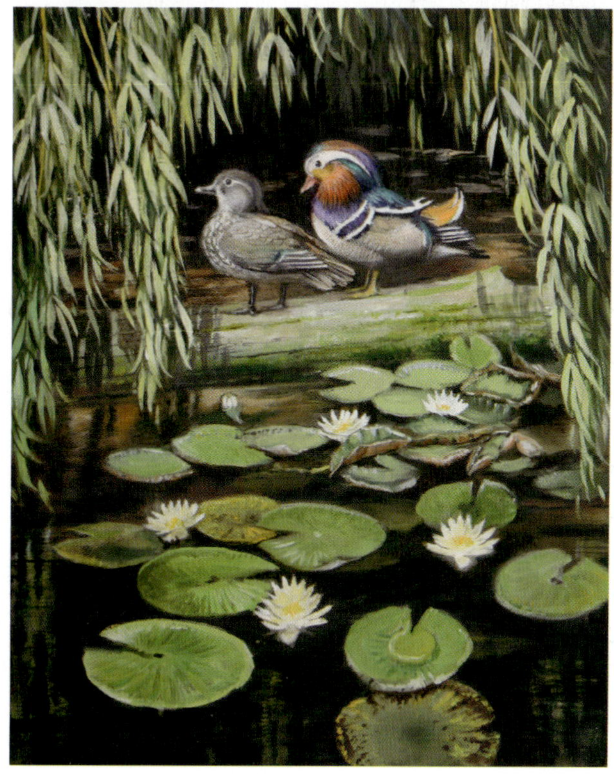

PARAKEETS
(Above)
From London to Marlow ring-necked parakeets are a familiar site along the Thames, but visitors assume they have escaped from captivity. This was the case in the 1960s, but generations later there are thousands of these birds living in the wild.

MERIDIAN LINE
(Right Above)
The Kew Observatory was built in Old Deer Park for George III to indulge his interest in astronomy. The foreground panel and the obelisks across the stream show the alignment of a meridian, set up in the days before the Greenwich meridian was universally accepted.

MANDARINS
(Right Below)
One of the most unusual and exotic birds to be seen on the Thames is the Mandarin duck. They are fairly shy and are more likely to be seen in backwaters and overgrown cuts to boat houses than on open water. They nest in holes in trees and are encouraged into large riverside gardens by the siting of nesting boxes for them.

RICHMOND RIVERSIDE
(Opposite Page)
The riverside walk a short distance upstream from Richmond Bridge.

ISLEWORTH

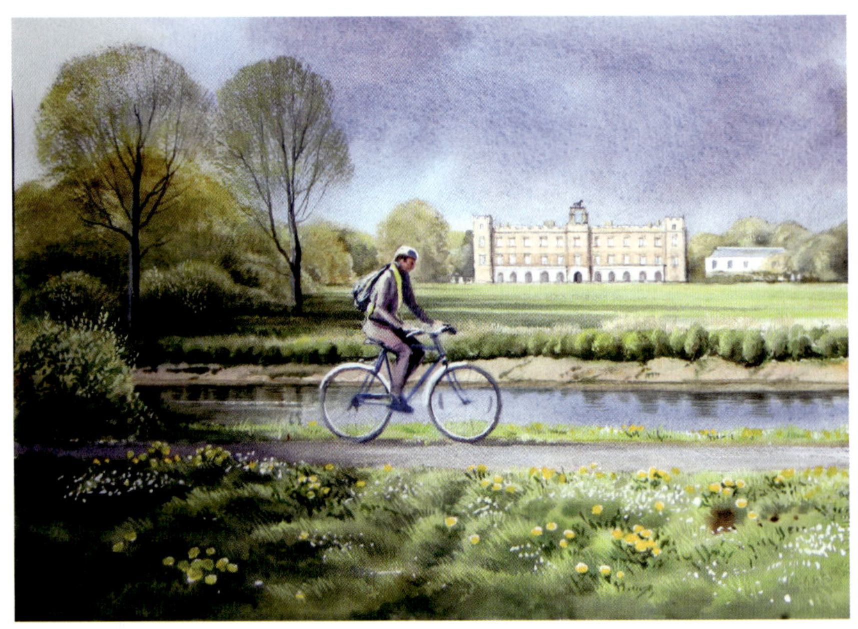

SYON HOUSE

Syon House is seen across the Thames from a viewpoint in Kew Gardens. The house was built on the site of a nunnery in the early sixteenth century for the Duke of Northumberland. Two queens were held here before their executions; Katherine Howard in 1542 and Lady Jane Grey in 1554.

SUCCESSFUL FISHERMAN

(Right below)

The Thames has a very high population of herons. From Corporation Island in the centre of Richmond to the riverbank at Syon House there are several heronries with the greatest number of nests along the Syon tidal meadows. Normally, these birds are quite shy but on the Thames they are used to people and can be approached fairly closely.

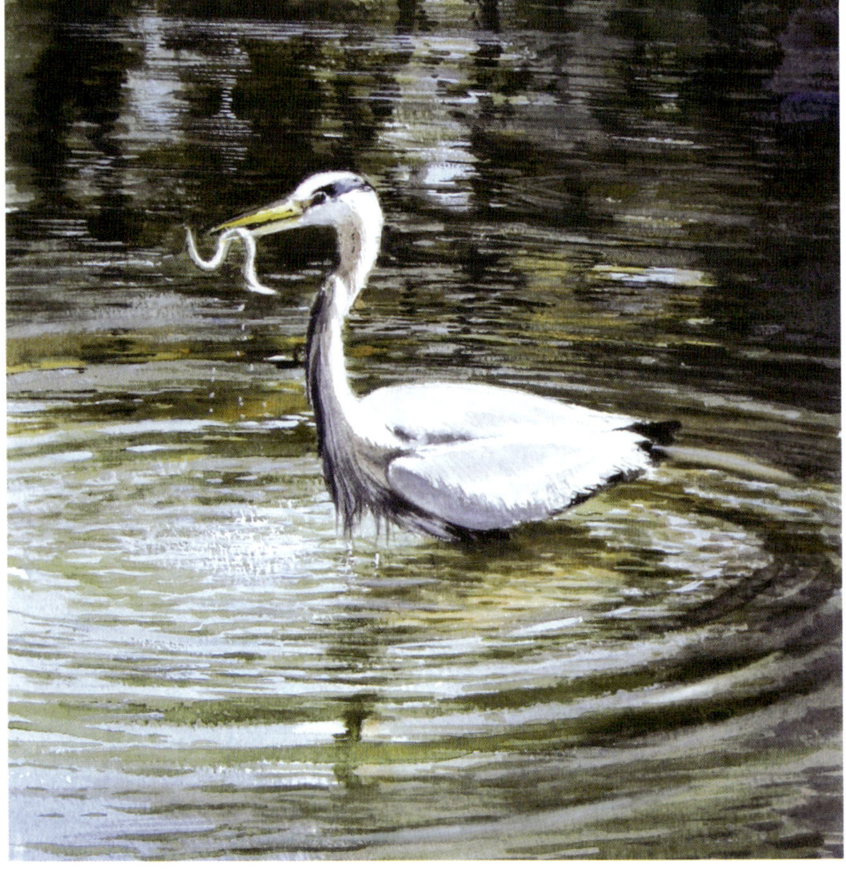

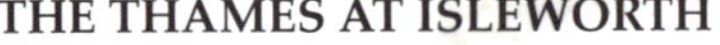

THE THAMES AT ISLEWORTH

(Opposite Page)

The Georgian waterfront and tower of All Saints' church make an appealing riverside setting at Isleworth. The church was actually burnt down in 1943 by some boys playing with matches and was rebuilt – the tower is all that remains of the original structure.

A riverside setting of attractive buildings and a church tower always provides a pleasing composition and from the south bank of the Thames the view of Isleworth is perfect except for one small problem; it's a little too far away for a detailed view across the river. In my case the answer was to take a boat from Westminster to Richmond, and photograph the scene as we motored past. A boat trip provides a unique perspective on the river and the services from Westminster to Hampton Court are excellent.

Lying almost in front of this view is Isleworth Ait, a nature reserve and breeding ground for numerous waterfowl. An ait or eyot is an old word for an island, and as far as I can establish, these are names used only on the Thames. Tidal change is marked at Isleworth after the passing of the lock at Teddingdon and the half tide lock at Richmond. The tidal meadows at Isleworth are unusual features and the twice daily tides run into creeks and channels and spill over to meadowland, bringing nutrients in their wake. A species of aquatic burrowing crab has found its way into the Thames (presumably from the ballast tanks of ships) and their holes in the riverbank are noticeable at low tides. The resulting erosion is giving cause for concern. Beyond the meadows sits Syon House, a fomer convent, appropriated by Henry VIII, and now the London home of the Dukes of Northumberland. The house has been remodelled several times and its rather dismal appearance hides a sumptuous interior by Robert Adam.

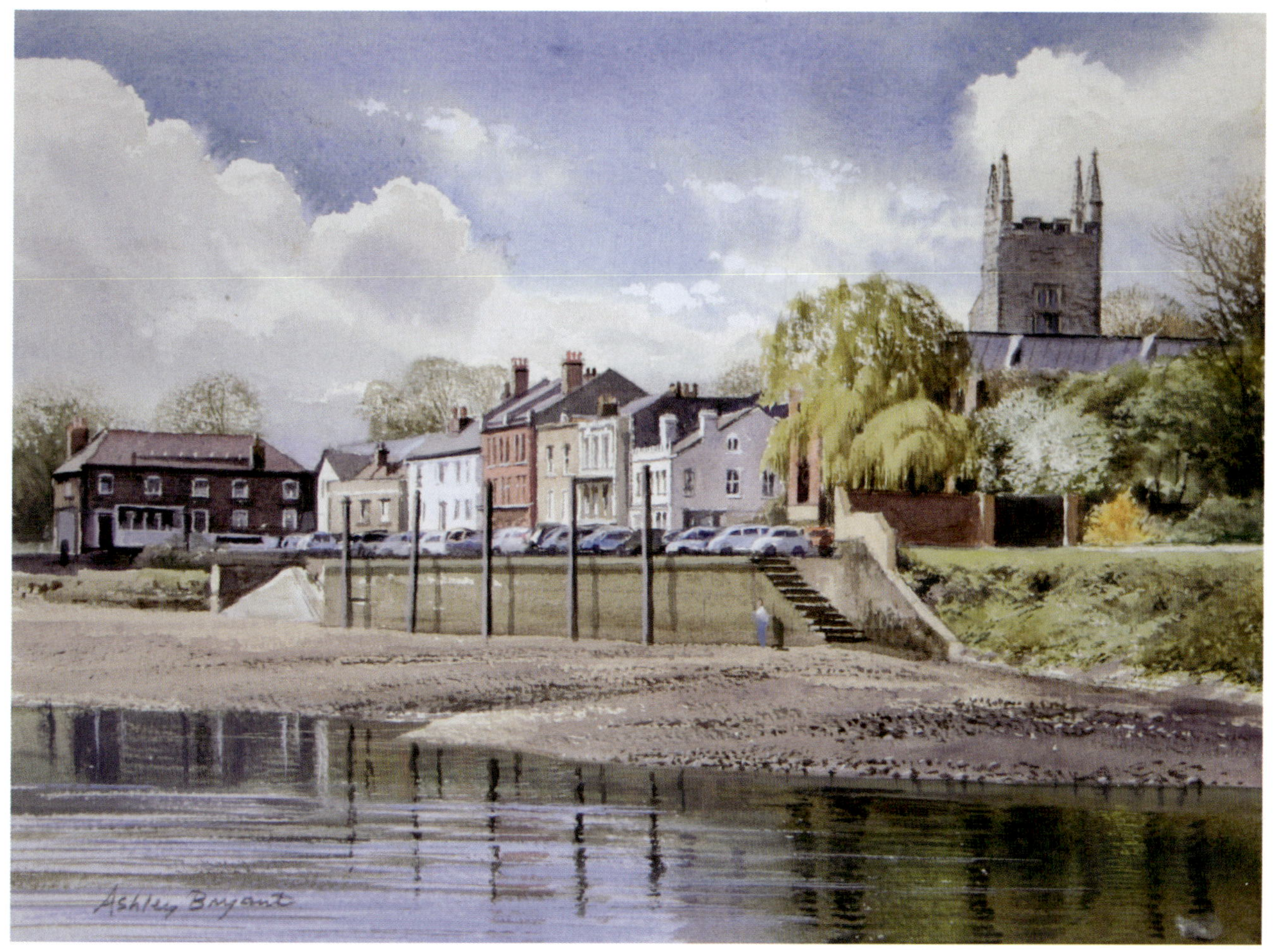

KEW

Kew Gardens lie alongside the Thames and glimpses of its magnificent vistas and the fragrance of bluebells in spring tempt many people from the Thames Path to this World Heritage Site. Starting in a small way in 1759, the gardens have grown to half a square mile and include 30,000 different plant species making it the largest collection in the world. Kew is an important plant depository and contains many rare and endangered species. The grounds are set out in a mixture of wooded parkland and gardens, with vistas and walkways leading to imposing focal points such as the Tropical Palm House, the Princess of Wales Conservatory and the Pagoda. Kew attracts many talented artists, especially those specialising in botanical studies.

A short distance from the river and adjacent to the Gardens, lies Kew Green, the venue for summer cricket matches. Sporting activities are amongst the most difficult of subjects to sketch because of the inevitable movement, but cricket is an exception. Every few moments the whole 'field' freezes with anticiaption, allowing sketching to continue. Although the name of Kew is synonymous with these famous gardens, the steam museum located near the bridge is worthy of a visit. The polished, antique machinery may not grab everyone's interest, but its purpose was to pump water directly from the river for use as drinking water in west London. If you lean over Kew Bridge and look down at the river flowing below, you can see the water our great-great grandparents drank! At least it was better than the cocktail extracted further downstream.

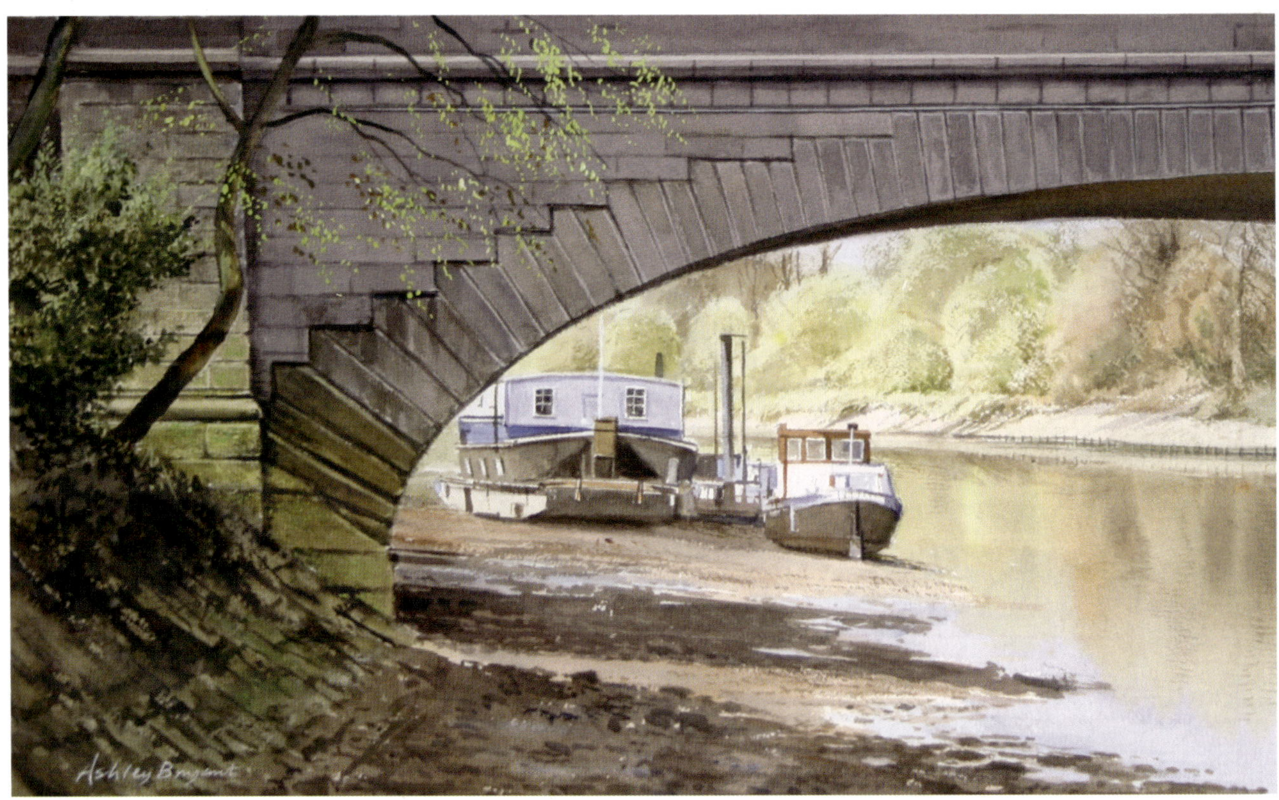

THE PAGODA
(Right)
Sir William Chambers' ten-storey pagoda is a famous landmark in Kew Gardens.

KEW BRIDGE
(Opposite Page)
Fashionable Kew and down-to-earth Brentford sit astride the Thames and are connected by Kew Bridge. This view looks upstream to the Brentford Ait at low tide.

THE WILD GARDEN
(Below Right)
A vista of bluebells in the oak wood makes an enchanting scene in the spring.

GROUND FLORA
(Below)
Bluebells, red campion and anenomies provide colourful displays in spring.

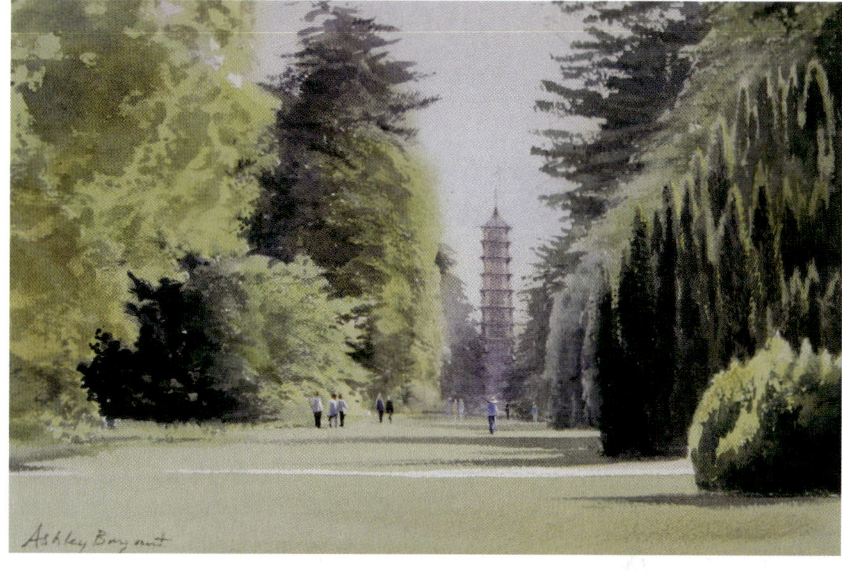

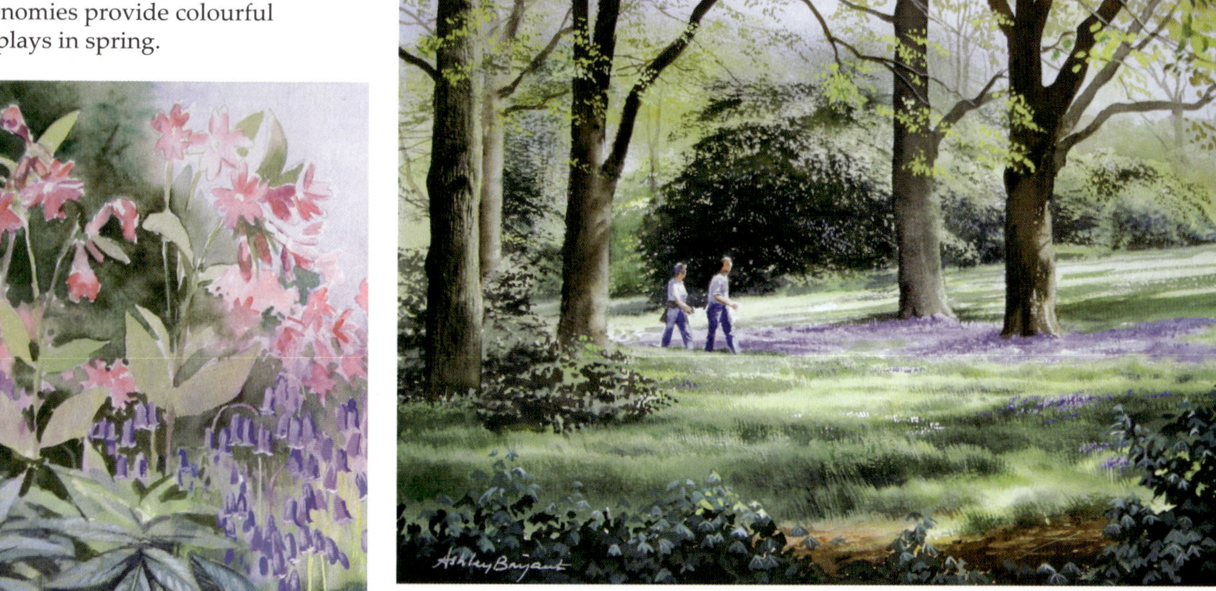

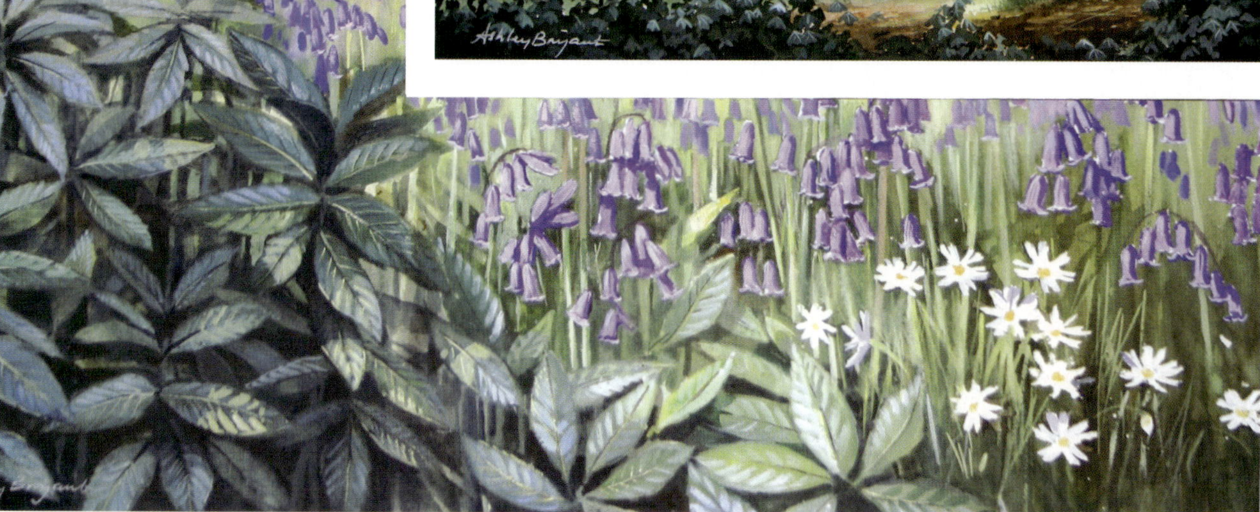

STRAND ON THE GREEN

The river alone often does not always provide sufficient interest for a composition. It is the surrounding landscape and its associated features, such as bridges, boats, the adjacent scenery and its reflections in the water, which provide the artist with a subject. Strand on the Green covers these requirements admirably, and the view upstream to Kew Bridge on the north bank of the river is flanked by lovely old houses and busy, characterful pubs. The ultimate view of Strand on the Green is from Oliver's Ait at low tide and with a sunset behind the bridge. From this island, the reds and golds of the evening sky are reflected in the water and wet mud banks, but I had to settle for the next best position on the towpath.

THE CITY BARGE
(Below)
One of the popular pubs along the towpath, the City Barge, took its name from the Lord Mayor's boat that was moored here in the late middle ages. In this watercolour, the Thames is seen at high tide and near the level of the towpath and sometimes customers have to tiptoe through the overspill. This pub has a flood barrier with watertight doorways, and various safety measures against flooding are adopted by the houses nearby.

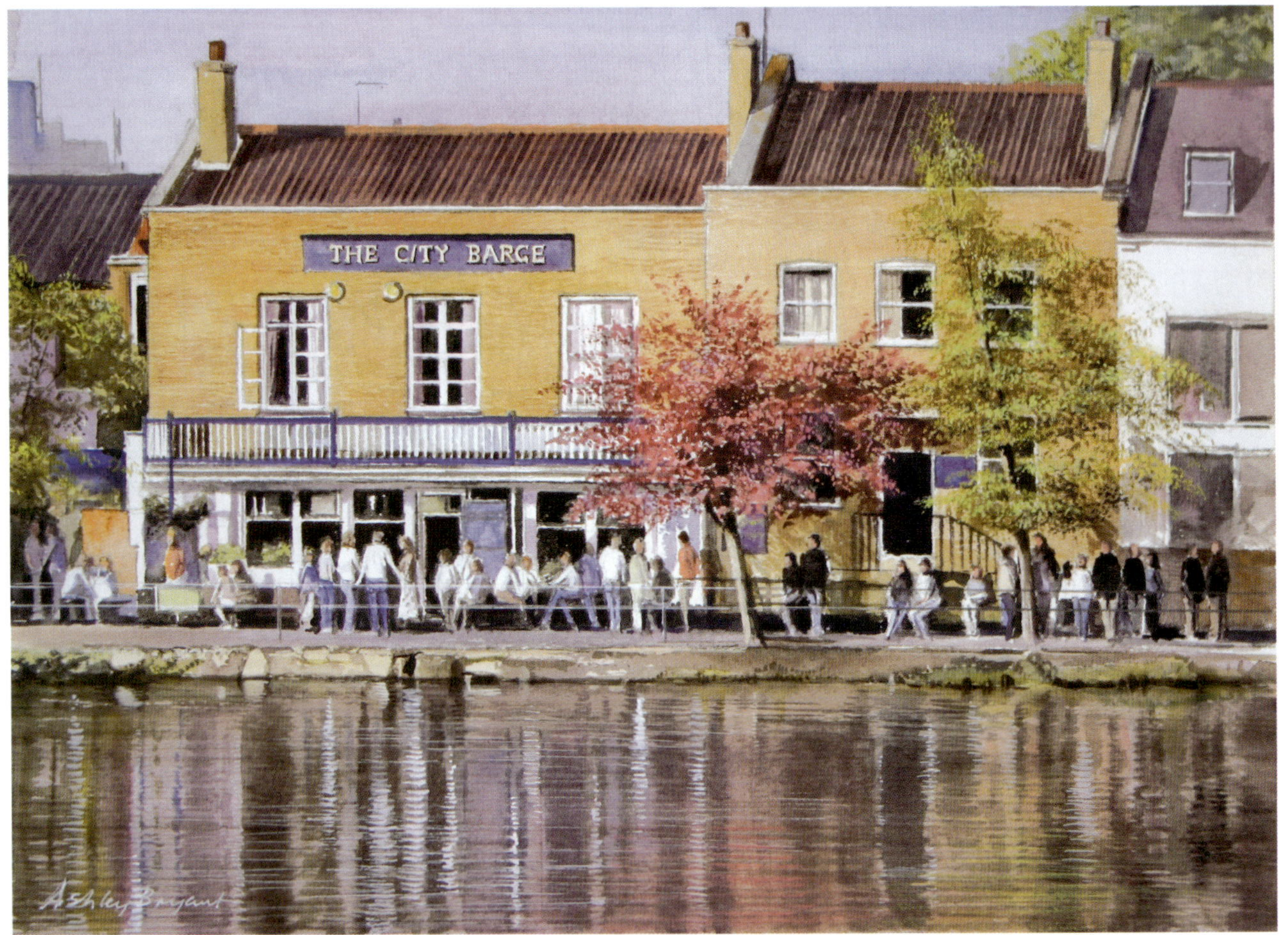

THE THAMES AT STRAND ON THE GREEN
(Opposite Page)
An evening view looking towards Kew Bridge. The official title of the bridge is the "King Edward II Bridge" since the king opened it in 1903.

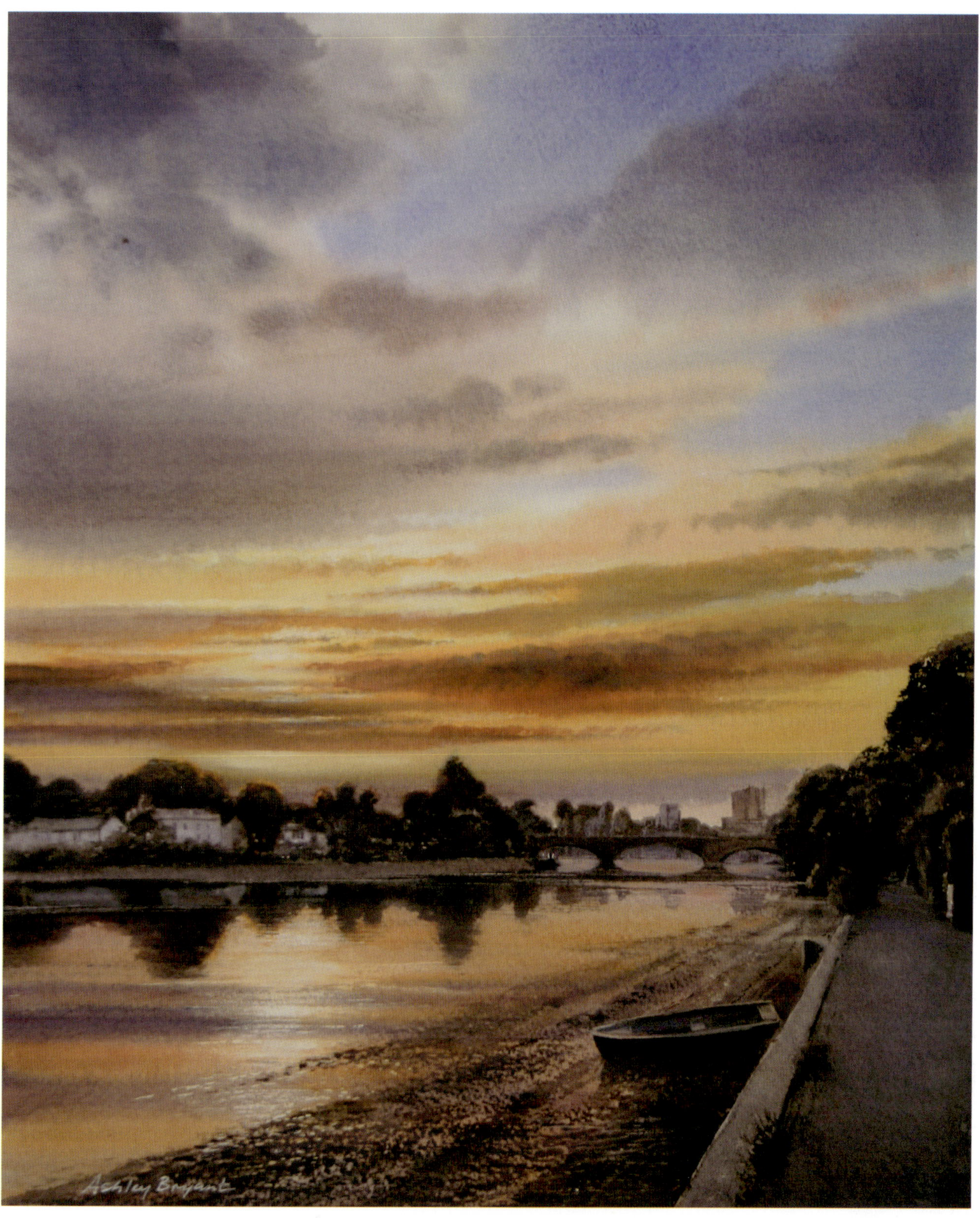

The Thames

HAMMERSMITH

There are several suspension bridges across the Thames but none so ornate as Hammersmith Bridge. Swirling acanthus designs sit on massive cast iron bases to provide anchorage for the suspension chains, and the towers are adorned with great golden medallions and tipped with finials. In truth, we could expect nothing less from its designer, the indefatigable Sir Joseph Bazalgette, a Victorian engineer in the Brunelian mould who worked tirelessly for eighteen hours a day on his ground-breaking projects. Bazalgette was also responsible for the design of a number of other Thames bridges, each one unique in design. His design for Tower Bridge, both practical and original, was rejected.

The highlight of the year at Hammersmith is the Oxford and Cambridge boat race, an event which sees the banks of the river packed solid with spectators. However, the best views are provided from the verandas of the riverside properties, and it is hardly surprising that they are packed to overflowing. The races – for there are two, since the main event is preceded by the "second string" crews of Goldie and Isis, pass by disappointingly quickly when you watch from the bank, but nobody worries unduly as it is party time in Hammersmith.

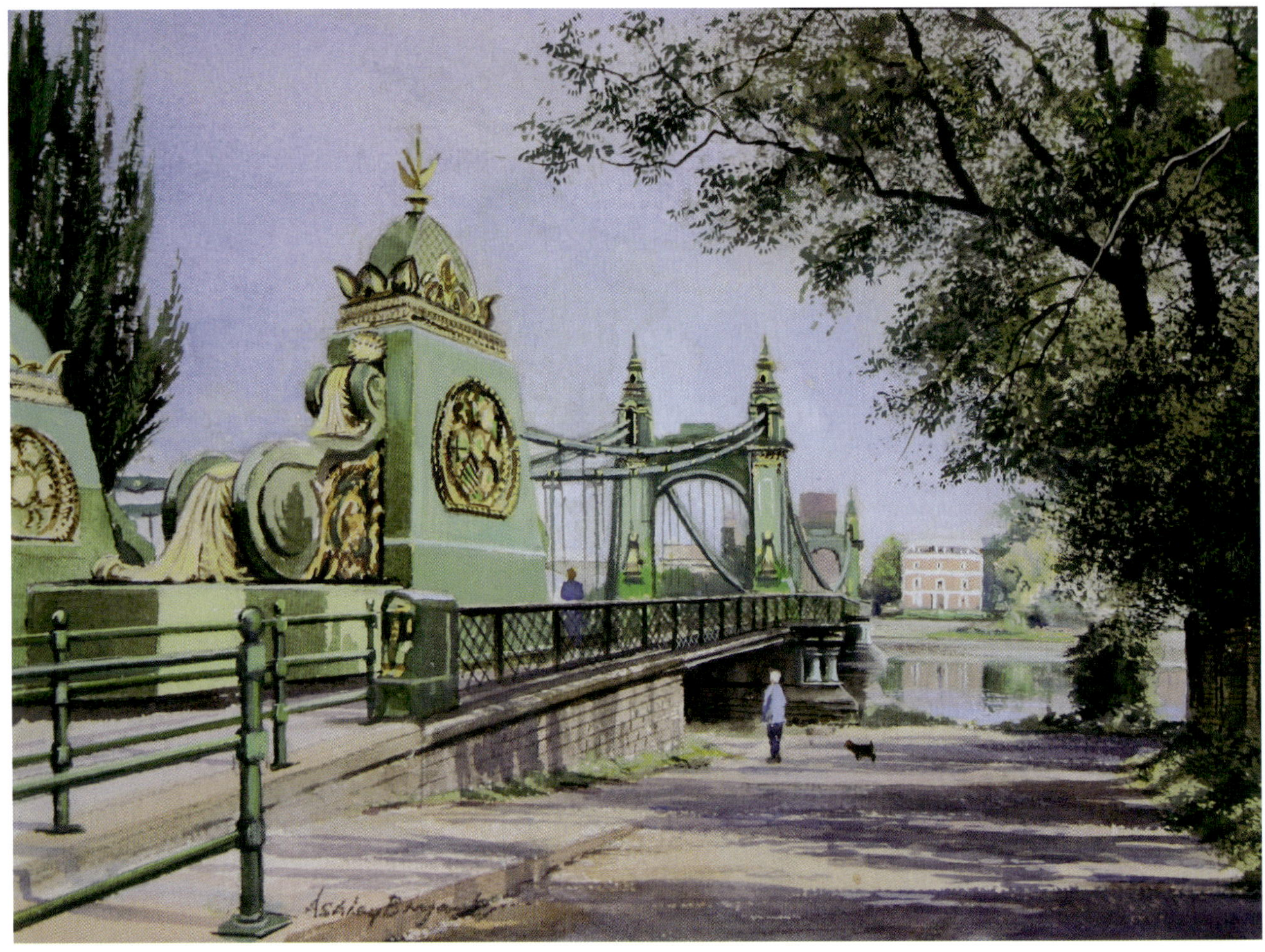

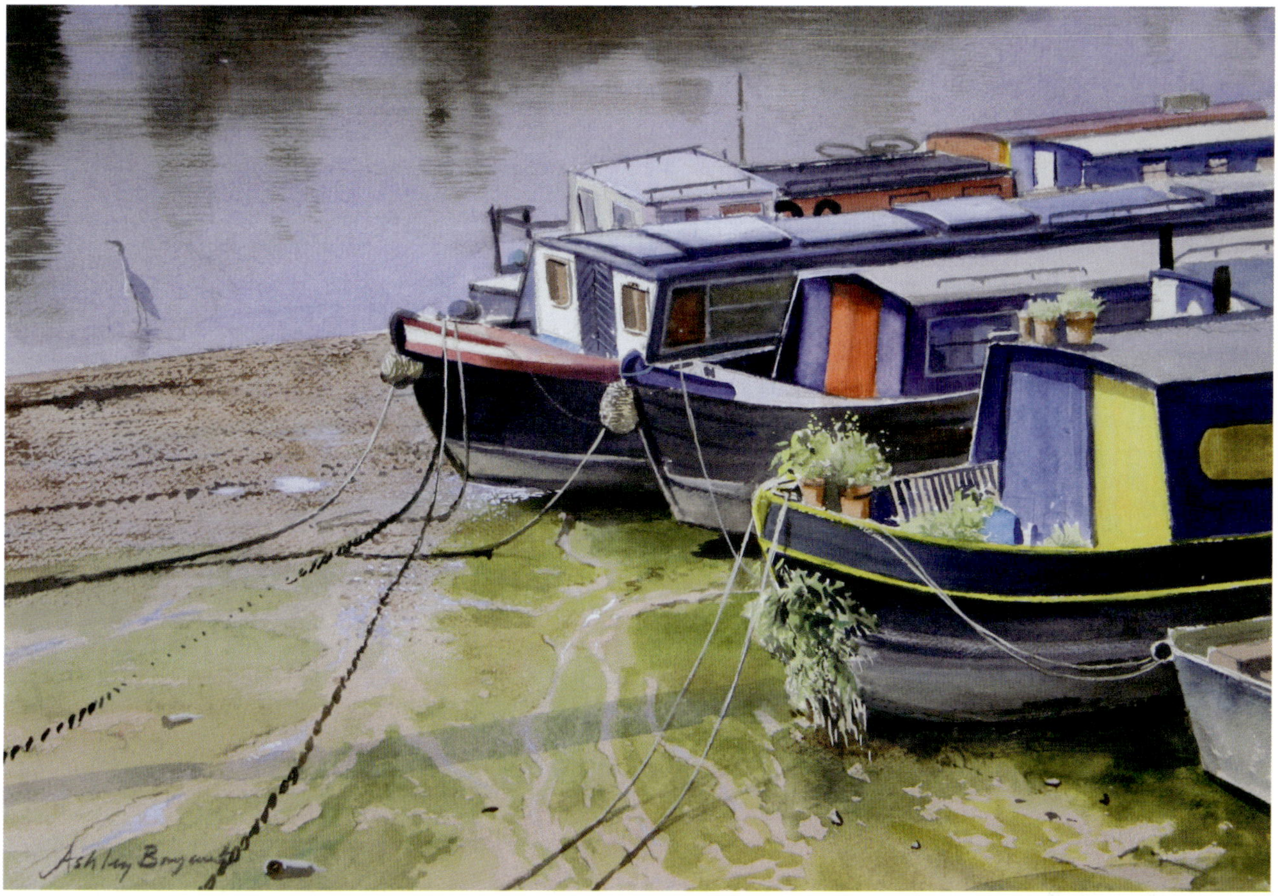

HAMMERSMITH BRIDGE
(Opposite Page)
The ornate structure of Sir Joseph Bazalgette's bridge is seen in this view from the south bank. Huge cast iron supports provide anchorage for the suspension chains although their bulk is disguised in the flowing lines and embellishment of the design.

HOUSEBOATS
(Above)
Several groups of houseboats are moored along the north bank of the river at Hammersmith, some appearing to be permanent fixtures. Numerous herons fish in the shallows, and one is seen ghost-like as it stands motionless in the water.

THE BOAT RACE
(Below)
In this quickly produced pen and wash drawing, Oxford and Cambridge are neck and neck near Hammersmith Bridge. Oxford in the dark blue vests is the nearer crew. This annual event draws huge crowds along the course from Putney to Mortlake.

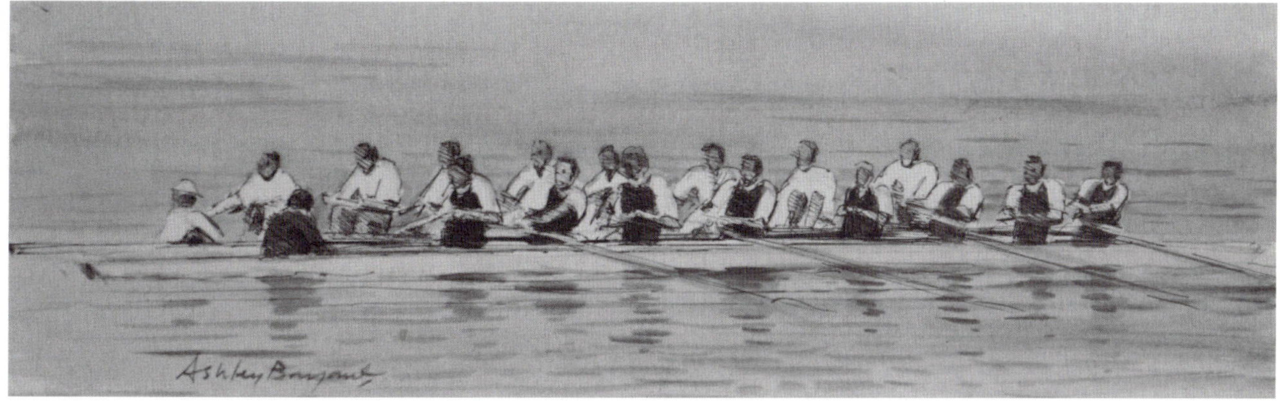

CHELSEA

The Thames at Chelsea provides a wide range of paintable subjects. Spanning the river is a favourite of many Londoners, the dainty Albert Bridge. It provides an eye-catching spectacle at night, lit up and mirrored in the Thames. It was opened in 1873, requiring strenthening a few years later, ultimately being propped up with piers in 1973. Amusingly, it still bears notices at each end cautioning soldiers to break step when crossing – the rhythm of marching was considered to be a danger to the structure. In contrast, the Lotts Road power station is an artistic challenge with its grime and stark functionality. It looms large near the riverside and is seen best from the Battersea bank. Industrial subjects are evocative of specific times in our history; they are interesting and even fascinating but do not generally make saleable paintings.

Chelsea Marina provides another change of scene. Here, angular geometry and slabs of bold colour – shapes of blue water, sleek white hulls and bold architecture of surrounding buildings stimulate the imagination. When a shift is made from representational art endless possibilities present themselves and I hope my next book will focus on these examples of creative art.

For my main painting I chose a view with a foreground of houseboats, of which there are many at Chelsea. Elegance is sacrificed for living space, but summer brings out plants and hanging baskets to enhance the scene. Living so close requires good relationships with neighbours, some of whom are rich and famous. Cheyne Walk boasted many famous names. Rosetti and Whistler were some of its greatest artists, whilst Brunel, Mrs Pankhurst and George Elliot added variety to the spice of the area.

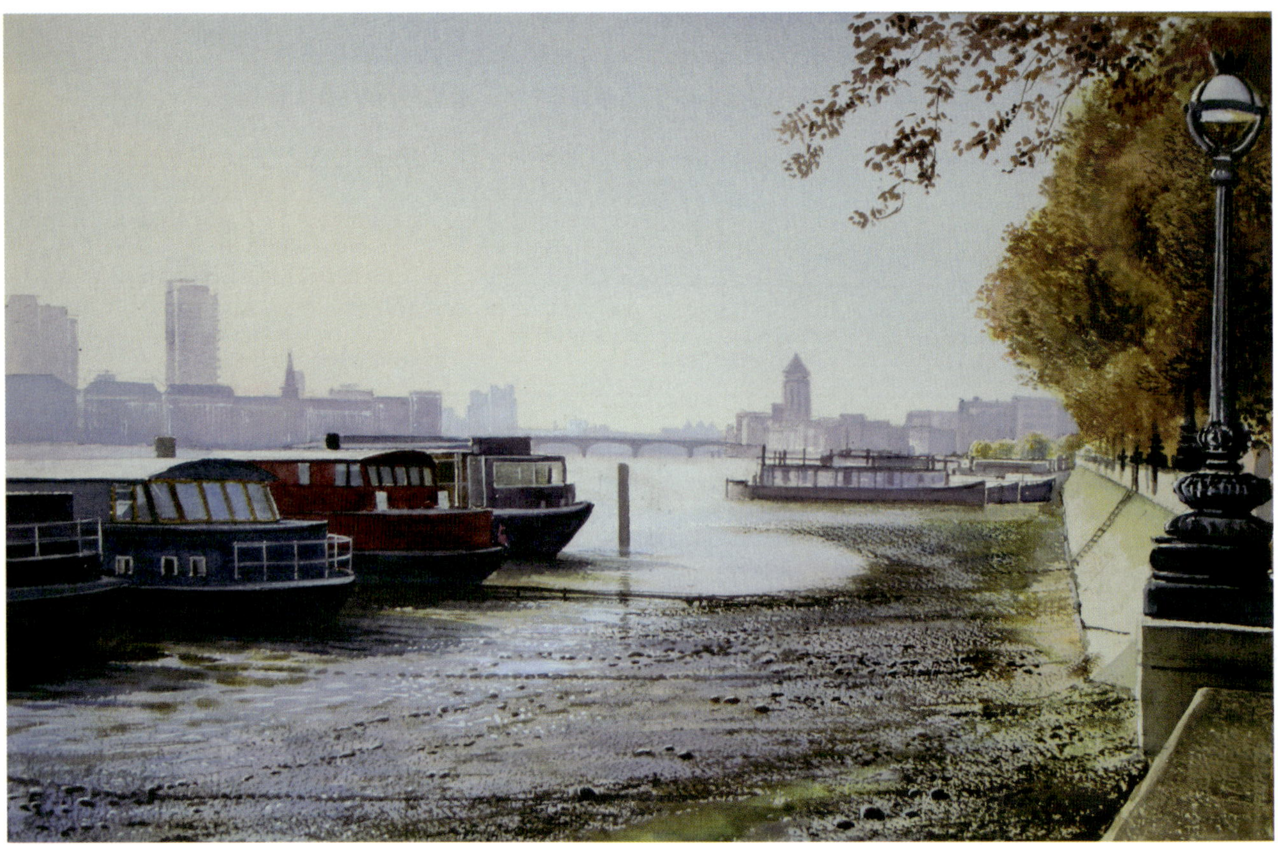

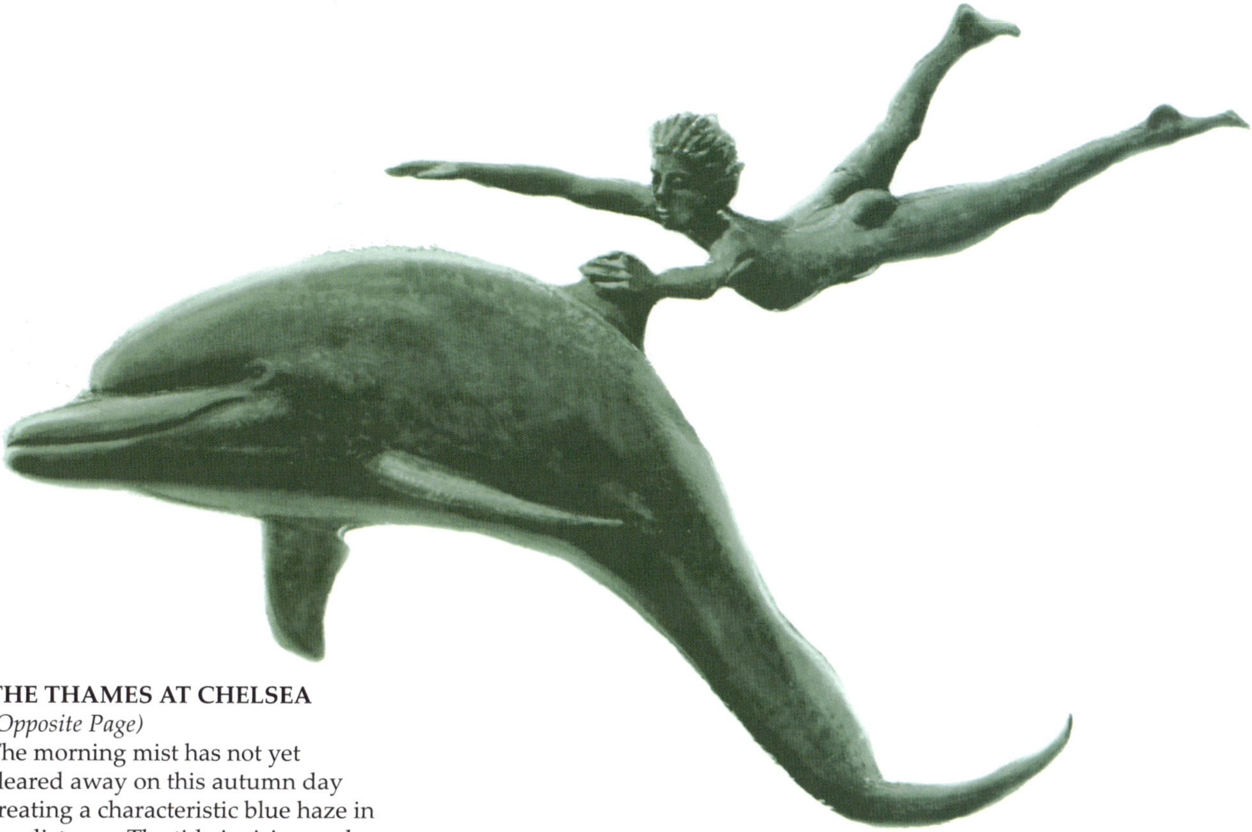

THE THAMES AT CHELSEA
(Opposite Page)
The morning mist has not yet cleared away on this autumn day creating a characteristic blue haze in the distance. The tide is rising and will quickly fill the gap between the house boats and the Embankment wall by Cheyne Walk.

BOY WITH A DOLPHIN
(Above)
I hope I have done justice to David Wynne's wonderful bronze sculpture that has graced the riverside at Chelsea since 1975. I have admired it since the day it was erected and it just had to be included in this book.

THE ALBERT BRIDGE
(Right)
I had all kinds of ideas for portraying this bridge and leaned towards a night time scene when the illuminations were reflected in the water. However, whilst on a boat trip from Kew to Westminster late one afternoon I took a photograph of the bridge and liked the way the water swirled behind the boat with the bridge practically silhouetted against the sky.

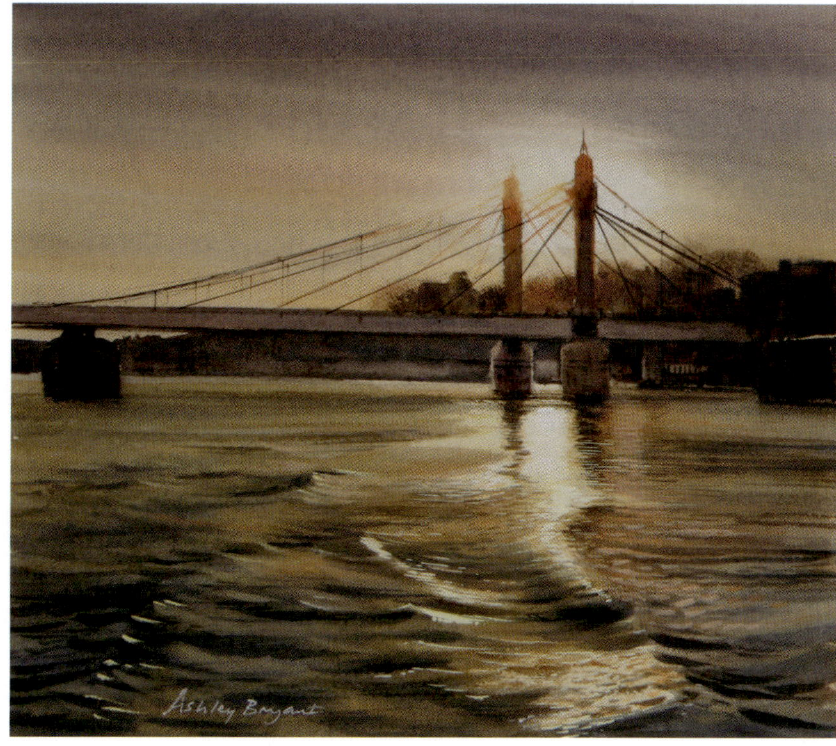

BATTERSEA

ST MARY'S CHURCH, BATTERSEA
(Below)
This church is reputed to conduct the highest number of weddings in Britain. It is undoubtedly in a delightful setting with opportunities for imaginative wedding photos.

BATTERSEA POWER STATION
(Opposite Page Below)
The distinctive outline of the power station looms above the river in this misty scene. It has featured as a setting or a backdrop to many films and television productions and has been portrayed on album covers, such as Pink Floyd's *Animals*.

Ask any Londoner to list Battersea's most famous features and they would have no hesitation in saying the power station, the park and the dog's home. The formidable power station, said to be the largest brick structure in the world stands by the Thames, its towering chimneys universally recognisable. It was actually declared a heritage site in 1980, three years before it ceased to generate electricity, and there it remains, a gaunt shell. A proposed redevelopment of the 38 acre site to include hotels, cinemas, shops and flats has met with much opposition.

The nearby church of St. Mary's stands almost on the banks of the river and makes a charming scene with its ever-present moored barges. The church is dwarfed by ribbon development of residential property along the Thames. Hundreds of thousands of people now enjoy riverside views and are developing affection and respect for the river.

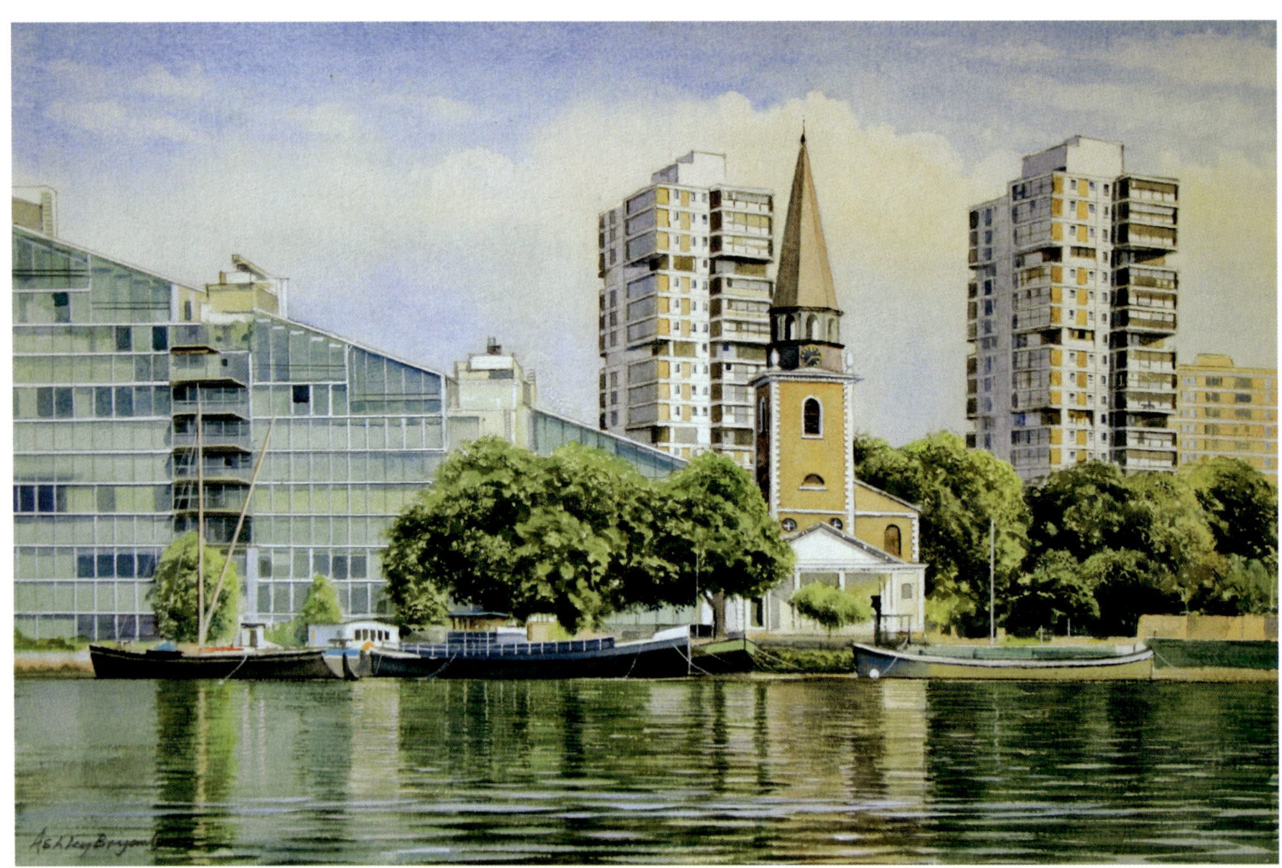

THE PEACE PAGODA
(Right)
A pencil sketch of this beautiful structure which serves to remind people of the goal of world peace. It sits beside the river in Battersea Park.

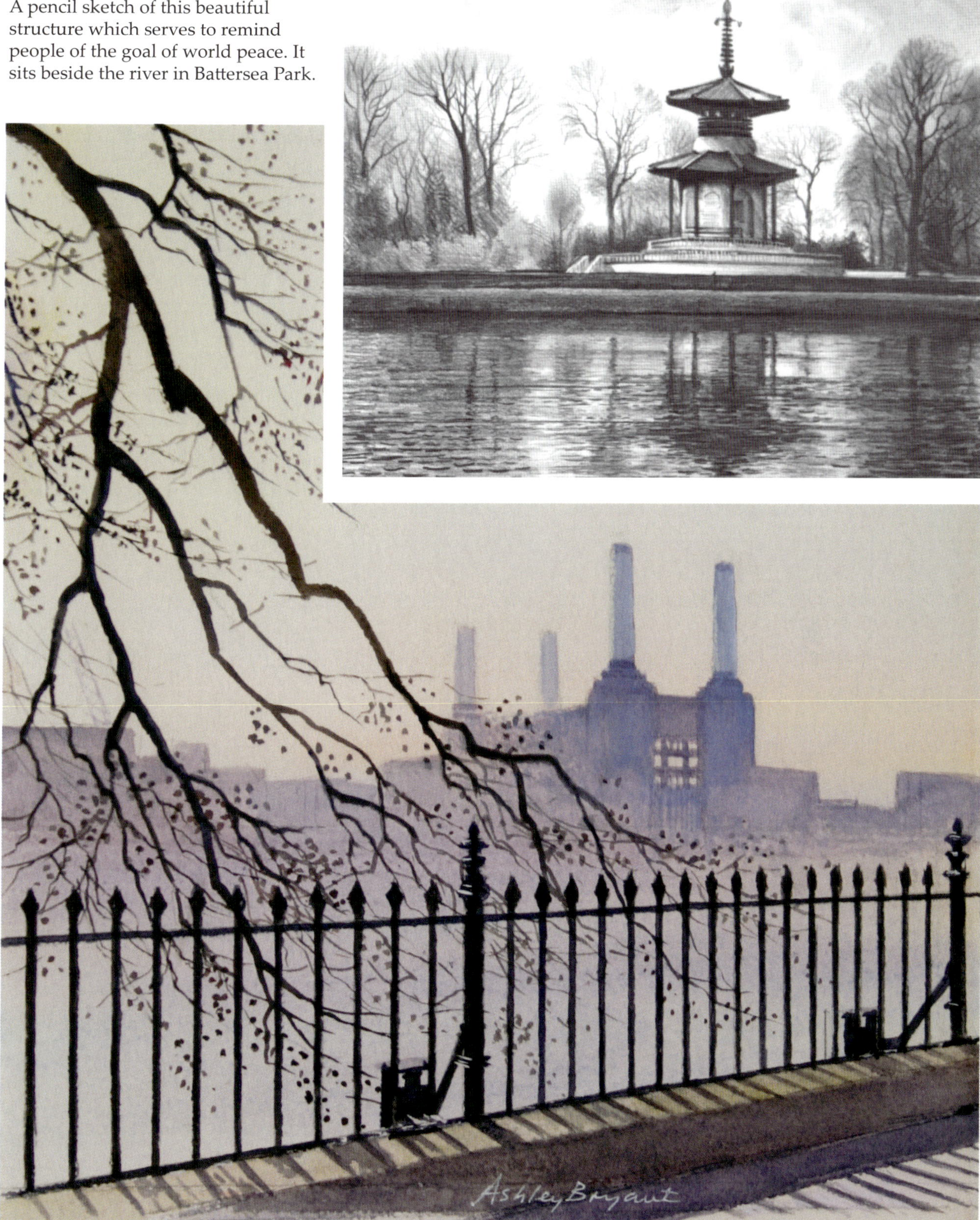

LAMBETH

Until the nineteenth century there was little development at Lambeth. The most historic building along this waterfront is Lamberth Palace, the London residence of the Archbishops of Canterbury. When it was constructed in 1207, the land was marshy and isolated, but it had the advantage of being close to Westminster and the king. Like other important riverside buildings, the main entrance to the palace was a water-gate, boats providing the main means of transport. The palace has been greatly modified since it was originally constructed; much that is visible today, including the great gatehouse, is Tudor. The palace garden is one of the oldest and largest in London. Next to the palace stands the church of St. Mary at Lambeth, now the home of the Museum of Garden History.

THE TUDOR GATEHOUSE
(Opposite Page)
The viewpoint for this painting is along the pathway to St Mary's church. It scans across the corner of the Tudor gatehouse to the palace and across the river to Westminster. The church incorporates the Museum of Garden History and makes an ideal conclusion to an interesting walk along the south bank.

THE THAMES AT LAMBETH
(Below)
In this sepia watercolour the palace is seen across the river on the east side of Lambeth Bridge. The church of St Mary stands on the right, whilst the "Gherkin" appears surprisingly on the extreme left. This modern building is located in the City but its position is distorted by the bends of the river.

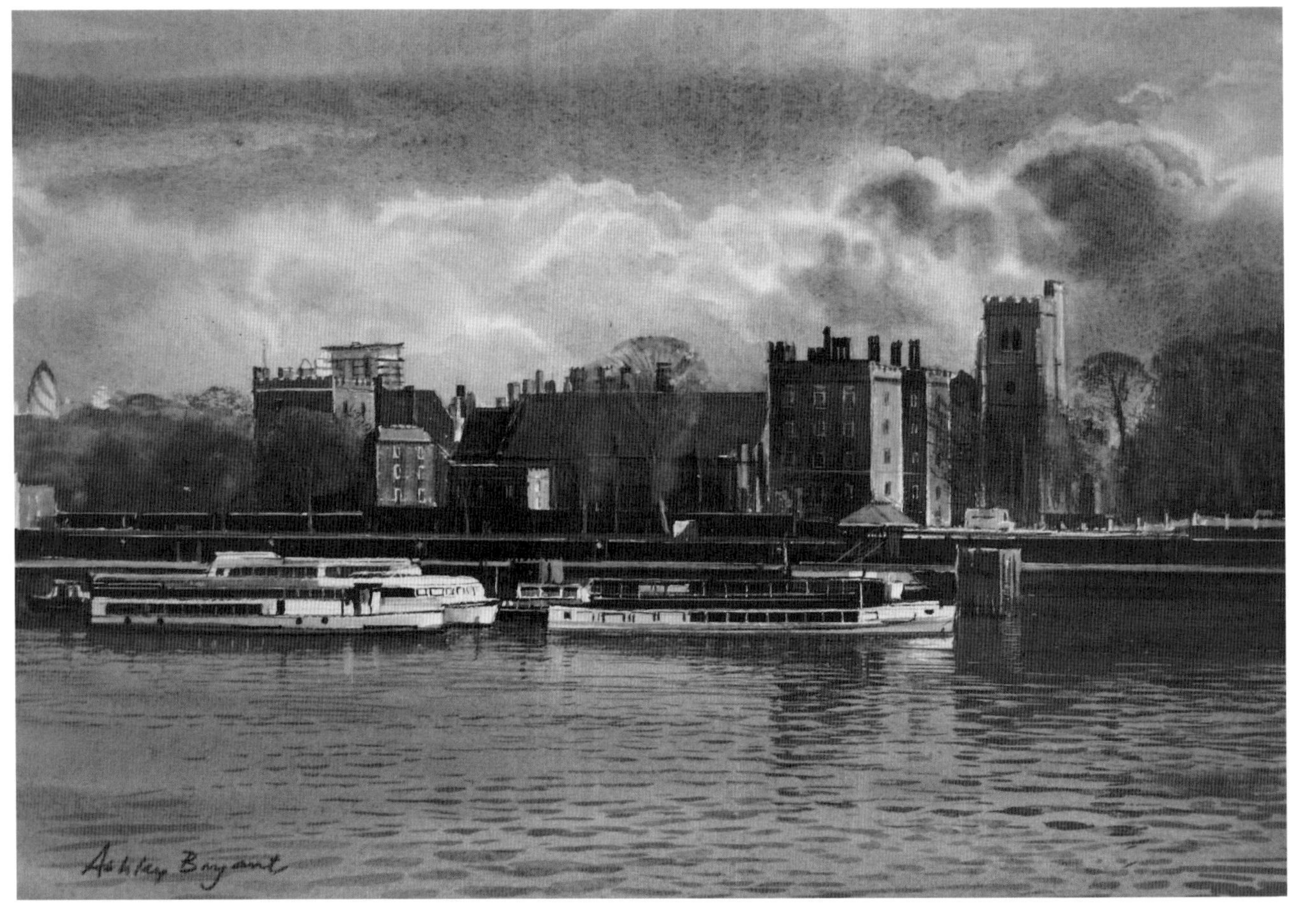

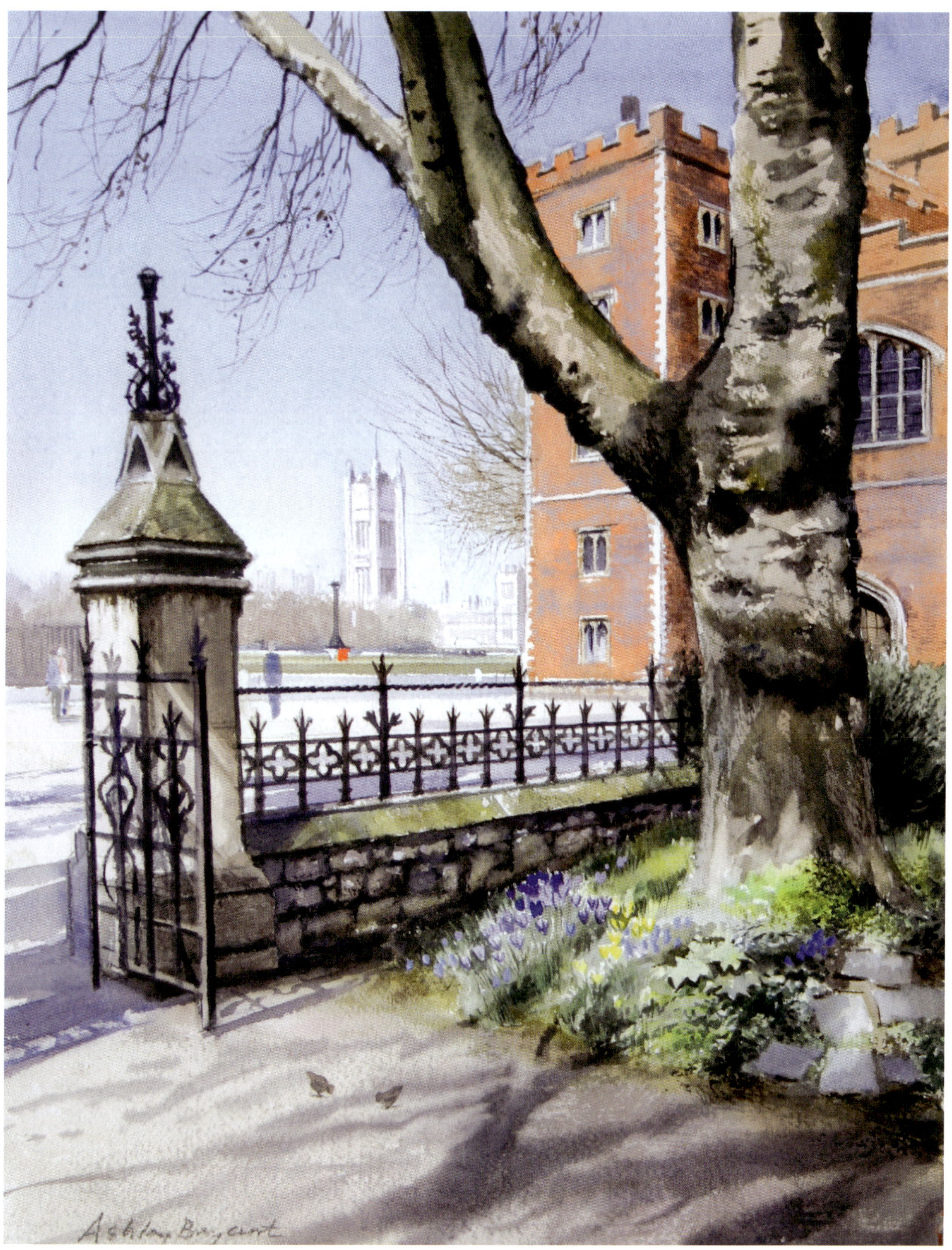

WESTMINSTER

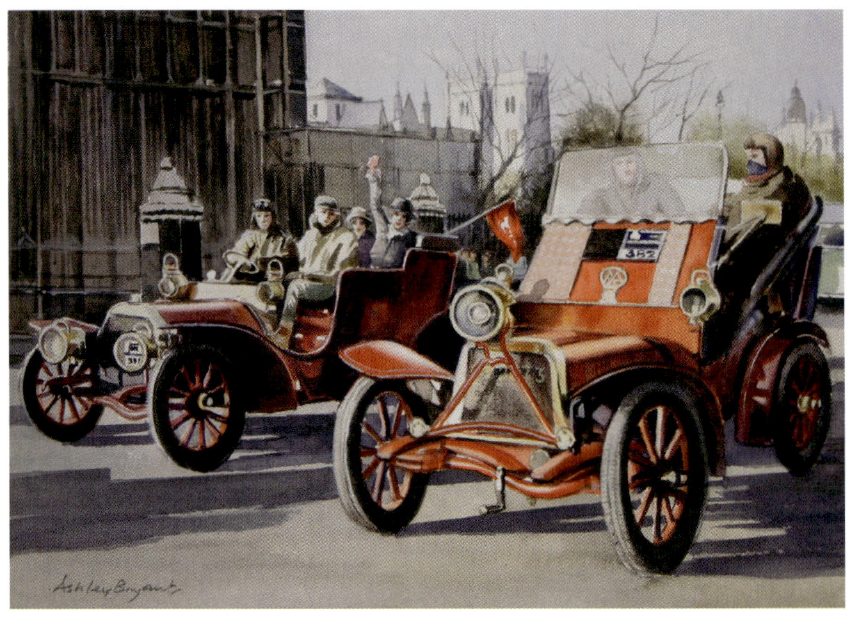

LONDON TO BRIGHTON RALLY
(Right)
An early start is required to reach Westminster for the annual London to Brighton rally of vintage cars. In the painting two vehicles are about to cross Westminster Bridge for their journey which could take up to six hours, with occupants open to the elements on a cold November day. Advice from a veteran campaigner was to "drink as little as possible".

THE PALACE OF WESTMINSTER
(Opposite Page)
The gleaming Victoria Tower dominates the Palace of Westminster and is framed by the arches of the plane trees in the adjoining gardens. Rodin's statue "The Burghers of Calais" is located near the foot of the buildings. The towers of Westminster Abbey are obscured by trees on the left, whilst the London Eye almost disappears off the right side of the painting.

BOUDICCA
(Left)
This dramatic statue by Thomas Thorneycroft shows a determined Boudicca and her daughters charging into battle. Its location at Westminster symbolises opposition against oppression and tyranny.

The Palace of Westminster presents a magnificent spectacle as it lines the Thames waterfront, its pale amber stonework glowing in the sunlight. The original, medieval Houses of Parliament burnt down in 1834, an event that was captured by Turner in several of his paintings. The re-building, to the designs of Charles Barry, ushered in a revival of Gothic architecture beloved by the Victorians. Almost any position across the south bank provides stunning views, but the London Eye now offers a completely different perspective and is especially interesting at night when the illuminated panorama is reflected in the river. Westminster's traditional views have been painted by some of the greatest artists, and none better than Monet, who produced several outstanding paintings, some in glowing colours and others in subtle renderings which captured the mist and gloom of London in the early 1900s.

The bustle of Parliament Square is left behind as you enter the gardens adjoining the Palace of Westminster. This is where I selected my viewpoint for the painting below, choosing a time of the year when leaves did not obscure the view of the Victoria Tower. Rodin's famous sculpture "The Burghers of Calais" is sited here in the gardens, and Westminster is home to other notable statues including a proud Richard the Lionheart, a stolid Winston Churchill and my all-time favourite – Boudicca and her daughters in a speeding chariot.

For centuries, London Bridge was the only bridge over the Thames in the capital. Proposals for other bridges were met with opposition from watermen whose interests and livelihood were threatened. Westminster Bridge was the first to break this stranglehold. It was completed in the mid-eighteenth century and paved the way for other London bridges.

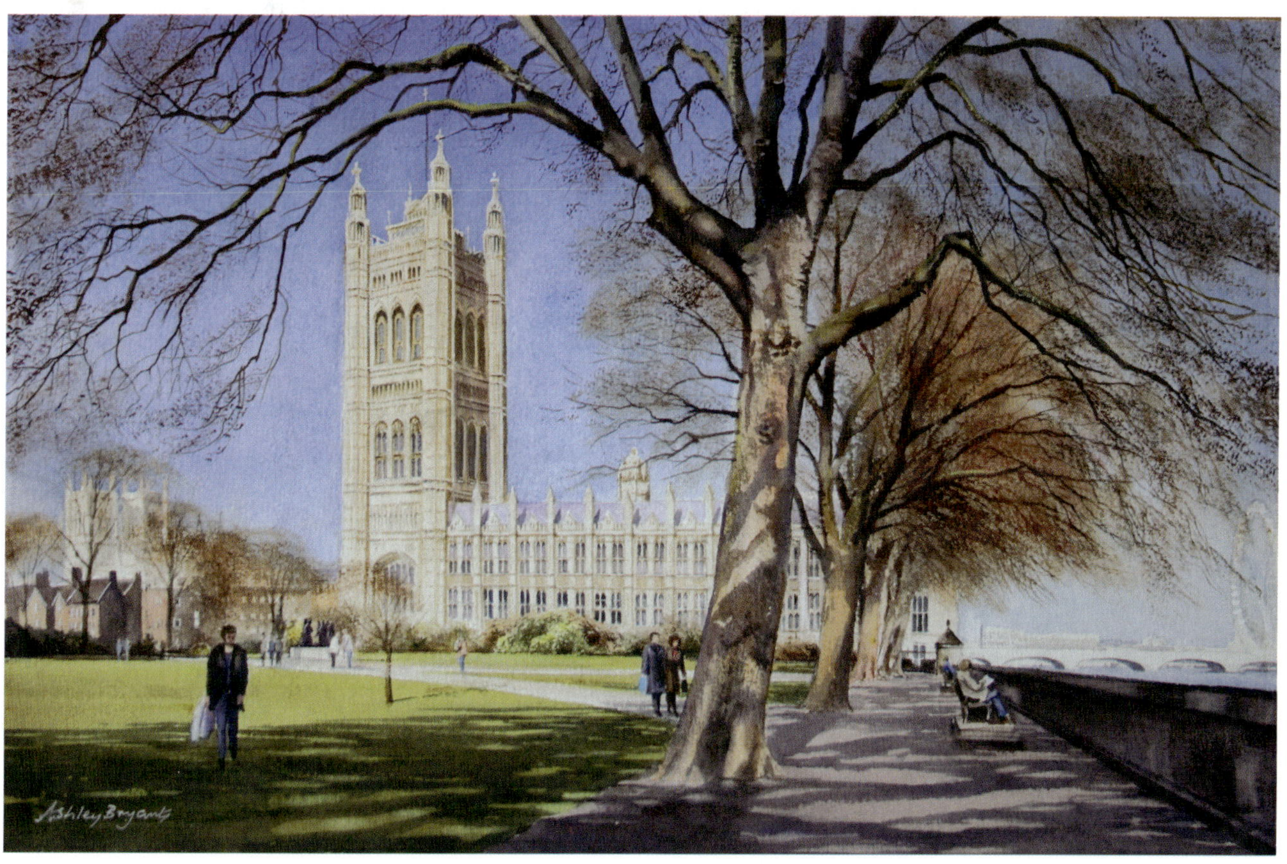

VICTORIA EMBANKMENT

CORMORANT

There was a time when people used to throw food to the black-headed gulls along the Embankment. There are not quite so many of these birds here now; on the other hand, cormorants numbers have significantly increased over recent years. At least this is an indication of the cleanliness of the river and the stocks of fish it supports. These birds typically perch on posts and moored barges holding out their wings to dry.

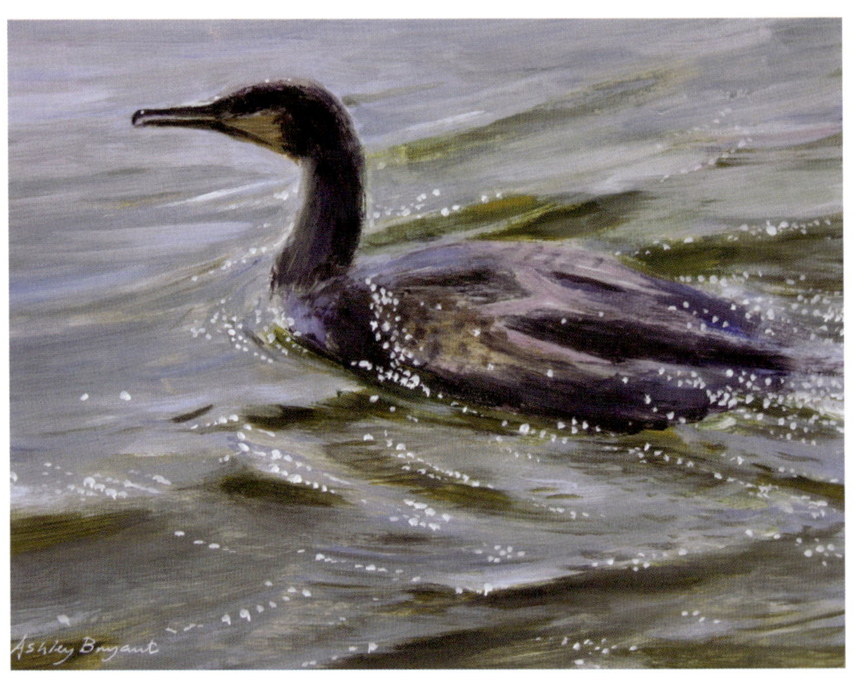

WET MORNING

This quickly produced watercolour captures a dreary autumn morning near Cleopatra's Needle.

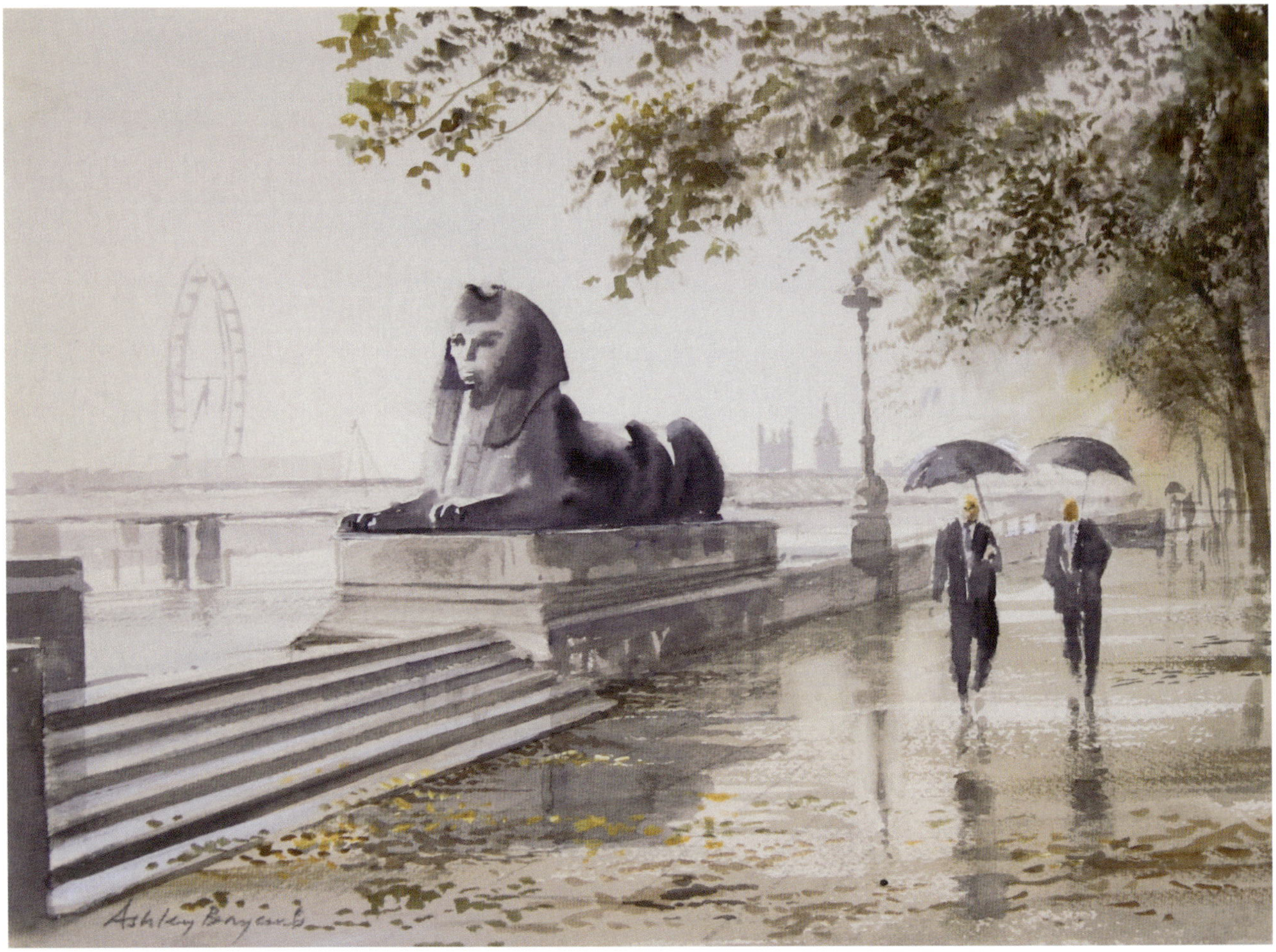

A walk along the Embankment reveals the broad scope of London's riverside with its diverse buildings, bridges, moored boats and bustling activity. These are scenes that inspire artists, poets, writers, musicians and film makers alike. This solidly engineered embankment with its massive granite walls and elaborate lamp standards is a bastion of the London scene. In historic terms it is fairly recent and surprisingly its construction was all down to sewage.

By the mid-nineteenth century the Thames in London was a festering depository of raw sewage. The tide moved it up and down but not away, and the problems escalated. Incredulously, the water companies continued to pump it out for drinking water, declaring it perfectly acceptable, but it had disastrous effects on public health. Dysentery was common, and there were even outbreaks of cholera. The "big stink", as the problem was termed, finally forced the government into action; both houses were, after all, sitting close to the problem. The hero of the hour was Sir Joseph Bazalgette, who completely rebuilt the sewer system of London with so much extra capacity that it is still in use today.

The Victoria Embankment was built to cover these giant sewer and later it also incorporated the Circle and District underground lines. Its wide expanse extended over the Thames foreshore and provided a walkway, road and several gardens – the Embankment we know and cherish today.

VICTORIA EMBANKMENT
This watercolour shows a hazy morning on the Embankment with a view towards the Houses of Parliament and Westminster Bridge. The famous clock tower incorporating "Big Ben" is glimpsed through the trees.

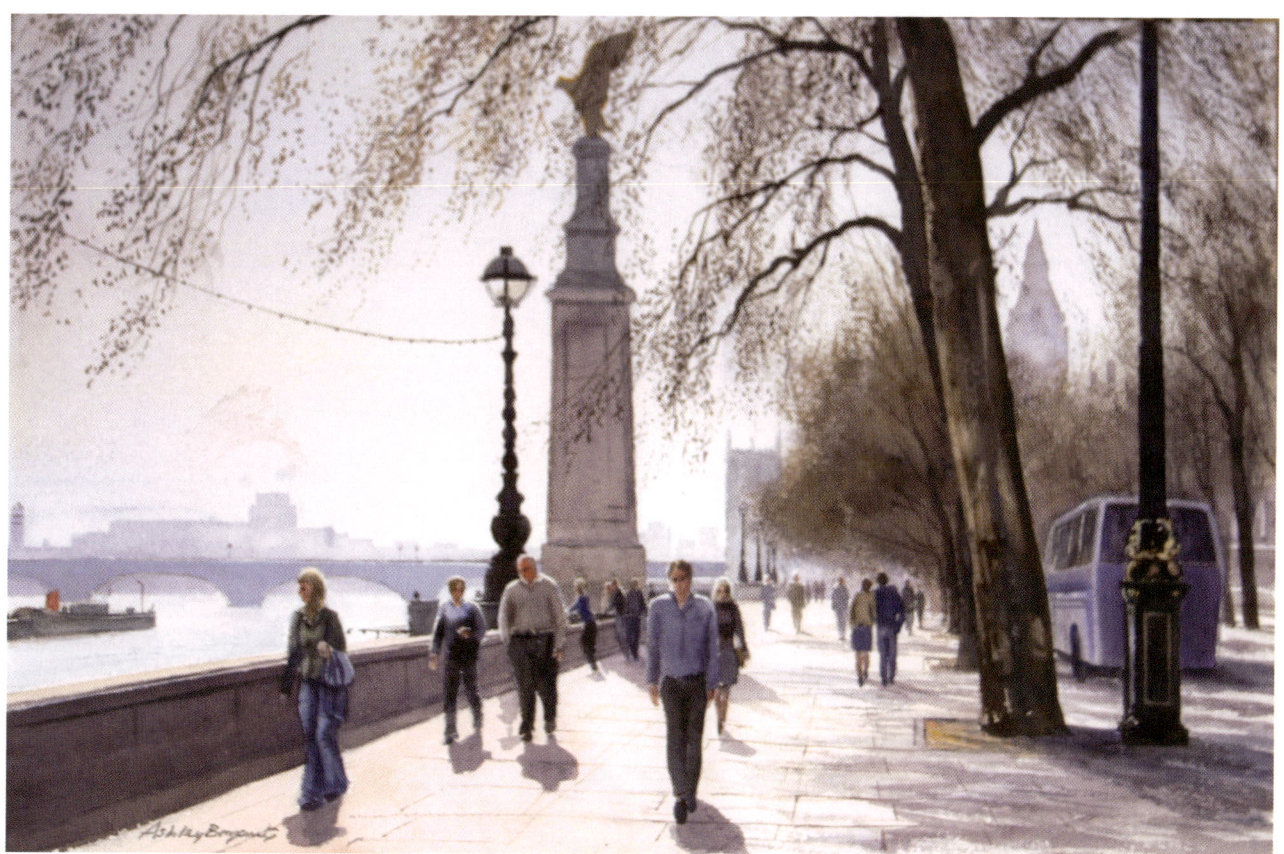

SOUTH BANK

One of London's most interesting walks is along the south bank from Westminster to Tower Bridge. Much has been done in recent years to illuminate the area's varied history and to develop its reputation as a centre for entertainment and culture. The London Eye is a huge attraction and gives a new perspective on the river as it snakes around before disappearing from view many miles away. This is the first of many attractions to take the tourist dollar, but there is no need to spend anything to enjoy this walk. There are street entertainers, bookstalls, green areas in which to relax, buildings to explore, and as always, people to watch. On one occasion I noticed two men fishing by Westminster Bridge; the tall one landed an eel, whilst the short one tried to unhook it from the line, in a kind of music-hall act as they demonstrated the saying "as slippery as an eel". A short distance downstream a street artist was painting a copy of Botticelli's "The Birth of Venus". A huge canvas was taped on to the ground so it could be removed at the end of her working day and taken home. Her rendition was magnificent; she had refused several serious offers from prospective purchasers as her hat steadily filled with £1 coins.

The daunting block of the old Bankside Power Station houses one of London's great new galleries – Tate Modern. Here you will find the cutting edge of modern art, sometimes beautiful, often bizarre, occasionally outrageous, but always thought-provoking. Further downstream, the Bankside Gallery, home of the Royal Watercolour Society, provides a more traditional selection of paintings and exhibitions.

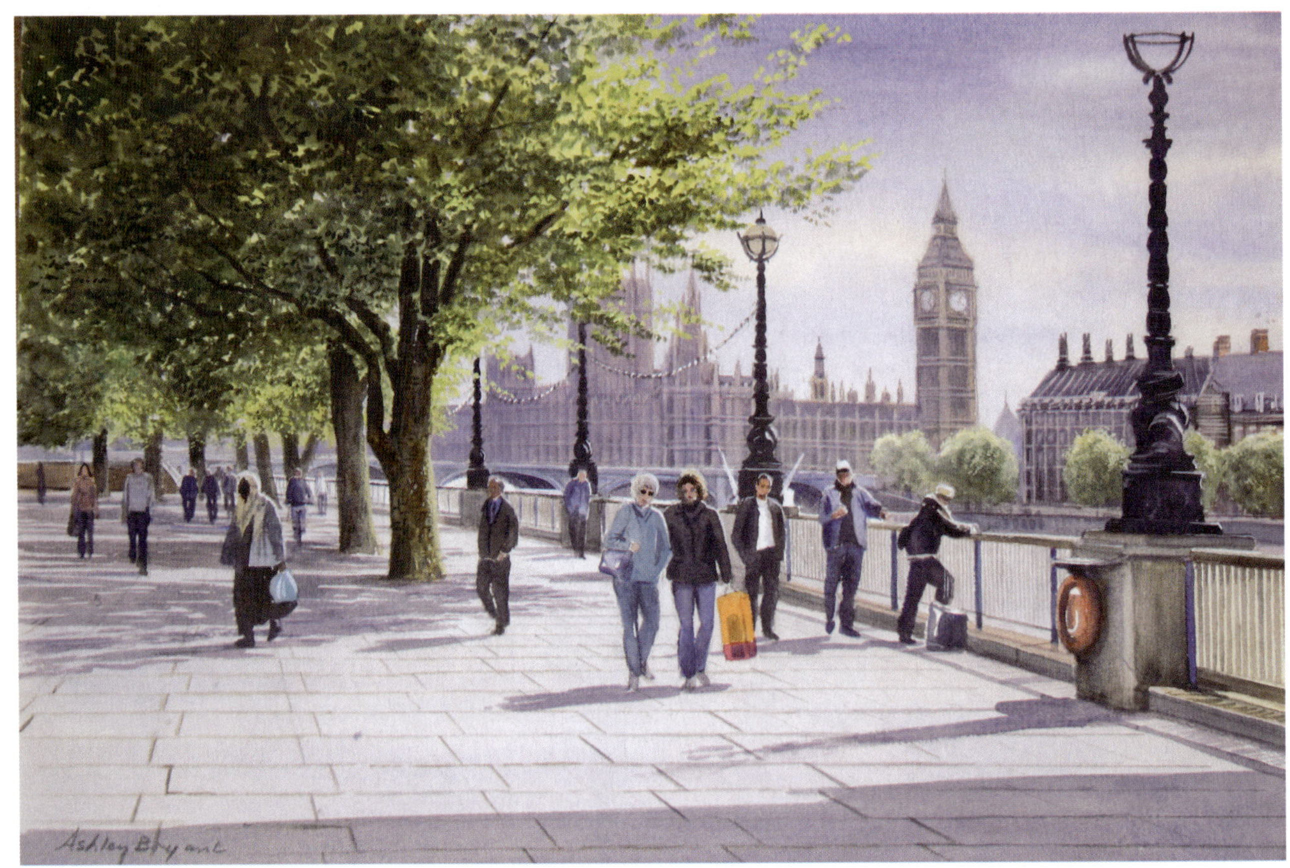

THE LONDON EYE

(Right)

Another quickly produced watercolour on a bleak January day, this view looks upstream towards the London Eye. This massive construction stands 440 feet (135m) high and from the top on a clear day you can see for 25 miles.

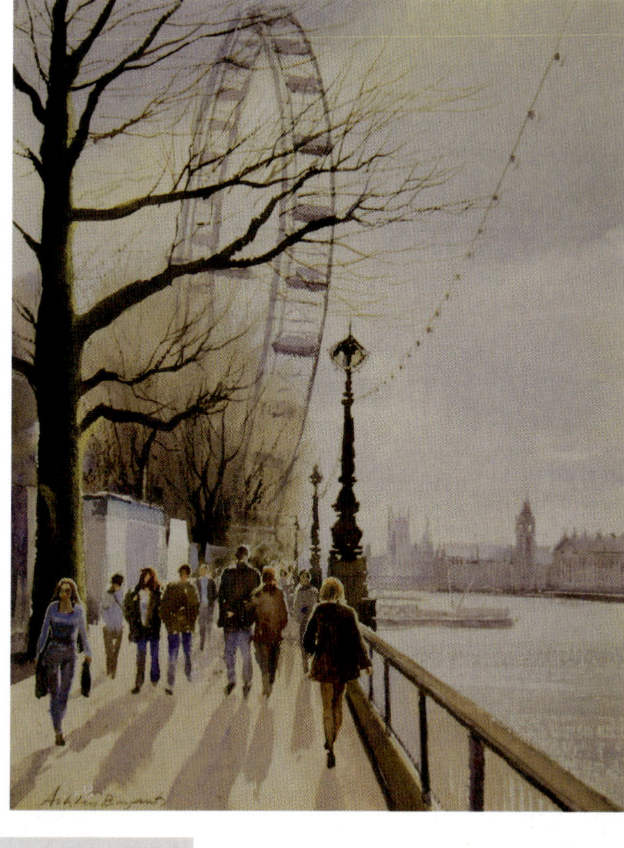

THE SOUTH BANK

(Opposite Page)

This broad walkway, a short distance below Westminster Bridge, provides an excellent view of the Houses of Parliament.

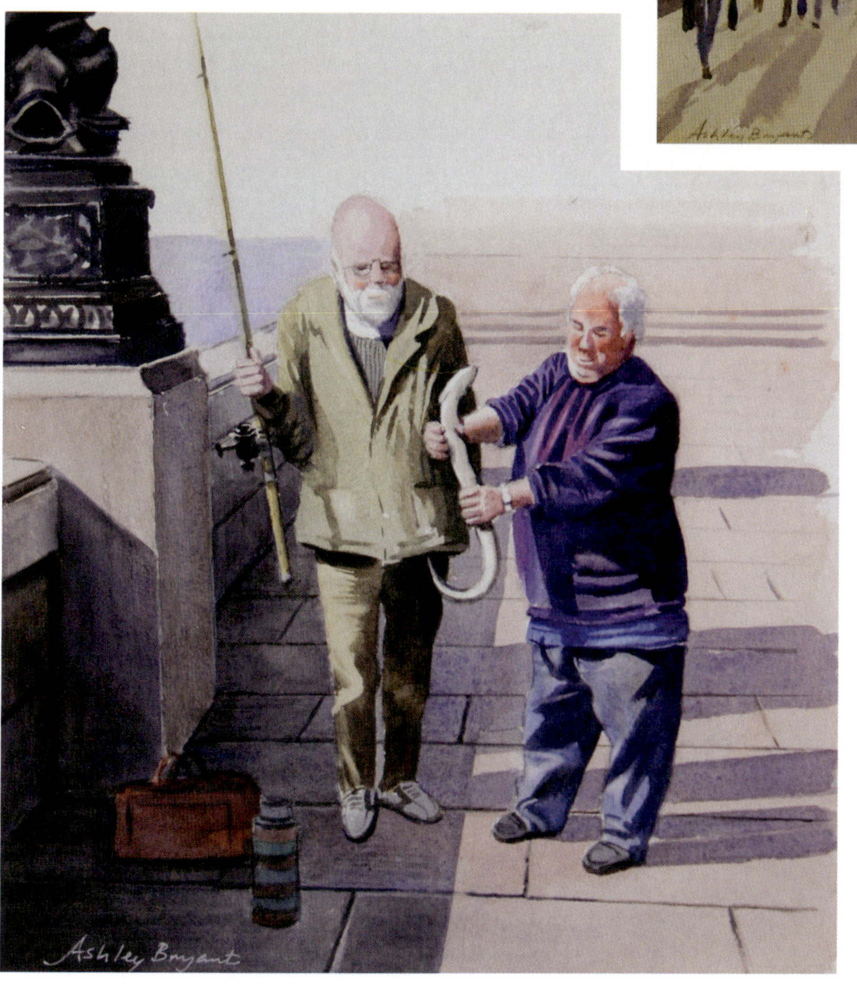

EEL CATCHERS

(Left)

A recent survey announced that eighty different species of fish are found in the Thames in central London, which includes salt water and fresh water varieties. The Thames is now the cleanest major river in Europe and even salmon have returned. I just had to include a painting of these two characters looking rather dubiously at their latest catch.

SOUTH BANK

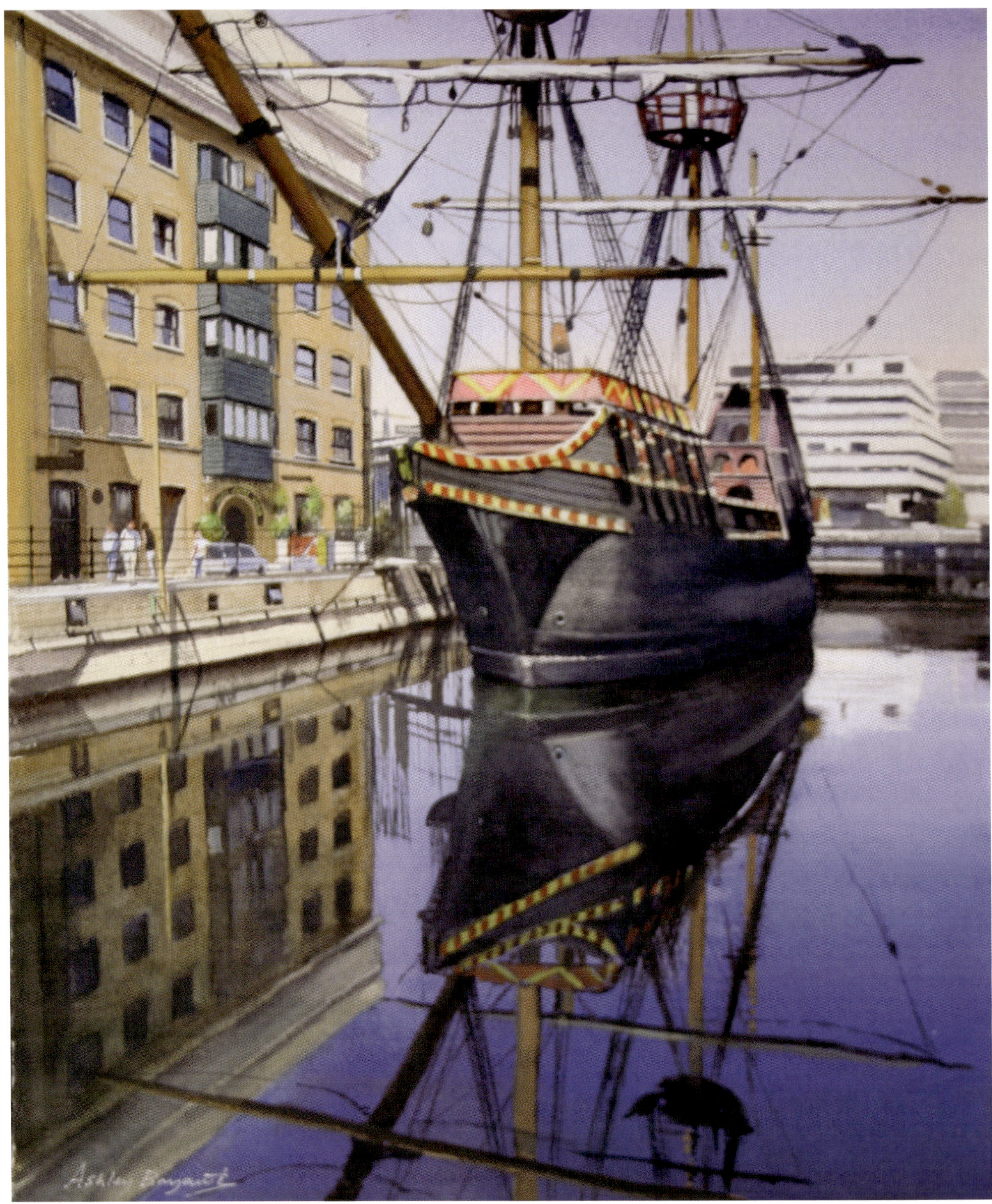

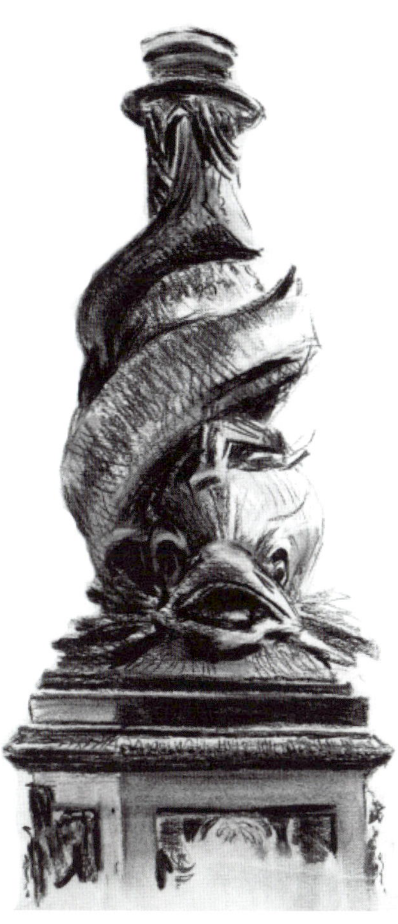

LAMP STANDARD
(Left)
The ornate lamp standards along London's embankments feature a mythical creature based on a sturgeon – some argue it is a dolphin.

THE GOLDEN HINDE
(Opposite Page)
An ocean going replica of Drake's "Golden Hinde" is moored in the docks near St Mary Overie.

STREET ENTERTAINER
(Right)
Weekends are the best times to enjoy a variety of street entertainment along the south bank.

THE REBIRTH OF VENUS
(Below)
This talented artist was carefully reproducing Botticelli's "The Birth of Venus" on a huge canvas.

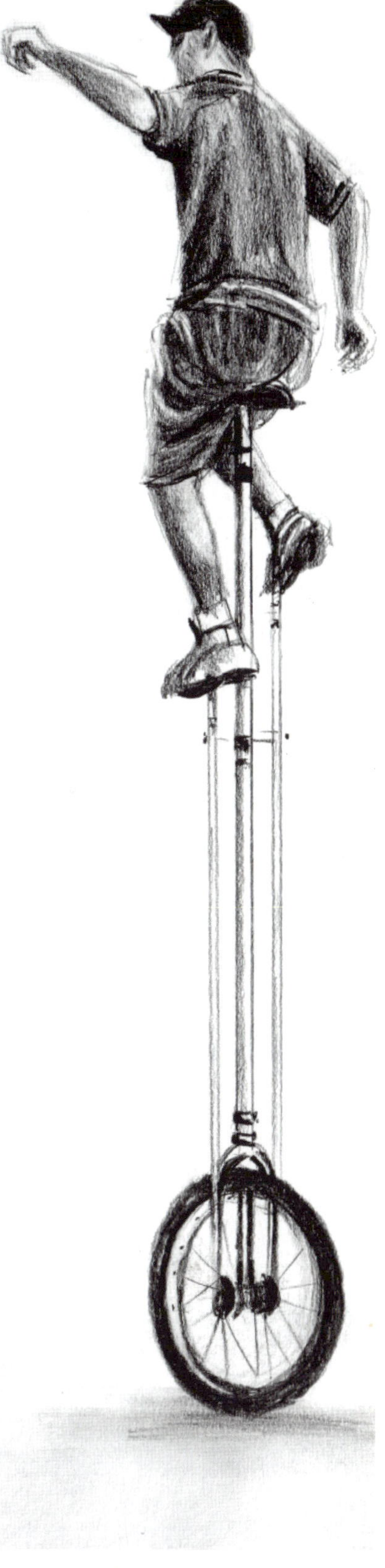

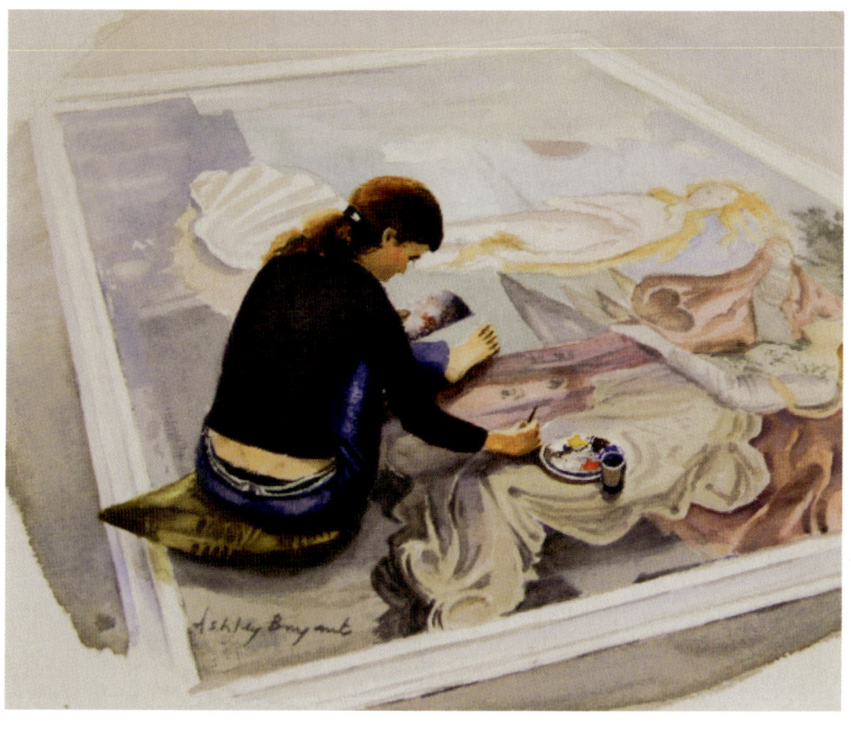

SOUTH BANK

Until about 1780, Southwark was the only significant development on the south of the river. Lacking the protection of city walls but avoiding the restrictions of the city fathers, the seedier side of entertainment developed here, with ale houses, bear baiting, cock fighting, brothels and theatres. It might seem odd to include theatres in this list, but they were considered to be dens of iniquity and sedition by the authorities. It was feared that plays could stir up all kinds of dissent and promote anti-establishment views to their captive audiences. It is remarkable that some of the greatest gems of English literature, including works by Shakespeare and Marlowe, flowed from these places. The original Globe Theatre has been recreated by the Thames and packed audiences enjoy the plays in the spirit of the original theatre.

Southwark Cathedral was built in 1106 on the site of previous religious buildings. It experienced a low point in Tudor times, when pigs were kept there, and was later reprieved and enlarged, finally becoming a cathedral in 1905. The nearby palace of the Bishops of Winchester also dates from the twelfth century, and a remaining gable wall with rose window offers a glimpse of its former glory. Another gem of history is the Clink prison, the ancient jail which gave its name to the term for imprisonment.

In a most enviable site by Tower Bridge stands the glass offices of the Mayor and Assembly of London, designed to convey the "transparency of the democratic process". A larger glass structure is proposed for the area – the London Bridge Tower, which is set to become one of Europe's tallest buildings, and is already known as the "Shard of Glass".

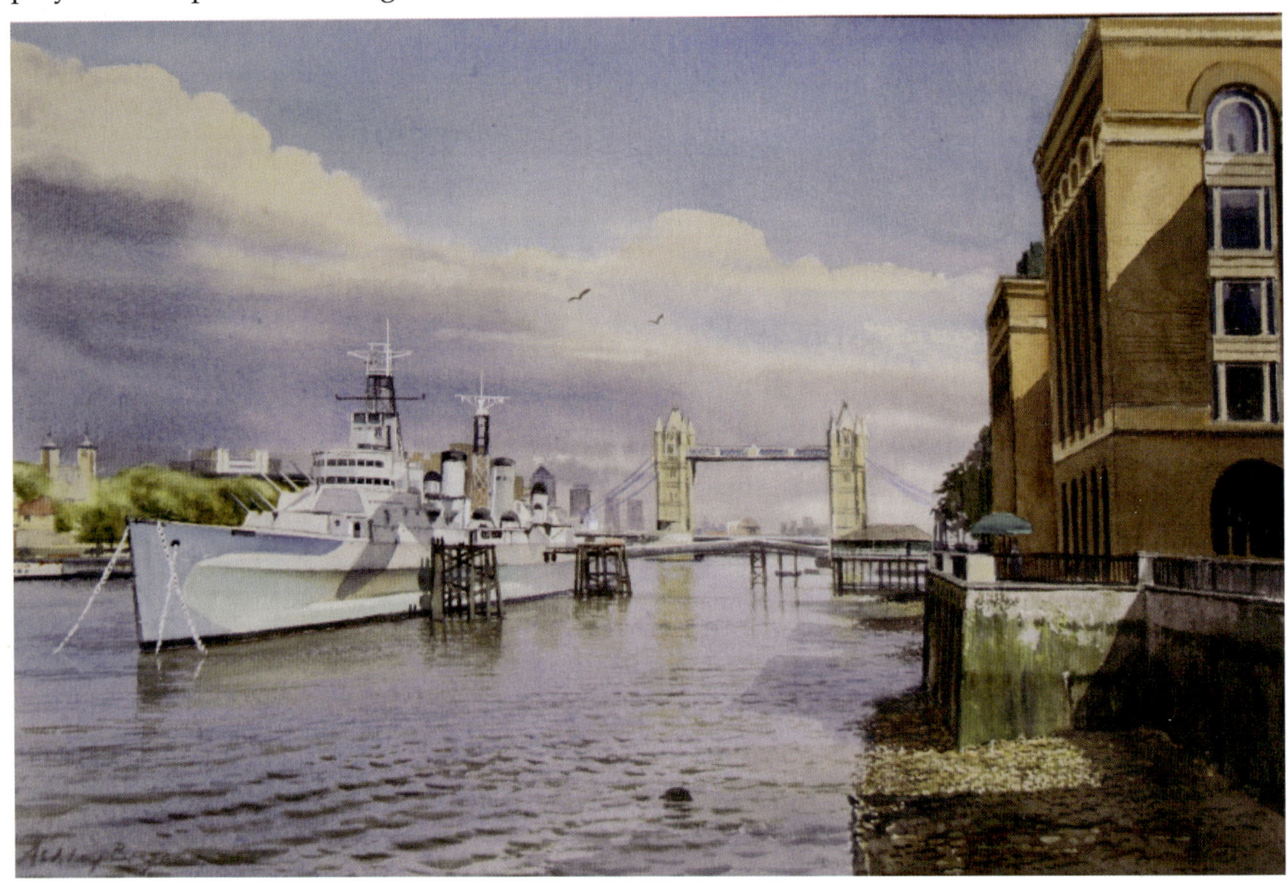

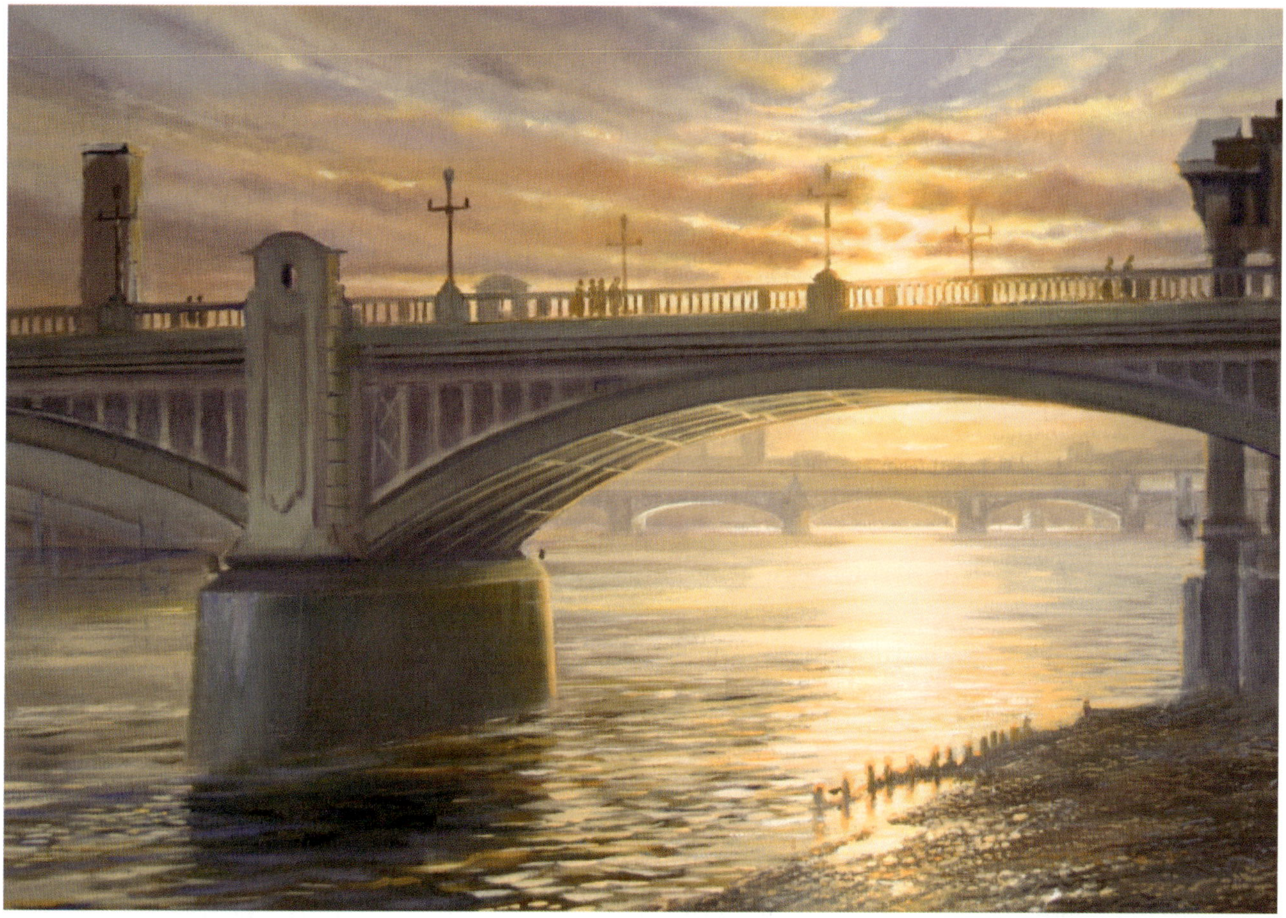

SOUTHWARK BRIDGE
(Above)
With the exception of the Albert Bridge and the new Millennium Bridge, all of London's bridges have been rebuilt. The original Southwark Bridge was built in 1814, and was later rebuilt in 1921.

GLOBE THEATRE
(Right)
The original Globe Theatre was destroyed by fire. The replica follows as closely as possible the original construction.

THE POOL OF LONDON
(Opposite Page)
The Pool of London would formerly have been packed with commercial shipping. Now HMS Belfast stands alone, with the Tower of London on the far left of the painting and Tower Bridge in the background.

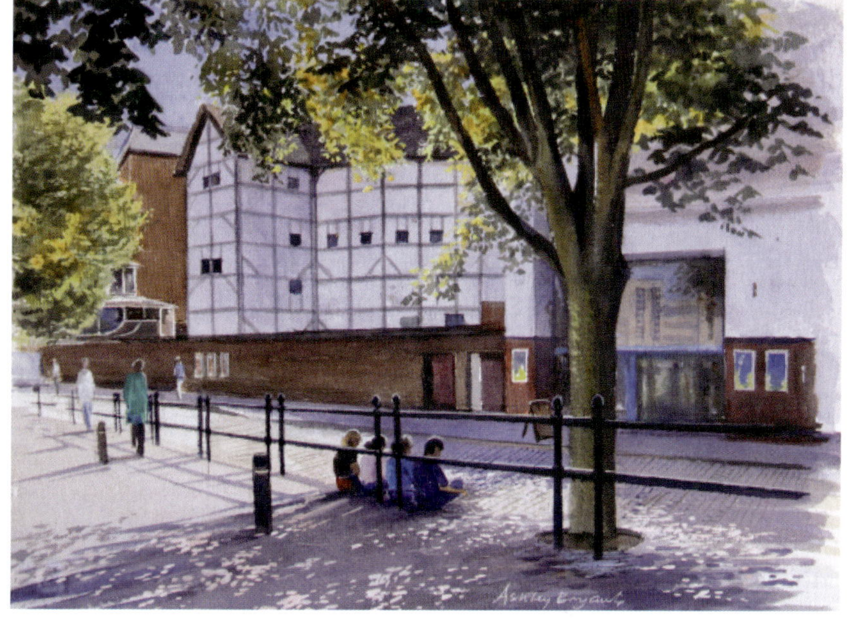

THE CITY

CITY EMBLEM
(Right)
The griffin is the emblem of the City of London.

ST PAUL'S AND THE MILLENNIUM BRIDGE
(Below)
In this pencil drawing the dome of St Paul's Cathedral provides a focal point at the far end of the Millennium Bridge, the latest to be built over the Thames in London.

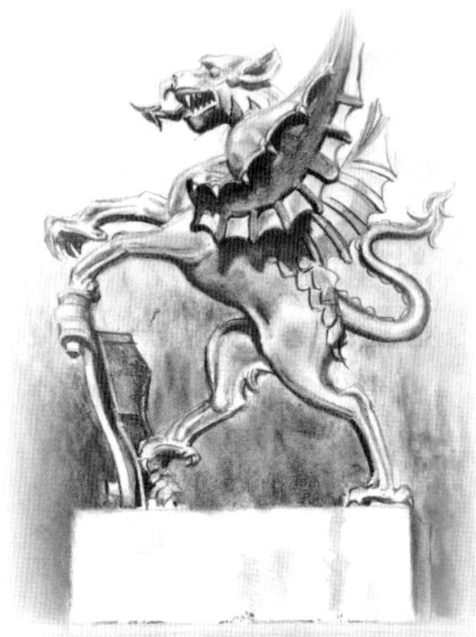

CITYSCAPE
(Opposite Page)
The now placid waters of the river were once a barrage of shipping. Next to the porticoed front of Billingsgate fish market stands the old Customs House, now veiled by trees, and once a hub of business activity. The "Gerkin" stands on the right, bringing to the London skyline a more adventurous form of architecture. Its shape is part of the movement away from the standard rectangular plan in building design.

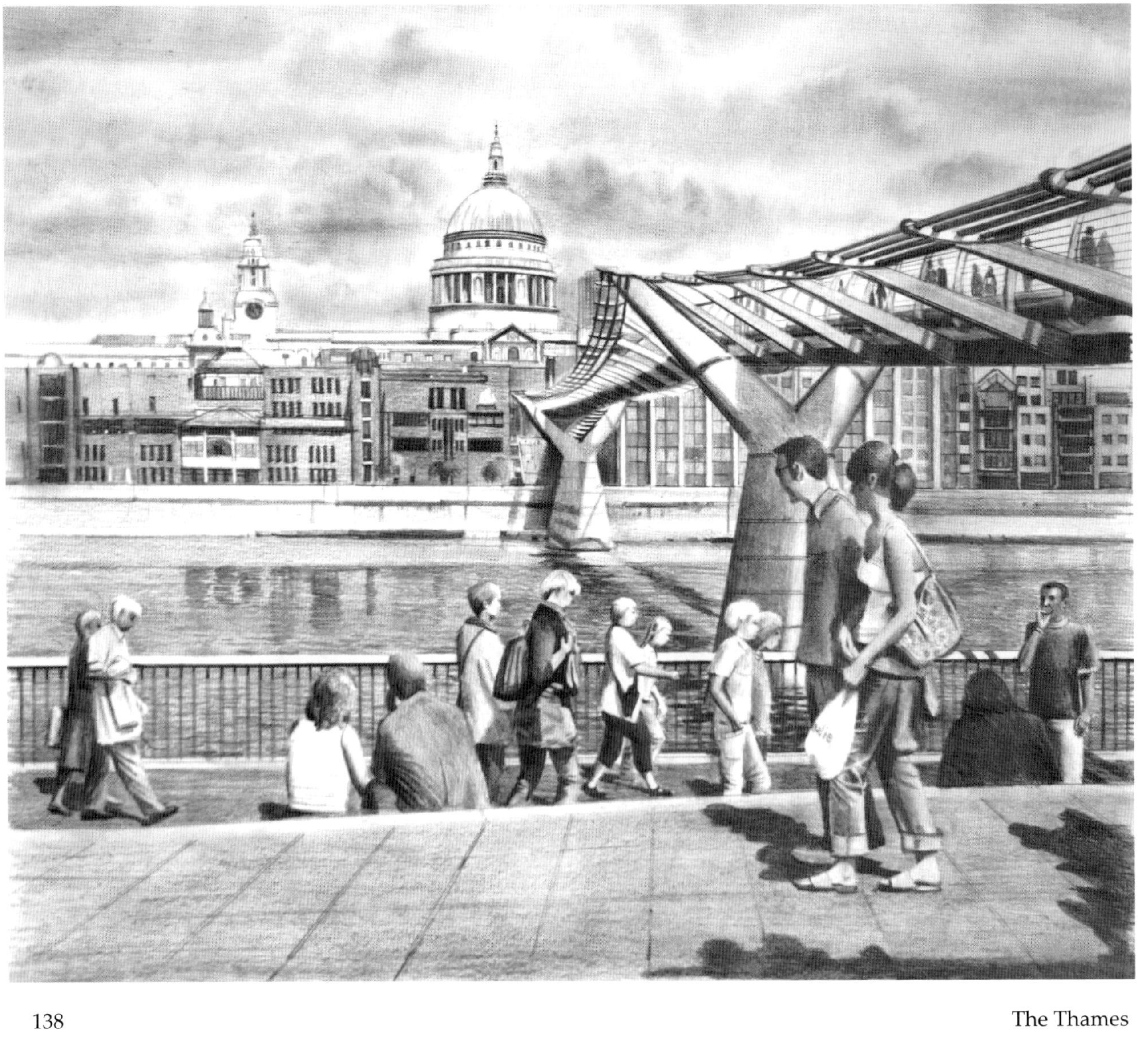

The City of London basically incorporates the area within the Roman wall, and its layout is largely mediaeval. After the Great Fire of London in 1666, proposals for a glorious new city were unveiled with wide avenues and piazzas conforming to an orderly, geometric layout, including as a centrepiece, Wren's masterpiece, the redesigned St Paul's Cathedral. Unfortunately the plot was lost when owners of destroyed properties quickly rebuilt as before, albeit it in stone. From an artistic point of view the city has great character especially in its older, classical buildings, but there are also exciting new developments, using modern techniques, and incorporating stone, glass and steel. However, it is sometimes difficult to get a good viewpoint on a subject in the narrow streets.

Space is created admirably from the Thames and the cityscape of new and historic buildings gels well together. For a capital city London is surprisingly low-rise with the Natwest Tower and the "Gerkin" as modest exceptions, but future plans will inevitably see it grow taller. The Bishopsgate Tower, rising to sixty storeys, will shortly dwarf London's older building. The watercolour painting on this page shows a view of the city over the Pool of London, which was once the busiest port in the world. Hundreds of ships brought commodities from around the world and it is this great trading heritage that ran hand in hand with the City's dominance in banking, insurance and the financing of merchant adventuring. Today it is one of the main financial centres in the world.

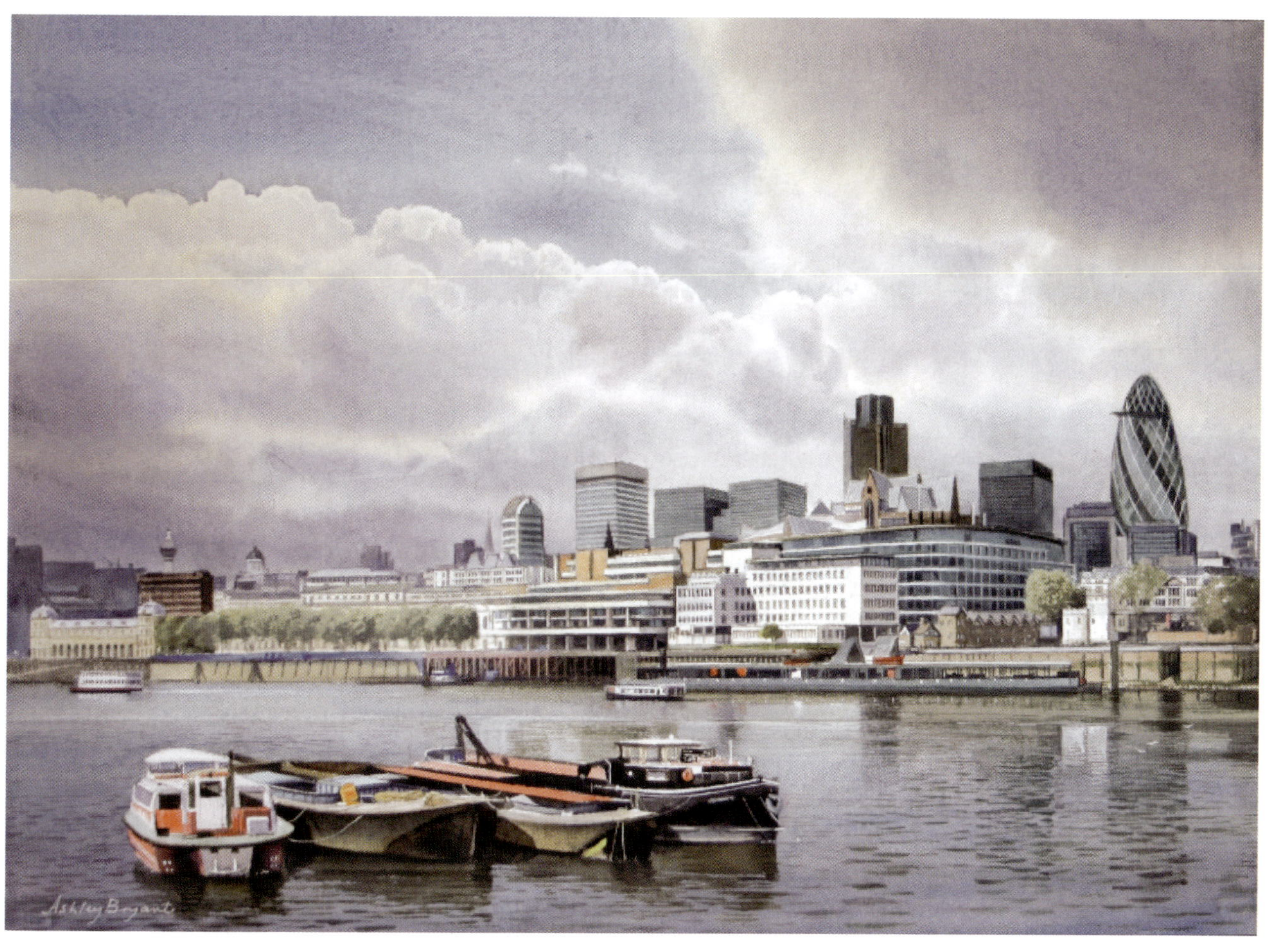

TOWER OF LONDON

William the Conqueror's great fortress built to strike fear into the hearts of rebellious Londoners must have seemed awesome it its day, rising imperiously amongst the simple wood and wattle houses of the town. It now appears quite tiny – such is progress. Nevertheless, for most of its 900 years it has admirably combined the roles of fortress, royal residence, armoury, treasury, mint, prison, and place of execution and its story mirrors the history of the nation.

In summer, its sparkling white stone, vivid green lawns and throngs of tourists barely disguise the Tower's grim history. Indeed, its darker side is promoted with enthusiasm – racks and thumb screws, accounts of executions, the fate of the two young princes and so on. The Tower is on tourists' "A" lists of places to visit, and visitors love the gory bits; the "oohs" and "ahs", their wide eyes and eager expressions call out for more. Crowds flock past magnificent suits of armour, shields and swords of the finest quality for the nobility and racks of weapons for the common soldier. How many of these visitors reflect on the thousands of poor souls who were on the receiving end of all of this hardware? At least the crown jewels make a change from death and destruction.

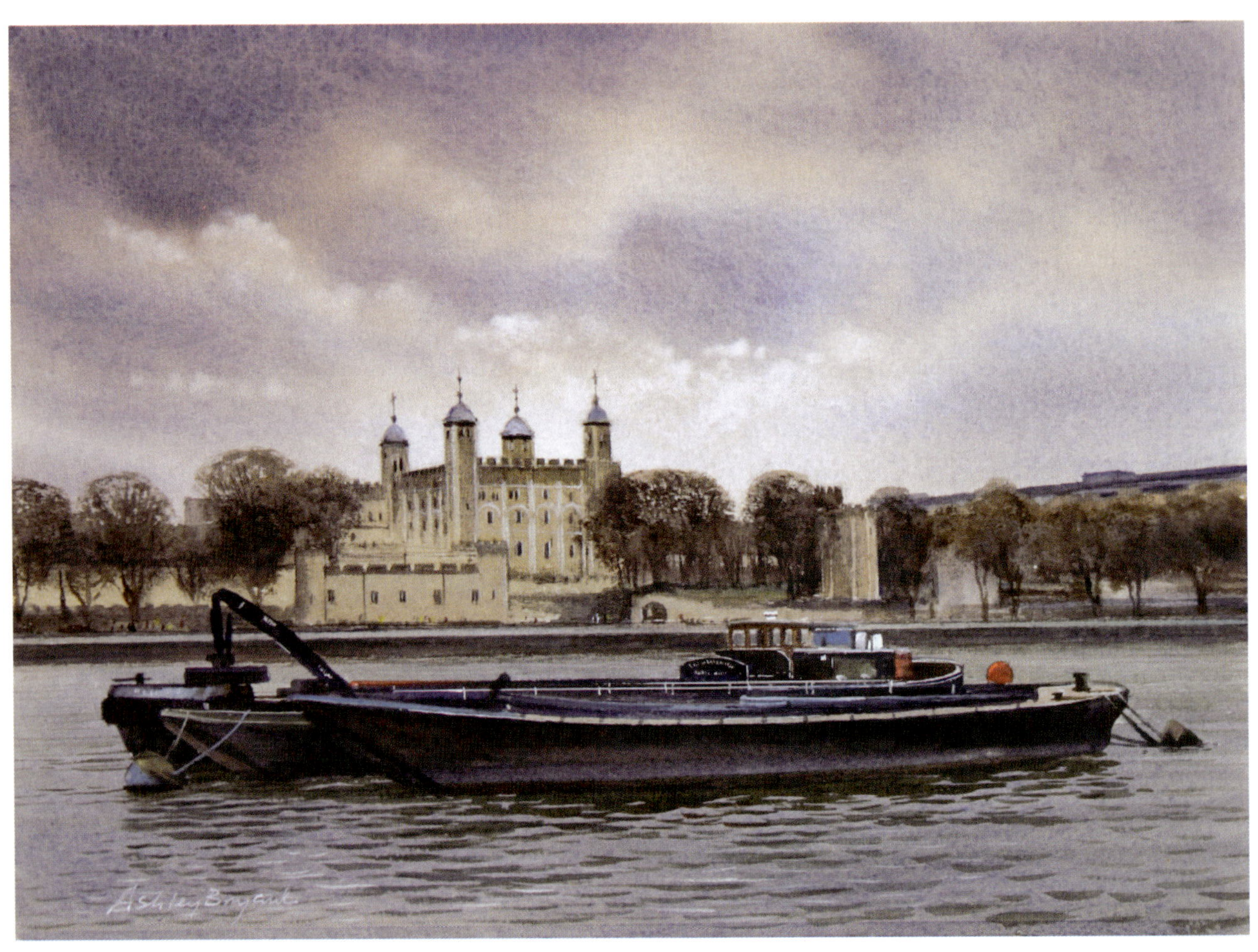

BEEFEATER
(Right)
A Yeoman Warder gives directions.

THE TOWER OF LONDON
(Opposite Page)
My feelings about the Tower's grim history are reflected in the choice of colours for this painting.

TRAITORS GATE
(Below Right)
This gate was used to slip prisoners quietly into the Tower, almost certainly a one-way trip.

THE GUARDIAN
(Below)
The ravens, supposedly present in the tower since its construction, are surrounded by superstition. It is thought that should they ever leave, either the tower, the monarchy or the country would fall. A group of tame birds are kept around just in case.

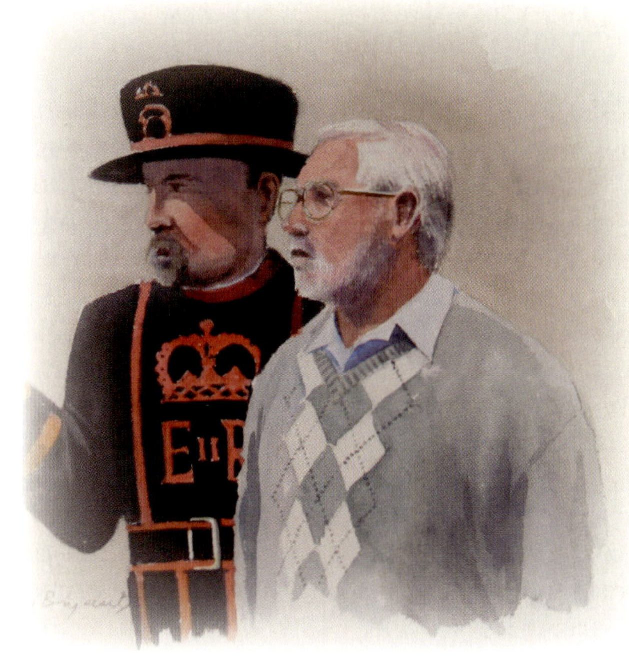

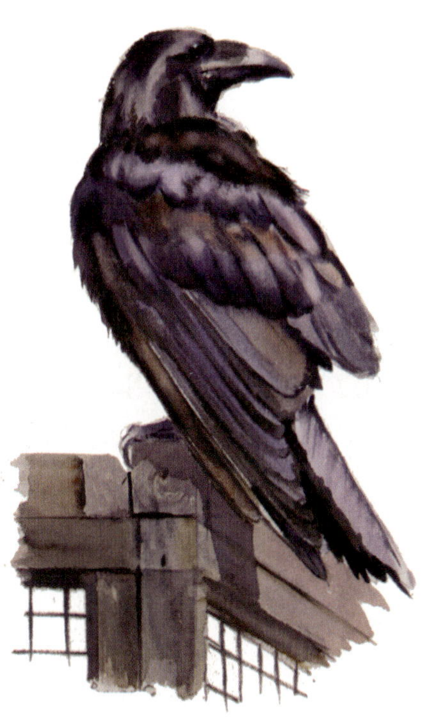

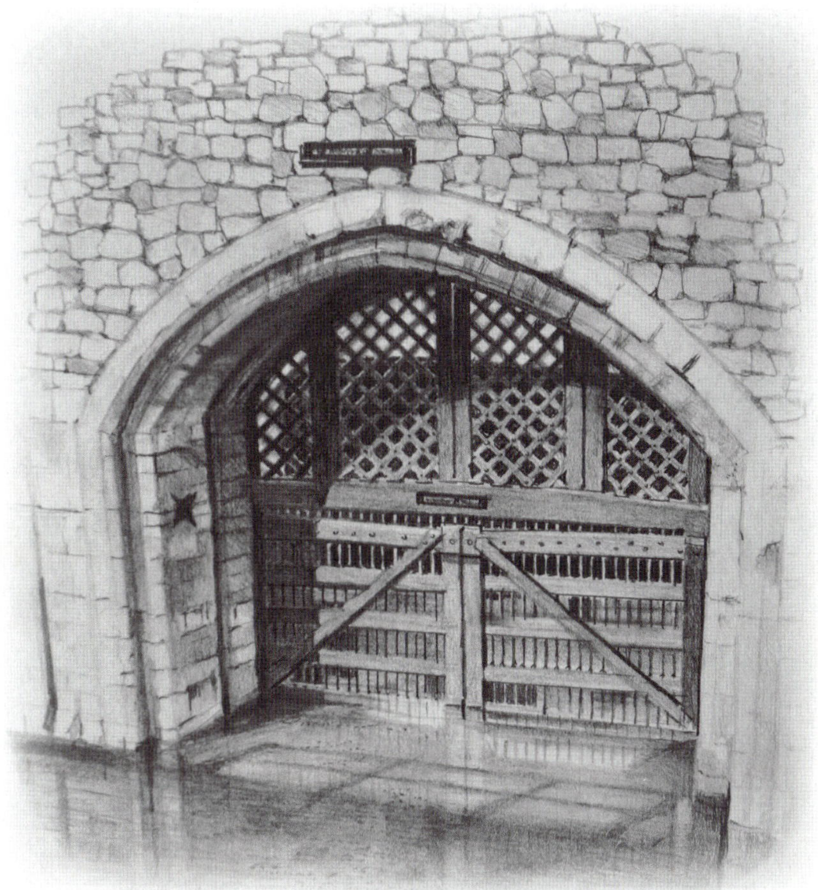

TOWER BRIDGE

This is one of the most distinctive and easily recognisable bridges in the world. Since it is the subject of thousands of paintings I thought I would create something original, and considered all the usual variations of different viewpoints, different times of day (including night time illumination) and different seasons. I was on the bridge when the London Marathon raced across and stood on the banks when a replica of Captain Cook's "Endeavour" passed underneath. I finally settled for something straight-forward, a view from the pier at Butler's Wharf.

The original specifications for Tower Bridge were daunting. Towards the end of the nineteenth-century congestion around London Bridge finally became intolerable and a new bridge was required further downstream, where seemingly insurmountable difficulties presented themselves. The authorities insisted on a clearance of 135 feet (40 metres) to accommodate the masts of ships. This would have required ridiculously lengthy ramps at either side for the horse drawn vehicles of the day, and Queen Victoria was not amused at the prospect of a huge structure next to "her" Tower. The bridge challenged the ingenuity of the civil engineers of the day, and a competition was launched. This led to ideas for swing bridges, rolling platforms, locks and lifting bridges. The winning design by Sir Horace Jones, who was actually on the judging panel, was for a double draw-bridge and was undoubtedly the most practical solution. The bridge was finally opened in 1894. It remains a technical masterpiece, built to last in true Victorian style.

DOLPHIN SCULPTURE
(Below left)
Another dolphin statue. This one is on the north bank, near St Katherine's Pier, and incorporates a fountain.

ST KATHERINE'S DOCK
(Below Right)
Situated near Tower Bridge, this early nineteenth-century dock was used for cargos of high value goods such as ivory and marble.

THE THAMES AT TOWER BRIDGE
(Opposite Page)
A view of the familiar Tower Bridge from Butler's Wharf with a Thames barge in the foreground.

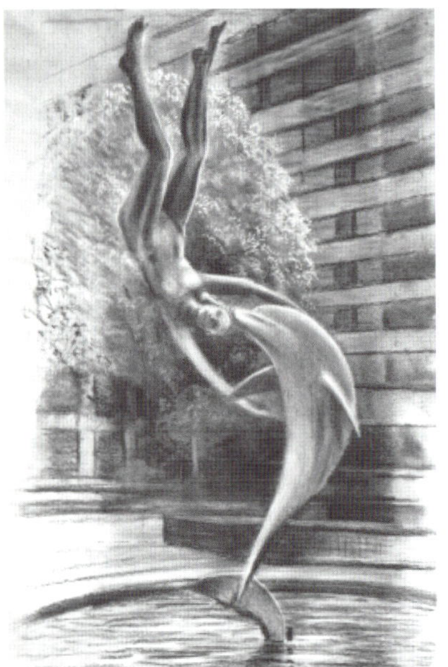

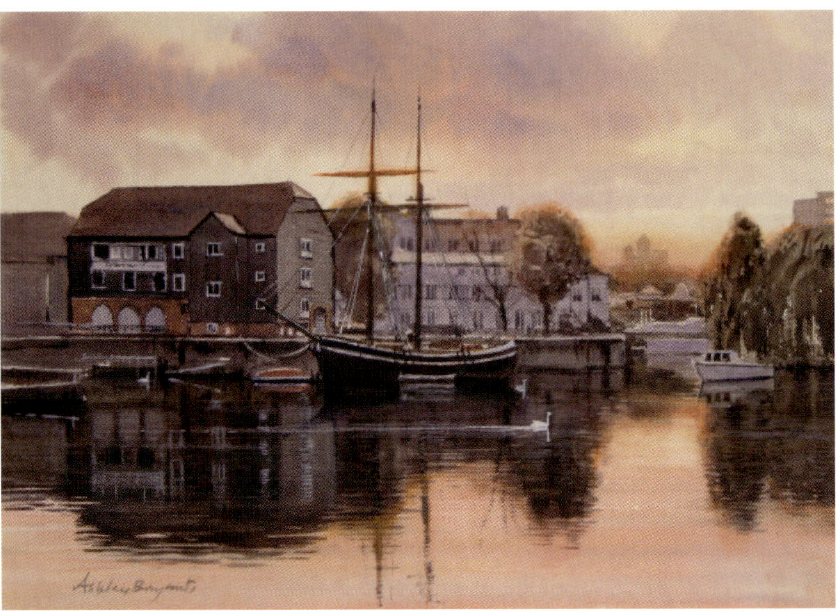

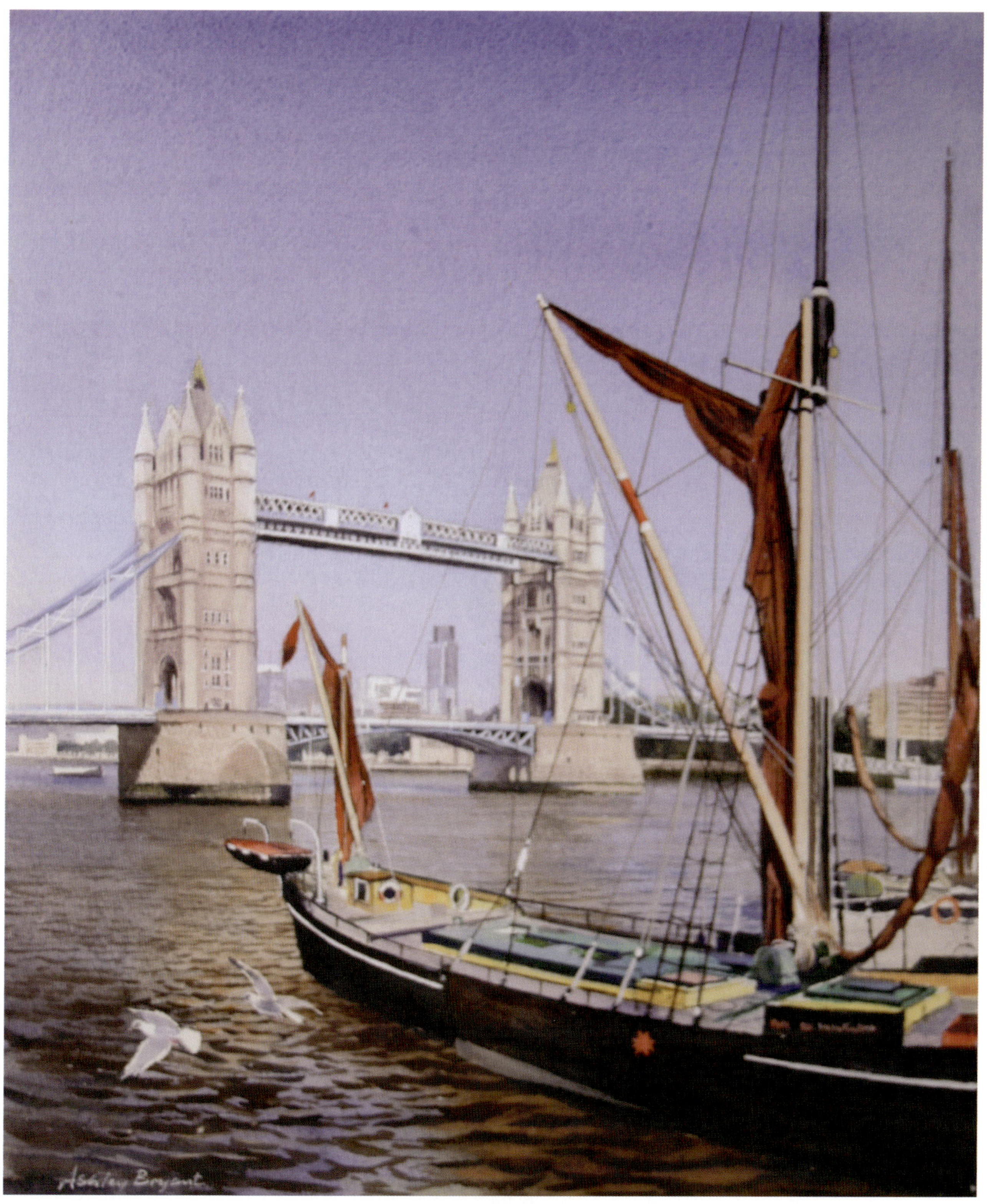
Ashley Bryant

ROTHERHITHE

THE THAMES AT ROTHERHITHE
(Below)
Old warehouses with crumbling brickwork, rotten timbers, flaking paint and rusty ironwork make wonderful artistic subjects but they are becoming rare in the race to convert them into smart residential property. There is a certain cache in owning a riverside apartment and developments quickly find eager buyers. Some of the riverside pubs still retain their old character, but for my main painting I decided on an open view of the river, with a collection of old barges to provide foreground interest and the towers of Canary Wharf just visible in the sunrise.

The riverside at Rotherhithe follows a never ending line of residential developments, many converted from old tenements and warehouses. The Thames Path dog-legs around these buildings in an irritating way, making Thames views infrequent and the journey longer. It has become a fashionable and expensive part of London, but many would ask why this has taken so long in an area so close to the heart of the capital. Right up to the 1970's many parts of Rotherhithe were dowdy, decaying and Dickensian. In fact, Dickens used the area for some of the lowest moments in his novels – Fagan died here in *Oliver Twist,* and to quote from *Our Mutual Friend,* "by Rotherhithe; down where accumulated scum of humanity seemed to be washed from higher ground, like so much moral sewage". Rotherhithe was also the last place in Britain to record Bubonic plague.

The area's traditional industry was shipbuilding, and many vessels were built along the foreshore, and docks brought in

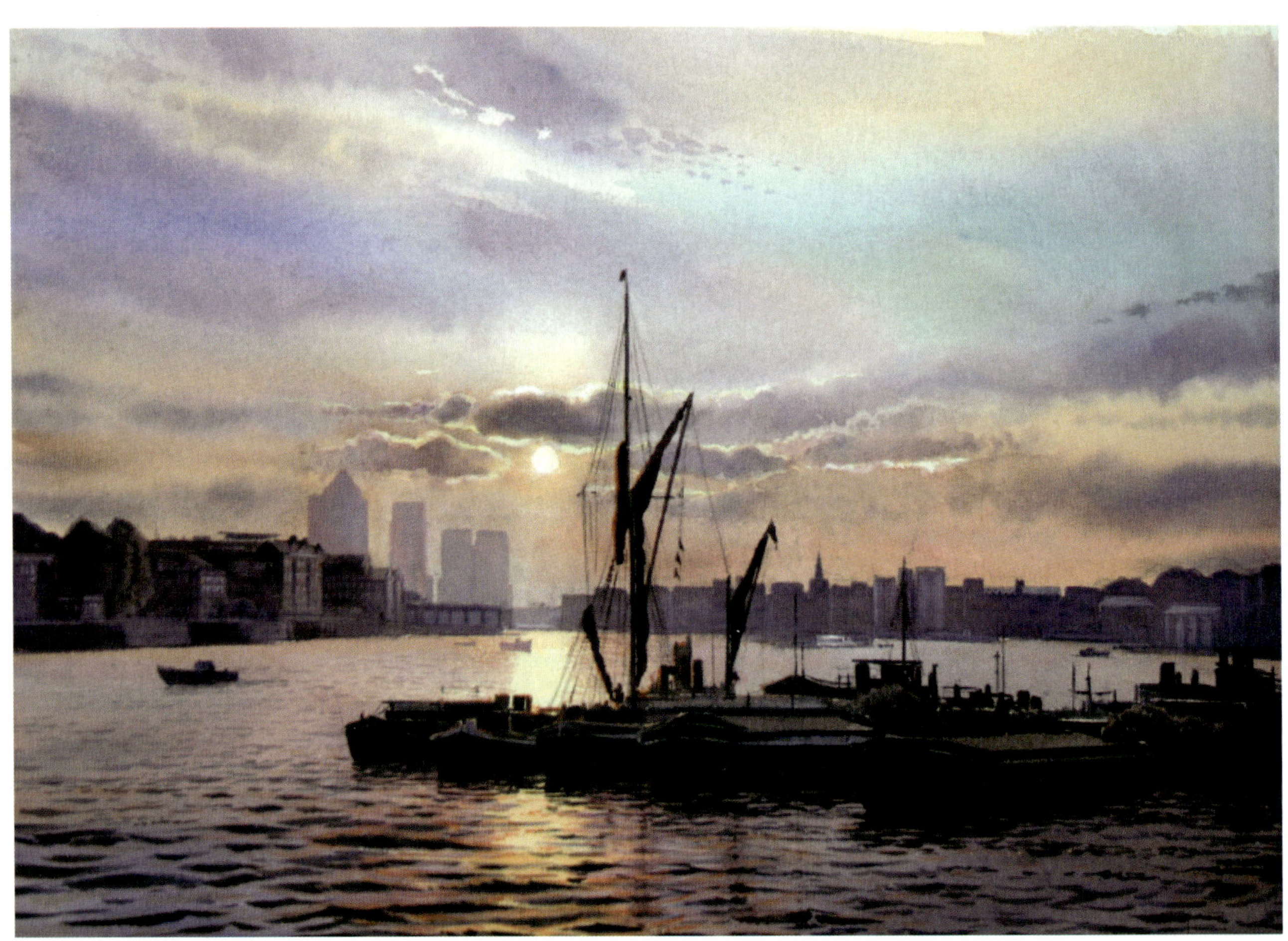

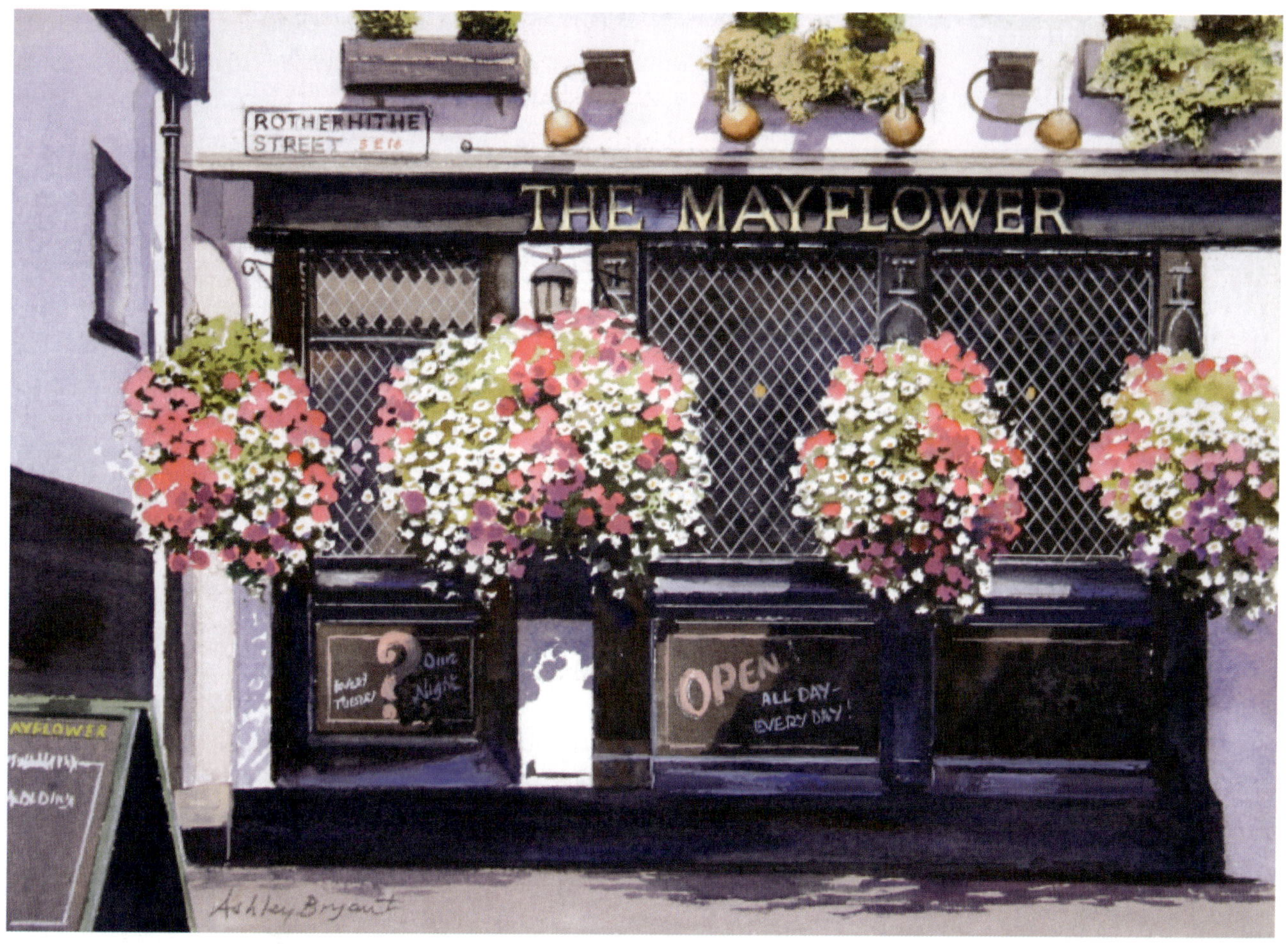

further employment. The first of these was Greenland Dock in 1700, so named as it was opened specifically to serve the whaling industry at a time when whale oil lit the lamps of the nation. The Surrey Docks were later additions, eventually closing in 1970. A great canal was promoted and work started to link these docks with Portsmouth but sadly, or rather amusingly, it only got as far as Peckham.

On a more up-beat note, Rotherhithe is home to Brunel's tunnel, which was described, when it opened in 1843, as the "eighth wonder of the world". Such an undertaking had been considered impossible, but with the invention of a revolutionary tunnelling shield and the determination of Marc Brunel and his famous son Isambard Kingdom, the world's first underwater tunnel was achieved after eighteen problematic years of construction. It is in use today as a London Underground tunnel and remains as dry as a bone.

THE MAYFLOWER
(Below)
In 1620 the Pilgrim Fathers set sail for America, where they became the first permanent European settlers. Their separatist views from the established church prompted this radical move and they embarked on their ship the "Mayflower" from a wharf next to an inn known as The Shippe, at Rotherhithe. The Pilgrim Fathers sailed via Southampton and Plymouth, landing in the newly named Plymouth Bay in Massachusetts on 21 December, 1620. After a period when it was known as the Spread Eagle & Crown, the pub changed its name to The Mayflower in 1957 to commemorate its association with this momentous voyage.

ISLE OF DOGS / CANARY WHARF

The development of Canary Wharf has brought a touch of Manhattan to London's riverside, and transformed what was until the 1980s a run- down area on the Isle of Dogs. This island, formerly known as Stepney Marsh, is where Henry VIII kept his hunting dogs. Its boggy nature, aided by breaches in the river, was finally drained by Dutch engineers in the seventeenth century. It continued quietly as rich farmland supporting some of the best cattle in the country until the early nineteenth century when it was transformed by extensive dockland development and tightly packed housing communities. London was burgeoning with trade, and the development of the East and West India docks in 1802 and 1806 respectively was followed by the Millwall Docks in the 1860s. The subsequent linking of the dockland complex created a true island.

Shipbuilding was an important industry in the nineteenth century, and at its height Isambard Kingdom Brunel's massive ship the "Great Eastern", was built and launched here. For many years it was by far the largest ship in the world, but it was a step too far even for Brunel, and its associated problems taxed his life's energy. After considerable difficulties getting this monster into the water, it was finally launched in 1859.

The docks finally disappeared, marking the end of an era for the Isle of Dogs. Canary Wharf has risen from the ashes, its ongoing development creating a virtual new city. Each day 65,000 people travel here, emerging from the cavernous tube station, the driverless Docklands Light Railway trains or from commuter water buses into this brave new world.

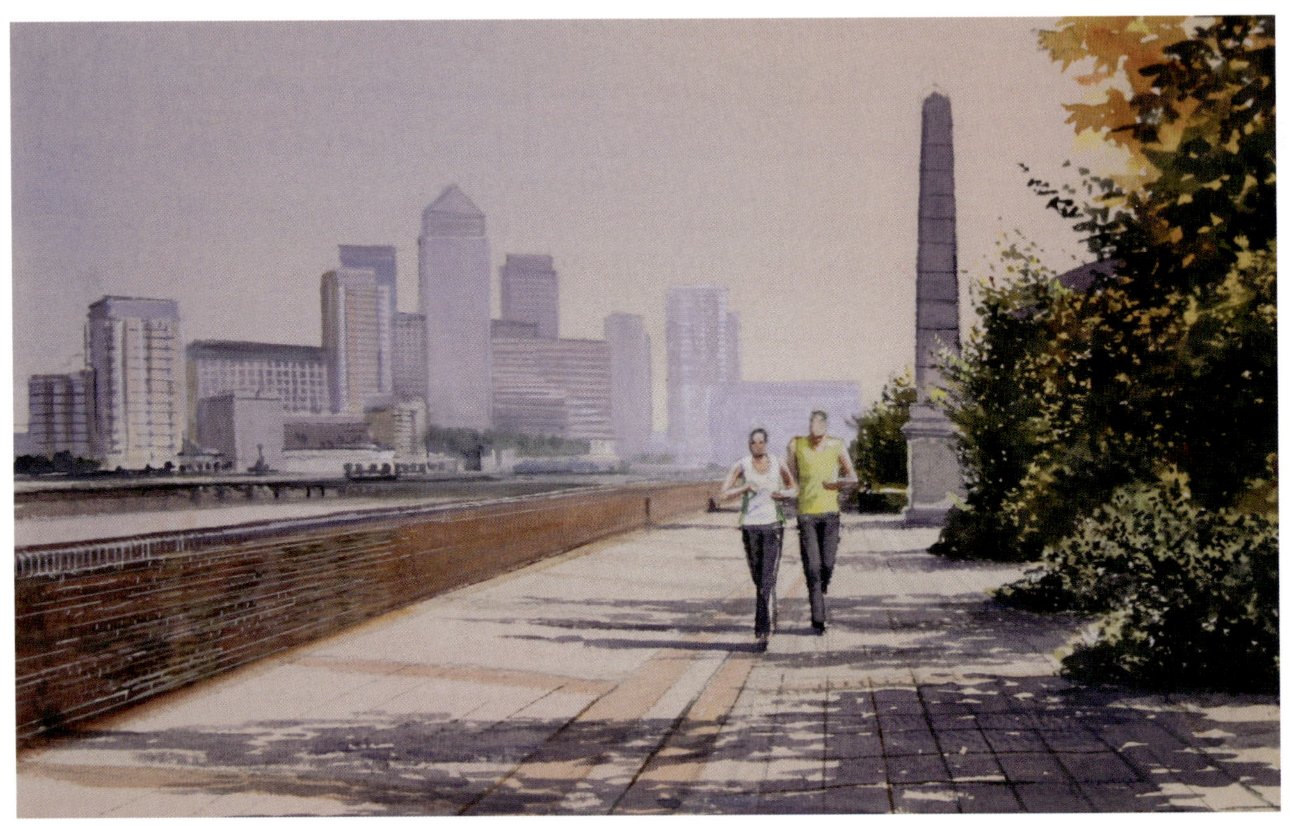

CANARY WHARF AND GARDENS

(Right)

The Canada Tower dominates the 8.5 square miles of London's Dockland Development and rising to 800 feet (260 metres) is currently Britain's tallest building. It was completed in 1990 and its fifty floors include 3960 windows – one reason why I avoided a close-up. Virtually all the employees in Canary Wharf work in service industries, predominantly in banking, insurance, publishing and the media. This view looks across the gardens which provide a welcome lunch time retreat away from all those computer terminals.

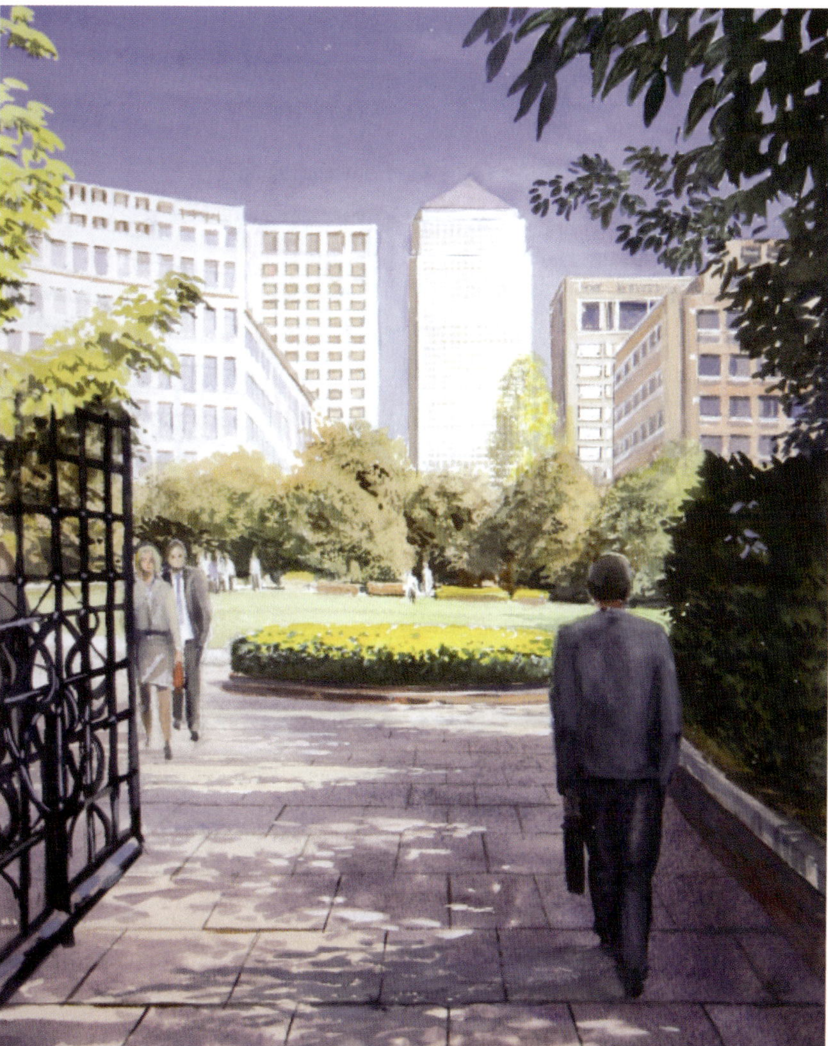

CANARY WHARF

(Opposite Page)

The full prospect of Canary Wharf is seen from the Thames path at Rotherhithe and Deptford along the south side of the river although the height of these buildings ensures they are seen from a great distance. The Thames walkways provide traffic-free avenues and are ideal for jogging. This couple were training for the London Marathon.

THE JETTY

(Below Right)

It is interesting that commuter waterbuses and taxis are reviving the old ways of travelling along the Thames. In earlier times boats were engaged from steps – like taxi ranks, where boats could be boarded. At low tide jetties along the foreshore enabled passengers to reach the boats without walking across mud. Many of these remain, their oak pillars sticking out of the riverbed like broken teeth. This jetty is sited on the south bank of the river almost opposite the Canary Wharf pier.

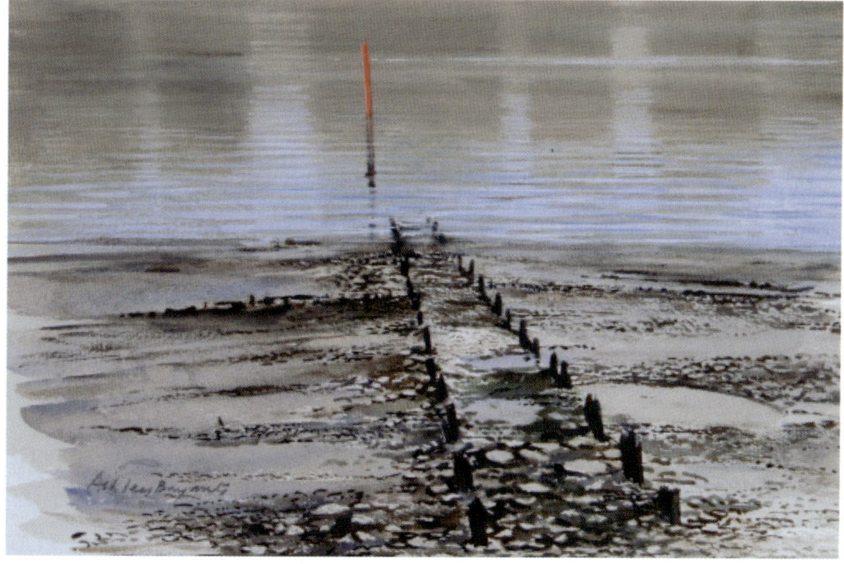

GREENWICH

GRADUATION DAY
(Above Right)
The University of Greenwich now uses the buildings of the Royal Naval College and students are privileged to use the chapel for graduation ceremonies. This magnificent building was completed in 1743 after Wren's death, but was later rebuilt after a fire. This watercolour shows some of the students as they gather around, chat about old times, and take the usual graduation photographs.

GREENWICH PARK
(Opposite Page)
This panorama incorporates Wren's Royal Observatory on the left, the Queen's House, buildings of the Royal Naval College at the foot of the hill and Canary Wharf on the far right. Glimpses of the river can just be seen.

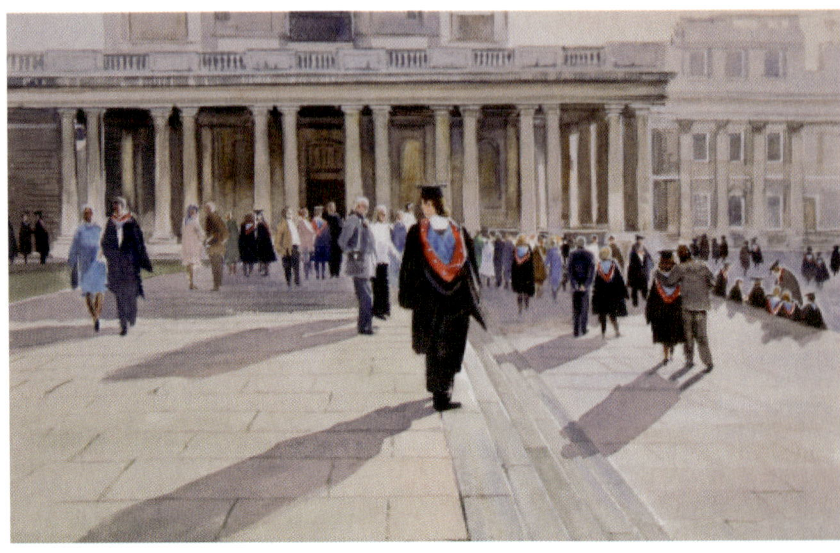

CUTTY SARK
(Below)
It would be remiss to leave Greenwich without a painting of this famous clipper, one of the last sailing ships to be built for deep sea voyages, taking cargoes of tea from China and wool from Australia. She was the sleek and stylish "Concorde" of her day. Sadly, the Cutty Sark is now in desperate need of attention, and millions need to be spent to combat the ravages of time.

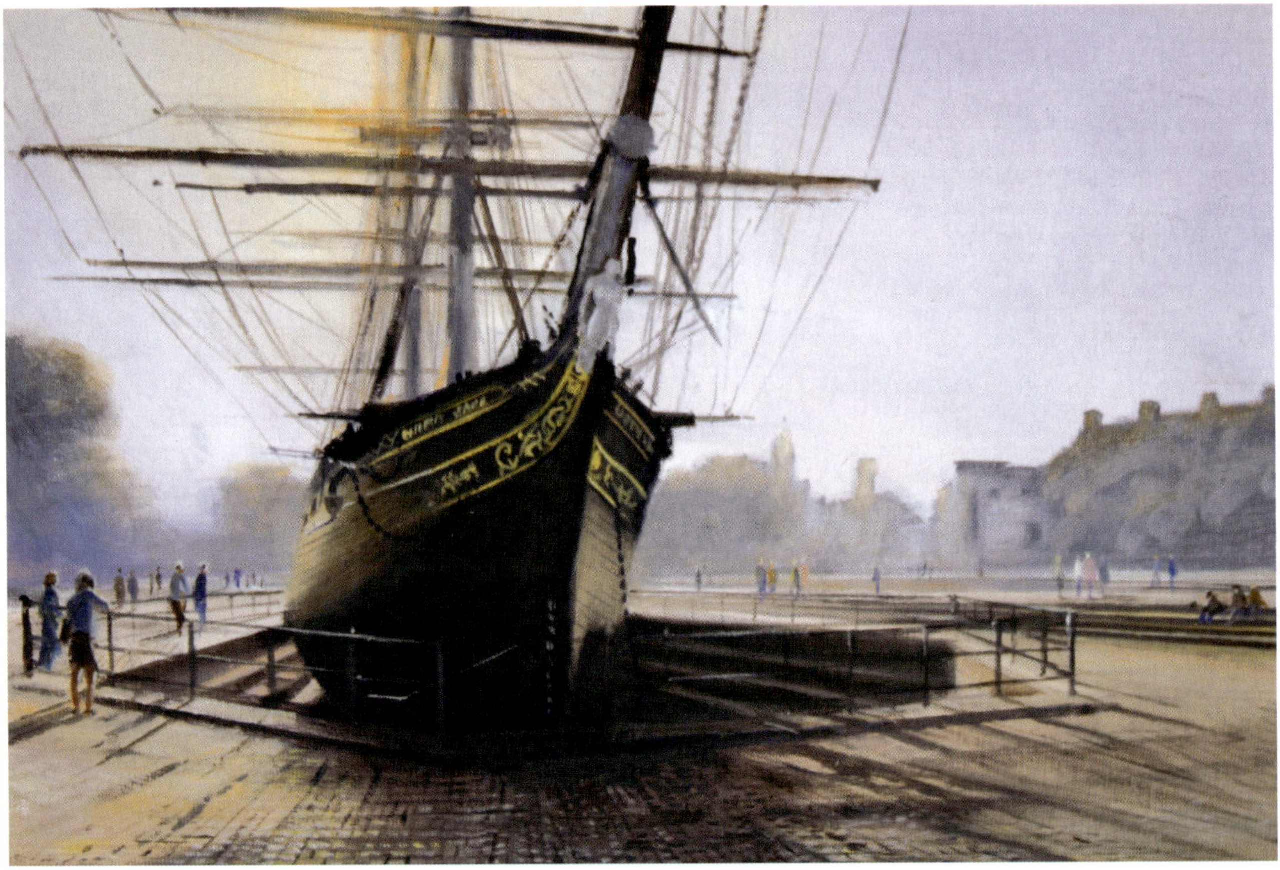

At Greenwich the architectural gem of the Royal Naval College stands in classical symmetry beside the Thames. It was inaugurated in 1873 in the buildings of the former Royal Naval Hospital. This great baroque masterpiece was designed by Sir Christopher Wren and completed in 1705. The buildings are now used by the University of Greenwich and Trinity College of Music. The adjoining National Maritime Museum includes some magnificent marine paintings; in these masterpieces you can see the smoke drifting across the battle scenes, hear the thunder of canons and smell the tar and black powder. The Queen's House occupies a central position in the symmetry of the complex. It was built in 1618 for Anne of Denmark, the wife of James I, and continued the royal association with Greenwich. Here, illustrious admirals and captains stare at you from the walls, the gold braid of their elevated ranks painted with such realism it defies definition as mere paint.

Greenwich Park is one of the magnificent green spaces around London with far reaching views. The Royal Observatory stands on the brink of the hill and was built in 1675 at a time when mathematics, science and astronomy were being brought into new focus. It is said that the first Astronomer Royal, John Flamsteed, had to use second-hand building materials to keep within a tight budget for the observatory. Nevertheless, it soon grew in stature and international recognition. The Greenwich Meridian was eventually adopted as the world standard, and thousands of tourists delight in being photographed as they straddle the line with one foot in each hemisphere.

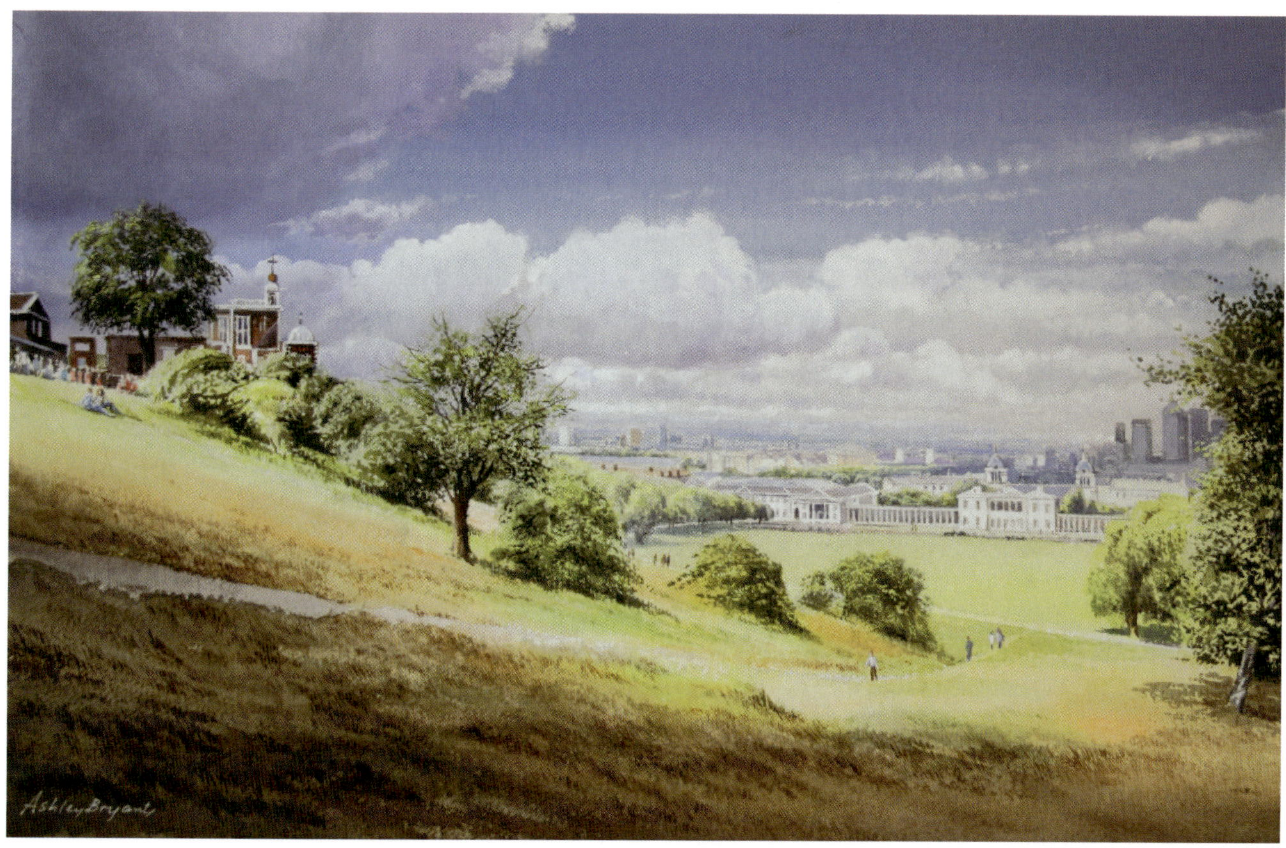

THAMES BARRIER

THAMES BARRIER
(Opposite Page)
The Thames Barrier is a masterpiece of engineering design and construction. There are ten separate gates which lie on the bed of the river and swing upwards when required between pairs of housings in steel-clad abutments, reminiscent of the Sydney Opera House. The four largest gates of the barrier are gigantic, each as high as a five storey building and as wide as the opening of Tower Bridge.

THAMES BARRIER PARK
(Below)
At Silvertown on the north side of the Thames Barrier an unusual park has been created from dockland, providing an attractive area of green space. The painting shows a sunken garden which follows the shape of the original Victorian dock. Wavy hedges create interesting flowing shapes which are emphasised in this frosty scene, whilst the contrasting colours of its flower borders add variety in summer. The surrounding parkland has been imaginatively designed; the clean sharp lines and the use of stainless steel and tinted concrete, together with granite edging for paths, gives the feeling of a large, modern garden.

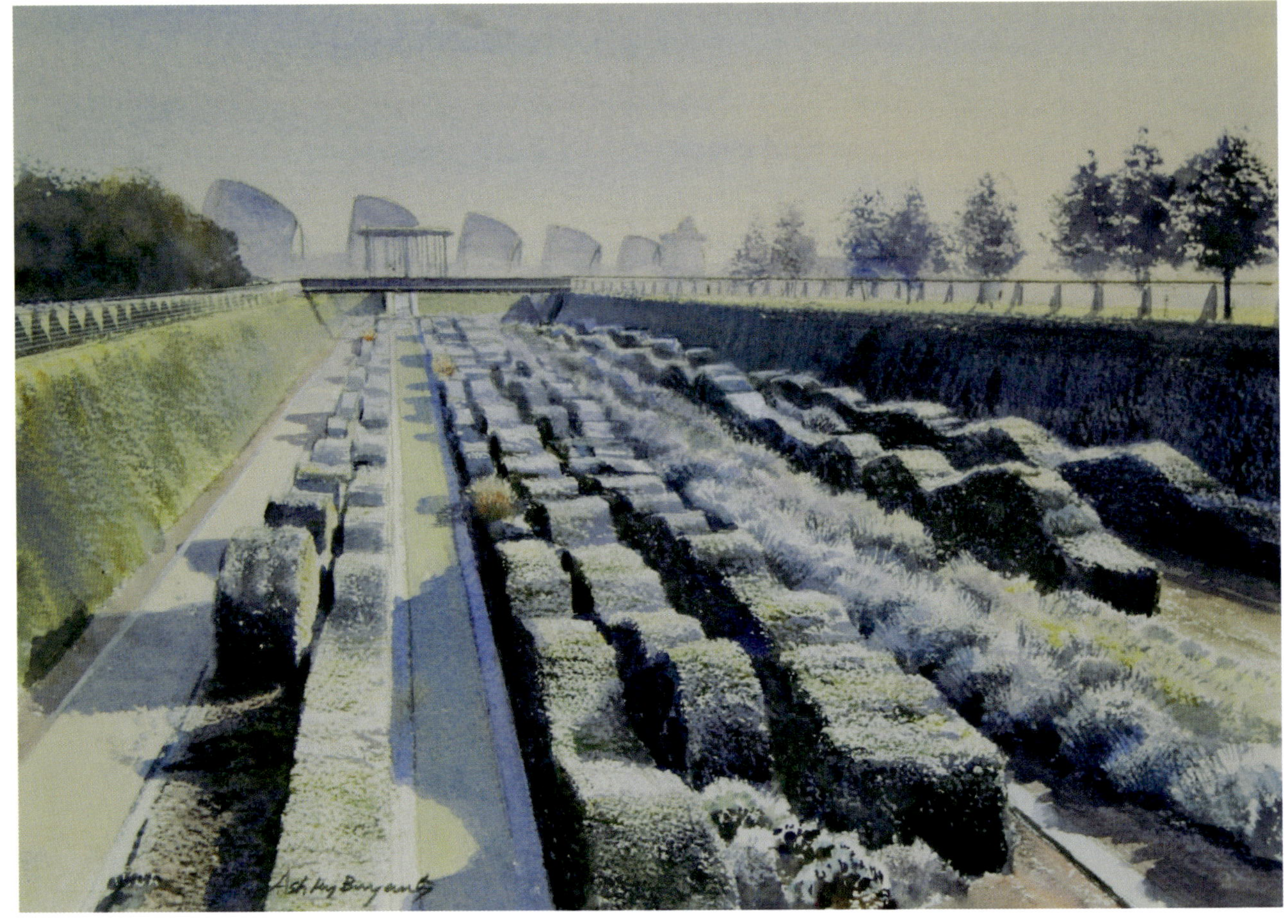

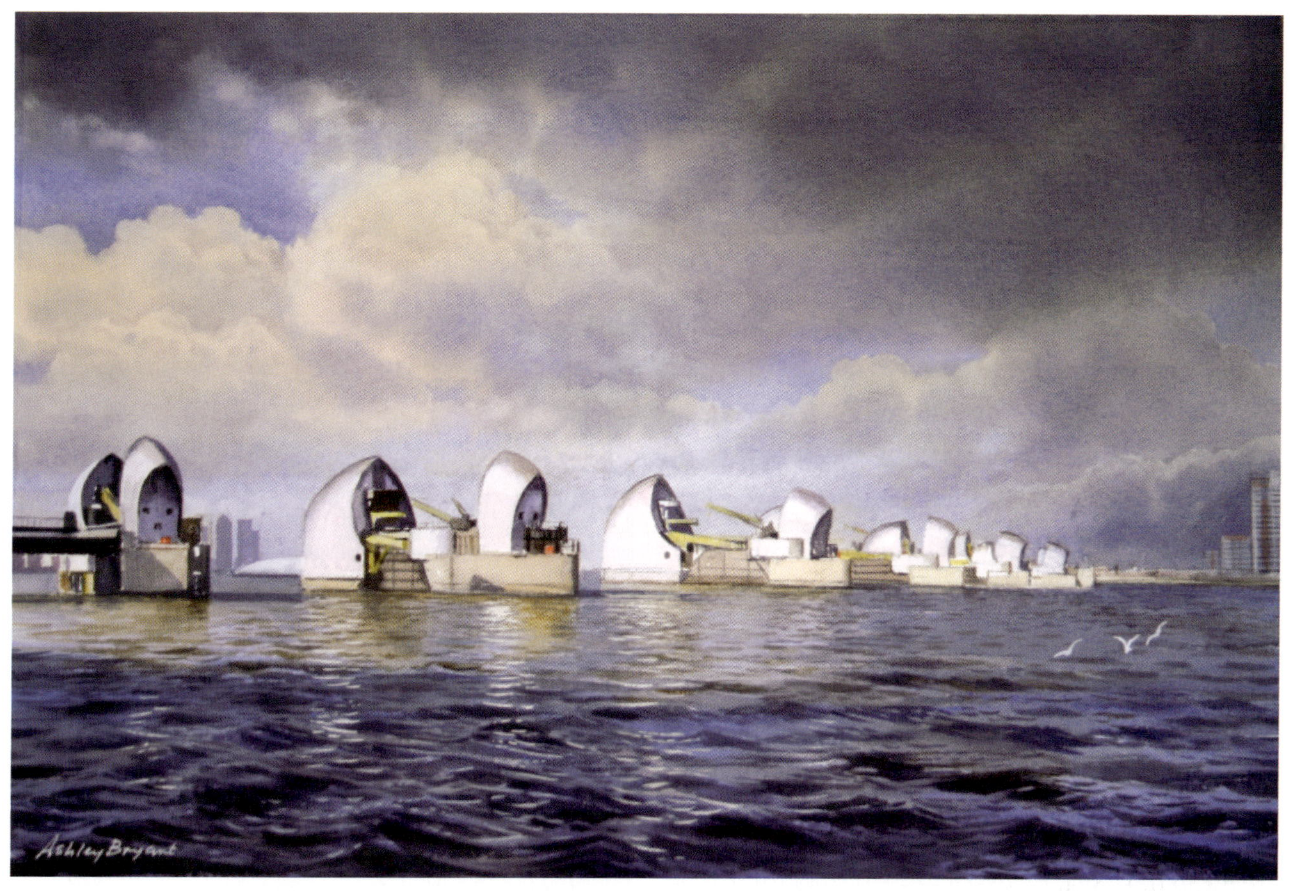

In 1953 an area of low pressure moved eastwards across the north Atlantic drawing up huge waves. It rounded Scotland, then move southwards down the North Sea, where the waves were increasingly funnelled between the encroaching landmasses of south east England and continental Europe. The effect was like a giant tidal bore in the mouth of the river, and the tide spilled over sea walls, flooded hundreds of square miles in East Anglia and Holland and raced up river estuaries with devastating results. Such a phenomenon is known as a surge tide. This event and severe high tides over the next two decades prompted the building of the Thames Barrier to protect the most valuable national asset of all – London. The flooding of the city and the disastrous aftermath was and is unthinkable. The resulting barrier was completed in 1982 and was a masterpiece of engineering.

When the design for the barrier was developed in the early 1970's, global warming was not recognised as a significant factor. Any future scheme clearly has to take into account new effects such as higher tides and the rise in sea levels. The present barrier is raised increasingly frequently and as this book goes to print, new solutions such as an even larger barrier are being considered. There is a limit to the height a barrier can reach since an equivalent height would have to be matched by sea walls from the barrier to the estuary. Where would this end? In other estuaries land has been allowed to flood and revert to tidal salt marsh to soak up high tides, and controlled flooding of the Thames estuary may be part of the answer. The media are fond of showing dire images of the effects of an increase in sea level. This possibilities are frightening.

RAINHAM

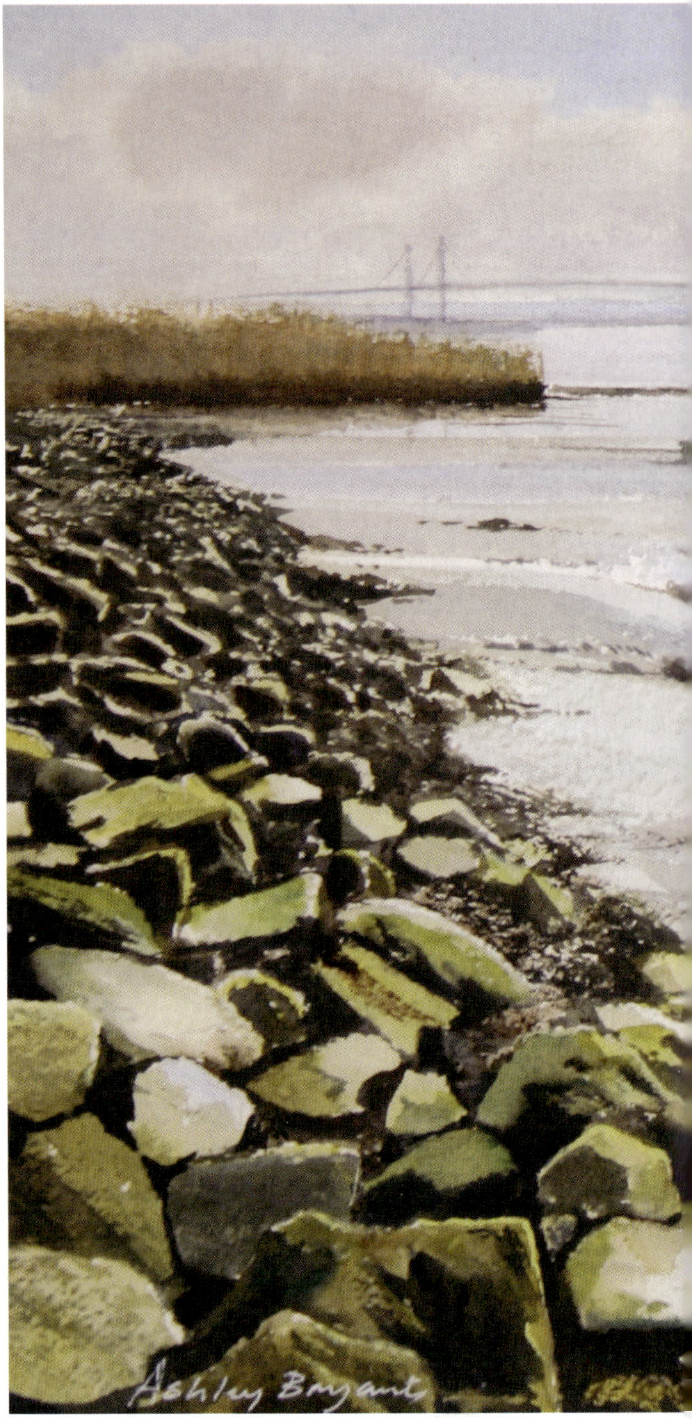

Much of the low lying land along the Essex and Kent shores of the Thames was formally marsh, and the building of sea walls from the fourteenth century onwards allowed the land to be drained and converted to pasture. The recent RSPB reserve at Rainham in Essex, including the Wennington and Aveley Marshes, is sited in this extensive ancient marshland and is a Site of Special Scientific Interest (SSSI). It is noted for the variety of breeding birds and the huge numbers of over-wintering waterfowl and waders. The reserve has recently witnessed an increase in the sightings of rare and unusual species, and the reputation of the reserve is growing quickly.

The preservation of this green space in an area hungry for building land is thanks to the Ministry of Defence, or War Department as it was known in 1906, when a rifle range was established, and flying bullets and shells kept the usual London overspill of housing at bay. This reserve is on the doorstep of a vast population, and is an educational asset for hundreds of schools.

VINNIE
(Below)
At the Rainham reserve young children become endeared to water voles through the character "Vinnie". The Reserve has a breeding programme for these mammals which are in national decline.

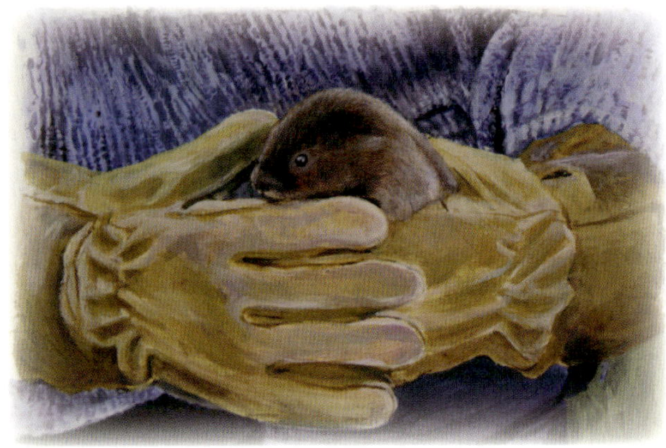

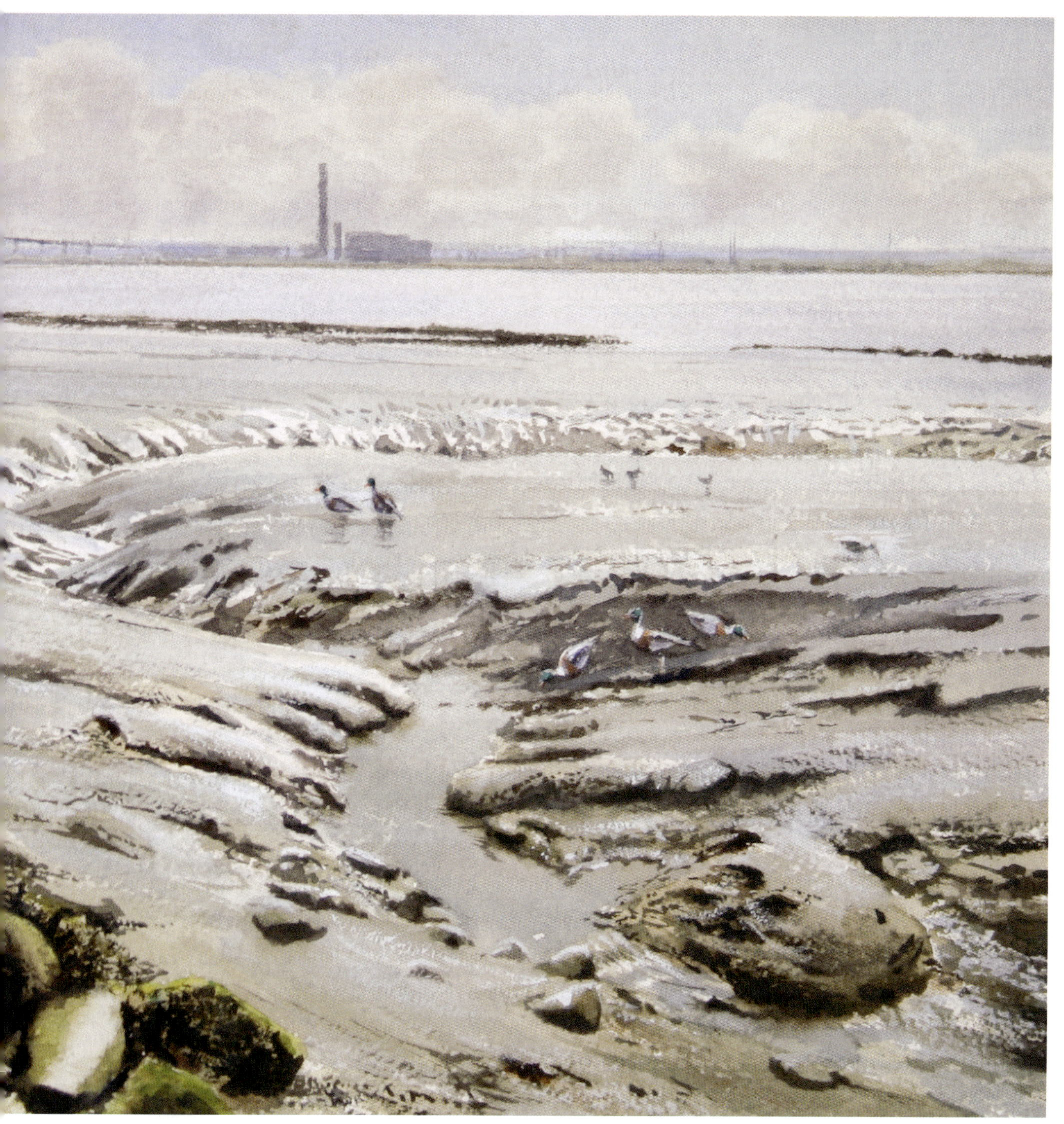

MUD GLORIOUS MUD
(Above)
Silvery mud flats and creeks line the Thames from the shore at Rainham Marshes. Here we are looking downstream towards the distant Queen Elizabeth II Bridge at Dartford.

GRAVESEND

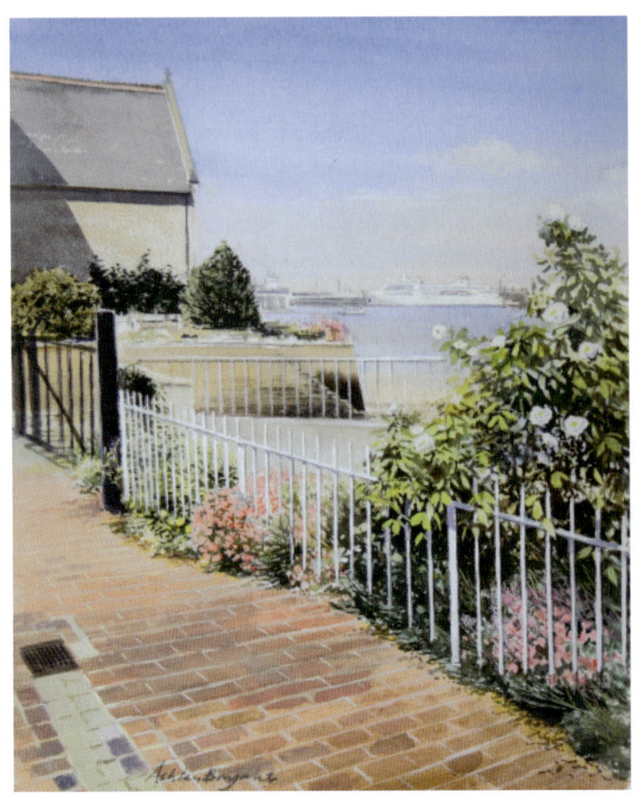

On the Kent side of the Thames, parts of Gravesend have the feeling of a seaside town and the promenade, flower beds, small piers, cafes and old hotels certainly add to that impression. Like many English seaside towns it has a faded glory, but great character nonetheless. Some would describe parts of Gravesend it as a poor man's Greenwich, which is praise indeed.

It was a fishing village and a port of embarkation for sailing ships, and passengers were rowed down to Gravesend to await departure. The town bristled with sea captains and crews, and provided lodgings, chandlers, provisioners and essential taverns. In Victorian times it blossomed as a tourist resort; its closeness to London and the usual trappings of seaside resorts attracted day trippers in their thousands. Today, the crowds have gone but its charm remains, with much to enjoy in the variety of interesting buildings, markets, quaint old pubs and of course its "sea front".

GRAVESEND RIVERSIDE
(Above Right)
This view looks towards the passenger terminal at Tilbury on another hot day in high summer.

THE THAMES AT GRAVESEND
(Opposite Page)
This picture shows the lawns, flowerbeds and riverside promenade which bring a touch of the Mediterranean to Gravesend. This pastel was produced in August 2003, when Gravesend officially reached 100° F (37.8° C), the first place in Britain to reach this temperature.

DISTANT COUSIN
(Below Right)
This black swan preens in the company of his distant relations as the tide laps back up the foreshore.

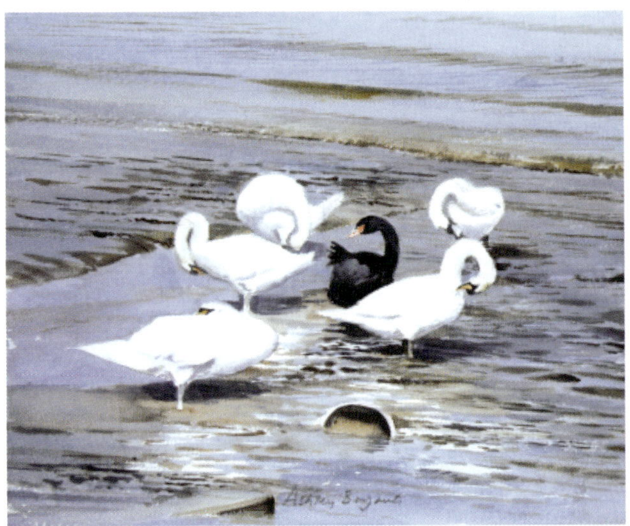

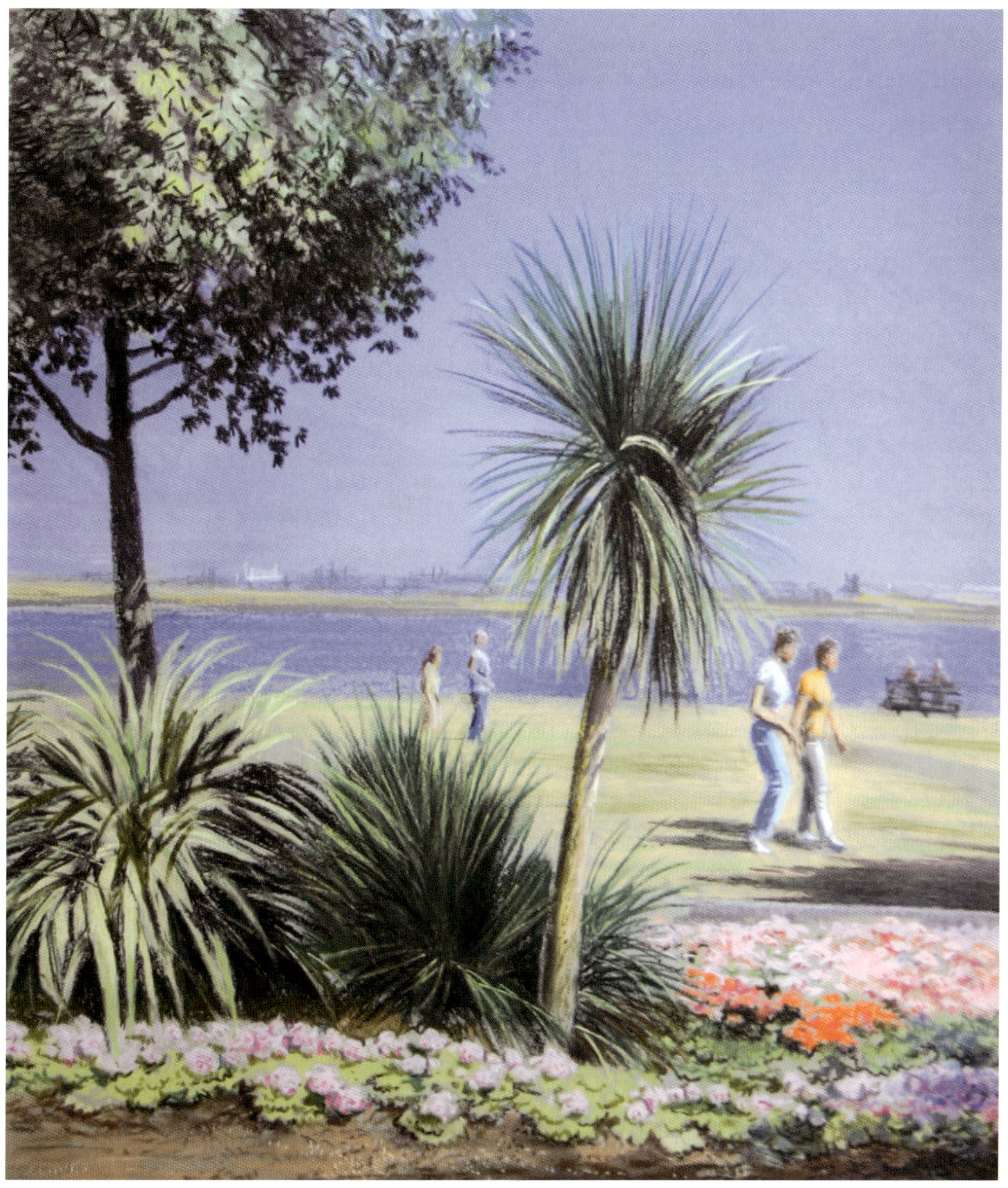

TILBURY

TILBURY RIVERSIDE
(Opposite Page)
The power station gives an industrial appearance to the banks of the Thames at Tilbury, and as with most power stations it provides a landmark for miles.

THE THAMES AT COALHOUSE FORT
(Right)
This view looks directly across the river at low tide from Coalhouse Fort towards the Kent coast on a cold winter's day. There are sections along this waterfront where you can collect enough timber flotsam and jetsam to build a log cabin.

APPROACHING COALHOUSE FORT
(Below)
The choice of monochrome for this watercolour and the distant, lonely figure creates a feeling of desolation. The strip of Thames on the left, the floodwater on the right and the low perspective emphasise the bleakness of the scene, whilst Coalhouse Fort sits starkly on the far right.

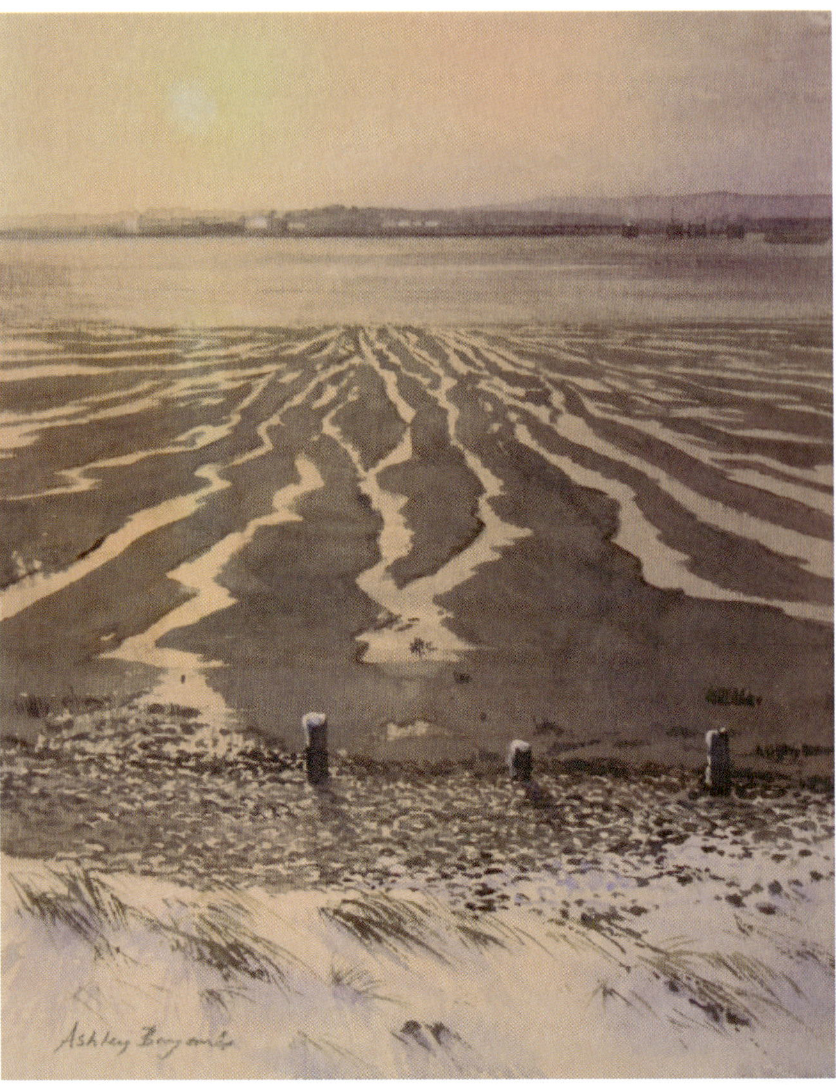

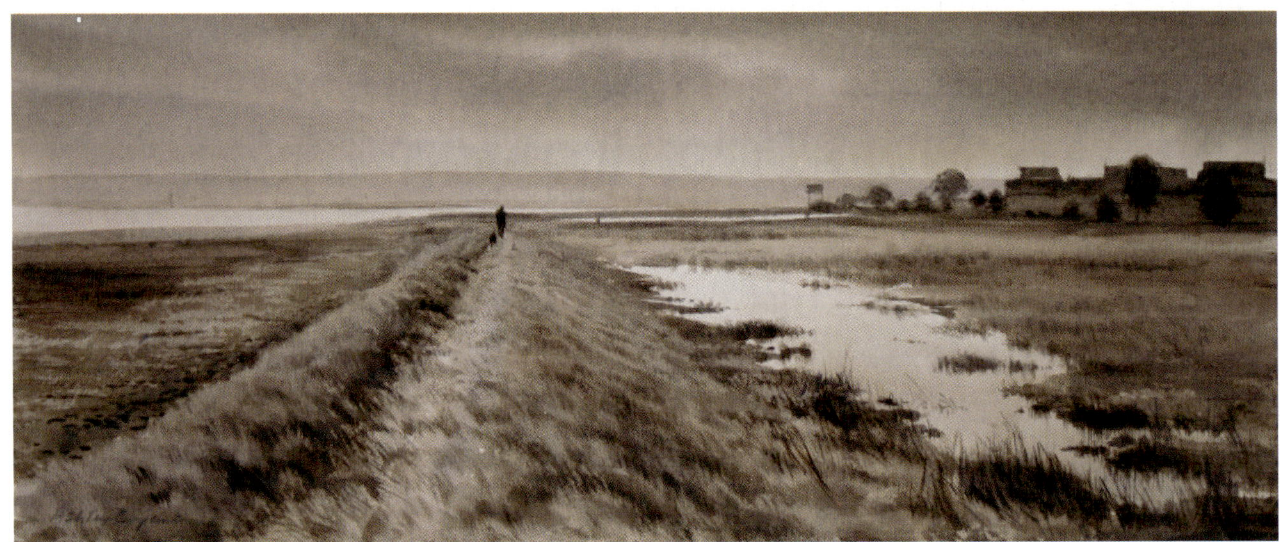

Tilbury in Essex stands some distance from the river, but its industrial complex is spread out along the riverside. The area is dominated by the power station, its twin chimneys providing a landmark for miles around. Tilbury has an enduring association with Elizabeth I, who addressed her army here during military preparations for the Spanish Armada, her famous speech rousing the support and fervour of her troops. Half a century earlier her father, Henry VIII, built a fort or blockhouse at East Tilbury, together with others at Gravesend and Higham on the Kent shore to repel an expected invasion. Tilbury Fort, three miles to the west, with the later Coalhouse Fort and those on the Kent shore, provided the mainstay of defences against enemy shipping along the Thames for four hundred years.

The huge Dockland complex at Tilbury absorbed much of the business of the East London docks, with the advantage of modern efficiency and economies of scale. In the 1960s and 1970s this brought a massive change to the communities and traditional livelihood of the London dockers. Now everything is computerised, containerised, sanitised and simplified; the days when nets of this and bales of that were swung over the sides of ships to be manoeuvred on to the quayside by muscular arms are (almost) forgotten. A passenger terminal still operates at Tilbury, and gleaming white ships take the relatively wealthy on cruises to exotic corners of the world. If you are not one of these passengers and Tilbury has caused a little depression you can always take the ferry across the Thames to sunny Gravesend.

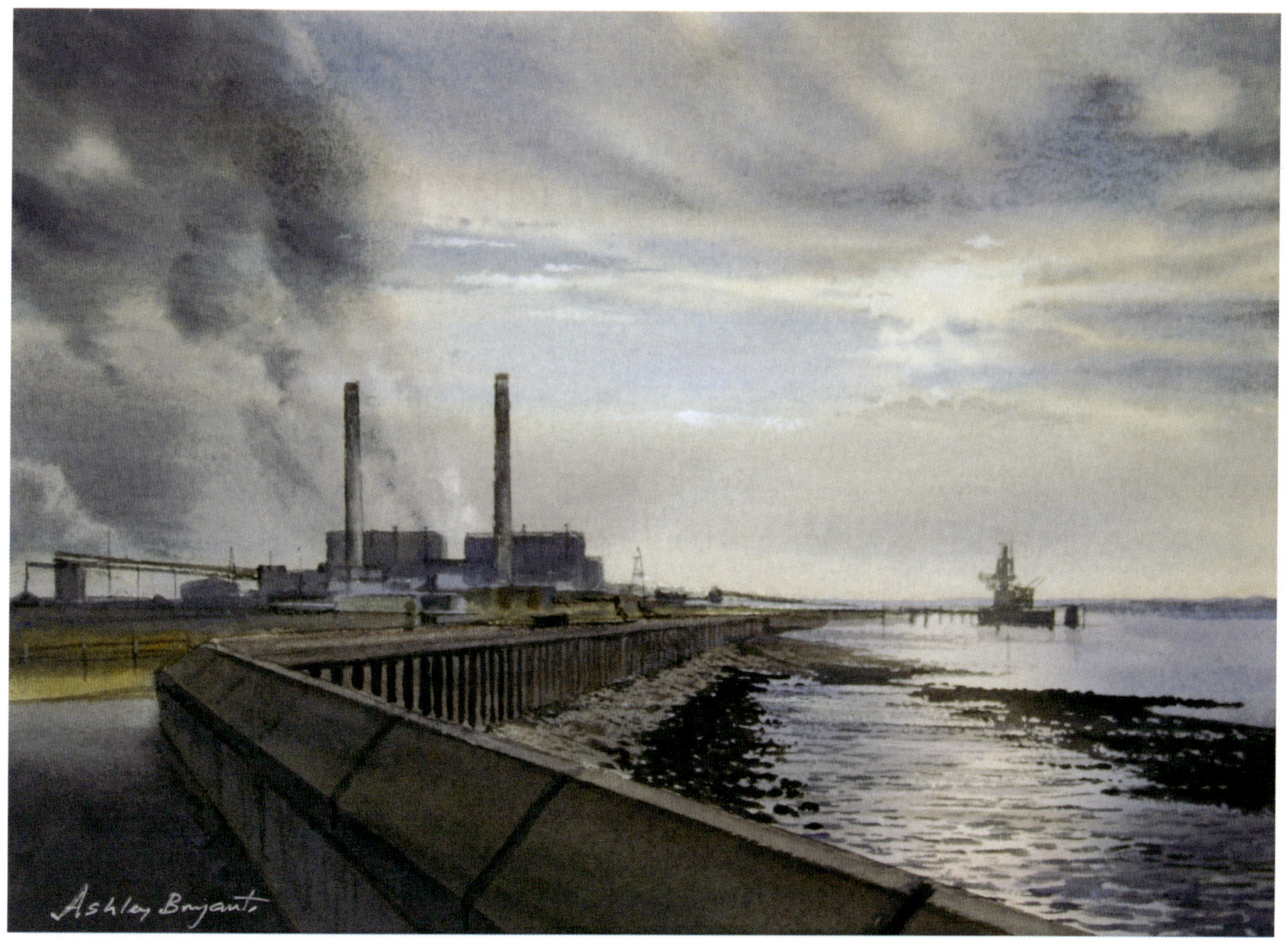

CLIFFE

BIRDS AT CLIFFE
(Opposite Page)
The marshes and lakes attract many species of birds, and here is a small sample of charcoal sketches and watercolours. Top left clockwise; wigeon, barnacle geese, snipe, oystercatchers, pintail and little egret. The last is now common but was a rarity in Britain ten years ago.

EVENING AT CLIFFE
(Below)
This large expanse of water is not the Thames but one of several lakes which attract thousands of wildfowl and waders, and is part of an RSPB Reserve. In the distance Tilbury Power Station interrupts the flat Essex skyline. Occasionally a large ship passes by along the Thames looking as though it is ploughing through the distant marshland.

From Gravesend, the Thames-side footpath, the Saxon Shore Way, takes the intrepid walker to the Isle of Grain. The word "intrepid" is used since this final exploration of the Thames on the Kent shore follows miles of empty landscape, broad mud flats at low tide, old salt marshes and pasture and intense, towering skies overhead. Distant tankers and container ships pass by on the river, and oystercatchers and curlews pipe along the creeks.

Along this stretch of river, Cliffe has been in the limelight in recent years. This village and the miles of surrounding agricultural land and marsh adjoining the Thames have been under the threat of a proposed fourth London airport. Cliffe found many supporters to protect its quiet interests, including powerful lobbying from wildlife groups such as the RSPB, and the proposal was eventually dropped. However, concerns for the future of this region have not completely disappeared. Pressures for new housing in the South-East, particularly in an area so close to London, make the Kent shoreline vulnerable to development, despite the prospect of flooding.

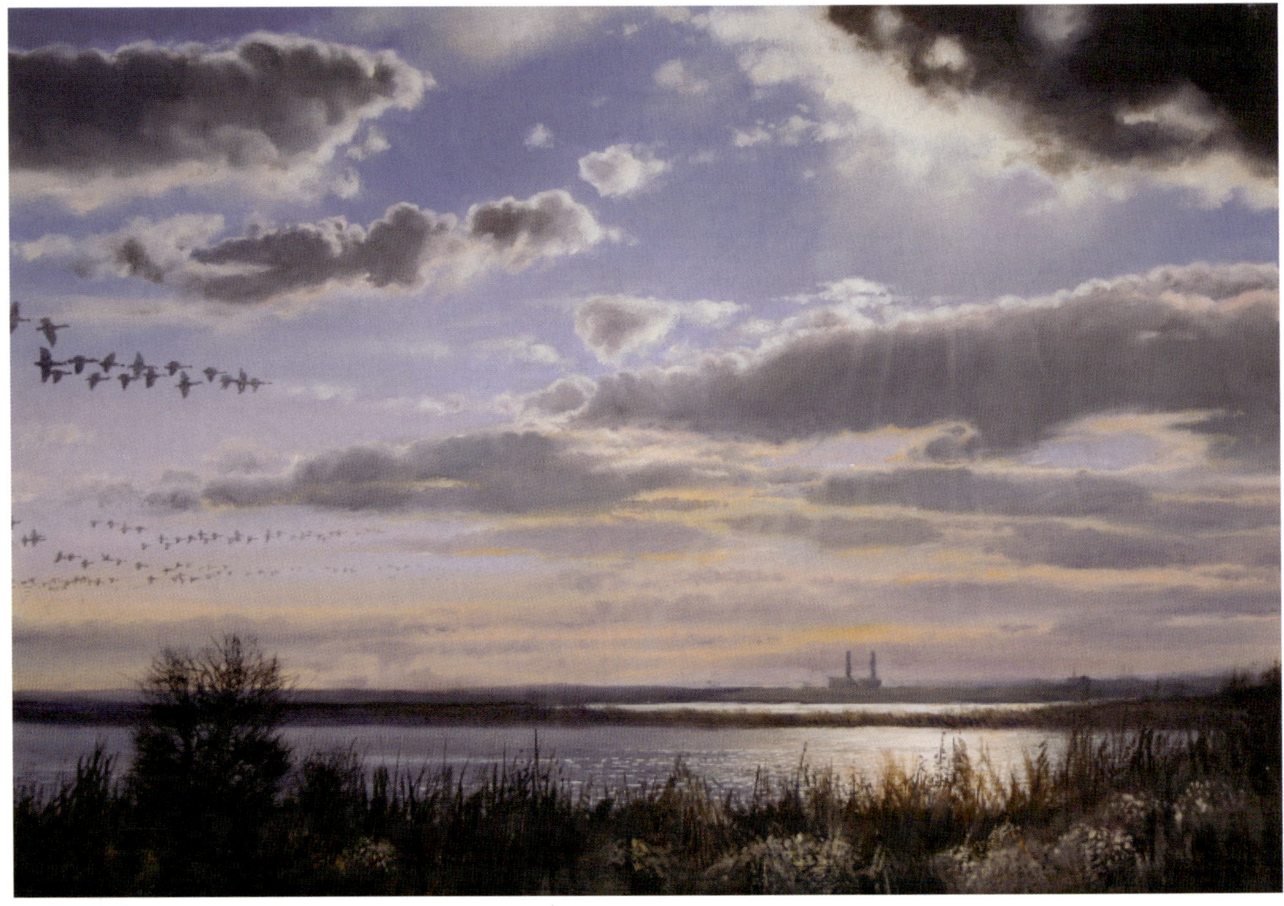

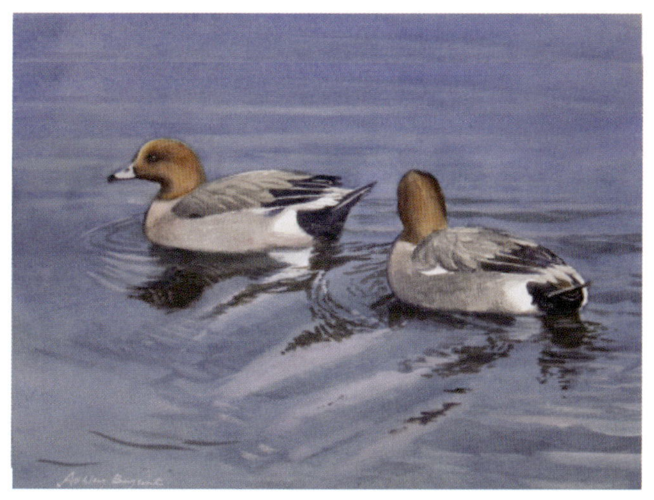

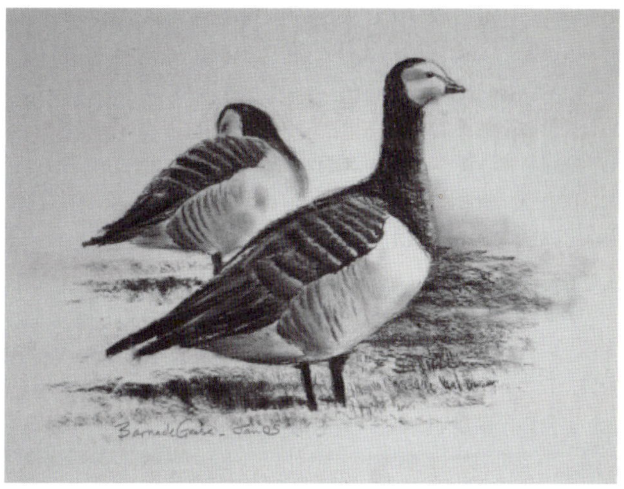

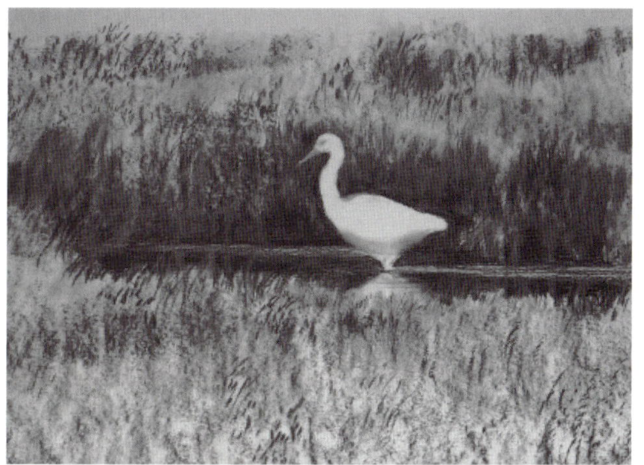

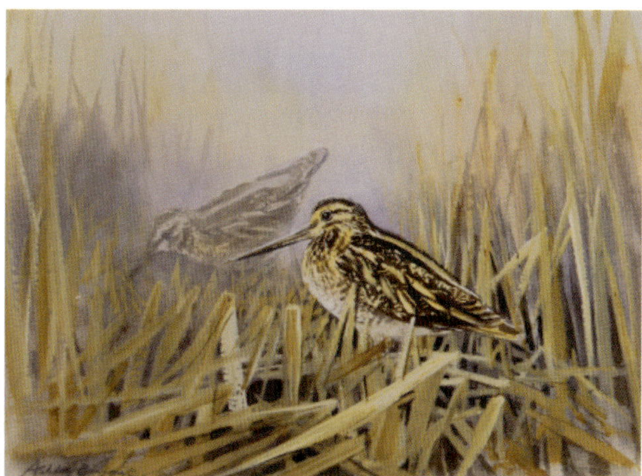

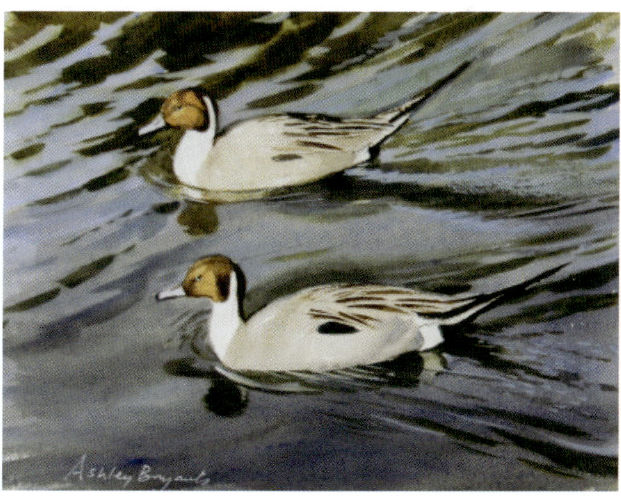

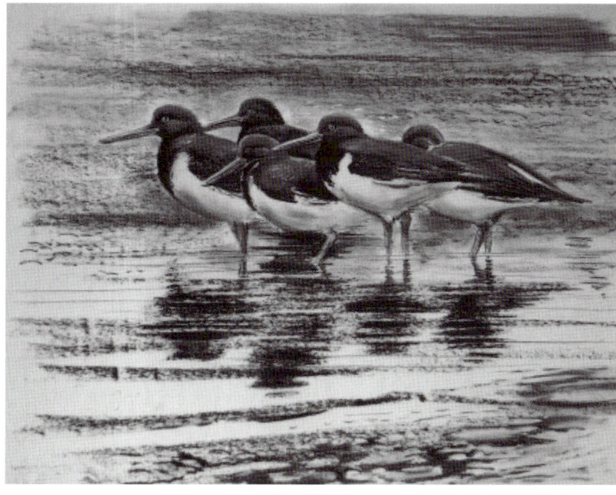

CANVEY ISLAND

Canvey Island is one of those maligned places in Essex and the butt of undeserved humour."Going to Canvey for your holidays?" may be a joke, but as an artist I am happy to spend time here. Industry and oil refineries challenge the artistic imagination, but the area offers some appealing subjects. Canvey is partly separated from the mainland by muddy creeks and salt-marsh, and atmospheric weather creates inspiring subjects. Early morning sun filtering through a light mist, reflecting on the muddy channels and foreshore, captures the atmosphere beautifully. A storm-laden sky provides a dramatic contrast with sunlit salt-marsh and illuminated distant sails. Theses scenes are truely Canvey specialities.

An intriguing notice "To the beach" invites curiosity. Over the sea wall emerges a tiny gem of a 1950s English beach front and seaside resort. Pale, golden sands sweep down to a clear river which is as blue as the Mediterranean on a summer's day. Children either swim in a concrete pool enclosed by the tide or build castles on the beach, whilst granddads queue for cups of tea outside a typical seaside shop, which sells everything from beach balls to bacon sandwichs. A small stretch of the sea wall is actually painted "lido blue" and provides a colourful backdrop to a scene that is evocative of seaside holidays of yesteryear.

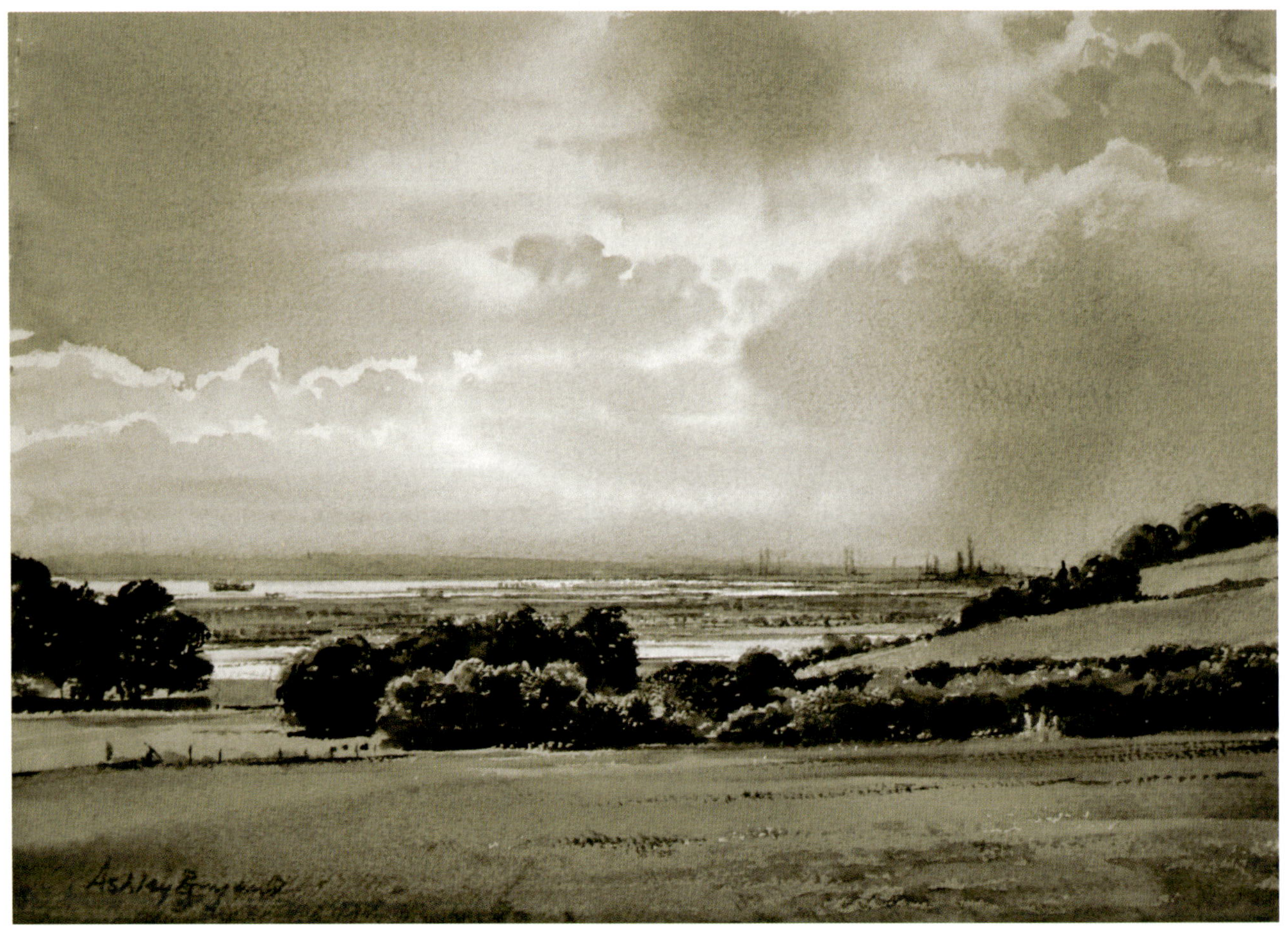

DISTANT VIEW – CANVEY ISLAND
(Opposite Page)
The industrial face of Canvey is contained in the distance in this view from the higher ground at Hadleigh Castle Country Park.

CRABBING
(Right)
These youngsters are having a fine time catching crabs, one of the simple pleasures at the seaside.

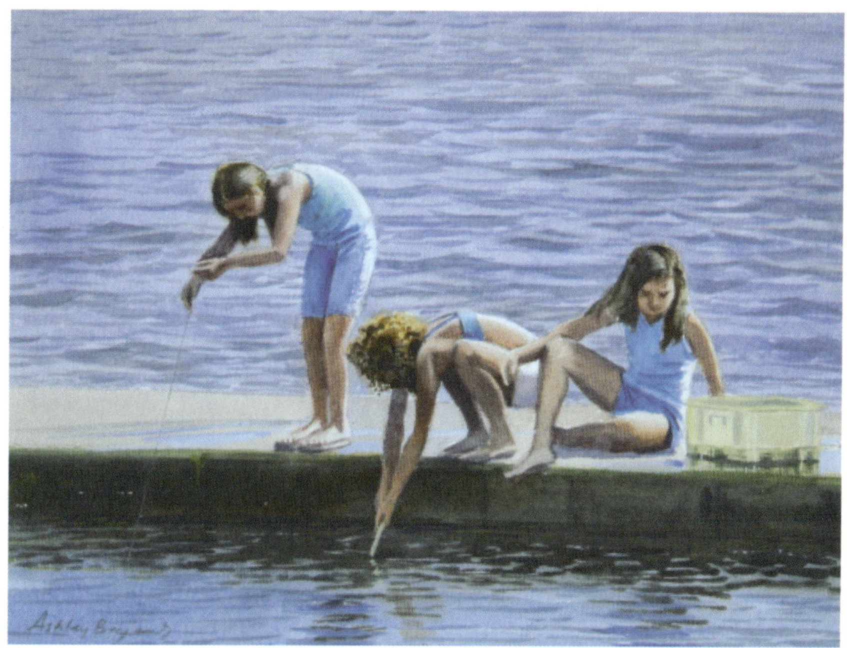

THE BEACH AT CANVEY
(Below)
All the fun of a seaside holiday is found at Canvey Island, with clean sands under a blue sky. Everything looks better on a sunny day.

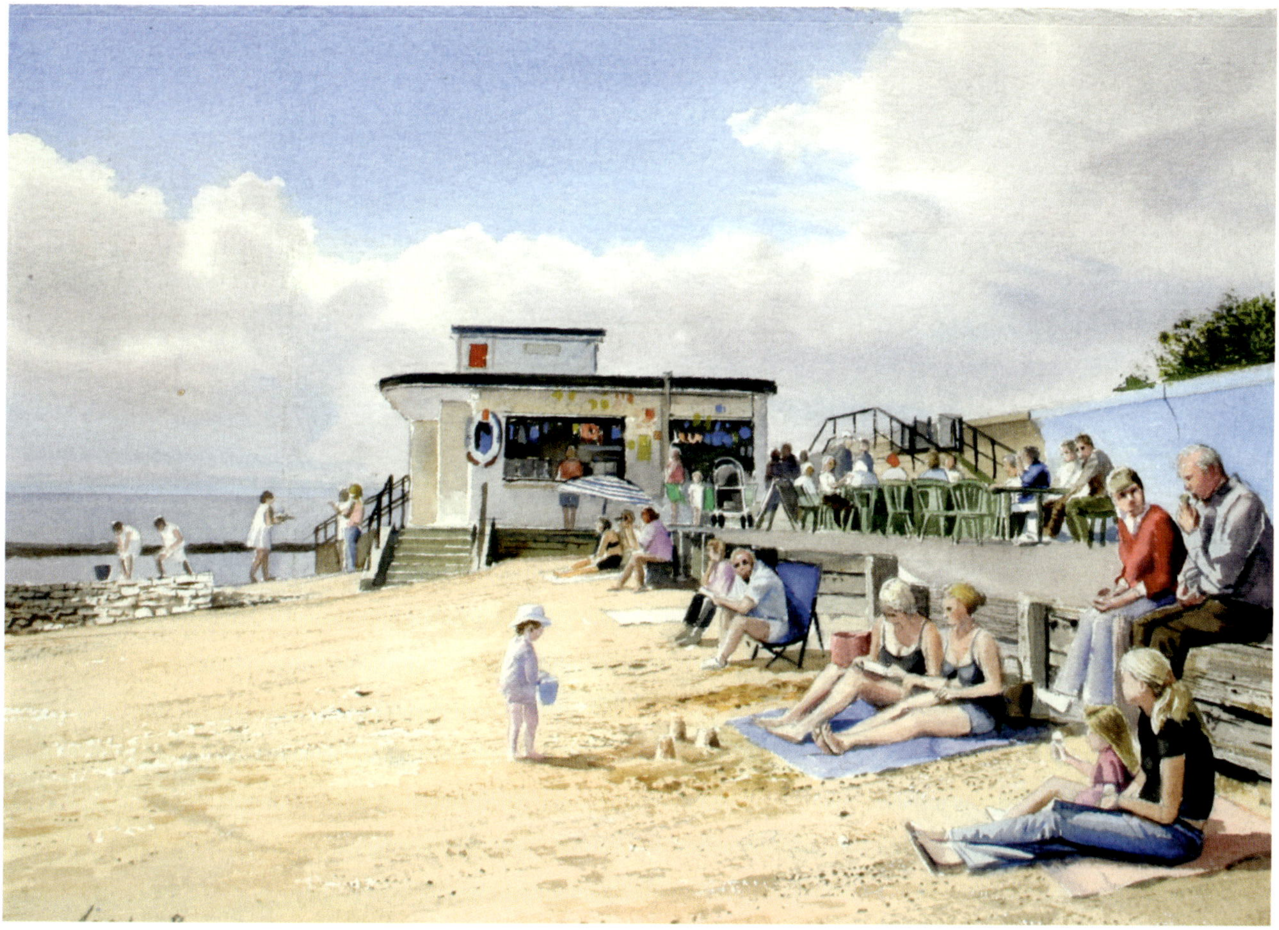

HADLEIGH

TWO TREE ISLAND
(Below)
This view looks south west along the distant Thames and the Kentish hills from one of the hides in the nature reserve at Two Tree Island. It shows the scrapes, the shallow lakes which attract a variety of wading birds and wildfowl. It is interesting to observe the various species as they feed here, the short-legged ones keep to the water's edge whilst those with long legs such as avocets and black-tailed godwits are able to use the deeper water. In this February view the water level is unusually high.

HADLEIGH CASTLE
(Opposite Page)
This frosty scene looks past the ruined turret at the corner of Hadleigh Castle and across the Thames estuary at low tide, which makes a small ribbon of the distant river. I feel honoured to have stood in Constable's footsteps to paint this view – quite literally, since there was no other satisfactory viewpoint I could have chosen. Apparently, I was standing in the garderobes, the old toilets of the castle, but if it was good enough for Constable, it was good enough for me.

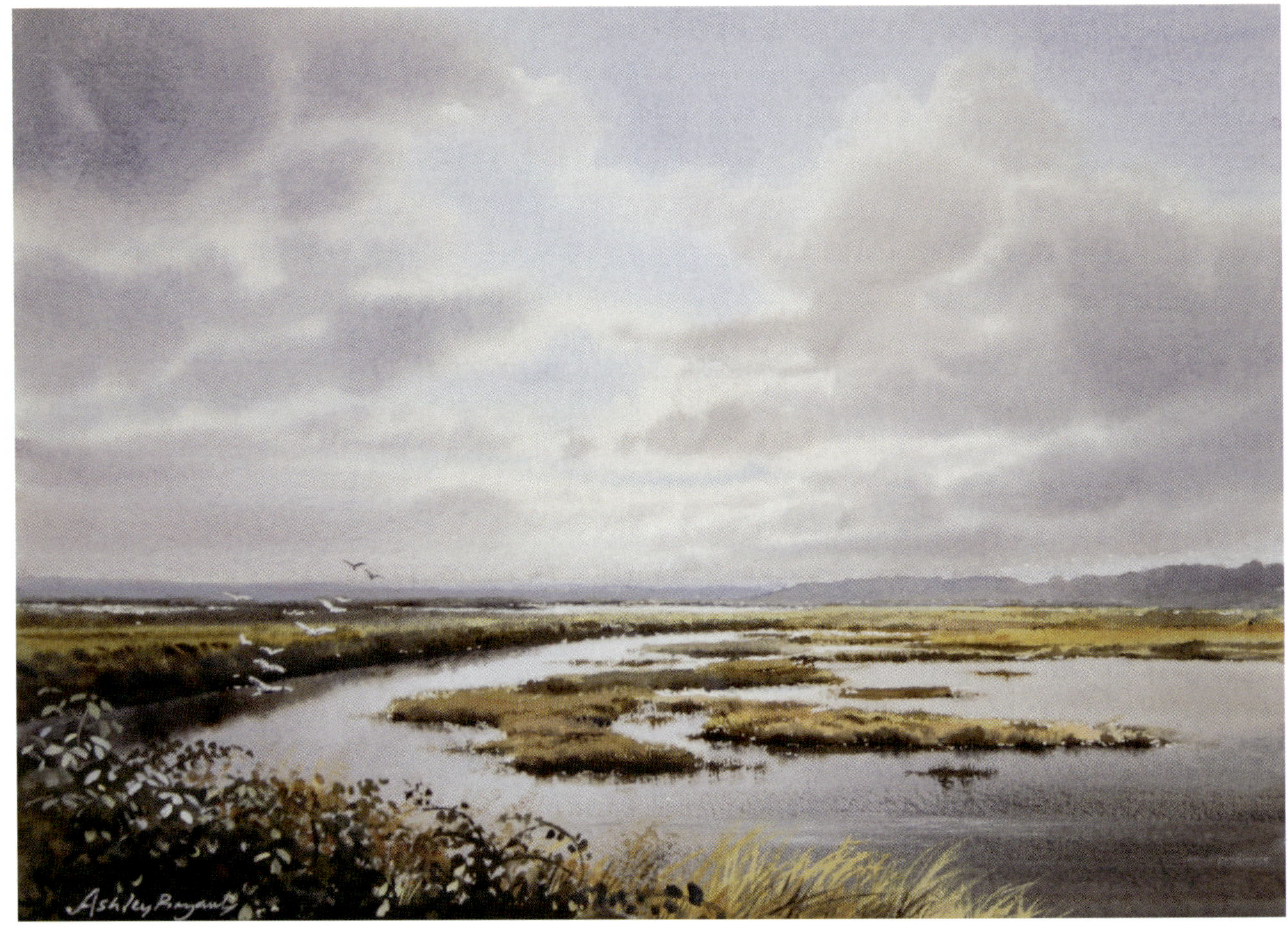

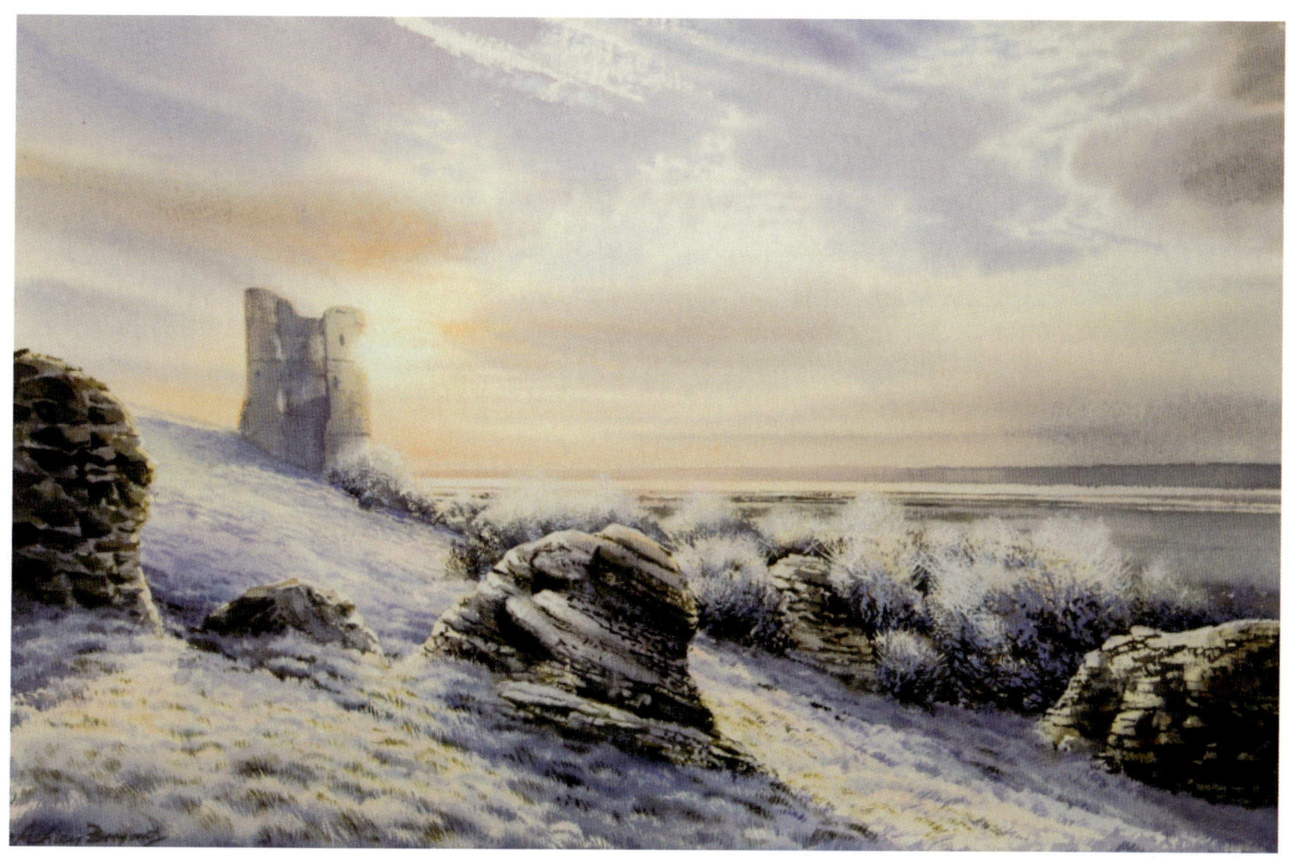

There are many splendid panoramic views along the Thames but the most extensive is seen from Langdon Hills in Essex. From this high ground it is possible to scan across from Canary Wharf to the Isle of Grain – the whole panorama of the Thames Valley from London to the sea. Several miles eastwards, Hadleigh Castle enjoys a similar outlook on the edge of this same strip of high ground. This early thirteenth-century castle was probably built as a rich man's toy and it is doubtful whether it had an offensive aspirations to protect the Thames, since ships could sail past undaunted along the distant river. The castle was enlarged in 1360 under the direction of Edward III but has lain in ruins for centuries, and when it was first sketched by Constable in 1814 it was pretty much in the same state of dereliction as it is today.

Beneath the castle lies Two Tree Island which was once a convenient place to dump London's rubbish. It is now an important nature reserve with a rich variety of habitats. The covered landfill provides grassland and dry scrub ideal for skylarks, whitethroats, kestrels and even short-eared owls. There are freshwater channels fringed with reeds from which the scratchy songs of warblers emerge in summer, but the major habitat comprises large areas of mudflats and saltmarsh. Avocets breed on the islands in "scrapes" – artificial shallow lakes which encourage a variety of waders, and wildfowl descend in their thousands to over-winter and feed on the eelgrass. Two Tree Island contributes to the international importance of the Thames estuary which, when considered as a whole, is one of the most precious wildlife sites in Europe.

LEIGH-ON-SEA

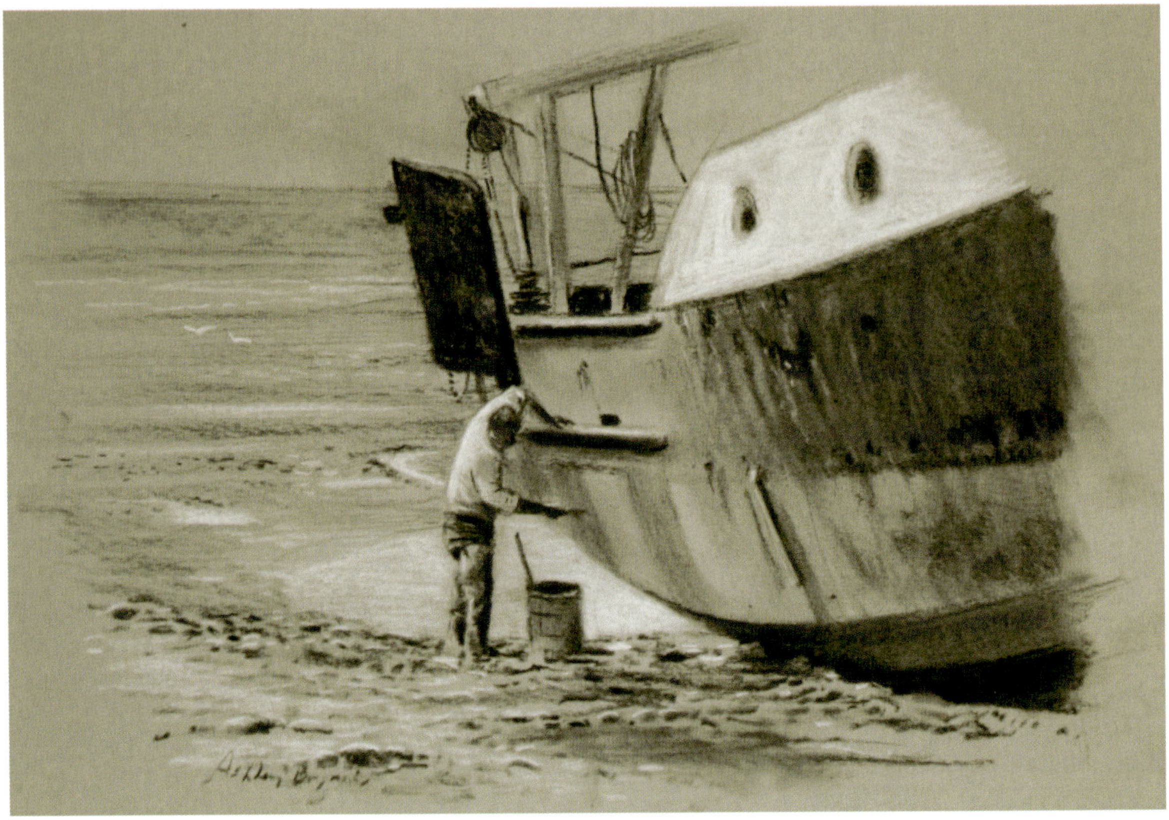

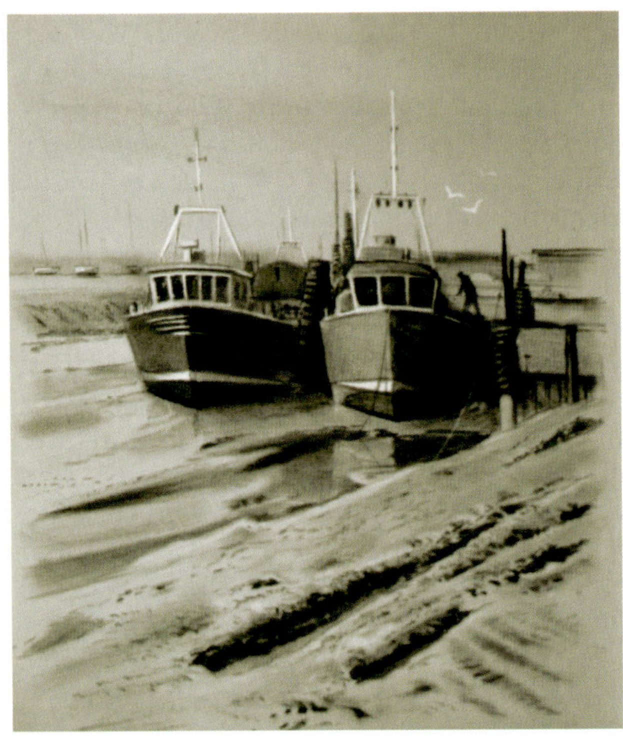

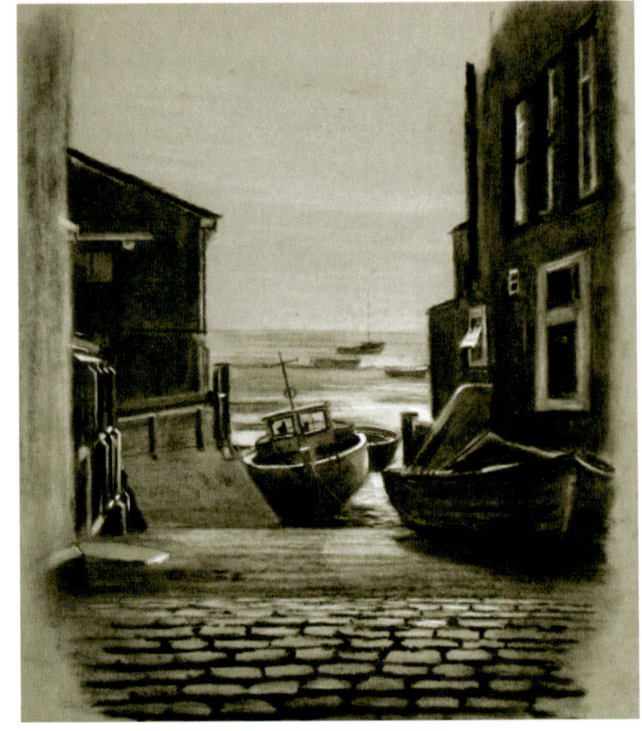

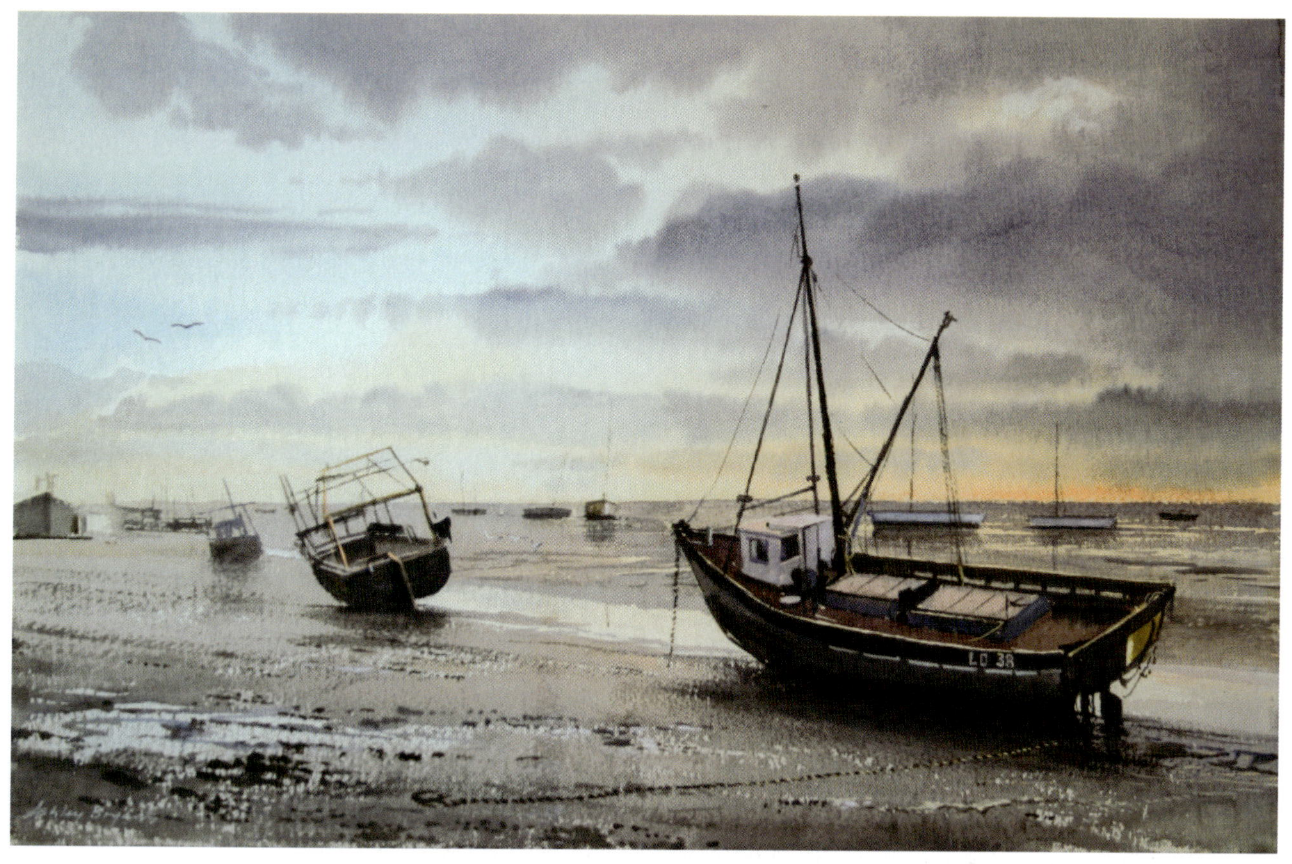

THE THAMES AT LEIGH
(Above)
A familiar view at Old Leigh with fishing boats resting on the vast expanse of mud. A narrow channel enables boats to find their way to the open sea from the quayside.

ESSENTIAL MAINTENANCE
(Opposite Page Above)
Painting and decorating are ongoing requirements for boat owners.

COCKLE BOATS
(Opposite Page Left)
These boats wait for the tide to fill the creek for their next fishing trip to the estuary.

COASTAL VIEW
(Opposite Page Right)
A glimpse of the estuary across a cobbled roadway.

Along the lower slope of Leigh-on-Sea sits Old Leigh, sandwiched between the railway line and the Thames. This is home to the professional seaman as well as the amateur, along with the boat repair yards, the chandler, and the yacht club.

The sea is in Old Leigh's blood, although the visitor is normally confronted by a sea of mud as the tide moves far out in these final reaches of the Thames. Fishing boats go out with the tide across the muddy waters of the estuary to trawl up cockles by the ton, yet these are replenished at the same rate. Such is the productivity of these waters. For many people a trip to Old Leigh would be unthinkable without a plate of seafood in the open-air café or a pint of beer in one of the well-worn pubs.

ISLE OF GRAIN

NEAR ALLHALLOWS-ON-SEA
(Right)
A bleak view across the side of the estuary towards the sea.

PROSPECTING
(Opposite above)
Metal-detecting is addictive especially when finds are frequent. Many interesting objects are uncovered in the mud at the mouth of the Thames.

BAIT DIGGERS
(Opposite below)
It is unnerving to watch the distant, tiny specks of bait diggers on the edge of the mud flats. They need to be alert to the turn of the tide and make a hasty retreat.

THE OLD CREEK
(Below)
Ponies graze on reclaimed land near the Isle of Grain power station.

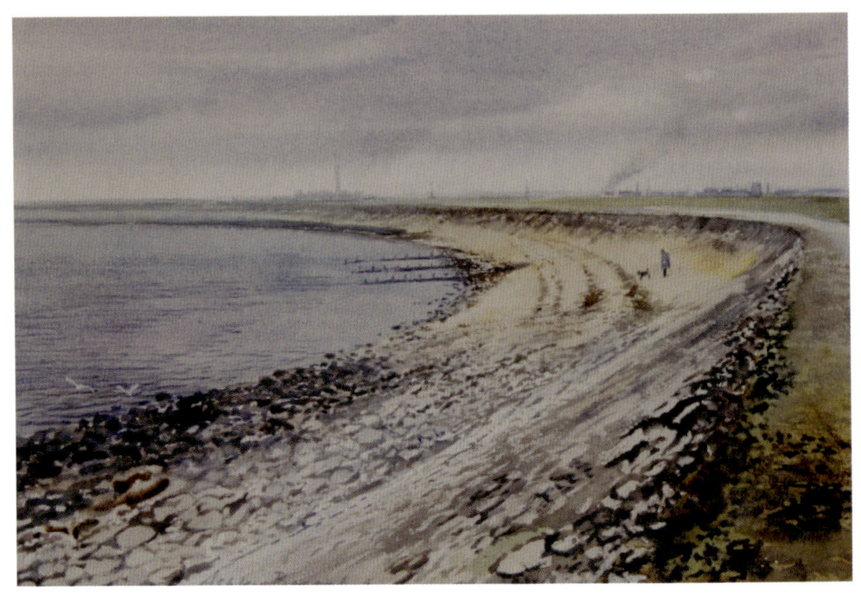

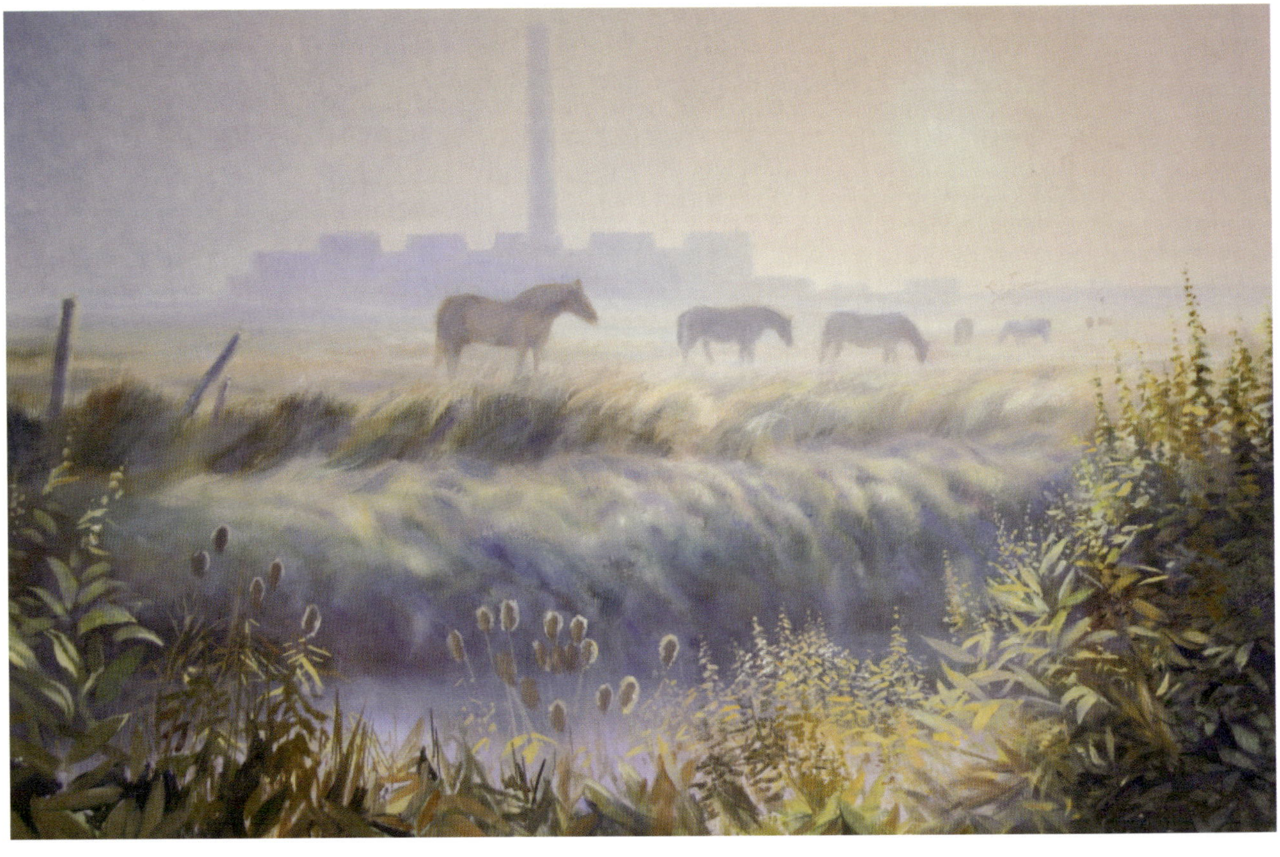

Much of this area near the estuary is forlorn and grey, the oil refineries and huge power station providing little charm on the flat landscape as we approach the river Medway and the Isle of Sheppey. Almost all of the views in this book show the Thames with its surrounding landscape but this is not possible on the final section of the Kent estuary, since a substantial sea wall separates river and landscape. For a painting you can choose one side of the barrier or the other but it is too wide for both to be incorporated into a composition.

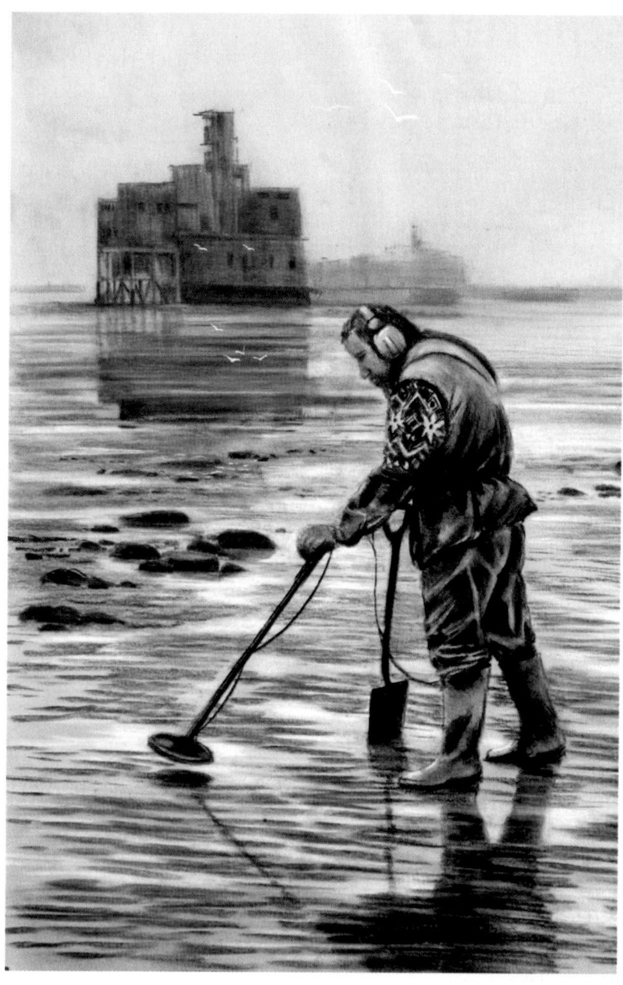

Much of the land is pasture and rough grazing, transformed from saltmarsh and an ever changing network of creeks by the building of this substantial sea wall and drainage of the land. Some of these blind creeks remain and I have shown one of these in the main painting along with the ubiquitous ponies that graze the land. The Isle of Grain power station is an imposing landmark seen for many miles around the Thames estuary. It is rather a brute and I chose to reduce its dominance in the painting with soft lighting.

The village of Allhallows-on-Sea and its Thames-side chalet camp occupy a more elevated position by the river. This is another so called seaside resort along the estuary. In winter the winds are biting, the dampness of the Thames is penetrating and the greyness is even gloomier. You may see one or two other people, bent into the wind as they walk their dogs. In summer the colourful sails of yachts under a blue sky, the smell of sun tan lotion and pretty girls in bikinis make for an amazing transformation from those winter months. The tide travels a considerable distance over the foreshore, exposing a vast plain of rich mud. It is a popular place for bait-diggers, their distant figures just visible at the edge of the tide.

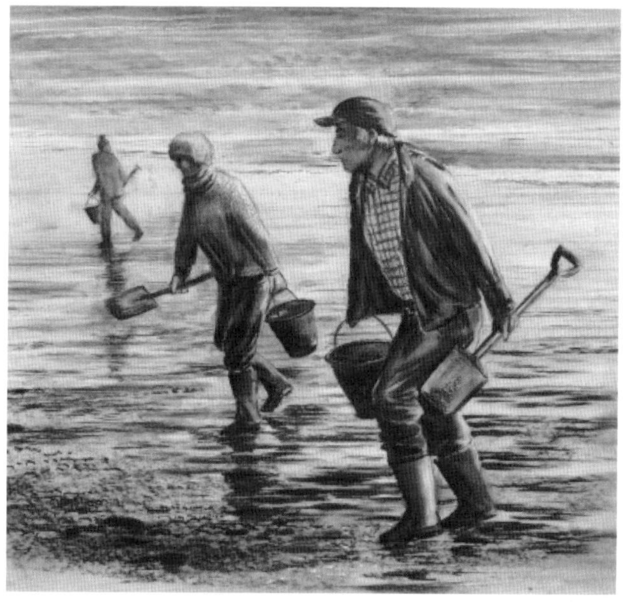

SOUTHEND

As Southend is reached, the Thames estuary is five miles wide and the mouth of the river is rapidly widening into the North Sea. This seaside town is a mecca for day trippers, attracted to its "Golden Mile" of glittering amusement arcades, Bingo halls, fish and chip shops, ice cream parlours, funfairs, pubs and hotels.

In common with this section of the Thames estuary, the tide travels a great distance over a sea of mud. In Southend a beach has been created by introducing sand, the finishing touch to a day at the seaside for those with young families. The pier brings a touch of fame to Southend since it is the longest in the world at 1⅓ miles; its length is necessary to reach open water across the mud. A small railway shuttles visitors along the pier. Fires in recent years have damaged the structure and unfortunately closed some of the pier-end facilities.

This last stretch of the Thames offers a new range of artistic opportunities centred on people enjoying the seaside. There are interesting compositions – people relaxing and the joys of the funfair – subjects that require a camera as well as a sketchpad.

SOUTHEND BEACH
A sunny morning in July and visitors are setting up their stations on the beach.

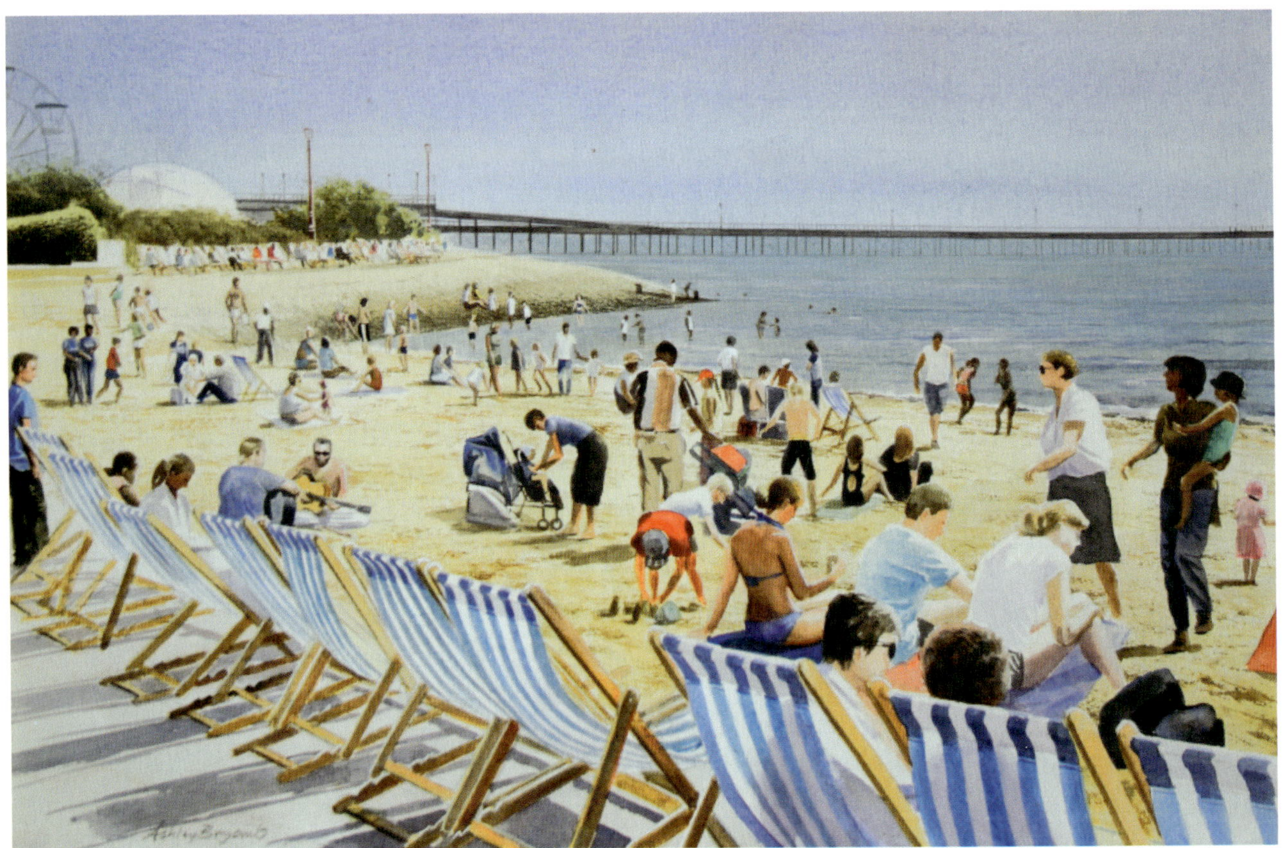

BARGE RACE
Thames barges were once a common site as they plied their trade around the coast and along the Thames with almost any type of cargo. This watercolour shows these boats making their way from Southend pier on the occasion of the annual barge race.

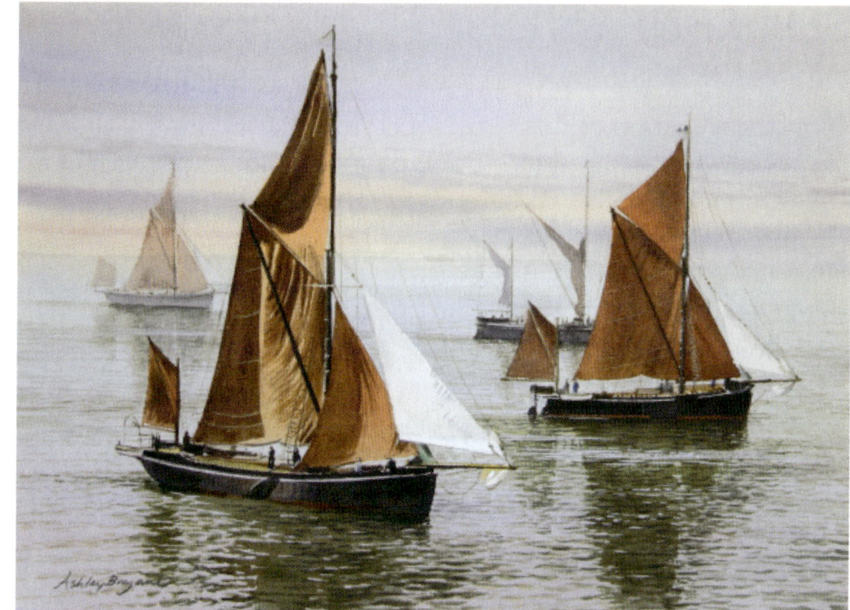

SOUTHEND PIER
A warm glow in the sky softens the starkness of the pier. The train carries the first passengers of the day, and a high tide covers the Southend mud.

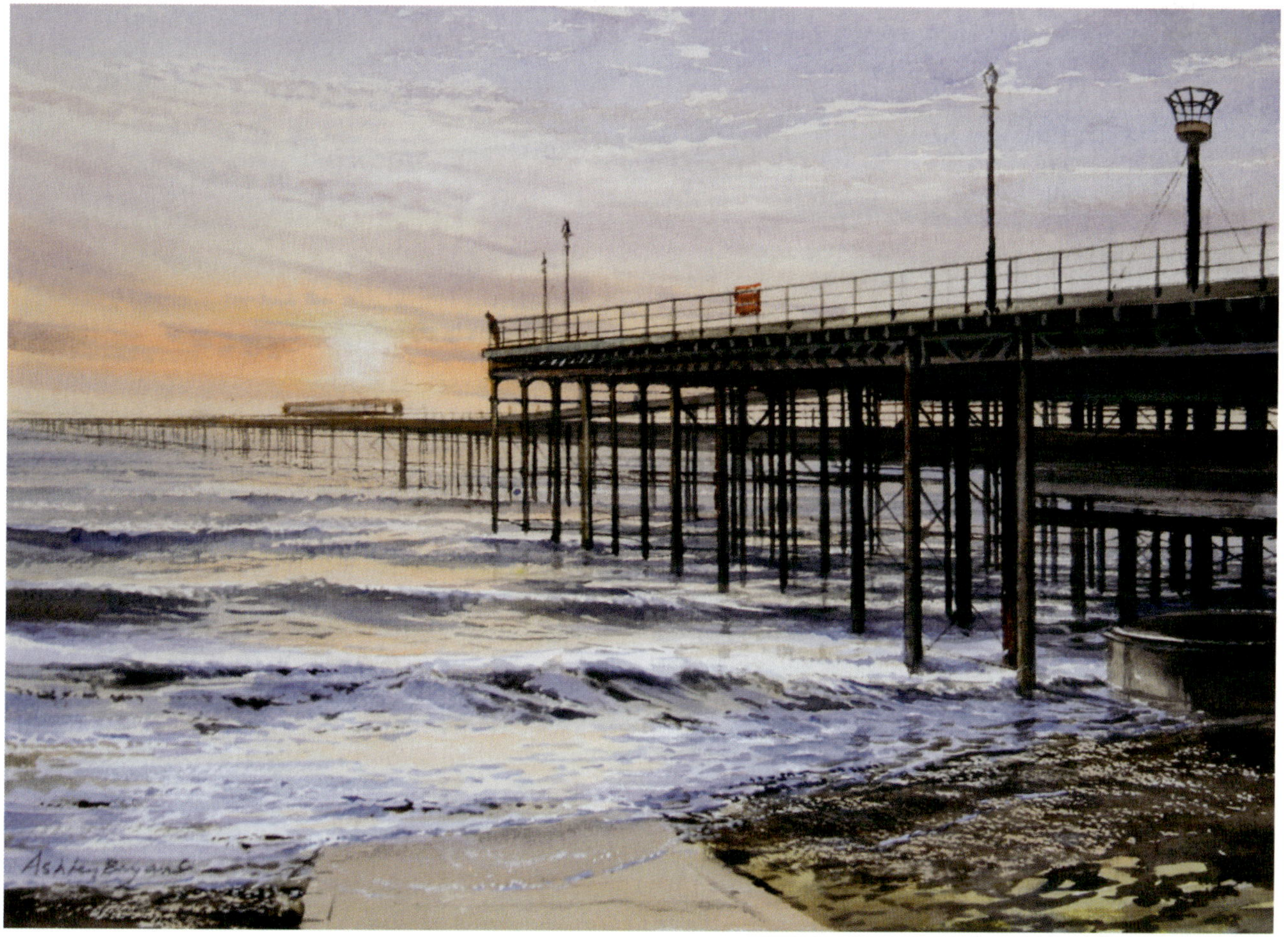

SHOEBURYNESS

In the first section of this book I recommended skipping briefly to these final pages to see the last phase of the Thames. It is now worth turning backwards to recall the source of the river as a small depression in a Gloucester field. The transformation from beginning to end has been astounding, and on the Essex and Kent shores at Shoeburyness the North Sea finally laps onto the beach at the end of a truly fascinating journey.

Here the coastline suddenly broadens, sweeping to the north. The area has been used by the Ministry of Defence for many years and its tenure, including that of the foreshore, has effectively protected the area from development and public intrusion. As at Rainham, this has maintained the natural environment and many rare plants have continued to survive, including those species that thrive on compacted sand and shingle. At Thorpe Bay on the Southend side of Shoeburyness, beach huts line the shore, and the colourful business of enjoying oneself at the seaside continues unabated as long as the weather permits. On a winter's day you have the place to yourself in splendid isolation apart from the little turnstones and sanderlings that run along the water's edge. Under an ever-changing sky the crash of waves and the rattle and roll of pebbles provide a timeless rhythm at the end of this journey.

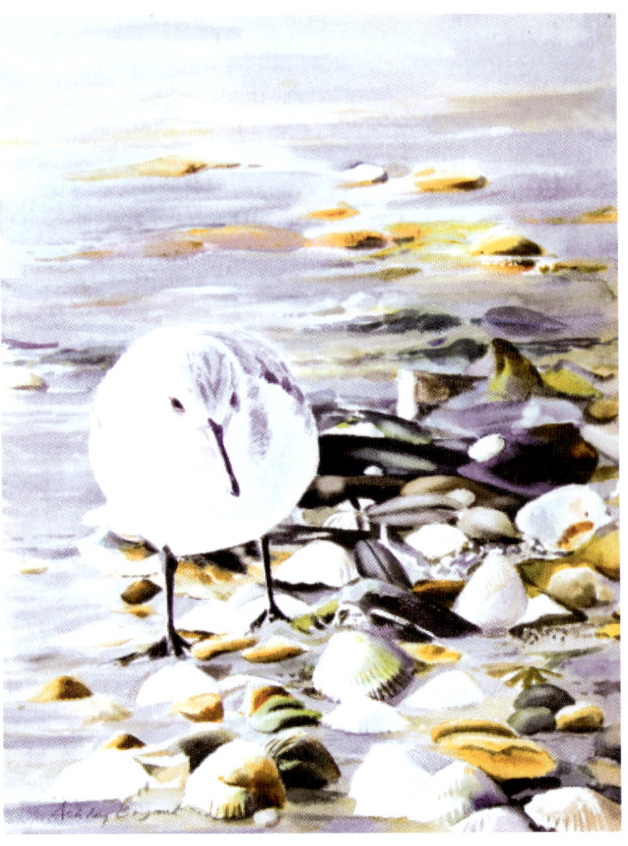

SANDERLING
(Above)
In sunlight the winter plumage of the Sanderling gives them the appearance of snowballs, as they puff out their feathers on a cold day.

OUT TO SEA
(Opposite Page)
This pastel shows a winter's morning at Shoeburyness beach looking eastwards across an empty sea. A build-up of clouds lends drama to this scene as the very mouth of the Thames.

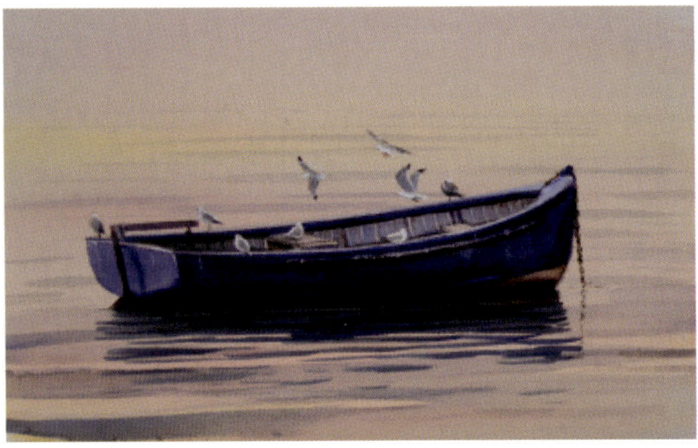

THE BLUE BOAT
(Left)
In the calm of an evening this boat is used as a vantage point by seagulls.

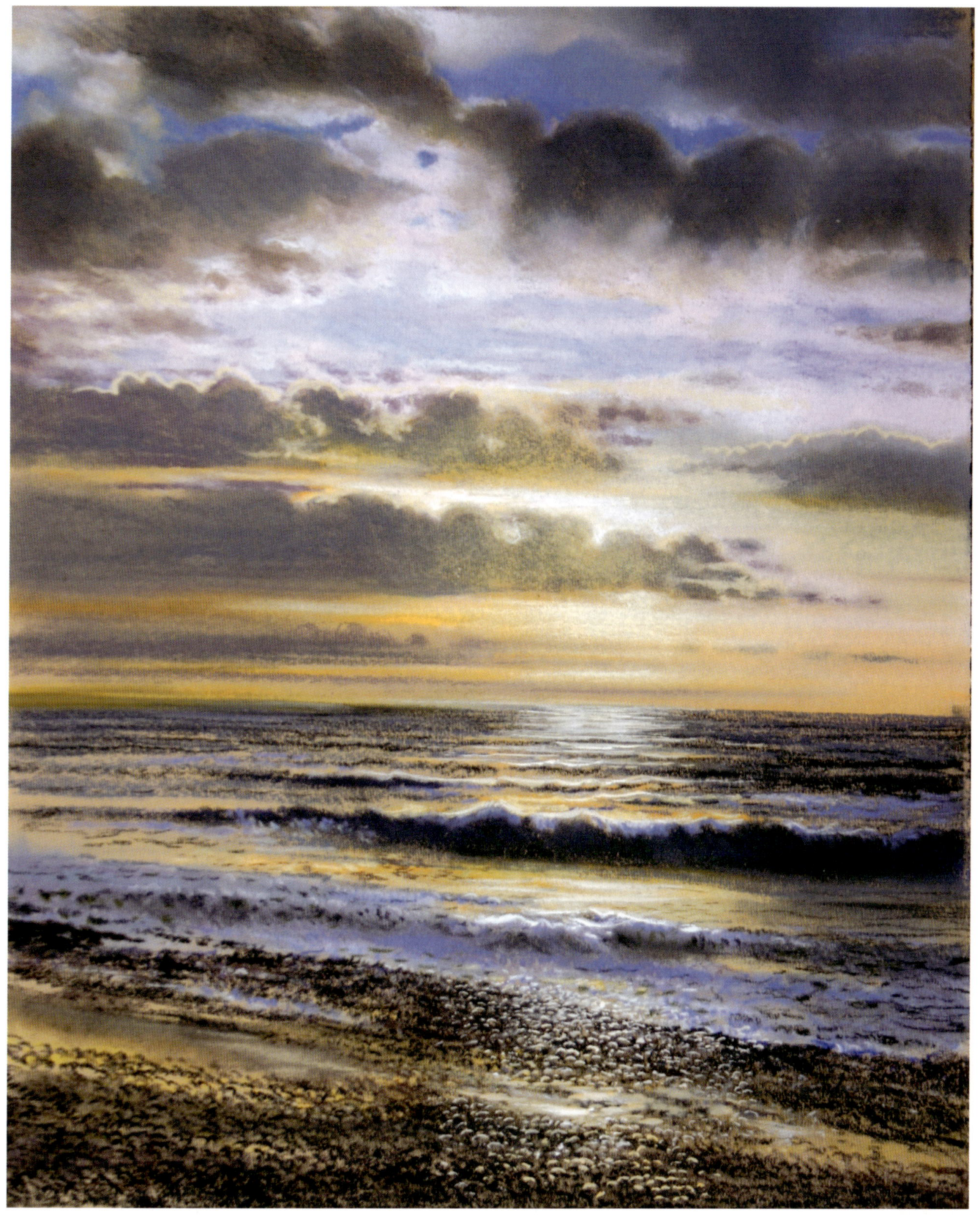

ACKNOWLEDGEMENTS

First and foremost I would like to thank my wife, Diana, who has been an invaluable part of this project from the outset. She has accompanied me on Thames walks and boat trips and emerged as a wizard on the PC with the manipulation of paintings. My son, Giles, has been of enormous help with typing; he has provided sound advice and good ideas, even acting as a model for some of my sketches. The rest of my family have been very supportive and also pressed as models.

My good friend Alan MacFarlane, who often had business in the Thames valley, would drop me off for a days rambling along the river and later pick me up miles out of his way. Mike Hill of the Port of London Authority provided helpful information on access points to the river. Liz Hull offered a tour of the new RSPB reserve at Rainham before it was open to the public and as always was a fount of useful information. Adrian Brink and his team at the Lutterworth Press have allowed me to forge my own timescale and have been very helpful throughout the project.

Finally I would like to express my gratitude to my students and friends who have given me continued encouragement and whose company I have enjoyed on walks along the river.

Further Reading

There are many books on the Thames, but while I have been working on this book, I have found those listed below, particularly helpful:

Access to the River Thames, PLA Review, 1996
J. R. L. Anderson, *The Upper Thames*, 1970
Paul Atterbury and William Haynes, *The Thames*, 2002
Ron Emmons, *Walks along the Thames Path*, New Holland, 2001
Paul Goldstack, *River Thames: In the Footsteps of the Famous*, 2003
Ian Harrison, *The Thames: from the Source to the Sea*, Cassell, 2002
London and the Thames: Paintings of Three Centuries, National Maritime Museum, 1977
River Thames and Southern Waterways, Collins/Nicholson, 1997
The Royal River, Bloomsbury, 1985
David Sharp, *The Thames Path*, Ordnance Survey, 1996

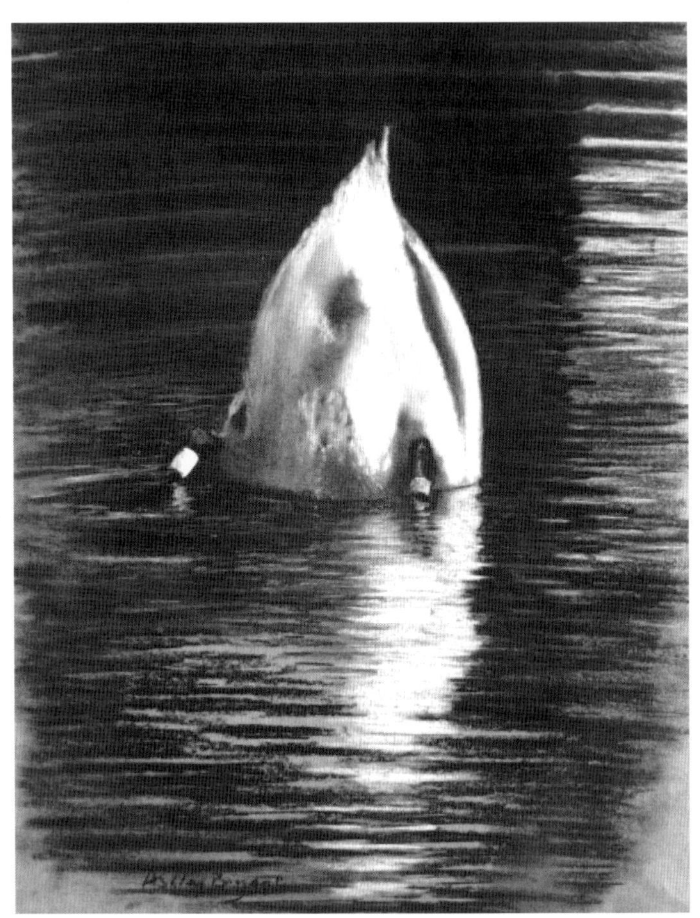

If you've enjoyed *The Thames*, you'll also love Ashley Bryant's

Riverside Journey

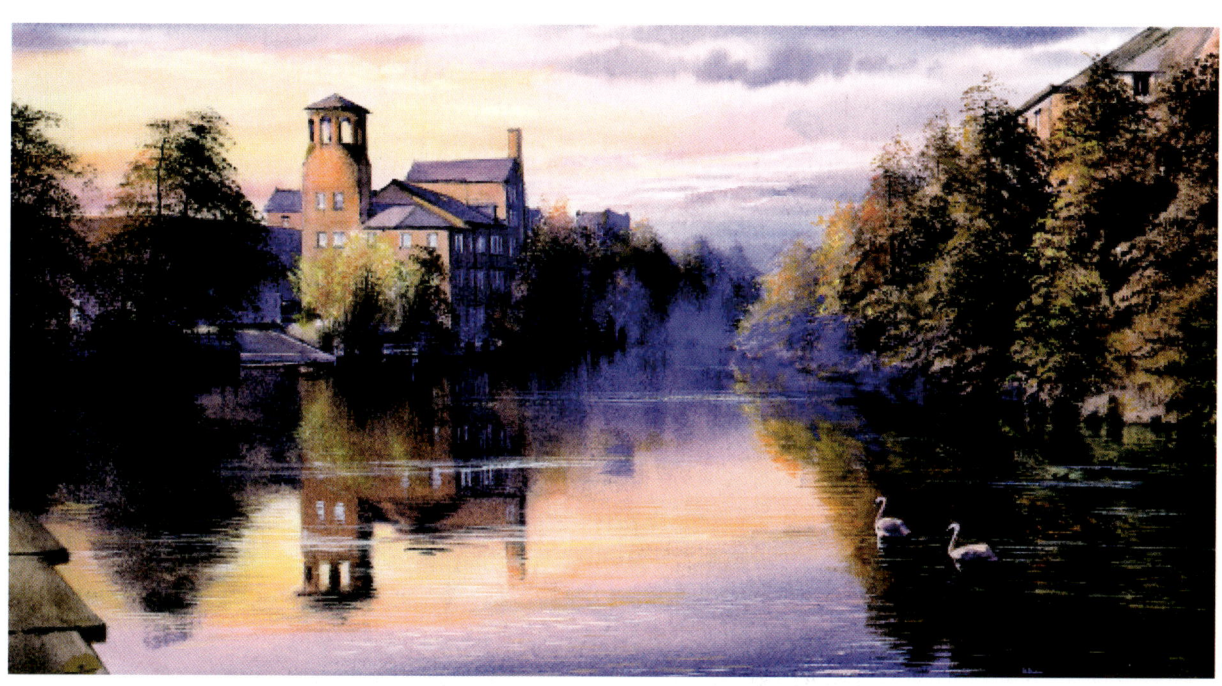

The Derwent flows through a landscape offering unrivalled beauty and variety. It rises in high moorland and tumbles along a steep-sided valley, dropping a thousand feet in six miles reaching a series of conifer-clad reservoirs and a limestone gorge at Matlock, with some of the most spectacular scenery in Britain – compared by Byron with "anything in Greece or Switzerland". It proceeds through thick woods to Derby, and then flows slowly over a broad flood plain until it joins the Trent.

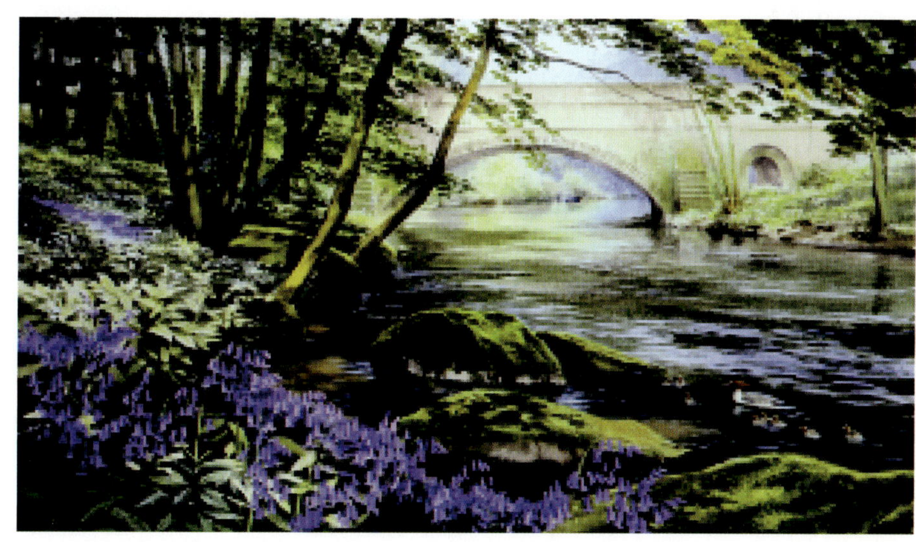

The Derwent hosts a diverse range of flora and fauna, sensitively captured by the artist. The place of the river in the history of industry is remembered too – one of the stretches, where its waters have driven various types of mill for centuries, has achieved World Heritage Status.

The paintings show many different points along the River Derwent, including the aqueduct at Cromford canal, the Belper Mills, and St. Mary's Bridge. As for the Thames, the illustrations are accompanied by the author's observations of the surrounding area including notes on local history.

This book records not only the wonderful landscape and wildlife but also illustrates people enjoying the countryside through the varying seasons and weather conditions. It is thus a record of the changing year, the inhabitants and the flora and fauna of a region, as well as a picture of one of the most beautiful and interesting parts of Europe.

ISBN: 9780718830137 Format: 210x297mm (landscape) hardback

Available direct from the Publishers:
The Lutterworth Press,
P.O. Box 60,
Cambridge
CB1 2NT

sales@lutterworth.com

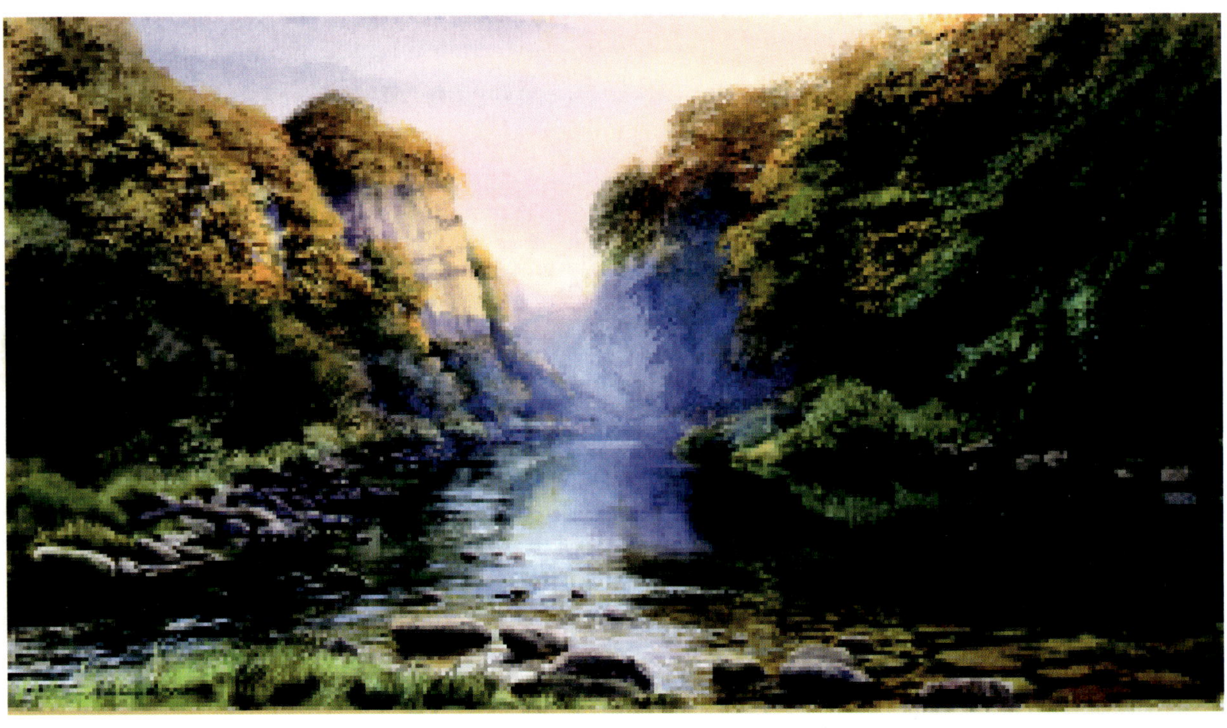